WHERE HISTORIES RESIDE

PRIYA JAIKUMAR

WHERE
HISTORIES
RESIDE

India as Filmed Space

DUKE UNIVERSITY PRESS | *Durham and London* | 2019

Printed in the United States of America on acid-free paper ∞
Designed by Matthew Tauch
Typeset in Garamond Premier Pro by Westchester Publishing
Services

Library of Congress Cataloging-in-Publication Data
Names: Jaikumar, Priya, [date]
Title: Where histories reside : India as filmed space / Priya Jaikumar.
Description: Durham : Duke University Press, 2019. | Includes biblio-
graphical references and index.
Identifiers:
LCCN 2018057039 (print)
LCCN 2019014500 (ebook)
ISBN 9781478005599 (ebook)
ISBN 9781478004127 (hardcover : alk. paper)
ISBN 9781478004752 (pbk. : alk. paper)
Subjects: LCSH: India—In motion pictures. | Motion pictures—India—
History. | Motion picture locations—India. | Motion pictures—Production
and direction—India. | Motion picture industry—India—History.
Classification: LCC PN1993.5.I8 (ebook)
LCC PN1993.5.I8 J29 2019 (print)
DDC 791.430954—dc23
LC record available at https://lccn.loc.gov/2018057039

TO TOM AND MEHA WITH LOVE

We die containing a richness of lovers and tribes, tastes we have swallowed, bodies we have plunged into and swum up as if rivers of wisdom, characters we have climbed as if trees, fears we have hidden in as if caves. I wish for all this to be marked on my body when I am dead. I believe in such cartography—to be marked by nature, not just to label ourselves on a map like the names of rich men and women on buildings. We are communal histories, communal books. We are not owned or monogamous in our taste or experience. All I desired was to walk upon such an earth that had no maps.

MICHAEL ONDAATJE, *THE ENGLISH PATIENT*, 261

When no heed is paid to the relations that inhere in social facts, knowledge misses its target; our understanding is reduced to a confirmation of the undefined and indefinable multiplicity of things, and gets lost in classifications, descriptions and segmentations.

HENRI LEFEBVRE, *THE PRODUCTION OF SPACE*, 81

CONTENTS

ACKNOWLEDGMENTS

This book came to me in fragments, as I hear second books sometimes do. Along the way, several people helped me understand how the pieces fit together. Important interlocutors have been graduate students at USC's School of Cinematic Arts, particularly those who enrolled in my advanced seminars on space and place and on postcolonial theory, many of whom are now colleagues and friends. Special thanks to Alex Lykidis, Veena Hariharan, Aboubakar Sanogo, Mike Dillon, Nadine Chan, Kate Fortmueller, Eric Hoyt, and Brian Jacobson. I am grateful to have been a beneficiary of Alex and Veena's research skills and Brian's close readings. Coming later in the trajectory of this book but important to my thinking on film and space were Michael Turcios, Darshana Shreedhar Mini, Sasha Crawford-Holland, Anirban Baishya, Eszter Zimanyi, Maria Zalewska, Harry Hvdson, Jonathan Mackris, Zeke Saber, Rumana Choudhury, Jon Cicoski, and Alia Haddad. Anna Ogunkunle, Michael, and Darshana helped with illustrations and tracking down bibliographic references. Thank you all for letting me participate in your intellectual lives and for sharing some of mine.

Writing and teaching at USC put me in the way of some fabulous people. With apologies to those I am assuming without naming here, thanks to Marsha Kinder for her inspiring mentorship; Kara Keeling and Tara McPherson for being fiercely smart, political, and outright fun; Akira Lippit for extending support when it mattered; Bill Whittington for friendship and conversations on film sound; Nitin Govil, an old friend whom I am lucky to call a colleague; Kyung Moon Hwang, a model of collegiality and university citizenship; David James for his warmth and encouragement and for being one of my favorite Marxists. Conversations about the research and writing process with Ellen Seiter, Anikó Imre, Rick Jewell, and Laura Isabel Serna were very helpful. Generative at an early stage were conferences on visual evidence at the USC and UCLA campuses organized by the incomparable Vanessa Schwartz, and a USC workshop on space conducted by Edward Dimendberg and Philip Ethington. Beyond my immediate colleagues, I am grateful to Angela Wood, Ashish

Rajadhyaksha, Aswin Punathambekar, Anupama Kapse, Charles Musser, Clare Wilkinson-Weber, Corey Creekmur, Dan Strieble, Debashree Mukherjee, Emma Sandon, Iftikhar Dadi, Ira Bhaskar, Jacqueline Maingard, Jane Gaines, Janet Bergstrom, Kartik Nair, Kaushik Bhowmik, Kay Dickinson, Luca Caminati, Manishita Dass, Manu Goswami, Matthew Hull, Moinak Biswas, Neepa Majumdar, Pam Wojcik, Paul Jaskot, Peter Limbrick, Peter Sarram, Ravi Vasudevan, Richard Suchenski, Ritika Kaushik, Sangita Gopal, Sarah Street, Shikha Jhingan, Stephanie DeBoer, Stephen Legg, Sudhir Mahadevan, Shubra Gupta, Tejaswini Ganti, Tom Conley, Tom Rice, Usha Iyer, and William Mazzarella for their suggestions, encouragement, and interest in my work. Rochona Majumdar's perceptive engagement with my writing buoyed me at important moments; Chuck Wolfe's scholarship, insight, and support helped tremendously; Gayatri Chatterjee enriched me with meals and conversations; reunions with Shohini Ghosh always felt like a homecoming; and scholars on UPenn's South Asia Center listserv served as reliable and generous consultants. Closer to home, Bhaskar Sarkar and Bishnupriya Ghosh inspired as scholars, community builders, and dear friends.

Several scholars and institutions gave unstintingly of their resources, time, and attention when they invited me to give lectures on material that found its way into this book. Thanks are due to David Rodowick and Erich Rentschler at Harvard University, Shelley Stamp at UC Santa Cruz, Steve Cohan at Syracuse, Dilip Gaonkar at Northwestern, Anjuli Raza Kolb at Williams College, Dan Morgan at the University of Chicago, Chon Noriega at UCLA, Josh Malitsky and Marissa Moorman at Indiana University, and the film and media faculty at Princeton, Rice, Tisch School of the Arts, University of Michigan Ann Arbor, The Ohio State University, Jawaharlal Nehru University, UC Santa Barbara, Columbia, and Stanford University, to name a few. It took Josh's invitation to make me understand that I had something to say about documentaries, and this realization came with the added bonus of getting to know Josh. Two hidden stars of this book are J. D. Rhodes and Phil Rosen. J. D.'s comments and encouragement clarified the project for me, and I greatly value our continuing exchanges and friendship. A fortuitous meeting with Phil led to his rigorous reading of a chapter that made me rethink it entirely. Thank you both for your unexpected generosities. Shanay Jhaveri's conversation with me on Jean Renoir's *The River* published in *Outsider Films on India* began what would develop into my long-term fascination with the film.

A Provost Fellowship at USC and the SCA Dean's Office Research Funds enabled me to take research trips to India and England. I am grateful to the

SCA Dean's Office, in particular to Michael Renov and Elizabeth Daley, for facilitating the latter. On my travels, acquaintances and friends helped with arrangements for accommodations, interviews, archival visits, and babysitting while also for being around for food, drink, and laughs. Too numerous to list here, primary benefactors were Anuradha Rasgotra Nayar and V. S. Gopalakrishnan in Bombay; Dipesh Jain and the indefatigable Raj Hate, who shared Bombay film industry contacts; Anil Kumar at the Films Division Office in Peddar Road; Christian Noevetzke, who assisted in Pune; and Amit Pasricha and Parul Chandra, my stalwarts in Delhi. Pragmatic and brilliant Urmi, whose friendship takes me back to a cozier era, always made the trek up from Brighton to London when I visited, to share meals and memories. Anonymous security guys at Chhattrapati Shivaji Airport in Bombay reunited me with my lost iPad. And my mother, Malati Jaikumar, manager extraordinaire, eased all my travels and made the 2009 trip to India memorable and comfortable for Tom, Meha, and me. Steve Tollervey always stepped in to help at the old BFI site and has sent me annual greetings from its basement for more years than I recall. Amit's photography and I also have a connection that goes back decades, and I am delighted to have his artistry on this book's cover. Edward (Ned) Comstock, Sandra Garcia-Myers, and Brett Service assisted with the photographs from USC's Archives of the Cinematic Arts, printed inside this book. Thanks also to Arti Karkhanis for assisting with the acquisition of visual material republished from the NFAI vaults in Pune.

It took two publications for me to realize that there was a book here. The first was research I initiated around the significant digital archive of films curated for the Colonial Film project by Lee Grieveson and Colin MacCabe. This research was first published as an essay in their anthology *Empire and Film*, which received the Society for Cinema and Media Studies best anthology essay award in 2013. The second was a piece I wrote for Jennifer Bean, Anupama Kapse, and Laura Horak's *Silent Cinema and the Politics of Space*. I am truly grateful to the editors of both these collections for giving me a platform to explore my interests. Lee miraculously reappeared near the completion of this book and has become an invaluable friend and ally. His questions on sections of my book were immensely clarifying. His advice and missives made the run-up to publication easier and more fun and continue to illuminate many things. I am fortunate that smart readers offered me formative feedback at various stages. Geeta Patel and Anjali Arondekar, sharp critics with big hearts, helped me refine this project early on. I could not have asked for a more incisive reader of the entire manuscript than Jennifer Peterson, whose feedback was all the more meaningful because we have shared a lot over the years, from graduate life in Chicago to motherhood in Los Angeles. Ranjani Mazumdar, with whom I share habits of the mind, has always been a key respondent as well as a friend in mirth. Thank you all. This book is richer and better for your insights.

A few people have been a part of all that I have written over the past twenty years whether they knew it or not, by virtue of the fact that they are lodged as voices in my head. I'm thinking of my late grandfather, G. R. Rajagopaul; cousin and kindred spirit Arundhathi Subramaniam; soul sisters Roopali Mukherjee and Madhu Dubey, whom I occasionally commission as readers; and mentor and friend Tom Gunning. Thank you for being enduring influences. Although you represent radically different worldviews, I am glad to have you as constant if mostly unseen and unwitting companions. There is also a cast of characters helping me by just being around me, and around for me. Thanks are due to Arun, Bronwen, and Nesta Holden, Gwen Jones, and Andrew, Martha, and Moe White for providing much needed respite in England over the holiday seasons. Bron's thoughtful reading of this book's introduction made me realize, yet again, how lucky I am to be related to her. She is a model of kindness, warmth, and intelligence, and I have much to learn from her. Harsha Ram and Christopher Miles are my beautiful cousin brothers and guardian angels in San Francisco, to whom I turn for wisdom and giggles. A global stream of cousins nourishes my extended family's diasporic quest for a more civic-minded and egalitarian world in multiple fields, so I acknowledge Lata Mani, Radhika Subramaniam, Swarna Rajagopalan, Sudha Rajagopalan, Kalpana Ram, Vandana Ram, Kavita Bedford, Lekha Joshi, and Nitya Ramakrishnan, as well as older and younger generations of the Govindapuram and Padi families, particularly our lyrical elder, P. V. Krishnamurthy, for inculcating and sustaining this ethic. There is also my geographically proximate Mt. Washington village of the Hayes, Kaegles, and Schachter-Regarde families, without whom my mothering as a writer would fall short. Above all, Anjali Arondekar and Lucy Burns have been devoted godmothers to my daughter Meha, giving me time to work and to be lazy. This is not counting the many ways in which Lucy and Anjali's intelligence and generosity make LA a familial place for me. Spending time with my brother, Prashanth, his lovely wife, Deepali, and bright young Mihir makes the separation from our parents a touch more tolerable. Prashanth provides me with an astrophysicist's detachment from the madness of everyday life. Thanks to you all.

The "sadness of geography" keeps me apart from too many people I care for, but I am incredibly fortunate to have their love. At the top of this list are my parents, Jaikumar and Malati, who still hold out an unrealistic belief that I can do anything I want. Appa and Amma, thank you for a lifetime of unconditional love that makes everything possible. Now that I have a child of my own, I understand what it must have cost you to support my decision to pursue a career so far away from home. I was oblivious to the consequences of my choices. You were not, but backed me up anyway. Thank you for that selflessness. Helping me along on these shores are also my grandparents. They lived a long life and left recently. My *thatha* was a vibrantly curious and intellectually formidable man, with an enigmatic smile and speedy vegetable-chopping skills. He continues to tower over the men I meet. And my two beautiful *pattis* visit me still, to smile over my labors. One rustles in, standing tall and perfumed in her pistachio green *chikan*-work sari. The other twinkles at me with her twin diamond nose studs. To you: *ayiram muthangal.*

The actual solicitation and production of this book lay in the capable hands of Courtney Berger, Sandra Korn, and their brilliant team at Duke University Press. This is my second book with Duke, and I am spoiled. Courtney is the perfect editor: a close, honest, and thoughtful reader, who will kindly yet firmly tell her authors what they need to know. Thank you for pushing me to make the revisions and cuts that this manuscript needed; for always responding to me promptly; and for actually reading my work. I take none of our substantial interactions for granted in this increasingly commercialized marketplace of academic publication. I am so grateful to have had the support of Duke's justifiably top-ranked team through it all.

I dedicate this book to the two people who have sportingly lived with it as they have lived with me, for the (too long) duration of its research and writing. My husband, Tom, who is my favorite skeptic and sounding board. ("Tom, is the word I want *entail* or *demand*?") And my daughter, Meha, who is my favorite conversationalist and writing coach. ("Meha, what goes into an introduction?") I am unreasonably lucky to have your abundant love, your patience during my solitary trips overseas and to the basement study, and your blind faith in following me everywhere else. Tom, there is not much I can do without you agreeing to take on half of everything. And Meha, you will be happy to know that this book is finally done! I hope you have not grown up too much in the meanwhile and still want to play backyard badminton with your mummy.

Los Angeles, December 2018

INTRODUCTION:
FILMED SPACE

Histories reside where we seek to find them. They are in our bodies and memories; in objects, archives, and territories; in words, images, committees, and communities; and they are endangered when unsought.[1] I accept all these possibilities in writing a history of films on places, and a history of places on film. Mrinal Sen's *Akaler Sandhaney* (*In Search of Famine*, Bengali, 1980) conveys the treacherous passage of a place—and what film scholars call the "profilmic"[2]—into visual history. In this self-reflexive film, a movie crew arrives from Calcutta to the village of Hatui in Bengal, India. The crew is on a location shoot to film a story set during the colonial Bengal famine of 1943, which caused approximately three million Indian deaths. Rained out of an outdoor shoot, lead actress, Smita (played by the late, acclaimed Smita Patil), devises a game to pass time. She holds up photographs of emaciated bodies and asks fellow cast members, sprawled across the director's room, to guess when the images were taken. Amid banter and incorrect answers, she reveals that the first photograph was taken during India's northeastern famine of 1959, the second in 1943, and the third during the 1971 Bangladesh war. She holds up a final photograph in jest. It is black. "Load shedding, power crisis," shouts someone, referring to India's frequent cuts in electrical supply. "Darkness at noon!" pronounces another. "Past, present and future," intones Smita.

Lacking context, the image becomes an unreliable witness of the place and time of its filmed subject: in this case, the irreducible human body in hunger

FIGURES I.1 AND I.2 Smita holding up photographs of famine in *Akaler Sandhaney*.
Courtesy of the National Film Archive of India.

and death, whose horror is more profoundly captured by an abstract black frame than by photographic realism. In this sequence, *Akaler Sandhaney* also conveys the fallacy of thinking that additional historical information with events and dates will bring accurate comprehension to those who do not share experiences and sympathies. The film is about the failure of a well-intentioned urban film crew that arrives on a location to shoot the story of a colonial-era famine but loses its way in the chasm between middle-class empathies for a rural past and the complex lives of thin-limbed villagers facing food scarcities in their present. Cinema is revealed to be a floundering cross-cultural and interclass encounter between a place and the filming of it. Frictions between the film and its location also point to the opacity and manipulability of the image itself, raising questions about the most accurate and ethical way to cinematically portray the stories of a place and its people given the limitations of perspective, gulfs of experience, and permeability of the past.

And yet it is a film, after all, that limns the differences between a location and its visual representation. This brings provisional faith in the cinematic medium, and in the possibilities of filmed space. *Filmed space*, that captured artifact of an encounter between a camera and its environment, serves as this book's focus and its point of departure. As a focus, it draws this project to feature-length commercial and art cinema and theatrical as well as nontheatrical shorts that are either shot in real locations or reimagine actual locations and built environments. Traces of reality in cinematic recordings and imaginations of it—appearances of "*the* world" in "*a* world" of fiction[3]—pull this book equally to the documenting impulses of cinema as to its abstractions, by disarticulating distinct forms of presentation while always considering the substratum of locations and architectures underlying such films. As a point of flight, this book is animated more by a sustained historical and philosophical investigation into the two handles of the phrase "film" and "space" than by the aesthetics, economic logics, or industrial practices of location shooting, though these remain important preoccupations.

I contend that a broad investigation of film and space is warranted because the full force of a spatial critique in film studies remains unrealized, despite influential discussions of screen space that were launched primarily in relation to the imaginary or implied subject's inscription within cinema's "narrative, apparatus and ideology"[4] in 1970s *Screen* theory and in more recent scholarship on spaces of film production, exhibition, urban life, and digital media.[5] Questions of space in film are taken up piecemeal in the analysis of one or the other aspect of the medium's materiality or immateriality, neglecting film's heterogeneous artifactual status as a framed and scaled visual image (and now increasingly an immersive environment) that is also an ideological apparatus, economic commodity, technological platform, site of exhibition and consumption, fragment of memory, and geopolitical instrument, *each* of which has its own particular spatial and social dimension.[6]

I refer to cinema's spatiality as artifactual here to underscore its constructedness; as something that calls on skill, craft, art, labor, politics, and commerce to facilitate the technology's mimetic and plastic capacities. The recurrent question "What is cinema?"[7] takes on a different inflection when we attend to the medium's spatial and social qualities. Whether construed as reams of stock footage or streaming digital content, film functions as a politico-economic commodity, aesthetic form, representational system, social object, and affective experience. In other words, we could deliberately misread the ontological question to say that cinema, in its functions, is many things. What this entails for the ontological question is the insight that cinema, with its referential powers (as a technology that can record or simulate reality) and representational apparatus (as an economic, industrial, and artistic form that can generate symbolic meanings), exemplifies and authorizes specific kinds of intersections between the material, social, and imagined spaces that constitute our world. Focusing on these intersections, my first task is to sketch out an itinerary of the social and spatial encounters that define and are enabled by film. That is, I need to outline the sociospatiality[8] of film as a multifarious object.

I start with the distinctions traditionally drawn between the terms "place" and "space" to explain how I think expansively about space (as a concept) in relation to cinema (as image and object) while involved in a fine-grained scrutiny of India's filmed place-images. A caveat: this book, with historical intent, primarily focuses on film in its celluloid form, but it should be understood as an open invitation to further discussions of the spatiality of film and media in their evolving formats. "Space," Yi-Fu Tuan notes, is an abstraction compared to the concrete materiality of "place," which leads us to understand, for instance, that finance capital's spatial reach is vaster than a particular steel-and-glass corporate building headquartered on a street in New York, London, or Bombay (now Mumbai).[9] Despite this deceptively neat division (inherent as well in Michel de Certeau's formulation of space as "practiced place" wherein the particularity of places are abstracted, vectorized, and temporalized by their use),[10] value-laden deployments of the terms "space" and "place" have provoked disagreement among social theorists. Place, Doreen Massey argues, is forced to play the part of a reactionary, fixed and outmoded idea or thing in the era of hypermobility and "time-space-compression" as proposed by Marxist geographers David Harvey and Fredric Jameson.[11] According to Harvey, "The incipient tension between place and space can get transformed into an absolute antagonism"[12] when localism and nationalism recuperate a reactionary politics of aestheticized place, against the annihilation of a place's particularity by the leveling forces of multinational capital. As Harvey notes, capital solves the problems of excessive accumulation through the spatial fixes of globally distributed risk, investment, and labor. In the face of this, disenfranchised and minoritized populations (and, in the Brexit and Trump era, we may add as well the majoritarian populations that perceive themselves as aggrieved minorities) articulate their resistance around place-based identities. To the extent that these constituencies are "disempowered" to define global space while being "empowered" to organize locally, they reaffirm a spatial fragmentation that "mobile capitalism and flexible accumulation can feed upon."[13] Massey finds such formulations of space and place constrictive because they shut out the possibility of a "progressive sense of place."[14] Place, for Massey, is not static and bounded but in a perpetual process of being defined by the "power-geometries"[15] of global capital in combat with those structurally denied access to geographical and class mobility.

Similar to Massey, Elena Gorfinkel and John David Rhodes express a comparable affinity for political and differentiated recuperations of place in the field of film studies. In their anthology on location filming, the authors note that space is "a uniform property of cinema" because the commercial cinematic apparatus is invested in conventions of perspectival and ideological coherence that, in Stephen Heath's words, habitually transforms the particularity of what is "seen" into the abstractions of a "scene."[16] Against this homogenizing tendency of cinema, profilmic place is understood as the "heterogeneous and specific element recorded by or sensible in film." It is in *place*, they argue, that history accrues and accretes, so that locations provide "the traction necessary for resonant and forceful political intervention" and critical recuperation.[17] For Gorfinkel and Rhodes, place becomes the "tactic" to unravel cinema's relationship to its hermetically sealed diegetic world, making place the "product of an agonistic relation" between the spatiotemporal world outside the film's frame and the fictional world constructed by its formal artifice.[18] This is an important point and makes intuitive sense. The cinematic lens's ability to capture the incidental and ephemeral makes each film frame potentially rich with visible realities that exceed those of a fictional narrative or plot.[19] Moreover, in industrial practice, actual locations frequently become proxies for other places, with North Wales doubling for Pakistan in *Welcome to Karachi* (Ashish R. Mohan,

2015), China for Afghanistan in *The Kite Runner* (Marc Foster, 2007),[20] and Toronto for Chicago in *My Big Fat Greek Wedding* (Joel Zwick, 2002). As Brian Jacobson shows with regard to early cinema in Southern California, locations served as a "studio beyond the studio," staged to play the role of *any* place in the world.[21] Spectatorial and scholarly acts that use the materiality of places to dislodge their visual representation from hermetically sealed frames and fictionalizations return interpretive command to the historian, the spectator, or the critic.[22] This intimacy with the real leads to what Gorfinkel and Rhodes call modalities of spectatorship that are "distracted and overcathected"[23] to visual details and ephemera not subsumed within a film's narrative.

I elaborate on the dialectics and frictions between the enframed and profilmic worlds as well, but find that the exclusive emphasis on place and location in film evades a few crucial concerns. First, place and space are experientially linked, which is why we can sometimes feel spatially alienated in our own bodies and homes, or spatially at home in strange locations and with strangers. Something that feels like "undifferentiated space becomes place as we get to know it better and endow it with value. . . . The ideas of 'space' and 'place' require each other for definition."[24] This is also the lesson taught by scholars such as Brian Massumi, Sara Ahmed, and Jasbir Puar, who point out that things (bodies, objects, places) may precede, coincide, or slide outside our rational recognition and knowledge of them, making feelings, intuitions, and mechanisms of interrelationship (affective spaces between us and other bodies, objects, or places) of interest.[25] I do not, therefore, share Gorfinkel and Rhodes's admittedly polemical and "stubborn insistence on place"[26] at the expense of space but give space its due analytic weight.

Second, and this is key: things *other* than place possess and generate spatial qualities. State power, capital, technology, and assignations within gendered, classed, racialized, and sexual hierarchies are central to how we measure our lives, delineate our borders and identities, experience our social worlds, and endow them with value. Thinking in sustained ways about how a place becomes part of cinema's enframed image, and how that cinematic image itself is produced and subsequently takes residence within innumerable spaces—of the state, industry, economy, aesthetics, regulation, ideology, memory, consumption, and everyday life—pushes back the horizon of historical analysis exponentially to multiple sites. If place in film draws our attention to a filmed location's layered histories, space demands an awareness of the *principles* underlying its organization and a sensitivity to the *systems* and *people* participating in the perpetuation or breakdown of that organization. To return to *Akaler*

Sandhaney from this perspective, the film could serve as the starting point of an investigation into a number of relational spaces that determine the look and fate of its place-images. These may range from Sen's access to camera and sound technologies for location filming in India in the 1980s to constructions of the film's cinematic space through shots and edits. It may include investigations into current challenges in finding prints of Sen's film to looking at *Akaler Sand-haney*'s images in relation to other visual records of India's famines. We could write histories that radiate out from a filmed place's relationalities to the other industrial, political, socioeconomic, and experiential sites that give it shape, form, and meaning. For this reason, *space* will refer to different but related va-rieties of (cinematic and social) space in this book. It will refer to the represen-tational space of a screen and its relation to profilmic spaces. It will refer to the institutional and pre-production contexts from which place-images emerge and to the circuits of their afterlives. It will also refer to the disciplinary, geograph-ical, social, embodied, and geopolitical contexts that give meaning and power to such moving images. Within the historical context of each analysis, I will be demonstrating how this expansiveness is essential to our apprehension of the relational spaces through which cinema is produced, organized, and assimilated, whether as artistic form, social, professional and private experience, or commer-cial product.

The critical impetus to write a capacious history of space—what we may think of as a deliberately *spatial film and media historiography*—is suggested by the sociologist and philosopher Henri Lefebvre.[27] According to Lefebvre, an analysis of the interrelationships between "physical, mental and social space" dismantles the "fetishization of space in the service of the state, philosophy and practical activity."[28] In other words, space can be as central a heuristic as place in writing film and media histories if we think about how any place becomes part of several (socioeconomic, political, disciplinary, and experiential) sites when it is transformed into an image, and how that process is itself implicated in the rationalizing logics and illogics of each of those social sites. For these reasons, the idea of filmed space performs a double shift in this book. It serves as the smallest unit of analysis, which concentrates our attention on what tran-spires when a place is filmed. This draws us to ontological questions of cinema's relationship to the real; to formal and aesthetic questions about how the screen or story uses the logic of spatial composition through narrative, edits, camera angles, camera movements, and so on to reproduce reality; and to the material circumstances of production crews and technologies. Filmed space is also the largest concept that drives this project's media historiography to shake out the processes through which states, institutions, economies, societies, and ideologies acquire an apparently objective status and self-evident territorial fixity.

In the long run, my claim is that spatial film and media historiographies can show us how apparently separate and immutable "physical, mental and social" spaces governing films and filmmaking are a part of interconnected historical and contingent processes. I am further claiming that to be alive to their mutuality is a way of thinking, writing, and mapping history *across* the different spatial registers of cinema as a material, ideological, affective, and social object.[29] I consider this book to be a spatial film historiography because it tracks the spatiality of cinema itself, whether as commodity, affective experience, or moving image; it also attends to cinema's constitution in relation to formal, socioeconomic, affective, and geopolitical spaces; and it attempts to adopt a critical self-reflexivity toward its own descriptive language and analytical categories, which spatialize knowledge by being at the front lines of disciplinary border constructions. This book aims to cut across different approaches to cinema with a methodological comprehensiveness to reckon with the medium's spatial identity in materially and socially rooted terms.

Any analysis of space must locate itself somewhere, in an act that hermeneutically foregrounds the fact that all theory and historical interpretation has an implicit or explicit geographical point of origin. *Where Histories Reside* is about the frictions and stories that have been attendant upon shooting different types of locations in India, rendering its territory and people cinematic.[30] In this book, I investigate the politico-economic and visual regimes through which places in India have been spatialized as moving images. I also write about the ways in which those images are in turn respatialized as commodities, artifacts, and objects of study, to designate a sense of place. My argument hinges on following the industrial infrastructures and representational apparatuses particular to film, so that while historical and anthropological scholarship on India's production as a national and visual space constitutes a significant precursor,[31] this book will be more attentive to the particular spatialities of film as image and commodity. The balance between the relative gravities of *film* and *India* to a project about films shot on location in India will be discussed further.

FILMED SPACE VERSUS FILMIC SPACE

My use of the term "filmed space," although colloquially a reference to the filming of places in India, aims for a conceptual precision that differs from the concept of filmic space in film theory. Annette Kuhn and Guy Westwell define filmic space in the following way: "The space created within the film frame as opposed to the space of the real world or of the profilmic event. Filmic space is a wholly distinct type of space, one that can only be created on the cinema screen through the techniques and language of cinema—one of the distinctive attributes of film as a medium being that it creates its own patterns of spatiality (and temporality)."[32]

Distinctions between profilmic or real space and filmic space were crucial to early developments in film theory because of a drive to establish the particularities of film language and the cinematic apparatus, with its formal tools of mise-en-scène, framing, lighting, editing, perspectival manipulation, layering of gazes, and so forth. These specificities, though crucial, diverted attention from the equally rich yield of thinking about entanglements between filmic and profilmic social places and relationships between the spaces of pre-production and production practices, which were taken up more vigorously under the historical turn in film studies. An example of this is Charles Wolfe's analysis of Buster Keaton's silent comedies, set in California. Wolfe breaks down Keaton's shorts into (a) the real locations where they were shot, (b) the fictional story world that unifies these spaces within the logic of the film's narrative, and (c) the cinematic field (of edits, lighting, movement, focus) of screen space. Finding links between these different kinds of spaces, Wolfe shows that Keaton's use of real urban sites along the California coast in *The High Sign* (1921) and *Balloonatic* (1923) contains clues to "how the experience of traversing and inhabiting this terrain found expression in cinematic form,"[33] even as it incorporated visual traces of the land's developmental and design history into its visual and narrative scheme.

The study of cinema and urbanism has contributed greatly to spatial thinking in film history, as in Edward Dimendberg's excavation of the histories of modernity and urbanism in the film noir genre, Giuliana Bruno's spatial mapping of Naples and lost Italian pasts in fragments of Elvira Notari's city films, Mark Shiel's work on early Hollywood, and David James's scholarship on the avant-garde in relation to the city of Los Angeles, to name only a few.[34] James examines how avant-garde films "document the spatialities in which they are set, but also the spatialities in which they come into being," to investigate the "relationship between the way a city figures in a film and the way it figures in the filmmaking."[35] This produces what James calls a "geocinematic hermeneutic," alive to the imprint of material histories in the visualization of cities within films.[36] Geocinematic readings and analyses of interlocking shifts in urban planning, cinematic design, film genres, and film fragments are part of an increasingly prolific and methodologically wide-ranging scholarship on cinematic space in relation to social, architectural, and material spaces. These include studies on the political economy of runaway productions; cinema as virtual travel and cinema's relationship to travel technologies; location filming; film and architecture; film in global, urban, and rural sites; film theaters, archives, and studio libraries; film labor in urban spaces; film and media in queer spaces; digital media's new spatial networks; emergent media's sociopolitical infrastructures and technological hardware; and more.[37]

Building on this expansive research but also traversing it with some disregard for differences in approach, I argue that in its disciplinary formation, film studies is hampered when it makes methodology itself a sort of spatial fetish.[38] Similar to Marxist ideas of commodity fetishism, fetishized spaces are spaces that hide their production processes to acquire a sheen of inherent value and objective reality. Methodologies become spatial fetishes when techniques of analysis are reified and begin to self-perpetuate (which is a risk borne by any discipline as it gets institutionalized), instead of remaining open to interrogation with every application. To grasp how film toggles between the material, social, aesthetic, and immaterial spaces constituting our world, writing about cinema must seek methods that cut across the techniques and intellectual habits of political economy, production studies, media ethnography, textual analysis, film theory, urban studies, and geopolitical analysis. To upend these divisions, I take my cues from the practices of a film's location scout as much as from any practice in film studies.

A location scout is charged with seeking out actual locations that can be used or adapted for a film shoot. The scout gleans a sense of this location from a film's script. She conceives of an ideal place for the shoot based on a photo bank of images, from her knowledge and experience of actual places, from preexisting images and imaginations, and from practical considerations of budgets and schedules. A 1994 manual for film location scouts in the United States defines "location" in the following way: "A location is a real place. It is a specific structure, an area, or a setting where action and/or dialogue occurs in a script. As differentiated from a 'set,' a location is a place where a production must go in order to have the right background to tell its story. A location mentioned in a script can be very specific such as 'the base of the Statue of Liberty,' or very general such as 'a cozy kitchen,' or something purely imaginary such as 'the planet Zargon.'"[39] Film historians interested in filmed spaces share with location scouts this intense interest in mediating between real and imagined places, but not their desire to make the transition seamless. The exchange between the real and the imagined becomes the focus of their study. For them, the terminology of a filmed space is of interest as much for its definitional ambition (it refers to everything that transpires when places are filmed and transformed into cinematic space) as for its definitional ambiguity (filmed places are defined by, and become a part of, so *many* different kinds of real and imagined spaces).

To attend systematically to the multiple spatialities that frame and are generated by the filming of a place, we can weigh the practice of location shooting against the three categories of social space suggested by Henri Lefebvre. Lefebvre scrutinizes institutions, objects, and ideas that we take at face value (instrumentalized spaces), and he reverse-engineers them back to the productive processes through which they acquire their apparent solidity. He does so to destabilize visuality and visibility's exclusive claim to truth. In what Edward Soja refers to as a "trialectics of spatiality,"[40] Lefebvre overlays material, mental, and social worlds in a *fluid* conceptual triad of perceived, conceived, and lived spaces—revealing his antipathy to knowledge itself as a catalogued and disciplinarily bound production of information—to describe their overlapping function in producing what we take as our reality. Lefebvre's trialectics of space serve as an enabling rubric to understand the different scales of cinema's spatiality and sociality for this study. Lefebvre uses a trialectics of perceived, conceived, and lived spaces in order to break away from the binarism of idealist versus materialist frameworks of knowledge and not to institute a new segmentation of space. In that spirit, what follows is less a rigid catalogue for thinking about cinema and space and more an acknowledgment of the intersecting histories that can be narrated when looking at the filming of places.[41]

The first of Lefebvre's triad, *perceived* space, refers to "materialized, socially produced, empirical space" that appears concrete, coherent, and institutional because it represents the ways in which any society "secretes that society's space."[42] This is quite literally the world whose systemic institutions define how we perceive it. For analysts of cinematic space, perceived space may highlight aesthetic traditions, political ideologies, and perspectival and representational conventions that frame images and guide narratives while effacing their own operation. Statist policies and corporate practices that legislate over film as art or commodity may also be understood as elements that make their own interests invisible, while defining the terms of a place's visualization. The second of Lefebvre's triad is *conceived* space, which refers to the design, knowledge, and order through which practitioners actively interpret, translate, and reproduce space. For historians of film, this may point to the codes, designs, and principles followed by film directors and executive producers as well as below-the-line film workers, such as production designers, location managers, line managers, sync sound engineers, location crew, and extras ("junior artists," in Indian cinema's parlance), all of whom do the actual work of translating a place into a visual space. It might also refer to the technologies for recording and duplicating the real, as well as professional practices around the adoption of audio-visual technologies. More expansively, the manner in which a place is transformed into conceived space after its filming could include frameworks of knowledge through which such filmed images are assessed by reviewers and critics, by historians and scholars studying cinema and media over time, and by the parameters of state and private archives cataloguing them. All of these create a context within which places circulate as recorded images in varied social spaces.

Lefebvre's last category of *lived* spaces refers to the ways in which spaces are experienced by their inhabitants and users. For film scholars attending to place-images, this draws their attention to the reimagination of places by filmmakers and spectators, and to the memories of places and built environments that linger on-screen well after a place's actual disappearance or destruction. It may also refer to the experience of inhabiting a place after it has been filmed or memorialized in particular ways. In distinction from Lefebvre's tripartite categorization, sociologist Pierre Bourdieu's notion of "habitus" combines elements analytically separated by the former into conceived and lived spaces. Defining "habitus" as "both the generative principle of objectively classified judgments and the system of classification,"[43] Bourdieu encourages us to think of practitioners who create the codes for reproducing social space as inseparable from their own lived embodiment of those codes. For film historians, this means that industry workers who materially depict and create a film's backdrop can also be understood in relation to their culture's social rules (the "production cultures" described by John Caldwell),[44] because they interpret, disrupt, or extend those rules through their own lifestyles, tastes, and professional as well as leisure activities. In this sense, when a film unit goes on location to film, it represents only one order of the event's lived space; that moment could be used to unbind the histories of its resultant images and their itineraries.

In its commitment to historicism, my project differs from media anthropologist Anand Pandian's deep ethnography of contemporary location-based Tamil films. Pandian studies location shoots to describe relationships between the contingent nature of filming and the "experiential texture of the film they yield."[45] Like Pandian, I am compelled by the "imminent potential of the situations in which these images arise."[46] Unlike him, I find that location filming discloses more than an account of the contemporary, the creative, and the experiential. Maintaining the initial encounter and enframing as a point of friction within instances of location shooting, this book is about the afterlife of such im-

FIGURE I.3 An image recognizable as an Indian village. Courtesy of Amit Pasricha.

ages when they transcend their moment of recording, almost instantaneously, to shape and become part of other social, experiential, and institutional spaces of regulation, exhibition, and memorialization in commercial theaters, state documentaries, school curricula, and archives. I study the production of filmed space in relation to these registers lest we take the apparent concreteness of an image and the seeming immutability of its enabling institutions at face value.

INDIA AS FILMED SPACE

Dark, semiclad, rough-kneed children in a Bombay slum; young lovers aboard Darjeeling's small-gauge train; village women with many pots balanced on their heads; ash-encrusted priests in the Ganges; bejeweled women in Jaipur's ornate *havelis* (mansions); Bollywood dancers in cosmopolitan cityscapes. These images of people and places telegraph India to audiences the world over. I organize my study around the filming of places that have represented India, and not around a history of location shooting in India's cinemas, to underscore a problem with how we categorize films in relation to geographical territories. This book's focus on locations and architectures demands an exploration of the cultural logics and disciplinary practices by which we cluster and categorize films when we inscribe them into historical narratives.

To put it differently, all books are haunted by the spirit of books that they could have been. This *could* have been a book about location shooting in India's mainstream, regional, or alternative cinemas. Such a shadow book could have shown that the Bombay film industry's sound films were predominantly shot in studios, back lots, and rented bungalows until the 1990s, with the exception of art and parallel cinema. *Where Histories Reside* will not be that book. Much as I would like to read it,[47] I am disinclined to write an account of location shooting in India's cinemas (although some of this history makes its way into chapter 5), because it leaves insufficient room to interrogate the institutions, practices, and ideologies that have defined a diverse region as a bounded, territorial, and national entity, to conjure "India" as a unified visual, fiscal, political, and regulatory space.

Michel Foucault memorably said, "A whole history remains to be written about *spaces*—which would at the same time be the history of *powers* (both of these terms in the plural)—from the great strategies of geopolitics to the little tactics of the habitat."[48] In this book, I am guided by a writerly commitment that lands somewhere between the procedures, strategies, and "minor instrumentalities" of institutions and discourses governing our social spaces (in a habit that I picked up from Foucault), and the negotiated "tactics" of working and living in those spaces at the local and individual scales (developed by Michel de Certeau).[49] Consequently, arguments about the geopolitics and aesthetics of filmed spaces emerge, in each chapter, in relation to smaller stories about particular production companies, film personalities, film professionals, cities, towns, and architectural structures, which collectively produce a sense of place. British film producer Bruce Woolfe's short geographical films on the Indian cities of Bikaner, Udaipur, and Darjeeling and Nepal's Kathmandu, shot for secondary school classrooms in the United Kingdom during the 1930s, are the focus of chapter 1 ("Disciplinary"). Chapter 2 ("Regulatory") is about the Kumaoni documentarian N. S. Thapa's theatrical and nontheatrical shorts on the Himalayan mountain ranges, made for the Films Division (FD) of India from the 1950s through the 1980s. In chapter 3 ("Sublime"), I discuss renowned French director Jean Renoir's journey to West Bengal to shoot *The River* (1951) on location in India, and in chapter 4 ("Residual"), I turn to North India's precolonial architectural ruins and mansions captured on film by US, British, and Indian photographers and filmmakers from the late nineteenth to the mid-twentieth century. The careers of Bollywood's location managers, junior artists, and below-the-line workers who are at the front line of current changes in location filming practices in the Bombay film industry today are the focus of chapter 5 ("Global").

The broad purview of a metacritical project on "India as filmed space" allows me to consider different kinds of films made by directors from around the world (specifically British, Indian, and European directors in this book), who used the country's locations and built environments as attractions, backdrops, or inspiration for their films. Filmmakers of different nationalities are of interest because abstract ideas about India have acquired visual coherence through a range of images and narratives about the country. Alongside feature-length fiction, moreover, nontheatrical, documentary, promotional, and short films have played a significant part in visual boundary construction and boundary maintenance. As the history of space has ever been a history of power, these images have served different ends when used by a British versus an Indian film production company. Until recently in India, instructional films, travelogues, newsreels, and documentary films were screened prior to the main feature in Indian theaters because of a governmental mandate making commercial theater licenses contingent on screening a percentage of state-approved films (chapter 2). By state design, this made documentary and nonfiction films a central part of how India's citizens encountered their nation as images on the big screen. In other words, in addition to commercial fiction films, nontheatrical and nonfiction films produced in India and abroad have equivalent purchase on a material history of images documenting or conjuring India as a place.

A few desires drive my grouping of films with a measure of irreverence toward their industrial typology, national origin, and historical period. The first is an imperative to show that a range of histories are embedded in the *processes* through which locations are transformed into moving images. To this end, each chapter tracks the history of a particular aspect of cinema's object status (as image, stock, commodity, archived document, curricular lesson) across a range of institutional, social, and experiential sites. The second is to argue that seeking these histories creates a historiography calibrated to spatial rather than exclusively temporal categories of analysis. The chapters braid together specific cases of location filming with broader questions of theory and geography to propose that our *historical consciousness* and *the protocols of film historiography* alter when history is foundationally driven by a critical focus on units of space in addition to units of time. Specifically, interrogating the spatial production of India through images of its places produces a historiography calibrated to the technological and regulatory processes involved in filming a place, the ontology of cinematic space in those images, the epistemologies framing the visualizations, the institutional and social actors involved in the film productions, and the categories of disciplinary knowledge through which those images are assimilated. So while there remains a repressed arc of periodization that moves this book from the colonial and national to the globalizing eras of Indian society and economy, my project's framework is conceptual rather than chronological, and attuned to spatial categories of analysis that create their own uptake of history.

This leads me to the third and related desire underlying my chapter divisions, which avoid periodizing Indian film history following the nation's dominant politico-economic orders as a colonized (pre-1947), nationally protectionist (1947–1991), and globalizing territory (1991–). Such a division tends to default into a scholarly bias toward studies of colonial dominance, national identity, and transnational exchange in film studies, even though relations of power, attempts at self-definition, and negotiations across political and fiscal borders have defined each of these periods. India's film history might well be narrated as one of colonial *exchange*,[50] national *dominance*, and global *identity* (or any recombination thereof). Qualifiers like "colonial," "national," and "global" as prefixes for "cinema" or "media" mean too many things (based on the context of intellectual debate or the political proclivities of those using the terms) for them to operate in the absence of detail. My proposal is not to lose the precision of historical analysis. Contrarily, it is to let the specifics of each case study take the lead in probing the efficacy of historical and theoretical categories in order to interrogate the categories of analysis that habituate us into unreflexive modes of thought. It is to keep alive the notion that ideas are, in many instances, the first line of spatial containment.

Each chapter of this book distills a particular construction of India within a regime of representation: India as an object of empirical study in British imperial geography (chapter 1), as an incompletely modern but teachable space in FD documentaries (chapter 2), as a possessor of metaphysical truths in Euro-American films (chapter 3), as a place haunted by specters of feudalism in the architectural structures and sets of post-Independence Hindi-Urdu commercial cinema (chapter 4), and as a postliberalized space of uneven mobile capital in contemporary Bollywood (chapter 5). If these selections seem arbitrary and far from exhaustive, that is because the ambition of scale and total history is replaced here by the need to explore the methodological assumptions of a spatialized film historiography with necessarily heterodox tools, including textual, aesthetic, policy, economic, and ethnographic analysis, to assess the varied (material, social, and immaterial) lives of film as an object. My contention is that a critical spatial film historiography unseats the self-evident unities that accrue around received industrial and critical typologies (such as those of genre or nation), to bring into the fold institutional and social histories that escape entrenched categories of analysis. Filmed locations are territorialized by the powers of state, dominant industrial practices, habits of visual perception, and the methods of film historiography itself (see the conclusion).

"Scenics," actualities, and newsreels abounded in the late nineteenth and early twentieth centuries to convey a sense of India as a place to international and domestic audiences.[51] Most of India's natural and built environments were first filmed to be part of nonnarrative shorts, and a cursory look at British, American, Indian, and French films shot on location in India during these early years brings up reams of nonfiction films, some now catalogued, annotated, and digitally accessible.[52] A random sample includes *Scenes on the River Jhelum* (1903, Charles Urban Trading Company, Britain), *Scenes in Ceylon* (1909, Hepworth Manufacturing Company, Britain), *Ruins of Delhi* (1910, Pathé Frères, Britain), *Le Travail des Elephants aux Indes* (1911, Pathé Frères, France), *Punjab Village: The Empire Series* (1925, British Instructional Films, GB), *People and Products of India* (1931, Empire Marketing Board, Britain), and newsreels from the prolific Fox Movietone News, such as *Turbulent Scenes of Bombay Riots* (1930, USA/Britain), *Bombay Boycott Parade* (1930, USA/Britain), and so on.

At first viewing, the overwhelming quantity of locational detail derails any effort at constructing a coherent analysis of location filming. A historiography calibrated to the plenitude of place across shorts, documentaries, and feature films offers a confusing welter of material for study. Like Jorge Luis Borges's character Ireneo Funes, who sees all objects in their immediate and extreme particularity and so loses the ability to generalize or make meaning,[53] a historian watching interminable reels of actuality and fiction films for the minutiae of geography, fauna, monuments, river banks, streets, crowds, villages, and cities will find herself at a loss for categories that do justice to the excessive visual data. Here again is the "distracted and overcathected" spectator that Gorfinkel and Rhodes speak of: someone too attentive to the things in a film's background to heed to their unification through narrative and ocular regimes.[54] However, this distraction and obsession provides a good model for a historian to whom, in Charles Wolfe's words, "cinema offers . . . the experience of moving in and out of different emplacements."[55] The disappearance of the unities of a film's genre-related or national categorizations leads to a dispersal in the historian's way of organizing and understanding films. Her sense of historicism now derives from a self-reflexivity gained by shifting grounds between the comparative visual perspectives and epistemic dispensations of the typological range of films she is watching, each of which frames the meanings of a place or location differently.

Five epistemic dispensations are named in this book: specifically, the disciplinary, the regulatory, the sublime,[56] the residual, and the global orders. Each dispensation organizes India as a place and a cinematic image in distinct configurations, to foster particular kinds of visual and institutional encounters with the land.[57] The five chapters of this book may therefore be read separately, but should be understood as disrupting each other's dominant spatial logic for organizing place. The effect of reading them should be one of reading a cumulative yet polymorphous narrative about the production of India as a location, rather than as a story composed of separate and disconnected episodes in film history.

Part I, "Rationalized Spaces," describes the rationalization of India as a colonial space in the tradition of British empiricism, and the renegotiation of that vision in newly independent India. At the turn of the twentieth century, a tradition of British empiricism privileging experience over pure reason exercised an intellectual influence on the study of geography in British classrooms.[58] Direct observation of a region gained traction as the essential first step toward mapping a territory and acquiring spatial knowledge. This logic of empiricism confronted particular challenges when it came to the curriculum on British colonies. Colonial lands were geographically distant and inaccessible to direct observation and experience. Moreover, the appropriate management of colonial territories was a topic of heated political debate by the 1930s. As I discuss in chapter 1, visual media about Indian towns and cities such as the *Indian Town Studies* series produced by Gaumont-British Instructional in the 1930s entered British geography classrooms as the best substitute for firsthand encounters with distant and combat-ridden places. Two decades later, these commercially produced but state-encouraged British shorts provided an institutional and aesthetic template for instructional films, travelogues, and military films made by FD, the Indian Ministry of Information and Broadcasting's film unit. The new state's emerging visual vocabulary combined the colonial legacy of empiricism with an apparently chaotic mix of supraregional nationalism, technological developmentalism, secularism, and spiritualism. Through N. S. Thapa's documentaries about India's northern mountain ranges, I consider the historical factors enabling a conjunction of nationalism, empiricism, secular rationalism, and myth in FD landscape shorts in chapter 2.

Antithetical to the rationalized discourses of the state were the fabulist and orientalist images of India, discussed in part II, "Affective Spaces." Cinematic images of India's villages and medieval palaces, holy men and ornate women, toiling peasants and lolling cows have been screened internationally at least since Gaumont and Company's single-reel attractions of the early 1900s. A cocktail of exotic images popularizing visions of the subcontinent's crowds, color, poverty, and mystery continues to entertain global audiences, most recently in Beyoncé's Bollywood diva/Mother Mary incarnation in the Coldplay music video *Hymn for the Weekend*.[59] Jean Renoir's film *The River* (1950), which was shot on location in West Bengal soon after India's independence, was hailed as a departure from orientalist depictions of the country. However, the film's combination of actuality footage with sublime themes of death and regeneration alienated some Indian critics and filmmakers who felt that the film reduced India to a moral canvas for white protagonists. This controversy makes the film a rich nodal text for exploring the artistic, social, and industrial frictions and collaborations provoked by a significant foreign location shoot in India. Against the grain of Renoir's visualization of India, but still using landscape to reflect on a sense of estrangement, Ritwik Ghatak's *Titas Ekti Nadir Naam* (*A River Called Titas*, 1973) and Roberto Rossellini's *India Matri Bhoomi* (1959) use Indian rivers to stage contentious dialogues with the trope of India as a sublime space. Looking at competing interpretations of India's waterscapes, I discuss how *The River*'s use of India as a location reverberates within the history of world cinema in chapter 3.

At hard edges to the Western lens on India as a sublime space, but also in response to it, is the anguished internal conversation that India's commercial cinema conducts with its own civilization, explored in chapter 4.[60] Ruins of cities and built environments in post-Independence Hindi-Urdu films such as *Sahib Bibi aur Ghulam* (Abrar Alvi, 1962) and *Lal Pathhar* (Sushil Majumdar, 1971) make muted references to the devastation of North Indian cities in the wake of India's traumatic entry into modernity through colonialism and Partition. Ambivalence surrounding the loss of an imagined feudal past becomes part of Bombay cinema's nostalgic mise-en-scène, particularly in its *haveli* films, which is my term for films that use an iconic type of precolonial mansion (the haveli) as a significant visual trope. Alongside European films that imbue India's landscapes with a sense of sublime spiritual transcendence are these commercial Hindi-Urdu films that are obsessed with the uncanniness of precolonial Indian ruins.[61] The films' narratives and cinematography saturate architectural relics with a sense of haunting nostalgia and melodramatic trauma, to write an affective history of the nation. European art cinema's sublime India and Indian commercial cinema's ruinscapes bring with them a representational and symbolic scheme that is not fully compatible with the sober (but no less ideological)

demands of empiricism extended by the disciplinary and governmental rationalizations of India's territories in statist British colonial and Indian FD films.

Earnest negotiations with the past through landscapes and ruinscapes were
rendered anachronistic by the late 1990s, when the Indian state inaugurated
paradigmatic shifts in the nation's economic policies. The past was put into a
radically different spatial relationship with the present when, starting in 1991,
the Indian state liberalized its quasisocialist economy to dilate the sphere of
commodification to every aspect of Indian society. Predictable and unpredictable transformations in response to privatization, as they unfold in present-day
India, can be seen across numerous socioeconomic registers, from changing
patterns of territorial, financial, and media ownership to increasing availability
and demand for consumer goods and the reorganization of familial and gen-
erational relations. The discussion of "commodified space" in chapter 5 deals
with India's globalization and rising right-wing populism between 2000 and
2013, to explore the mutually entangled processes of India's economic reterritorialization, the Indian middle class's social reorganization, modifications in the
nation's labor forces, and shifts in Indian cinema's aesthetic styles. I tell these in-
terlacing stories by attending to the rise of new below-the-line professionals in
Bollywood who are changing the look and craft of Hindi cinema's backgrounds
and filmed locations. I conduct media ethnographies to write a history of the
contemporary, when a potentially volatile mix of people from India's varying
social classes and regions join the skilled and unskilled work demanded by location filming in Bombay and Bollywood today. As I show, India's transitional
economy is reshaping the social and professional relationships within the film
industry's workspaces while also impacting the microspaces of the film workers' aspirations and desires.

In this book, archival, biographical, and institutional analysis of films from
India's colonial and early national periods are presented alongside textual, cultural, and aesthetic readings of commercial Indian and European art films from
the mid-twentieth century. In distinction to these approaches, the history of
contemporary Bollywood demands ethnographies of the present. There is historical relevance to each of these approaches, and a pleasure distinctive to each.
But the push toward methodological heterodoxy is essential because ecumeni-
cal analytic tools bring sensitivity to the many artifactual facets unique to cinema as an artistic form, sociocultural medium, statist institution, commercial
enterprise, and professional practice. No singular mode is sufficient to uncover
the variegated registers of space constituting, produced by, and implicated in
cinema. Following the injunction to think more carefully and historically but

also more capaciously about cinema and space, I suggest a few lines of possibility for spatial thinking in film studies. These are broad invitations—based on lessons learned from my more focused research into films on or about Indian locations—to go beyond the apparent chasms between the realities of social space and the formal particularities or ideological constructions of filmic space. Filmed spaces are a part and a product of cinematic, social, industrial, imagined, and political spaces. The study of filmed spaces can expose how cinematic and real spaces carry each other's imprints if, to use E. M. Forster's familiar injunction, we "only connect!"[62]

- CONNECT CINEMATIC SPACE WITH THE SOCIO-SPATIALITY OF MEDIA: The two handles of the phrase "filmed" and "space" make it oscillate between recorded screen spaces and profilmic spaces to draw out histories generated in the encounters between film and place. One end of the dyadic phrase opens out to the recorded image incorporated into formal filmic spaces. The other end hints at different kinds of social spaces, such as the world of ephemeral encounters during filming; the statist and capitalistic frameworks of image production; the theatrical or nontheatrical venues where images are distributed, exhibited, consumed, and archived as a range of spatial objects (film stock, video, or digital data); and the social sites where images linger as memories of places since altered.

- CONNECT MATERIAL WITH IMMATERIAL SPACE: Filmed space is substantial and insubstantial, material and abstract, in the Benjaminian sense of representing the "temporal core of history . . . where evolution halts for a moment, where the *dynamis* of what is happening coagulates into *stasis*."[63] This temporary freezing of time can serve as a functional definition of what happens when a place is filmed, crystallizing its fluid time into an enframed unit of space as an image, object, and commodity. These images and objects are subsequently remade in multiple sites of distribution, exhibition, politicization, commodification, memorialization, and experience, each with their own temporality. In this sense, perhaps places transforming into images experience the same fate as a person who is about to be photographed, in Roland Barthes's poetic account.[64] Despite lacking the singular subjectivity of a person, a place that is about to be filmed and that subsequently has a life as a cinematic image is material *and* spectral. It exists simultaneously within the time-bound present of the now and within a differentially temporalized and posed world of an image, remade in preparation of its imminent recording, and perpetually remade in its reuse as an image.

- CONNECT FILMED SPACE WITH A SPATIAL FILM HISTORIOGRA-
  PHY: A history written from multiple sites necessarily interrogates what
  such a perceptual shift does to the disciplinary practice of film historiography. Using filmed space as a historical unit of analysis rearranges how
  we think about film history as a spatiotemporal and disciplinary practice,
  because such writing prioritizes a different optic: *not* chronology or a
  film's form, style, production, genre, technology, and authorship; *nor* the
  global against the national or local scales of production and capitalization. Rather, it simply begins with the question, What transpires when a
  place is filmed, and why? Seeking the rationale unravels the factors definitive of and contingent upon that moment. Abandoning familiar organizational frameworks produces not a randomization of film and media
  history but a history narrated as a constellation of particular regulatory,
  economic, political, affective, and personal forces that define encounters between a camera and its locational environment within any given
  context. Such a historiography is less a rejection of other optics than an
  incorporation of them through a focus on (a past of) determining factors,
  (a present of) enabling encounters, and (a future of) artifacts produced,
  preserved, or forgotten when something is filmed.

- CONNECT THE FLUIDITY OF CINEMATIC TIME WITH THE
  INSTRUMENTALITY OF SOCIAL SPACE: Postmodern geographers
  have complained that the habit of treating "the production of space as
  rooted in the same problematic as the making of history" has subordinated spatial questions to temporal ones, resulting in the projection of
  "geography on to the physical background of society."[65] Ironically, filming
  a real location or built environment is a process by which any place is
  literally converted into a visual background and usually subordinated to
  a film's narrative or thematic elements.[66] Retrieving a film's background as
  a point of focus and analyzing it as a distinctive aesthetic and produced
  entity performs a few strategic inversions. It disarticulates the different
  stages of a film's pre-production process prior to its manufacture as a
  unified textual and visual experience; it focuses on the ontological moment of the camera's capture of the profilmic; it studies the ordering of
  the world within the film's narrative and aesthetic schema; and it tracks
  the embodied and spatial experiences generated by that captured artifact
  of place in the afterlives of films as social objects. The concept of filmed
  space is thus founded on the assumption that all spaces are instrumen-

tal, in the sense that they are shaped by state and institutional power, aesthetic and narrative regimes, market forces, and social hierarchies.

- CONNECT THE INSTRUMENTALITY OF SOCIAL SPACE WITH THE PARTICULARITIES OF ITS EMBODIMENT: If economic and sociopolitical determinations influence how we draw our boundaries, how we manufacture our identities, and how we cast our fantasies, then moving images also exercise their own determinate power on us and *through* us. We each bring our own idiosyncrasies, particularities, bodies, and experiences to them. As regulated object, consumed commodity, and subjective as well as collective experience, filmed spaces are sites of power and politics, but equally of encounter, imagination, and dissidence.

THINKING SPATIALLY ABOUT CINEMA

Film was not constituted as a uniform object under the purview of the Indian state. Rather, it was dispersed into many different categories within the taxonomic framework of India's Constitution. Constitutions are fundamental principles that officially transform a territory into a nation by establishing certain precedents for its people and their lives, laws, labor, and products. The constitution of any state partitions national space politically and economically through "its own particular administrative classification,"[67] to provide a framework of operation that designates fundamental shared values regarding the extent and limits of a state's power and its people's rights, adopted and occasionally adapted within the land. According to the Indian Constitution, legislative issues are divided into separate lists to determine whether the union's parliament (equivalent to the federal authority in the United States but with more power) or an individual state can legislate over it. All issues fall under three lists: the union list (those under the jurisdiction of the central parliament), the state list (under state legislatures), and concurrent list (shared by the center and the states). From 1947 until 1998, the constitution remained obfuscatory on how to apportion legislative powers over cinema. Cinema fell into different jurisdictions based on its categorization as an object of censorship (which brought it under the union list), a luxury product (which was on the state list), entertainment (on the state list), flammable commodity (union list when film was part of the petroleum industry, and state list with the introduction of safety films when it moved out of the flammable category), theater and dramatic performance (under the state list), and so forth.[68]

In other words, the manner in which film was defined and organized—how it was bounded and placed in relation to other products and aspects of social life[69]—could affect the domain of its jurisdiction. Additional confusion came from the fact that the union list was supposed to cover all industries "expedient in the public interest," but the Indian government's low estimation of the commercial entertainment industry made it an uneasy fit within that category. Film was, by default, on the state list for most concerns, although the "sanctioning of cinematograph film for exhibition" was assigned to the union list, which gave the center authority over censorship.[70] Fuzziness around sorting film as an object allowed the center to exert moral authority over cinema with its power of sanction, although individual states retained most of the constitutional rights over film with their power to license theaters and tax entertainment. At stake was the spatial distribution of state power over the cinematographic industry across the scale of a nation, from its local, provincial, regional, and central levels, which depended on how the national territory was defined in relation to film *and* how film itself was categorized.

Spatial thinking makes us review a liberal state's regulation of media as a territorialization of its power over time, defining the extent and the limits of its intervention. The state's management of film as a commodity has been one of many factors in the historical territorialization of state power (as explored in chapter 2). In India's case, the vagueness of the Indian Constitution over sorting films across different lists continued for five decades after Indian independence, despite recommendations to the contrary from three significant official reviews of Indian cinema: namely, by the 1927–28 Indian Cinematograph Committee (*Rangachariar Committee*), the Film Enquiry Committee of 1951 (*Patil Committee*), and the Working Group on National Film Policy of 1980. Each of these inquiries recommended that film be transferred to the concurrent list, in significant measure to protect the commercial film industry from the innumerable regional and national regulatory authorities overseeing theater licensing and taxes.[71] In 1998, the constitution's categorization of film finally changed when the then minister of information and broadcasting, Sushma Swaraj, made a parliamentary proposal to place film on the concurrent list. The film industry was brought under the center's legislative powers in order to give it official industry status, with the ability to attract finance capital, insurance, and other benefits of industry that it had demanded for decades. The Indian state's inauguration of media globalization and the consequent international popularization and monetization of "Bollywood" was part of this restructuring of national space as a privatizing market.

Referring to the maze of regulations that commercial film producers, distributors, and exhibitors had to battle merely to survive in the era of economic protectionism, the *Patil Committee Report* of 1951 quotes a verse from the Urdu/Persian poet Mirza Ghalib's lyrical love poem titled *"Aah ko chahiye ik umr asar hone tak,"* translatable as "It takes a lifetime of longing for a sigh to make a difference."[72] The commercial film industry's desire for an open market was realized when, after decades of the industry's longing, the erotics of profit overtook rituals of public responsibility in the relationship between film business and the Indian state. As I show in "Rationalized Spaces" and "Commodified Spaces," statist measures to regulate or liberalize cinema had an impact on the production practices governing representations of national topography, just as much as they found expression in the aesthetics of film and media images.

Tracking the government's wrangling with the film industry nevertheless make too much of institutional power. What potentially slips past such an account is the *fantasy* of consumerism, which predated India's economic deregulation and underwrote both the film industry's lobbying for lower taxations and on-screen images of free-market consumption.[73] In other words, the success, visibility, and power of institutional spatializations of territory should not throw us off the scent of desired, repressed, and partially articulated spatial imaginaries. Whereas consumerism and privatization were not officially endorsed by the Indian state until the 1990s, spectacles of consumerism, romance, and travel had a much longer presence in Indian cinema, and were expressed in significant measure through representations of landscape. In these cases, histories gleaned by following the regulation and commercialization of film as an economic commodity are insufficient in revealing the affective meanings generated by filmic space. In "Affective Space," I study these alternative cartographic imaginations of land, architecture, and geography on-screen, as they manifested themselves in imaginations that exceeded the ambit of statist visions.

Despite these differences, all location and place-based films discussed in this book explicitly or viscerally contain elements of a travelogue,[74] which is an archetypical cinematic form conveying the sense of an encounter with or inhabitation of new lands. Unfamiliar places are introduced to viewers to educate or entertain them when British students learn about Indian geography through film (discussed in chapter 1) or when Indian viewers learn about their own country's geography in documentaries (chapter 2). European audiences travel virtually to India in films shot there and distributed internationally (chapter 3). In other instances, places and architectures conjure dystopian or wish-fulfilling alternatives to social realities, as in reincarnation films set in havelis, or in consumerist

FIGURE I.4 A visual spectacle from *Throw of Dice*.

spectacles of global travel (chapters 4 and 5). Arguably, in a colonized land, there is a profound sense of encountering one's homeland against and through the colonizer's image in early cinematic visualizations of topography. Self-representation can feel like a form of revisitation when it occurs in the context of first renditions by an imperial power and its proprietorial ownership by an imperial state.[75] Divergent treatments of film's backgrounds present these contesting impulses of self-representation. When actor and producer Himansu Rai worked with Bruce Woolfe's British Instructional to shoot the palaces of Jaipur and Mysore for an international audience in *Throw of Dice* (*Prapancha Pash*, Franz Osten, 1929), he creatively adapted an outsider's perspective on Indian landscapes by making regional architecture, flora, and fauna into a cosmopolitan spectacle. Dadasaheb Phalke, on the other hand, transformed Prabhat Studio's grounds into a mythological setting in *Raja Harishchandra* (1913), incorporating outdoor locations into tableaus of stories already familiar to domestic Indian audiences.[76]

A touristic sensibility migrates as well into the bureaucratic imagination of FD, which produced documentaries that took the spectator/citizen on a cinematic journey of the nation's regions. People and territories marginal to the new Indian state—such as the Gorkhas and Lepchas of North India, or the terrains of India's northeastern states—become objects of a national touristic gaze under the visual regime of FD landscape documentaries. Contrarily, in India's commercial Hindi-Urdu films, on occasion those very places and people positioned by the state as minoritarian, marginal, or exotic become a haunting trace of the environmental uncanny. If appeals to India's syncretic past make FD documentaries instruct all Indian citizens on the national credo of "unity in diversity" by synthesizing India's varied topographical and ethnographic types into an imaginary whole, it pushes a strand of commercial Hindi-Urdu films (such as its Muslim socials) to explore repressed traumas in North India's cities and architectures. Markedly different from either of these visual regimes are today's corporatized Indian media images that shrink-wrap and brand post-modern spectacles of Indian geography. Their self-conscious style either assumes a media-savvy, global, and consumerist audience, or defies Westernized cosmopolitanism with a stylized and self-conscious provincialism. This aspect is described in the chapter on "Commodified Spaces," where space itself becomes a commodified and consumed thing.[77] Each cinematic iteration—whether produced as rationalized, affective, or commodified space—generates a particular relationship between territory and its perception. Each suggests a different mode through which India has been organized and visually spatialized on film.

RIVAL HISTORIES AND GEOGRAPHIES

In *Culture and Imperialism*, Edward Said's analysis of the "rival geographies" of place in art and literature captures the extent to which metaphoric struggles over representing places accompanied material contest over territories.[78] In film and media more so than in literature, given media's commercial need to solicit markets as capital-intensive commodities, geopolitically marginal territories became popular backdrops and news items when rapidly mechanizing technologies of vision coincided with expanding Western politico-economic interests around the world. Photographs and films of places such as Lucknow in 1857, Kashmir in 1948, Palestine in 1967, Mai Lai in 1968, or Fallujah in 2004 became globally familiar at the same time that a spectacular and violent suppression of their sovereignty implanted a local sense of alienation and unhousing for the inhabitants of those locations. One of the challenges confronting historians writing about filmed locations is the manner in which political events at the international or national scale unleash the sense of a place's multiple significance for different populations. A splintered and subjective sense of time comes to be embedded in the same images of place. Another challenge is to consider how historians may reduce the effect of what Susan Sontag has called "proximity without risk"[79] endemic to the mass circulation of any photographic image, which is the experience of feeling that we know a place and a people because we have seen them represented frequently on media, without questioning the basis of our knowledge or endangering the comfort of our assumptions.

This book aims precisely to disturb the complacency of such perspectives and assumptions. References to the Himalayan "hill station"[80] Darjeeling appear here in relation to the Gaumont-British Instructional short *A Foot-hill Town: Darjeeling* (1937). Darjeeling also makes an appearance in K. L. Khandpur's FD documentary *Darjeeling* (1954) and in the classic of parallel cinema *Kanchenjungha* (1962), directed by Satyajit Ray. It features in a different form in the commercial moneymaker *Aradhana* (1969), directed by Shakti Samanta (chapters 1, 2, and 5). The hill station Darjeeling is part of a montage of alternative images in this book. Soviet filmmaker Sergei Eisenstein suggested that architectural ensembles reflect montage computations to a moving spectator, but for a stationary one, the creator needs to juxtapose "in one unique point the elements of that which is dispersed in reality, unseizable to a single gaze."[81] For Eisenstein, cinematic montage was thus a "means to 'link' in one point— the screen—various elements (fragments) of a phenomenon filmed in diverse dimensions, from diverse points of view and sides."[82] In my more linear chapters, case studies draw together different visual perspectives on particular cities, towns, and architectural structures in India. My effort is to undercut the singularity of each cinematic gaze, and indeed to show how each text produces its cinematic space through the management of other potential relations between time and place, memory and history, society and subject. Against the singularities of statist, commercial, or populist mappings of India as territory, this book offers an alternative cartography (discussed further in the conclusion). At the same time, this book's comparative histories and modes of visualizing places are not intended to create an impasse of representational relativism. Nor is it my intention that we halt at historicizing each particular spatial imagination. Rather, my argument is that spatial film historiographies—undertaken, in this instance, through a study of films shot in India—allow the discipline of film and media studies to tackle two challenges: first, the challenge posed by Henri Lefebvre and geographers in his wake to all historians; and second, the challenge posed by subaltern historians to Western historiography.

With my analysis of filmed places through the historicization of representational and social spaces, I concur with Marxist geographers Henri Lefebvre,

Edward Soja, Doreen Massey, and David Harvey, who argue that we need to redress a disproportionate focus on temporality and historical consciousness in European social thought, to show that space is not a passive canvas for human action but an active product and shaper of human life and social relations. This book's concluding chapter expands on the ways in which this project adds to an already rich range of scholarship on cinema and space. On the other side, in debate with Western Marxist geographers, subaltern historians have asked for an account of the persistence of *other* spatial logics—the feudal, the fantastical, the tribal, the ethnolinguistic, the caste-based, the communal, the superstitious, the mythic, the nonlinear—that are partially but never wholly comprehensible within vocabularies of modernity, capitalism, and hypercapitalism, as they persist to produce differentially capitalistic and differentially modern (off-modern, in Svetlana Boym's terms)[83] places around the world. Without refuting the centrality of capitalism to the history of modernity, subaltern historians challenge the primacy given to capitalism's territorial reorganization of the world at the expense of alternative spatial mappings that linger to assist, reformulate, or disrupt the order of economic globalization in microspaces. They dispute the enshrinement of one (Western) modality of capitalism and modernity as normative.

Accepting the second challenge in sustained ways throughout this book, I contend that spatial film historiographies are well equipped to respond to the subaltern critique of Western historiography to convey what Spivak refers to as "the uneven diachrony of global contemporaneity."[84] As others have noted, in any given slice of time, time itself is experienced differently across and within locations.[85] Framing the films and histories of nations such as India as non-Western or anomalous evades the substance of this critique. The sharp point of the argument is that fundamental categories that explain the world, such as history (in this case, of cinema's past) and philosophy (in this case, of cinema's ontology) are indexed to events and texts that belong to what Dipesh Chakrabarty calls a "hyperreal Europe."[86] Others are explained by their qualifying particularity. In film theory, this discrepancy is entrenched in the citational practice of using films, events, and experiences of twentieth-century Western Europe and the United States to explain abstract ideas about cinematic form, although no singular type of place, race, gender, or sexuality can claim ontological normativity.[87] A study that focuses on the filming of locations is necessarily cognizant of the source, object, and intent of cinematic knowledge production. It offers a refutation of the possibility of innocent epistemologies.

To realize the scope of spatial film criticism, we need to consider space as an ontologically central but politically and historically contingent force in cinema. This book acknowledges the earlier and important turn to screen space in 1970s *Screen* theory, but shifts focus away from an exclusive emphasis on the implied subject within the filmic text to consider the tensile relations between onscreen and social, disciplinary, capitalist, affective, and geopolitical spaces. Escaping the territorial trap of different ideational approaches in film studies calls for writing across three registers: across cinema's ability to manipulate time and space to account for the medium's ontological referentiality and plasticity;[88] across the methodologies of film theory, political economy, and cultural studies to account for film as a formal, material, and social object; and across differentiated geopolitical contexts to account for cinema's emergence in the mutually implicated histories of global modernity. While questions of temporality rather than spatiality have been of primary concern to subaltern historians, the revelation that modernity must be understood in relation to disparate historical subjects and contexts has an immediate (if unstated) spatial dimension. To borrow digital humanities scholar Todd Presner's words from another discussion, "What this means for the temporal field is that multiple, nonsimultaneous histories are considered as if they were simultaneous; for the spatial field, it means that multiple, noncontiguous geographies are linked together as if they were contiguous."[89]

Colonial histories and geographies, often effaced from dominant accounts of Western modernity, were temporally contiguous and, more important, causally central to the production of modern industrial Europe. Colonization and slavery were the material practices that made the world contiguous and contagious under the sign of modernity and must remain a historical reference point for spatially decentered writing in the era of neoimperialism and globalization. Seeing the world in this way, with what may be considered a radical spatial equivalence despite reified political asymmetries, makes us ask why knowledge appears placeless in some forms and situated in others; theoretical when produced in relation to some geographical locations, and empirical in relation to others.[90]

This perspective allows me to raise but also sidestep the question of whether this book is about cinema or about Indian cinema. I do not feel compelled to answer that question, because I am proposing that thinking about filmed spaces through a sustained interrogation of locations in film is an opportunity to feel the rub of epistemic and territorial categorizations in all of film history and film theory. What such a study makes clear is that the history of filming a location, in India or indeed in any place in the world, is necessarily a history of the competing assumptions, knowledges, experiences, and practices that underwrite the production of a territory as a visual environment. Apparently coherent spatial perspectives or grids for organizing space give visual and political definition to that place, much as the place and its people exert a determinate influence on an image's visuality and politics. The following historical account of the disciplinary spaces of geography, regulatory spaces of the state, affective spaces of human encounter, residual spaces of memory, and commodifying spaces of capital collectively present space as a template for understanding Indian locations on film. They also orchestrate five arguments and methods for the practice of a spatial film historiography.

PART I

RATIONALIZED SPACES

I

DISCIPLINARY:
INDIAN TOWNS IN BRITISH
GEOGRAPHY CLASSROOMS

My first argument for a spatial film historiography is inspired by films whose historical exegesis involves breaking the old pact between territorial power and epistemic truth. Disciplinary assumptions that lie behind the categorization of places are exposed when we treat epistemic questions of category in pedagogical practices—in this instance, of geography and film studies—as fundamentally spatial. We begin to see how curricular and disciplinary practices create the borders and limits of knowledge to claim their status as institutional truth.

Abstract yourself from this book; realize where you are at present located, the point where you stand that is now the centre of all. Look up overhead, think of space stretching out, think of all the unnumbered orbs wheeling safely there. . . . Spend some time faithfully in this exercise. Then again realize yourself upon this earth, at the particular point you now occupy. Which way stretches the north and what country, seas, etc.? Which way the south? What way east? Which way the west? Seize these firmly with your mind, pass freely over immense distances.

WALT WHITMAN, *HANDBOOK FOR GEOGRAPHY TEACHERS*

These films project the Empire, providing for the people of this country a means of surveying a domain too wide and strange to be described otherwise than by film.

J. B. HOLMES, "G.P.O. FILMS"

In 1919, H. (Harry) Bruce Woolfe founded British Instructional Films (BIF), which came to be known for its educational, expedition, war, and science films. Soon reconstituted as British Independent with some of the same production team, and as Gaumont-British Instructional (GBI) by 1933,[1] the company's short geographical films made for British schoolchildren from the ages of ten and above used a hybrid format of actuality and animation that is evident in the *Indian Town Studies* series. The series includes *A Thar Desert Town: Bikaner* (1937), *A Central Indian Town: Udaipur* (1937), *A Foot-hill Town: Darjeeling* (1937), and *A Himalayan Town: Katmandu* (1937), some of which are available for viewing online at the Colonial Film archive with a running time of approximately seven to ten minutes each.[2] These shorts enjoyed limited Saturday morning educational screenings in 35 mm format at select Gaumont-British theaters across twelve cities in the United Kingdom, starting with Manchester, Bristol, Newcastle upon Tyne, and London. Their primary purpose, however, was to supplement the geography school curriculum as 16 mm films for substandard projectors in classrooms.[3] Film historian Rachael Low notes that a market niche in science films, classroom films, and instructionals may have contributed to Bruce Woolfe's and British Instructional's survival during the

FIGURE 1.1 *Indian Town Studies*
series on Bikaner.

difficult postwar years of British film production onward of the 1920s, making it "one of Britain's most innovative production companies" of the time.[4] The company's catalogue of films for nontheatrical exhibition reveal that shorts that fall under the category of "Geography" dominated their film productions, alongside films on "Natural History."[5]

Viewing the *Indian Town Studies* films some seven decades later at the British Film Institute (BFI) on Stephen Street in London in 2009, I experienced an uncanny sense of visual familiarity and intimacy with the people on screen. Transcending the film's leveling narration, details of Bikaner and Udaipur and close-ups of faces and gestures registered vividly when, with each replay, people moving in their environment took on an insistent reality distinct from the voice-over's ideological script. Retrospectively, however, these first impressions strike me as somewhat delusional. Whatever similarities a twenty-first-century film scholar may share in terms of features or skin color with the colonized subjects visually captured in such films, politico-historical distance and disciplinary training constitute differences. As noted by early theorists of cinema, film possesses the ability to lead viewers to unexpected "encounters with contingency, lack of control, and otherness"[6] when a camera's involuntary susceptibility to its material surroundings disturb the discretionary forces of an image's placement, framing, editing, and narrative control.[7] Contemporary viewers who oppose the politics of a film desire to seek contingencies and resistances within racist and colonial film texts in order to read against their grain. But such critical gestures have limited historiographic value beyond the immediate satisfaction of upending a racist text.

A useful if somewhat schematic tripartite framework for a spatial analysis may follow David Harvey's distinctions between "absolute," "relative," and "relational" spaces.[8] I could say, for instance, that in the summer of 2009 I sat in the absolute space of an archival consul at the BFI; I was relative to other consuls and viewers, just as the film was relative to other films made during and since the 1930s; and my encounter with the film was relational to an infinitely collapsing epistemic frame of references, ranging from the original intent of those geographical films, their institutional and industrial contexts, the processes through which they came to be archived, the questions that led me to them, the vocabularies through which I now seek to make them comprehensible, and so on. The British instructional shorts on India can be historicized in relation to each of these spatial levels. As I argue, in their specifics, the shorts display the uses of visual media in teaching Indian geography to British schoolchildren in the 1930s. As graphic evidence that helped stabilize a field of disciplinary knowledge, they reveal how the status of imperial geography was tested and formalized through visuals about colonies between the two world wars. As projections of colonial India deployed in educating British pupils addressed in the films as future citizens of a nation and empire, they highlight intersections between the visual practices of geopolitics and geography. In the longer perspective, their scrutiny necessitates a reflection on the modes of film historiography that frame contemporary acts of interpretive contextualism, as we respond to such archival films today.

A spatial film historiography calls for a history of these location shots in relation to each of these rungs of meaning: specifically, as assessed within their own conditions of production, and from the position of other times and spaces that possess the ability to "contest and invert" their politics and perspective.[9] Paula Amad's deployment of the returned gaze of subjects of colonial documentaries to think about "a more deeply contextualized and less deterministic" trope of "visual reposte" calls for a similar historiographic turn.[10] If images of the colonized subjects staring back at the camera in early colonial photographs, documentaries, and nonfiction films provide us with the thrill of potential disruptions within colonialism's visual regime, an interrogation of the politics of the camera's gaze and its enabling infrastructures demand rigorous historical inquiry into the contexts of production and the forces behind them. A critical dismantling of the politics of a colonial visual archive must therefore accompany its historical study.

Film historiography faces particular challenges in discussing and codifying the colonial visual archive, because a crisis of categorization was endemic to the colonial process, where the acquisition of sovereignty over bodies and resources across diverse political formations accompanied the constitution of Europe's liberal democracy. If unable to confront the legacies of Europe's contradictory political affiliations, discourses on colonial film risk being trapped in modes of description that merely reinforce the problematic place of colonialism in European liberalism. Questions about the conditions under which colonial territories became part of the imperial cartographic imagination remain at arm's length when the field of film studies neglects to examine the ways in which its own narratological and disciplinary practices graph the world in constructing cinema's historical trajectories. For any discipline to enlighten us on colonial cinema, it must comprehend and disrupt the logics of seeing, being, and thinking that made such films possible in their own time and assimilable within a longer history of cinema, politics, and industrial practice. A historiography that questions the truths of a colonial vision is as yet incomplete if it does not simultaneously assess its own conceptual spatialization.

Colonial films (actualities, newsreels, travelogues, or feature films) have been typically thought of as the range of films made *in* colonies or *about* colonies during a period of Euro-American and Asian territorial imperialism, which largely ended by the mid-twentieth century. Such a periodization nevertheless raises other questions. Should "colonial films" refer to films produced by imperial nations exclusively for exhibition in the colonies? Alternatively, should they refer to all films circulated within the imperium? Could they also refer to *any* film produced by a nation in possession of colonies? More narrowly, should they refer exclusively to films on the *topic* of colonies? If some of these definitions appear too broad or too narrow, setting viable limits exposes the assumptions that underlie any working definition of colonial cinema.

As Edward Said proposed in defining British literature in relation to British literature specifically about colonies and dominions, "We should try to discern . . . the counterpoint between overt patterns in British writing about Britain and representations of the world beyond the British Isles. The inherent mode for this counterpoint is not temporal but spatial."[11] In other words, new symmetries become evident when we place British literature about Britain adjacent to British literature about the rest of the world that was produced during the same period. Translating this emphasis on synchronic (rather than diachronic) modes of literary history to visual images, it becomes important to remember that films relevant to an imperial imagination partook of structures governing domestic visual representations as well as imperial ones. Structural affinities between media content that was directed inward to Britain's domestic population and outward to the imperium were based in the formation of a larger *geopolitical* optic shared by both kinds of texts, and reading for this optic reveals imperialism's centrality to the constitution of a modern British nation that was simultaneously liberal and imperial.[12]

Geopolitics emerged as a crucial strategic concept in British political theory during the late nineteenth and early twentieth centuries, founded on the "understanding of states as divided between land- and sea-powers, as engaged in territorial competition, and as becoming empires through war, trade, and protection."[13] Films about territory and geography were materially relevant to the evolution of this new concept of geopolitics. The incorporation of films about colonial landscapes and built environments into geography classrooms, and the production of GBI's short films representing Indian towns in the late 1930s, occurred in the context of political developments pushing Britain to assert and reevaluate its strategic global position during the decline of formal colonialism. Opening with the specifics of the *Indian Town Studies* series, I consider them within the comparative frameworks of other shorts produced by Bruce Woolfe's film companies, including nature and insect films that are typically *not* gathered under the umbrella of colonial documentaries. My categorical reassembly highlights the role that seemingly minor instructional films played in larger geopolitical and disciplinary formations in Britain, exemplified by a range of topically unrelated films. Places in India were spatialized by these geopolitical and disciplinary regimes of comprehension when they were incorporated into geographical shorts.

GAUMONT-BRITISH INSTRUCTIONAL'S GEOGRAPHICAL SHORTS IN COMPARATIVE CONTEXTS

The GBI shorts about the Indian towns of Bikaner, Udaipur, and Darjeeling share several formal similarities.[14] They all start with identical maps of India identifying the physical markers of the Plain of the Indus (west), Plain of the Ganges (east), Himalaya Mountains (northeast), and Deccan (south), and the political markers of Delhi, Bombay, and Calcutta. These maps are animated by arrows, letters, moving dots, and lines that show, in the case of Bikaner, gates and wells in the walled city and, in the case of Darjeeling, the route from Siliguri and the path of a two-foot gauge railway. All the films use voice-overs that are as laser pointers to an image and engage in "visual pointing," to use Joshua Malitsky's phrase.[15] "Take a good look at this map of India. The arrow points to the Deccan." "Take another look at Bikaner on the map." "If you look at the people in the market, you will see all kinds of North Indians." "Notice . . . the different kinds of faces." Creating a similar visual trajectory for the lands, a frictionless path of arrows and dots takes the viewer on an ever-narrowing journey, from the map of India to a township. Our sequential introduction to modes of

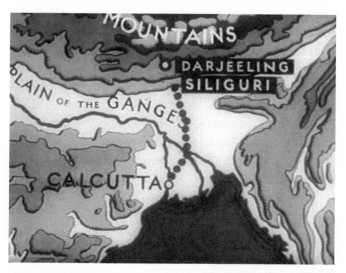

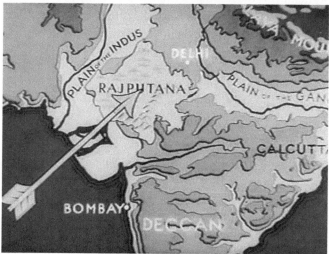

FIGURE 1.2 Map of India in *Darjeeling*. (ABOVE)
FIGURE 1.3 Map of India in *Bikaner*. (BELOW)

FIGURE 1.4 Display of different transportational modes in *Bikaner*.

transportation and the marketplace, with its vocationally or ethnically varied consumers, leads to key built environments such as temples at the spiritual end, and observatories and irrigation systems at the technological end. The tour culminates with architectures of governance, ranging from the Maharaja's Palace in *Bikaner* to the Government House in *Darjeeling*, which was residence to the governor of Bengal in the summer months. In this pattern, the films are similar to an earlier silent BIF geographical film about Afghanistan, *The North West Frontier* (1928), which ends with a humble mud fort that is noted by an ironic voice-over as "the last outpost of Britain on the central Asian Road."

Four places in India with distinct roles in imperial administration—Afghanistan, a frontier of nomadic tribes and invasions; Darjeeling, which served as a British summer resort and tea plantation; and Bikaner and Udaipur, Rajputana Princely States under the sovereignty of the British monarch—are leveled by visual tropes. Repeatedly, viewers encounter vocational or ethnic types of inhabitants (a cobbler, a metalworker, a potter, a *pan-wallah*, and "a cartridge maker" in *Afghanistan*; North Indians, Tibetans, Nepalese, and Europeans in *Darjeeling*), using an incongruous range of transportation (camels, motor cars, bicycles, and horse carts in *Bikaner*; trains, oxcarts, and coolies in *Darjeeling*) and quaint modes of entertainment (dancing dolls in *Darjeeling*; the royal procession in *Bikaner*), portraying the place's awkward relationship to modernity and temporal progression.

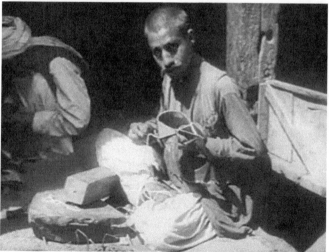

FIGURE 1.5 A bazaar of pots in *Darjeeling*. (ABOVE)
FIGURE 1.6 Vocational types: a cobbler in *Afghanistan*. (BELOW)

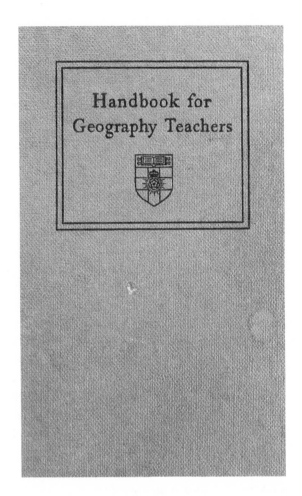

FIGURE 1.7 The 1955 revised edition of a 1932 handbook by the Standing Sub-Committee in Geography in Britain.

The visual building blocks of these geographicals are location shots and ethnographic images edited together with maps and diagrams. Semiotically speaking, the cinematic image and the diagrammatic map are at odds with each other. Maps are symbolic designations of a place drawn from a cartographic system rather than from the lexicon of technologically reproduced reality.[16] They are part of an iconography of enumeration, whereas actuality footage of locations and crowds can register photographic detail in excess of framing discourses. But maps and photographs overlapped as orders of representing reality within the imperial context, when British schools encouraged mapwork based on photographs that represented an experientially tested realm of the familiar. The British *Handbook for Geography Teachers* (1955) recommends that photographs of one's neighborhood or holiday visits serve as the basis for map drawings in order to establish maps as "representations of reality."[17] Abstractions were discouraged, as was the tendency to tell "picturesque but inauthentic stories . . . under the heading of Geography" in dealing with "Life on Other Lands."[18] Consequently, of greater interest than a geographical film's use of maps as text or image is the idiom of scientific nominalism that these films share with the map-making process.

Regional map making was to serve as the training ground for students of colonial geography because it could nurture the student's faculties of *accurate imagination*, a phrase I pursue further because it was crucial to the abstractions that accrued empirical status with regard to colonies. For schoolchildren, colonial maps, photographs, and films were sanctioned by truths not ratified by their daily experience but by institutional knowledge, because unlike familiar local neighborhoods that served as factual corollaries of early map-drawing efforts, colonies were geographically inaccessible except through the imagination. Lacking reliable observational accreditation, the credibility of colonial geography films came from second-order sources sanctioned by the authority of educational institutions and the state. They reflected standards of accuracy acceptable to imperial geography and to its vocabulary of visuality, rather than observational truths. Institutional adjudications over questions of visual veracity and emergent notions of an accurate imagination gained significance in this context.

Two aspects of this observation are worth carrying forward. First, geography's empiricist claim to accuracy was made through the realm of the imagination, specifically defined as a visual and aesthetic realm. This legitimated the entry of literature and film into geography classrooms because fiction and filmic record served as illustrative evidence, and reciprocally conceived of geography as accessible to the imagination in addition to being a field of verifiable study. The ideal balance between an aesthetic imagination of landscape and the ability to accurately survey territories was precisely what became the crucial issue in debates over the best ways to inculcate geographical training and outlook among the British youth during the first half of the twentieth century. Second, although formally and affectively different, both cinema and cartography were linked to the visual truths of imperial geography. Or more bluntly, both geographical films and maps prescribed an imperial outlook on the world. Geographical films that formally combined the artifice of cartographic symbolism with a photographic registration of detail reveal linkages sanctioned between Britain and its empire, and between empire and visuality, in the spatial education of the modern British citizens.

In order to be of greater practical use to curricular geography, the GBI's *Indian Town Studies* series utilizes stable, somber, and data-centric visual regimes, suppressing the fantastical aspects of commercial colonial films (such as those produced in the 1930s by Alexander Korda[19]). Distinctions that mark this series as curricular as opposed to theatrical productions became institutionally entrenched with the formalization of film in education. Before focusing on the function of these shorts in consolidating imperial geographical education, however, I want to lay the grounds for denaturalizing the category of "colonial cinema" by studying the material and aesthetic links between the *Indian Town Studies* series and Bruce Woolfe's other productions. The company's wide-ranging films served as source films or precedents—by providing actual footage or by offering aesthetic influences and narrative frameworks—to the GBI geographicals. Close readings of other GBI films associated with the geographical shorts, either through shared film footage or shared aesthetics, show the crosshatched influences of an internationalism appearing alongside appeals to British industry, colonial cooperation, peer patronage, and geopolitical leadership in the instructional material aimed at Britain's expanding electorate in the 1930s.

WINGS OVER EVEREST, *Gaumont-British Picture Corporation*

Directed by Geoffrey Barkas and Ivor Montagu, *Wings Over Everest* (1934) was a central film for the reeditage footage used in the *Indian Town Studies* series. It was produced by the Gaumont-British Picture Corporation (GBPC), which was the umbrella company of the subsidiary instructional wing GBI.[20] Winner of that year's Oscar for best short subject, *Wings* itself plundered footage shot during three pioneering flights over Mount Everest in 1933. The first two flights were the stuff of British tabloids: they were funded by a chorus-girl-turned-millionaire, they were shot on biplanes flown by dashing young Scottish aviators (one of whom was a titled marquis), and they set out to track the path of two missing British mountaineers, George Mallory and Andrew Irvine. Although cameras malfunctioned on the first attempted flight, subsequent efforts provided the Royal Geographical Society with a detailed survey and meteorological information on mountainous areas that had been previously inaccessible, permitting the incorporation of new data into the mapping of Everest.[21] An editorial from the period pointed out that if US flights over the North and South Poles signaled America's national edge in aviation over Great Britain, the Everest flights marked "the triumph of British grit and also British materials, beside resulting in an extension of human knowledge of the planet we inhabit."[22]

Flight lieutenant David Fowler McIntyre and Douglas Douglas-Hamilton (Marquis of Clydesdale, commander of 602 City of Glasgow squadron of the Royal Auxiliary Air Force, and member of Parliament for Paisley) commandeered the first two of the pioneering flights over Mount Everest that provided footage for *Wings*. The third flight, led by air commodore Peregrine Fellowes, was over Kanchenjunga. *Wings* combines camerawork from these three expeditions to show documentary evidence of the aerial conquest of Mount Everest and to present a narrative about British technological prowess, native superstition, Indian cooperation, and aristocratic charity. *Wings*, available for viewing at the BFI, edits together several different kinds of places in Britain and India to convey what the opening voice-over describes as the "spanning of mountains and continents," which needed "the care and work of many hands." The first of these places are the Himalayan mountain ranges. *Wings* opens with two men, presumably McIntyre and Hamilton, walking up a mountain toward the camera with the ranges behind them. They turn to gaze at the summit, challenging each other with the prospect of flying over the mountain ranges in three hours. "Are you ready for a first-class show?" This fragment appears to be the only recognizable sequence reused in the *Indian Town Studies* short *Darjeeling* (1937), albeit without any dialogue. The other reused material is either difficult to trace visually or was part of footage captured during the three expeditions that was not used in the final cut of *Wings*. The mountain shots in *Wings* set up an early contrast between the "white men" to whom Himalaya's "peaks are a challenge," and the "races that live in the shadow of the grand Himalayan range," to whom they are "the thrones of Gods who visit destruction on men who invade their Holy places." Proleptically, the voice-over tells us of earthquakes that visited the region immediately following the British flights over Everest, proving the power of divine retribution to the locals but dismissed as coincidence by the pilots.

From the mountain shots, the film moves directly to London's iconic urban topography, with aerial views of the city and pans of office interiors as the explorers seek "a company of men fitted for this high adventure." Clydesdale visits Lady Houston, soon to be the peer patron of the flight. Here the camera pans over furs, pillows, and Lady Houston's turban, as she demurs from the danger of the mission but ponders that "what appeals to me is that the people of India—if this is a success, and it is going to be a success—will then know that we are not the decadents that their leaders are trying to make us out to be. That's what appeals to me." The demonstration of purpose and technological triumph are aimed at colonial nationalist dissidents as well as Britain's domestic labor

FIGURE 1.8 An image from *Darjeeling*, possibly reused from *Wings Over Everest*.

force, as demonstrated in the extended sequence about how the enterprise is "setting Englishfolk to work." This sequence of machinic and human work is a montage of physical activity, with multiple images of hands drawing diagrams of airplanes, Englishwomen stitching suits, chemists measuring liquids, plumes of smoke from chimneys, automated machines matching sheet metal, and mixing fuel. The parts are now ready for assembly at the Royal Air Force in Karachi. The film's spatial return to British India is framed by an animated map of crates of equipment reaching Karachi by sea, followed by fully assembled planes flying to Jodhpur. As the animated maps transport viewers seamlessly to different places in the British empire, they also facilitate a synchronization between location shots and statist visions of the territory. The British state's territorial ideology inscribes itself upon visual expositions of the profilmic world, in which location footage is treated as the live-action detail of a section of an animated map in a technique that would be repeated in independent India's FD documentaries on landscapes (discussed in the next chapter). Following the film's return to British India, viewers are treated to low-flying shots over the Rajputana states and Delhi. We have to imagine the footage shot in these towns and archived for later use in the *Indian Town Studies* series. The remainder of *Wings* maps out the mission from the flying base in Purnea, Bihar, which is the launch site for the flight over Everest, and expertly intercuts between aerial shots and interior shots of the plane in flight.

Despite being culled from three different flights—mounted with still "pistol" cameras that could take vertical and oblique images for "a series of survey strips," as well as 35 mm and 16 mm kinematograph cameras[23]—*Wings* effectively conveys the sense of a single flight. The narrative is not tight enough to build dramatic tension, but it creates an arc concluding with the restaged crisis of broken oxygen masks aboard the plane, which accurately portrays what occurred on the first flight over Everest. "What was it like?" the men ask Clydesdale after he completes his flight. "Alright" replies Clydesdale, as the film ends amid a close-up of faces laughing at his understatement. The raw immediacy of documentary footage coexists alongside this staged theatricality of dialogue and attempted humor in an unevenness that conveys the film's hybrid ambitions to display, record, instruct, and entertain. The dispersal of the film's visual idiom across different registers—including images of manual work, surveillance of landscapes, projection of nationalist propaganda, and depictions of the team of workers, engineers, and aviators—offers a testimonial to the competing demands that were placed on a commemorative documentary of this period. The representation of technological challenges, aristocratic patronage, and human triumph accentuated in *Wings* disappear entirely when some of its footage is reedited and integrated into the GBI shorts about India. Although a few stylistic tropes from *Wings* do endure in subsequent instructionals on India, particularly the combination of documentary with restaged fiction and simple animated maps, the colonial shorts fundamentally shift focus from British industry to Indian topography and ethnography, erasing the process by which the films were produced in favor of making the place appear transparent and natural. A comparison between the form and address of the source film, *Wings*, and the repurposed theatrical short *Secrets of India* and the curricular short *Indian Town Studies* opens the way to disarticulating the aesthetics and purpose of colonial geography films.

Secrets of India *Series, Gaumont-British Instructional*
Material shot by teams filming flights collated in *Wings* made their way into GBI's *Secrets of India* series (1934) as well as the *Indian Town Studies* series, which were produced three years apart.[24] Based on catalogue descriptions and surviving films, it appears that despite some shared footage, the *Secrets* series differed considerably in style of presentation from the *Town* series, which came later.[25] In the *Secrets* series on Udaipur, for instance, a voice-over informs us that the King's Palace is the dwelling of "his Highness the Maharana of Udaipur, direct descendant of the sun god, and natural leader by birth and tradition of

all the Indian leaders of the Hindu faith." This display of exotica and superstition affiliates the *Secrets* series with a long tradition of presenting Indian locations through the idiom of fantasy, which British geographical films set out to mitigate with their social scientific tenor of their maps and facts.[26] Mythic and orientalizing images (and music) have no place in the *Indian Town Studies* shorts, which are formally curricular and favor realistic descriptions. This sets them apart from a majority of shorts in circulation during the 1930s for theatrical exhibition.

One example of the exotic fare of short film is *Romantic India* (1936), provided by the Government of India and reedited by C. E. Hodges Production for the British market, which was deemed unsuitable "in the teaching of geography" and more appropriate for general interest or theatrical audiences.[27] A film composed of scenic shots of Indian temples, monkeys, praying Hindu priests, gushing rivers, Himalayan mountains, glaciers, village bazaars, camels, the timber industry, and elephants, *Romantic India* uses stock footage of Indian attractions and iconic locations that would have been familiar to British audiences. Within the context of teaching geography, however, the fact that the places shown in *Romantic India* are treated as generically "Indian" and neither identified by place names nor separated typologically by their flora and fauna or vocations and ethnic types of people made the film unsuitable for classrooms.[28] As appraised in the *Monthly Film Bulletin*, one of the BFI publications that reviewed short films for their curricular or theatrical interest, "their combination in a single film gives an impression of incoherence. Maps showing the areas filmed should be provided and furnished with a scale."[29] The film was not assessed as appropriate for educational venues, having more in common with the sensationalism of commercial fare.

Edward Said notes, "Orientalism is absolutely anatomical and enumerative; to use its vocabulary is to engage in the particularizing and dividing of things Oriental into manageable parts."[30] Similarly pursuing orientalism's systematizing function, Arjun Appadurai distinguishes the "heat of the novel, the light of the camera" from the "cool idiom of number" when it comes to describing colonial populations and territories. "Illustrating literally the power of the textual 'supplement' . . . numerical tables, figures, and charts allowed the contingency, the sheer narrative clutter of prose descriptions of the colonial landscape, to be domesticated into the abstract, precise, complete and cool idiom of number."[31] Geographic films occupy a liminal space in this regard, to the extent that they use an iconography of enumeration with maps and voice-overs to describe the metrics of a place and people, while also enhancing the aesthetic appeal of a

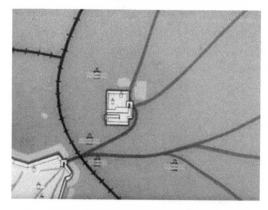

FIGURE 1.9 Classificatory images locating the palace in *Bikaner*.

FIGURE 1.10 Aesthetic images detailing palace architecture in *Bikaner*.

place through a visual elaboration of its difference and exoticism. Imperialism's numerical and nominal impulses of classification are entwined with a measured appeal to aesthetic sensibilities in geographical films.

This in-between aspect of colonial geographical films, oscillating between the heat and light of the affective and the "cool idiom" of the enumerative, creates an unstable mix that was controversial in its own time. Promoting the register of aesthetic appreciation in his presidential address to the Royal Geographical Society in 1920, explorer and archaeologist Sir Francis Younghusband stated, "I am not claiming more than that knowing natural beauty (and being aware of it) is part of geography."[32] Younghusband is quoted by G. J. Cons, academic supervisor of the GBI's *Indian Town Studies* series and general editor of the *Handbook* in 1955, in his introductory statement on geography's incorporation into school syllabi. Discussed in detail further, the *Handbook* provides a fascinating insight into the arguments in favor of introducing experiential, novelistic, and cinematic encounters with land in the teaching of geography, a notion that was resisted by conventional approaches that prioritized facts and empirical data.

Showing an affinity to John Dewey's notion that active participation was the best path to education, and directly influenced by Halford Mackinder's ideas about geography being about an active social relationship between man and the world, Cons champions the routing of factual knowledge through social and sensory experiences. Citing a series of books—such as Whitehead's *Science and the Modern World* lectures from 1925 and V. Cornish's *The Beauties of Scenery* from 1940—Cons makes a case "to resurrect the aesthetic tradition of geography."[33] Referring to these authors' "plea for aesthetic education" with the argument that "when you understand all about the sun and all about the atmosphere and all about the rotation of the earth you may still miss the radiance of the sunset," Cons pushes for an incorporation of fieldwork, literature, poetry, and films into geography classrooms.[34] The curricular *Indian Town Studies* series had to strike a balance between abjuring the wild exoticism and fanciful claims of the *Secrets* films, while maintaining a sensory appeal to the visual over the dry narration of facts. The aesthetics of place had to be incorporated but not dominate the metrics of a geographical film, which aspired equally to the evaluative detachment of a scientific eye. This was less a binarism between aesthetics and nominalism than a negotiation between the two, founded on the belief that sensory and social appeals would provide the best pathways for a sound geographical education.

Secrets of Nature *series, British Instructional Films*

Bruce Woolfe's earlier and more popular *Secrets of Nature* (*Nature*) series (1922–1933) influenced both the *Secrets of India* films that delivered an exotic India to theatrical audiences and the curricular *Indian Town Studies* films. Mary Field was a key figure in several of these productions. Self-described as "the only Englishwoman at present directing talking pictures,"[35] Field was a leading figure in educational films during the 1920s and 1930s.[36] She was the producer of the *Indian Town Studies* series and had worked as editor on the *Nature* series in collaboration with Percy Smith, who was a plant, insect, and underwater cinematographer. Field was sensitive to the drama of nature documentaries emerging from reality itself, rather than from narration or staging, and she would carry this sensibility over to her work on the *Secrets of India* and the *Indian Town Studies* series. Field wrote about the precise tension between reality and theatricality in the *Nature* series and recommended shooting as much film as possible while making a nature or travel film: "So the Director of the nature picture will film everything that may come in useful, the natural surroundings of his subject, the other creatures that impinge upon its life history, long views, close-ups, and shorts from unexpected angles."[37]

The *Nature* series proved so successful that film historians give it primary credit for securing the viability of Woolfe's production company during the 1930s.[38] After its success, Woolfe would recruit Field to serve as director for some of the *Secrets of India* series and as producer of the *Indian Town Studies* films, which diversified her subject matter to "geography, history, language, physical education, and hygiene syllabi in schools."[39] Consequently, beyond analogous titles of the two *Secrets* series that promise to reveal something hidden, the production teams of both the *Secrets of Nature* and the *Secrets of India* series largely overlapped, and they would continue to collaborate on the geographical shorts of 1937. A defining aspect of all these shorts, despite differences in topics, was the relationships they posited between real environments and the cinematic form. Edits combining narrative and actuality in GBI's expedition, nature, insect, and geographical films were part of an evolving understanding of how the cinematograph could grasp the "real," with its emergent rather than imposed sense of drama. Field opposed dramatic films to "nondramatic" (travel or nature) films by saying that "all you can do is to have a general idea of what your film is to be about and then set to work to collect material that may prove useful in making it."[40] Most of GBI's nondramatic films were edited to convey stories gleaned from the world with broad directives and in the absence of a prior script.

The production teams for these films occasionally played up the similarities between short topic documentaries on nature and those on human geography with a self-conscious sense of humor. Field's *Mystery of Marriage* (1932), for instance, compares human and insect mating rituals to comedic effect, and her larger body of work "humorously adapted the wildlife genre to the human and political concerns of rationing, agricultural production, and the use of pigeons as messengers by the army."[41] As discussed by film historian Oliver Gaycken, Percy Smith's scientific films draw viewers into the ambit of nature's secrets through tropes familiar from other genres, such as crime melodramas and detection.[42] An important aspect of the "scientific detective's" exposition lay in the element of sleuthing. As Field and Smith write, given an animal's sensitivity to light and filming equipment, the challenge lay in filming them to seem as if they were "in the absence of any visible person or object."[43] Aspects of this approach to filming are evident in the *Indian Town Studies* series as well. As with the nature series, there is a desire to observe Indian towns and rural Indians at work (typically to the exclusion of urban Indians) while erasing traces of the filmmaker's presence. Although the documented subjects frequently look back at the camera in defiance of this trope, geographical films have a strong element of visual ethnography. Strikingly, the royalty from India's princely states (Udaipur and Bikaner) are accorded single static shots and a direct frontal position and gaze toward the camera.

Presentist and nominal modes of classification characterize nature films and geographical films alike, akin to ethnographic films.[44] There are ominous aspects to creating these reciprocal echoes between the natural and human worlds, because it puts into relief some stark differences. The manner in which BIF's nature films transition from creature to product highlights a key omission of geographical films, which never name the conditions under which products are extracted from laboring entities. Differentiating between the Ailanthus and Admiral silk moths, an intertitle in *Skilled Insect Artisans* (W. P. Pycraft, 1922) tells us, "To secure the silk it must be unwound before the moth spoils it by dissolving the end of the cocoon." This is followed by a shot devoid of moths and focused on a spindle winding thread from cocoons instead. "When the silk, which sometimes is a double thread more than a mile long, is wound off, the dead body of the pupa comes to light." A human hand now enters the frame, giving scale to the visuals and holding the dead pupa from different angles. The destruction of the moth on which the production of silk is predicated is visually emphatic, receiving dramatic close-ups and multiple points of view, marking raw-material extraction as an aesthetically distinct stage within the industry of production.

The cinematographic capture of the beauty of the insect (the dark dead body of the pupa) combined with an instrumental attitude to extracting a product (spooled silk) that renders the creature redundant cannot be transported to geographical films. The elided middle of economic imperialism that transformed a feudal territory into a colonial source of labor and raw material is not included in the geographicals that enumerate and categorize ethnographic and vocational types of people. Transforming colonial labor into a naturalized ethnographic vocational typology suppresses imperial industry as the rationale behind the subcontinent's production of commodities such as jute or timber or ammunition, and behind the erosion of traditional trades. This is reminiscent of Achille Mbembe's discussion of the colony as "a formation of terror" that combines "massacre and bureaucracy."[45] Geographical shorts suppress the violence in the frame of bureaucratic vision. Civilizational explication and organization remains the preferred mode of representing India as a geographical location in the curricular shorts.[46]

Shiraz *and* A Throw of Dice/Prapancha Pash, *British Instructional Films*

Before turning to the role that geographical films played in the educational formalization of geography, it is useful to consider one final comparative context regarding their cinematic form. Gaumont-British Instructional's geographicals can also be read against Bruce Woolfe's theatrical productions under the BI banner, which involved shooting on location in India. British Instructional's films *Shiraz* (Franz Osten, 1928) and *A Throw of Dice / Prapancha Pash* (Franz Osten, 1929) enjoyed considerable critical and commercial success in Britain. These films were cofinanced by Germany's UFA through presold rights and were part of the creative vision of an international team composed of Himansu Rai (an Indian actor/entrepreneur), Niranjan Pal (an Indian scriptwriter), and Franz Osten (a German director). As oriental fantasies, the commercial films are of an entirely different order than the curricular geographicals. Made explicit by the film's full title, *Shiraz: A Romance of India* is a romance featuring a twice-abducted princess, a lovesick emperor, slave raiders, fortunetellers, and duplicitous ladies-in-waiting. The potter in this film, the fictional Shiraz, is entirely unlike the tradesmen of geographical films. Played by Himansu Rai, he is a man who comes close to being trampled by an elephant and blinded by hot steel prongs for his beloved, eventually fulfilling his destiny by building the celebrated Taj Mahal in memory of the empress Mumtaz Mahal, whom he loved without hope of reciprocation.

Despite its overt exoticism, there are several overlaps between films that are commercial fantasies and curricular productions. *Shiraz* and *Throw of Dice* place the same emphasis on India as a filmed location as the geographical shorts. British Instructional Films' commercial features use built and natural locations, such as a bazaar, a desert, and a palace, which are iconic places recorded as well by GBI's subsequent geographicals. *Shiraz* opens with these lines: "'Shiraz' was produced entirely in India. No studio construction or artificial lighting has been used. The actors are all Indians." Both kinds of films, in other words, emphasize the authenticity and accuracy of their representation. Like the geographicals, these dramatic films pay devoted attention to the cinematicity of landscapes and monuments. The Indian princely states (particularly the Rajputana states) are a favored location in both kinds of films.[47] The British Crown administered the princely states as sovereign entities distinct from British India provinces. British recognition of royal Indian titles made princely states ready collaborators of Indo-British film companies interested in utilizing them as material resources and vistas of opulence. Filming at these locations was facilitated by the "beautiful scenic motifs and cheap labor" of the princely states, in the words of Naval Gandhi, a filmmaker of the period.[48] The princely states of Jaipur, Udaipur, and Mysore extended their assistance for BIF's productions, with the maharajas (kings) making their palaces, land, and people available to Himansu Rai. Reviews of the commercial films commend these aspects of the film's authentic mise-en-scène. Of *Shiraz*, the *Bioscope* notes, "A notable feature of the production is the admirable work contributed by vast native crowds."[49] A review of *A Throw of Dice* in the same trade journal praises the film for "Beautiful palaces, gorgeous dresses and state ceremonials and vast armies" that "form the picturesque background," activating the conventional appeal of authenticity in publicizing a location-based film.[50]

Geographical films were sanctioned by different productive rationalities than commercial films, given that the shorts were guided by an instructional mandate to cultivate an accurate imagination, against the latter's profit-oriented sensationalism. But to the extent that they were produced in this instance by the same company, and circulated location shots of India during the same period, both participated in creating seemingly axiomatic visual truths about the colonial place. This returns us to the earlier question of whether—given overlaps in production personnel across the BI and GBI films, and traces of parallel tropes in colonial geographicals, nature films, and insect films—we can presumptively delimit colonial films to films *depicting* colonies or even aimed at colonies. It appears, in this instance, that GBI's Indian geographical films are better explained when placed in the context of Woolfe's production companies (BIF and GBI), rather than exclusively in the political context of colonialism. In fact, foundational to the BIF/GBI's range of cinematic content was a perspective of visual objectivity and cosmopolitan affect that drew from (and hybridized) actuality footage, fiction, news, and scientific and travel discourse.

This is significant because the fields of anthropology, human geography, and comparative politics were as yet not clearly demarcated disciplines in the 1930s. My analytic reshelving of curricular geography films next to nature, insect, and commercial films that had overlapping personnel and companies discloses shared visualities and desires across different film forms and genres. The recommendation that the *Indian Town Studies* series be aimed at students of ten or eleven years of age in geography classrooms was itself an act of disciplinary disaggregration and formalization. It highlights the processes by which imperial geography as well as film were being institutionalized.[51] Geography was formalizing its parameters in educational institutions, particularly with regard to visual material. Preemptively isolating its visual practices when it was still rationalizing its disciplinary gaze would be anachronistic. What is more to the point is the rationale legitimating the entry of particular kinds of films into geography classrooms, discussed next.

AN ACCURATE IMAGINATION

One of the chief functions of geography in school is to help children *to imagine accurately* places, people, activities which lie beyond immediate experience. . . . Using always the experience of the child as the starting-point, the geographer has, in addition to many other aids . . . a wide range of visual aids to assist him.

G. J. CONS, *HANDBOOK*

These words open the section titled "Visual Aids" in the *Handbook for Geography Teachers*, in which the writer evaluates lantern slides, filmstrips, films, wall charts, diagrams, and three-dimensional models for geographical teaching. The idea of an accurate imagination, which relied on the development of empirical methods to extrapolate one's mode of understanding the world by moving from its known (seen and experienced) to its unknown (unfamiliar or seen through facsimile) realms, derived from the geographer James Fairgrieve's textbook *Geography in Schools* (1926). Fairgrieve, who would supervise BI's short on Afghanistan, *The North West Frontier*, in 1928, states that the "function of geography is to train future citizens to *imagine accurately* the conditions of the great world stage and so help them to think sanely about political and social problems in the world around."[52] The connection between visuality as a technique for developing an accurate imagination and accurate imagination as conducive to building a sense of world citizenship played an important part in the acceptance of films as tools for teaching geography. The path to cinema's inclusion as a legitimate aid to geographical education was paved by claims about the centrality of certain kinds of visualization to geography and to citizenship.[53] The two words in the phrase—"accurate" and "imagination"— betray geographical education's empiricist claims made through appeals to the senses, particularly the visual.

G. J. Cons, supervisor of the GBI's *Indian Town Studies*, general editor of the *Handbook for Geography Teachers* in 1955, and senior tutor and lecturer of geog raphy at the University of London's Goldsmith College, named geography an "outlook subject," orienting an "educated person" to the "geographical perspective" of an age.[54] "Outlook," "educated," "perspective," and "age" are key terms, pointing to a collaboration between the late Victorian formalization of empire and popular education in Britain, alongside the institutionalization of disciplinary geography and the emergence of a visual (perspectival) imagination of the world in the early twentieth century. Degree-granting geography departments didn't open at British universities until 1917, but discussions on how to instill in the growing citizenry a sense of place and point of view within their region, nation, and world emerged with the consolidation of empire in the late 1800s, leading to the incorporation of geography into school curricula.[55] Imagination was an important way to reach broader audiences who may have had less exposure to world affairs, particularly with the expansion of suffrage and the mandate to educate the working classes. The paradigm of an accurate imagination in British geographical education appeared in the context of expanding popular education and citizen building. Colonies served as limit-sites that proved or disproved the viability of a conceptual weld between imagination and accuracy, because their physical inaccessibility and the preponderance of fantastical visual representations challenged the ideal of a broad-based rational education in imperial affairs, while also making it more urgent.

GEOPOLITICS AND AESTHETICS

In his definition of an accurate imagination as a means to train future citizens in rational thinking about world affairs, James Fairgrieve owed a debt to his professor Halford Mackinder, a pioneer of modern geography and the concept of geopolitics. Member of the British Parliament and the Royal Geographical Society, champion of the Oxford University extension lectures, proponent of a "new geography" and liberal imperialism, and key architect of the concept of geopolitics, Mackinder was the first to systematically connect geography with what he called a "special form of visualisation."[56] Beyond establishing the significance of visual aids in classrooms, Mackinder influentially proposed that "imagination or visualisation was the specifically geographical mode of thought."[57] In a lecture delivered in 1911, titled "The Teaching of Geography from an Imperial Point of View, and the Use Which Could and Should Be Made of Visual Instruction," Mackinder suggested, "The power of visualisation was meant for real things, rich in shape and colour.... Let our literary teaching appeal to the mind's EAR, and our geographical and historical teaching to the mind's

EYE."[58] While fiction was to be appreciated for its cadences, the scientific study of reality demanded pictorial comprehension. As geographers James Ryan and Gerry Kearns show in their extensive histories of Mackinder, he was central to the promotion of geographical education through the use of visual slides. He assisted in the creation in 1893 of the Geographical Association as an organization of schoolteachers promoting the subject through sharing slides, based on the principle that geography, as much an art as a science, was fundamental to the teaching of civic responsibility and local, national, and world citizenship.[59]

Despite disciplinarily straddling the natural and social sciences, in the wake of explorers like Younghusband and educators like Mackinder, there was a consistent push to reclaim an appreciation of natural beauty in modern geography, defined by them as a discipline encouraging factual analysis and comparative thinking sustained by the sensory faculties.[60] The "visualising eye and the rationalising eye"[61] had to work in concordance to appreciate simultaneously the scientific *and* aesthetic significance of topographical forms. This was the basis for putting together the term "accurate," premised on knowledge founded on scientific facts, with "imagination," premised on the ability to stretch the mind beyond the immediately visible and verifiable world. As the opening epigraph from Walt Whitman quoted in the *Handbook* suggests, the *thinking* mind had to train itself so that it could *sense* the world at all times, accurately, spatially, comparatively. Political consciousness was to enter at a reflexive level as an (unconscious) affectivity that grew out of (tutored) ratiocination. "The real geographer *sees* the world drama as he reads his morning paper. He gesticulates unconsciously as he thinks. . . . In other words, he sees it in perspective of space."[62] What geography had to produce was an instinctive sensory comprehension of spatial meaning, so that visualizing actual topography offered a condensed enactment of Britain's imagined historical destiny.

Central to this formulation was Mackinder's notion of Britain's topographical "insularity and universality," which the *Handbook* proposes as a cornerstone fact used to structure the teaching of British geography.[63] Britain's insularity and universality were measurable topographical features and values and constituted the progressive stages in the education of a pupil. A student's primary school education (ages seven to eleven) began with an intimate knowledge of Britain as an island group or a "homeland" by focusing on its insular regional features. Britain was also privy to the "great human contrasts" of nature and biology because the British Isles were offshore to Europe and territorially pivotal to the world's "universal history."[64] So secondary education (ages eleven and above) oriented students to colonies and lands farther afield from England.

Topography was understood to encourage a geographical vision, and this vision could serve as evidence and valuation of territorial space.

The movement was outward because a perspectival encounter with one's humanity demanded the ability to visualize the entire world within a comparative framework, anchored in a locational position that was simultaneously territorial and evaluative. In a Heideggerian sense, the being was inserted into the world picture and into the world *as* picture with a secure scientific understanding of the being's place within this visualization.[65] Early twentieth-century imperial geographers in Britain embraced Whitman's mental exercise in spatial abstraction because it reinforced such a concrete positionality. As Mackinder reminded his audience, "Let our teaching be from the British standpoint, so that finally we see the world as a theatre for British activity. This, no doubt, is to deviate from the cold and impartial ways of science. When we teach the millions, however, we are not training scientific investigators, but the practical striving citizens of an empire which has to hold its place according to the universal law of survival through efficiency and effort. The special virtue of thought by visualization is that it prompts *doing* rather than merely *knowing*."[66]

The pronouncedly spatial and visual transaction between being and the world is significant in a couple of ways. First, as scholars of visual studies note, the Heideggerian notion of a representational and consequently controllable world highlights the imperializing impulse of European modernity,[67] which seems to be a cognate notion to Mackinder's idea of a "knowing" that promotes a "doing." Second, and this is crucial to Heidegger's thesis, it creates an expanded role for the aesthetic under modernity. In "The Age of the World Picture," Heidegger dwells on aspects of modernity that, according to him, provide "a certain conception of beings" and "interpretation of truth" enabling the emergence of scientific thought.[68] The metaphysical grounds for the formation of modern sciences, he argues, rests upon the emergence of mathematical principles of research procedure. Scientific knowledge is institutionally formalized because of repeatable methodological techniques that require the transformation of the world and its experience into manipulable units of representation, which serve as objects for disciplinary technologies. Under modernity, the world becomes a picture as it is translated into conceivable, knowable, and graspable forms into which beings insert themselves to measure, research, and calculate its related parts, becoming modern through acts of representation and manipulation.

Within this regime of modernity, aesthetics no longer points to rarified objects of art but becomes the framing grid through which the entire world is transformed into measures of representation, open to manipulation by the state and disciplinary practices. In other words, aesthetics is no longer synonymous with art but with the symbolic realms of paramount importance in the management of political and economic life. Walter Benjamin would write of a similar expansion of the aesthetic realm under modernity, and make us see the complex texture of life through it. While valuations of the expansion of the aesthetic into the everyday may have varied (for Heidegger, it reflected an alienating objectification of life and a suppression of the incalculable aspects of life), the idea itself was accepted by several philosophers and theorists of modernity.[69] Mackinder hailed the expanded realm of the aesthetic as a key rationale for including visual material into disciplinary geography. For him, as championed by Cons in his promotion of visual material in classrooms, it was central to the production of future citizens who would be cognizant of the world, because their citizen-mindedness was contingent on a particular visualization of the world.

David Lloyd and Paul Thomas have argued that educing a modern citizen from a subject requires an education of the senses because, for representative democracies—where the part stands for the whole, and the state for its populace—a prior ethical formation invested in the universalization of particular experience is essential.[70] The cultural realm acquires a larger role when the state's survival depends on the perpetuation of a certain disposition or predisposition of its citizens. Although this sounds remarkably similar to the Foucauldian thesis of governmentality, best articulated by Lee Grieveson for its relevance to media's function in the evolution of liberal and neoliberal state rationalities,[71] Lloyd and Thomas are critical of Foucault's neglect of the representative liberal state as a utopian aspiration. Despite this elision, what Foucault clarified was the dispersal of the state's disposition toward the subject across a range of microdomains, corresponding with (and facilitated by) the decline of transcendental sovereignty. Secular liberal states became boundless when they were remade through the management and disposal of all things governing human conduct and life.

With liberalism, states began to function not only as an explicit authoritative agent but more profoundly as something that was reformulated into a logic guiding everything, from disciplinary practices to everyday encounters. While this does not imply incontrovertible state power (as the suasiveness of a liberal political regime can be manifest or repulsed across intimate spaces of subjective experience and public spaces of collective decision), it does highlight the pervasiveness and permeability of state rationalities. With such dispersal, decisions on how the world could be visualized and representationally negotiated became crucial to the liberal state. In other words, aesthetics became the terrain for a struggle over power. Most recently, Spivak has revived the call for an "aesthetic education" as the only way to *combat* contemporary forces of hypercapitalism and corporatization within and outside the university.[72] Understood in this context, a few bland geographical shorts on India with omniscient voice-overs, animated maps, and location shots can be seen as exemplifying a very particular use of aesthetics in the struggle for power. The *Indian Town Studies* combine facticity with the impulse to excite the imagination of British schoolchildren through cinematic maps and location shots to picture "distant lands" for imperial Britain's expanding domestic electorate.[73]

AN AESTHETIC EDUCATION

In Britain of the late 1920s, a collaboration between imperial and liberal ideologies underwrote the advancement of geography as an aesthetic appreciation of the world.[74] It also opened the way for novelistic material and visual media to enter British school curricula. Early twentieth-century British educationalists invoked Romantic poets (such as Keats and Wordsworth) and American humanists (like Whitman) to propose ideals of imagination and understanding in the face of an overstretched and imploding empire. The version of the *Handbook* from 1955 discusses the success of a book titled *The Teacher Was Black*, a study that proved that the "introduction of two Negresses to a school staff led to a very marked improvement in the attitude of children towards Negroes in general."[75] To simulate this experience, world geography lesson plans were proposed that could show "the foreigners concerned as real, live people." To counter the belief that all Africans were "primitive people" living in a jungle, for instance, it was suggested that students be shown *photographs* of Africans as "carpenters and engineers, dentists and judges." Alternatively, students could see a film that "not only showed some of the modern development in Accra, but also showed a woman doing the family shopping," to spot similarities between the English market and a market in Accra.[76] Human and physical geography were to be inhabited imaginatively to expand one's sympathies. Photography and film played a central role within this mandate.

British education could claim a demonstrable difference from the overtly political and propagandistic uses of visual instruction by Fascist and Communist nations in the 1930s because of these subscriptions to an institutional mode of neutral observation and empathetic appreciation. The goal of geography, as framed by Mackinder and embraced by subsequent British geographers, was to promote "imperial *understanding*," although notably for Mackinder this was not an empathetic route to dismantling empire but a vigilant state's pragmatic response to the need to maintain its geo-strategic position because the political principles of liberal imperialism best qualified Britain to be a world leader.[77] Geographical films of 1937 were suggested for school curricula because they utilized referential tools—maps, factual voice-over narrations, ambient sounds, location shots, and occupational and architectural detail—to create an empiricist framework for understanding the similarities and differences between familiar domestic surroundings and unfamiliar faraway Indian towns. This method rejected older fact-oriented geographical gazettes learned by rote, encouraging instead comparative and analytic thinking that required classrooms to incorporate a range of visual aids and literature on exploration and travel fiction alongside traditional textbooks. In sum, the GBI geographicals came into existence because appeals to the notion of an accurate imagination in the interwar period created an expanding role for the visual medium of film in education, based on the belief that film produced the closest approximation to firsthand experiences of other lands, and was capable of expanding a student's geographical sensibilities while affirming the advantageous position and responsibilities of being British. These films were part of an ideology that favored inculcating an appreciation for natural beauty while affirming the political stature of the British Isles when placed in scalar comparison to a world,[78] in which the imperium was cast as a cohesive and comprehensible unit.

APPROPRIATE FOOTAGE AND INSTITUTIONAL LEGITIMACY

Finding appropriate visual material that could foster an "accurate imagination" of colonial geography—in other words, material that cultivated a perspective combining observation with a sense of experientially grounded empathy that affirmed Britain's political superiority—was therefore crucial. Colonies presented tactical challenges. They were physically further afield, unavailable for field trips, less familiar, and, within the calculus of British governance, more chaotic than domestic lands. They were prone to becoming subjects of fantasy, and in need of stronger monitoring by texts of scientific observation, travel, or administrative record. As a space of representation, colonies presented problems to the evolving discipline of modern geography and to the aesthetic education of British citizens, both of which placed faith in the rational cultivation of imaginative, visual, and perceptual faculties.

One of the first concerns raised about visual material for the teaching of imperial geography was the relative paucity of appropriate images or footage.

Mackinder notes that colonial images had "usually been collected either without system by passing visitors whose main object was other than educational, or by residents who . . . are apt to omit pictures of the contrasts which for the stranger are the most salient."[79] Arbiters of what counted as legitimate visual material for the educational market increased in significance with the emphasis on an accurate imagination. The first organization that studied appropriate educational images for circulation in the empire appears to have been the Visual Instruction Committee of the Colonial Office, started in 1902 to gather lecture slides. Their project was to spread visual instruction on Britain "on the same lines in all parts of the Empire," beginning with Ceylon, the Straits Settlements, and Hong Kong, and expanding to include material on India and the dominions.[80] Between this early period and the 1950s, institutions producing visual geographical material for education multiplied to include several public and private institutions in Britain, such as Aims of Industry, the British Film Institute, British Instructional, the Central Film Library, Educational Foundation for Visual Aids, Encyclopaedia Brittanica, the Gaumont British Film Division, the Imperial Institute, Scientific Film Association, Sound Services, and Wallace Heaton.[81] Publications reviewing films and visual material for education included *Film User, Journal of Education, Look and Listen,* British Film Institute's *Monthly Film Review, School Government Chronicle,* and *Visual Education* (which reviewed filmstrips).[82]

As this list indicates, state-run public institutes and private companies participated equally in the production and circulation of imperial images for education, making untenable any definitive demarcations between the state's mandate for a geographical education and the market's orientation toward similar material.[83] Bruce Woolfe's BIF/GBI specialized in films and filmstrips, while the state-funded Imperial Institute was a key source for photographs, slides, lectures, museum exhibits, photo posters, dioramas, and study kits. Both organizations provided material to supplement teaching material on the Dominions, India, and the colonies in British classrooms.[84] Educational literature of the period indicates a peaking interest in how to adapt material on the empire for classroom teaching. On May 27, 1937, immediately following the production of the *Indian Town Studies,* G. J. Cons, supervisor of the GBI series, held a lecture and screening for a mixed audience of film, education, and BBC representatives to explain "how the [geographical] shorts came to be edited" from entertainment films.[85] Exchanges between educationalists, film production companies, and film reviews in educational publications demonstrate an emerging interest and domain of sanctioned opinions regarding best practices in the use of films for geographical education.

Geoffrey Nowell-Smith and Christophe Dupin's historical account of the BFI's complex inheritance of the role as a one-stop institution for film archiving, culture, and education in Britain is borne out by the smaller tale of GBI's colonial geographical films. In 1927, the Imperial Institute wrote a letter to the British Board of Trade in support of Bruce Woolfe's BIF as a private company ideally suited to get a commission to film different parts of the empire. Confidentially criticizing their own educational film holdings to the Board of Trade, Major Keating, secretary to the Imperial Institute, noted that short films from colonies "have been sent over intact [to the Imperial Institute] for display in this country without any attempt at re-editing. Titles are obvious translations from the native tongue. . . . Certain pictures of native rites and customs are altogether unsuitable for display to a non-adult audience."[86] Here again was the problem Mackinder had pointed out, about the dearth of suitable material from the colonies that could be used for educational purposes. As Keating observes, Woolfe's company had proved itself a trustworthy source for high-quality short films because it did not depend solely on contributions of film footage from colonial governments, as evidenced by BIF's successful fulfillment of a commission from the Committee of Colonial Representatives to make a series of films between 1925 and 1928 publicizing colonial life and products. Discussed by film historian Tom Rice, BIF's "Empire Series" was a collection of short films reedited from prior films shown at the 1924 British Empire Exhibition at Wembley, combined with footage shot by the BIF crew during a Special Squadron's Empire Cruise in 1923 and the Prince of Wales's tour of Africa.[87]

On the strength of this work, in 1927 A. E. Bundy of BIF sought a commission from colonial governments on behalf of Bruce Woolfe to "make cinematograph pictures of an educational nature" and for "preferential rights in the distribution of fictional subjects produced in the Empire." British Instructional Films did not finally earn this contract (notably, the request was a frequent if futile one in the 1920s, in the wake of the successes of *Shiraz* and *Throw of Dice*), but the bid reveals a perceived potential for governmental cooperation with private firms on educational and nonfiction films on empire.[88] Corresponding with a Colonial Office inquiry in 1923 about BIF's qualifications to receive preferential rights in producing educational empire films, Major Keating of the Imperial Institute ranked Woolfe's company highly and "in every way superior" to similar films sent to the institute by colonial high commissions, the Colonial Trade Commission in London, and private companies like Levers and Cadburys. According to Keating, Woolfe's filmmakers took "the trouble to seek the advice of eminent authorities . . . from an educational point of view";

they limited "each subject to one reel of about 1,000 feet"; and they succeeded "most happily in introducing little scenes of native life, recreations, native types and customs into nearly all their films. These tend to hold the interest and impress the memory."[89]

Established in 1887, a year after Britain's Colonial and Indian Exhibition, the Imperial Institute (restructured as the Commonwealth Institute in 1958) had a stake in promoting colonial educational films in British classrooms. The Imperial Institute was home to a permanent museum of materials to publicize imperial trade and foster education and research into empire life and trade in Britain. In 1935, the Imperial Institute also took charge of housing and managing the Empire Film Library, which had been founded in 1926 by the Empire Marketing Board (EMB) to store and circulate short educational and trade films about the empire in service of interimperial trade.[90] This library was taken over by the General Post Office (GPO) following the EMB's dissolution in 1933, eventually moving from there to the Imperial Institute two years later. Home to its own theater and screening facilities as well, the institute screened instructional and empire-related films on-site in addition to loaning them out to "some 2,500 schools and other organizations" domestically, as of 1937.[91]

By the end of the 1930s, however, the British government was losing interest in supporting visual material that looked too much like propaganda. Dwindling endowments and grants from the British Parliament and dominion, Indian, and colonial governments to the institute meant that the organization found itself chronically short on funds and resources. The institute repeatedly issued appeals for funds from the British Cinematograph Fund (founded under the Entertainment Act of 1926 to "encourage the use and development of the cinematograph as a means of entertainment and instruction") to assist in the replacement of film prints and the upkeep of the Empire Film Library.[92] The appeals were rejected in 1938, making the running of the Imperial Institute and its library increasingly unviable. By this time, the BFI's entry into film education had in any case made the Imperial Institute's roles as repository, research center, and arbiter of educational and imperial promotional material seem redundant.[93]

In the face of competition from the BFI, the embattled Imperial Institute sent an enumeration of its remit to the Department of Overseas Trade, revealing the depth of contention over issues relating to what composed a good education in imperial and world geography and who was best qualified to store, circulate, or screen relevant visual material. The Imperial Institute's director, H. A. F. Lindsay, indicated areas of overlap and disagreement with the BFI and argued that their library of films should coexist with BFI's holdings because they had separate jurisdictions. "That [British Film] Institute is chiefly interested in documentary films of National importance.... The Imperial Institute is concerned only with films of all-Empire educational interest and its Empire Film Library circulates throughout the United Kingdom chiefly in schools and societies too poor to pay more than the cost of carriage.... We consider that there is room and need for both organisations."[94] Unfortunately for Lindsay, the BFI was fast establishing itself as a center for the cultural and educational assessment of short films and publishing reports on the use of films on the teaching of history, science, foreign language, and geography in schools. The BFI had also criticized the Imperial Institute's Empire Film Library holdings for being out of date because they were furnished by high commissioners and colonial governments for whom British school education was neither a priority nor an interest. This was, of course, exactly what the Imperial Institute had attempted to rectify in its attempts to improve its collections, although to little avail. Officials at the institute well knew that several of their archived and "loan films" sent by colonial governments, such as the aforementioned *Romantic India*, were chaotically assembled. The collective awareness of a need to define acceptable norms for the visual material on colonial geography reveals an emerging consensus over what constituted an accurate imagination of the empire and which institutions were authorized to provide films to furnish such an imagination for the British citizenry.

READING FOR LIFE ITSELF

So far I have argued that GBI's geographical films about India demonstrate the anatomy of what was considered an "accurate imagination," which was influential in introducing visual media into British geographical education. I now depart from this mode of historiography to question the assumption that there was any consensus over accuracy in the first place. While the aesthetics of British visual geography provided the matrix for delivering a liberal imperial ideology to students, such aesthetics belied actual *rifts* in what counted as accurate. During the 1930s and 1940s, there was great political ferment over territories and territorial boundaries, which was reflected in controversies over maps and photographs as key symbolic renditions of territories. Animated maps and location shots of colonial places were the visual means by which GBI's geographical shorts acquired their referential status. But the claim of the accuracy of a map or a location shot was predicated on suppressing contemporaneous contestations over the use of maps, photographs, and images as tools for governance.

The notion of an accurate imagination was aided by the concept of accurate representation, which gave imagination to the "logic of visualisation."[95] Towns in India were visualized as transparent within GBI's representational regimes, which transformed a place, its people, and the fullness of their lives into an abstraction that could be easily communicated to a viewer. Without claiming to restore to fullness those lives and places that were flattened by visualizations of imperial geography, the primacy of a geographical film's disciplinary perspective in delivering a colonial place to us can be unseated if we look for alternative records of the place to understand the exclusions on which such geographical visions were based. If, as Lefebvre contends, "People *look*, and take sight, take seeing, for life itself," then it is worth seeking out that which escapes these visualizations to mark the failure of any representational account to encapsulate all of life.[96]

Mobility and Visibility in Geographical Films

In ways that have been rehearsed several times since the 2001 US invasion of Afghanistan, the North-West Frontier Province was proving to be ungovernable by the British in the early twentieth century. In 1937, the Government of India received complaints about the entry of nomadic Afghans into British India with improper travel documents, such as passports without photographs or unauthenticated photographs. The Afghan passport rules provided for "the issue of passports without photographs to nomads, carriers and labourers—presumably because of the difficulty in obtaining photographs in Afghanistan—and because nomads etc have been locally exempted in the N.W.F.P and Baluchistan from the Indian Passport Rules."[97] This exemption was set to expire in 1938, which provoked discussions in preceding years between the Ministry of External Affairs and the Home Department over the best course of action. Eventually, the administration accepted that while it was desirable for the Afghan government to "encourage the art of photography in Afghanistan by sending some of their subjects to India for training" in photography, it wasn't possible to enforce photographs as a requirement to travel across the frontier. The Afghan border was too large and porous, photo studios and visa acquisition points too far apart, and booksellers in India not in possession of Afghan almanacs.[98] R. B. Elwin, undersecretary to the Government of India, Home Department, concluded caustically that "any Afghan can cross the frontier when and where he likes without meeting anybody."[99]

These nomadic Afghans who escape photography, or leave a frustrated trail of bureaucrats pursuing their accurate visual trace, are not part of the lexicon of images in BI's short, *The North West Frontier*. Geographicals are intent on

FIGURES 1.11 AND 1.12 Cartridge makers portrayed in *Afghanistan* belie the photographic challenges of tracking nomadic Afghan subjects.

showing a rootedness of locals in their environment, so they present information with an exegetic lack of ambiguity that anchors the viewer within clearly demarcated views and spaces. "This is a view of the walls from the outside," says the narrator about the walls of Bikaner. "And now we are looking at the walls from the inside of the town." Similarly, we are told of the different vocational types in Afghanistan, and then we are shown the cobbler, the metalworker, and the cartridge maker.[100] The stability of our status as spectator in relation to colonial places contrasts with the chaotic conditions surrounding photography as a mode of comprehension, visualization, and control in the colony.[101]

Irregular Realities versus Standard Symbols

The same may be said of cartographic symbols (of topography and political boundaries) in the films, whose nominalism conveys none of the challenges of standardizing maps of India during this period. Maps share with film screens the quality of flattening space.[102] Accurate cartography is contingent on the acceptance of certain standards for transcribing latitudinal and longitudinal distances onto alternative shapes such as cylinders, cones, and planes. Film screens, like maps, distort the scale of a spherical globe by their two-dimensionality. Under the leadership of the British government in 1909, an international conference of interested (imperial) nations was convened to publish a series of sheets mapping the entire world following uniform standards.[103] This standard was referred to as the International Million Map of the World or the Carte Internationale du Monde, according to which a map of the world on a scale of one to a million (1/M) was proposed.[104] The publication of such maps ushered a new era in cartography, promising a uniform idiom for comprehending the world.

> A map of the world on a uniform system, in which all sheets are arranged to fit together along the margins—uniform in their manner of reckoning longitudes from the meridian of Greenwich; uniform in their manner of reckoning heights in meters above the mean level of the sea. They will have the same method of indicating the relief of the land, the same conventional signs for towns and roads, the same styles of lettering to distinguish between physical and political features. In a word, the whole map will be written in the same language, without difference even of idiom.[105]

In 1937, Colonel D. J. Campbell, director of Map Publication in India, and Brigadier C. G. Lewis, Surveyor General of India, led a conference on the viability of replacing the varieties of maps available on India with "only one 1/M series" that would conform to the Carte Internationale.[106] However, conforming

Indian topography to international standards posed problems. The Carte Internationale road classifications allowed for only three kinds of roads, unlike the Survey of India maps that recorded a variety of thoroughfares more descriptive of Indian topography. In maps of the subcontinent, three classes of roads were reserved for "wheeled traffic" alone. Then there were the "generally motorable" "transfrontier" roads (fourth category); "transfrontier" roads for "other wheeled traffic" (fifth category); "pack animal" roads (sixth category); and "footpaths" (seventh category).[107] The heterogeneous forms of transport pictured in the GBI geographicals, ranging from camels, horses and oxcarts to pedestrians, rickshaw-wallahs, and automobiles were precisely the problem in fitting Indian topography within any recognized criteria within the international series. On September 2, 1937, a letter went out from the Surveyor General's Office in Calcutta to the secretary at the Central Bureau of the Ordnance Survey Office in Southampton, England, requesting special exemption for Indian terrain, which was not an easy fit for the standardized international grid: "Sir, I have the honour to state that we are contemplating a change in our 1/M map policy . . . we would like, if we can do so without seriously impairing the international value of the maps, to facilitate and expedite the change, by adopting a more convenient contour and layer interval than those laid down . . . we would like the liberty to adopt say one more classification, the necessary modifications being made in symbols used."[108]

Needless to say, the request from India to add "one more classification" necessitating some "modification" to international standards was not granted by the Ordnance Survey Office in England, which noted, "Central Bureau has no power to authorise modifications of the style of the Carte Internationale du Monde au Millionieme," since those were standards set by an international community of nations.[109] Official-seeming cartographic symbols standardized across the *Indian Town Studies* edited out the resistance of the land to productions of visual regularity, to allow an international comprehensibility otherwise impeded by alternative graphic visual translations of the landscape more useful to motorists, army officials, aviators, and residents on-site. The geographical films fulfilled the fantasy of cartographic accuracy and cosmopolitanism by erasing the particularity and quotidian uses of the land.

Gaumont-British Instructional's *Indian Town Studies* series delivered visual and factual information about colonial locations to British classrooms but abstracted the very thing at the center of their disciplinary address: namely, location. Conceiving of such locations as products rather than objects of study reveals the colonial visual geographical as an artifice in itself, while also allowing colonial places a reality greater than their artifactual status within GBI's frame of disciplinary knowledge. This perspective is available to us now, not only because of a temporal distance that allows us to situate colonial geographical films in their historical contexts, but also because we can see them in relation to alternative and actively anti-imperial ways of knowing, recording, and ordering colonial space. Inspired by the greater availability of colonial and historical films in digital archives, our sifting through the material offers us the rare opportunity to reorder matrices of comprehension through which colonial space was grasped at a previous time of imperial filming, screening, and archiving.[110] With its new platform and accelerated access, the digitization of colonial cinema revives concerns about the colony as a space produced through the organization of knowledge in archival and disciplinary practices. The digital reintroduces dreams of accuracy through its (illusory) promise of more complete preservation and access as it stores infinitely more material in infinitesimal spaces, while making that material available to the imaginations of a wider public. It gives the idea of an accurate imagination traction beyond its precise historical usage in imperial geographical texts of the 1930s, because it revives long-standing frictions between the desire for a total history and the questionable faith in the visual as evidentiary proof of accuracy and presence. A geographical and historical imagination's desire for accuracy is opened up for reimagination from within the contemporary.

In order to recast the quest for a so-called accurate imagination of colonial places in GBI's geographical shorts, I have assessed their spatial tropes (of recombined location shots, animated maps, and voice-overs) relative to other productions by Bruce Woolfe's companies and evaluated their significance in relation to discussions of visual media usage in geography classrooms between the 1930s and 1950s. My effort has been to contextualize the *Indian Town Studies* series in relation to the institutional and disciplinary legacies of British liberal imperialism. The discussion shows that the act of writing a film historiography of imperial Britain and colonial India in the 1930s is not just about Britain or India or the 1930s, although it is also most certainly that. Undertaking a spatial film historiography of colonial shorts forces us to confront the categorical assumptions we make when we attempt to historicize colonialism.[111] It requires a confrontation with the archival inheritances of colonial documentation. A spatial film historiography of the *Indian Town Studies* series offers us the opportunity to break with the conspiracies between disciplinary categorizations and epistemic assumptions, allowing us alternative ways to produce historical knowledge about the shorts. This alternative emerges from recuperating a sense of "differential space," which is Lefebvre's phrase to describe the differences that are eliminated when lived realities are transformed into abstract spaces.[112] Seen through the lens of differential space, GBI shorts aimed at British schoolchildren can be understood as much more than curricular innovations that utilized visual media. Their analysis brings to the fore the formal and epistemic assumptions of cinematic and noncinematic documents that work, in their time and over the years, to erase the dense realities of colonial locations and people despite expressing an avowed interest in representing them. Analytically dismantling the spatial tropes of the GBI films, expanding the category of colonial films, and understanding their part in producing a discipline and an episteme allows us to seek an appropriate and ethical historiography for places that were wrenched from their own geographical contexts through acts of imperial film production and circulation when they were preserved in time as filmed, mapped, and catalogued locations.

2

REGULATORY:
THE STATE IN FILMS DIVISION'S
HIMALAYAN DOCUMENTARIES

My second argument for a spatial film historiography uses travelogue, expedition, and mountaineering shorts from the state-run Films Division of India to suggest that as visual artifacts and material objects, films offer two distinct but interrelated ways to analyze state power in the historical transformation of a place into a scopic landscape and politico-economic territory. First, moving images shape our spatial imaginations of the world by using cinematic techniques such as framing, editing, and camera movement to revisualize the topography of real locations as cinematic landscapes. Second, films are technomaterial objects or "things" that circulate and acquire functional definition in relation to a civil society and a marketplace, whose contours they also express.

Being a child of the mountain was a disadvantage for me. Films Division assigned me [a] majority of the documentaries to be made on the Himalayan regions.

N. S. THAPA, *THE BOY FROM LAMBATA*

The State establishes the peculiar relationship between *history* and *territory*, between the spatial and temporal matrix.... National unity or the modern unity thereby becomes *historicity of a territory and territorialization of a history*—in short, a territorial national tradition concretized in the nation-State; the markings of a territory become indicators of history that are written into the State.

NICOS POULANTZAS, *STATE, POWER, SOCIALISM*

In 1940, at the age of sixteen, a Kumaoni Rajput boy from Uttrakhand changed his family name from Dhami to Thapa. Thapa was a common Nepalese Gurkha surname, and the boy hoped to blend in with the 2/10 Gurkha Rifles of the British Indian Army, composed mostly of recruits from eastern Nepal, Sikkim, and Darjeeling.[1] This act of self-transformation to escape a life of poverty in mountainous Pittorgarh by joining the military during World War II plunged young Narain Singh Thapa into a biographical script that reads like something plotted by bureaucrats. Within a year of joining the Gurkha regiment, he was reassigned to the Indian Army's Public Relations Films Unit in Tollygunge, Calcutta, recently established to train Indian Army personnel in newsreel and documentary filmmaking in order to record troops in Britain's Burmese, Middle Eastern, and Italian war fronts. Captain Bryan Langley, who had worked with Alfred Hitchcock at British International Pictures prior to joining the army, schooled Thapa as a combat cameraman. Thapa also trained under Major Peter Goodwin, who introduced the young man to a love of literature, including an eclectic mix of Dickens, Tagore, Kalidas, and Pearl S. Buck.[2] The unit submitted footage and short films for the army's internal use and to the Information Films of India (IFI) as well as its weekly newsreel, the Indian News Parade (INP).

The predecessor of INP and IFI was the Imperial Department of Information's Film Advisory Board (FAB), which closed down in 1943. The FAB had been tasked with drumming up support for World War II in India, a war effort unpopular with Indian nationalists who saw it as part of a European machinery largely indifferent to the condition of the colonies and colonial troops.[3] Created under the command of the British India government, the IFI and INP expanded this war-mobilization mandate to educate Indians in political events, domestic affairs, and international relations. Despite their larger remit, the propagandist origin of the organizations made them anathema to India's new government. Within sight of the transfer of power in 1947, both IFI and INP were dissolved. In the tumult around India's independence and partition, Thapa's film unit was demobilized. He found work as an archivist of footage collated from Britain's theaters of war, joining Major Goodwin in Shimla and briefly transforming himself into "Tim," the "Editor and Supervisor of the Film Subsection of Inter Services Historical Section." By 1948, the newly formed Films Division (FD) of India had recruited Thapa as one of its newsreel cameramen.[4]

Started by independent India's Ministry of Information and Broadcasting (I&B), FD was a state-funded film organization "literally plucked from Nehru's dreams."[5] India's first prime minister, Jawaharlal Nehru, "believed that the short film could be used just as effectively in peace time to further the interests of a developing nation as it was used in wartime for propaganda purposes," as noted by documentarian Sanjit Narwekar.[6] Despite anticolonial nationalist resistance to imperial film units, India's I&B Ministry formed FD along the lines of colonial film organizations,[7] The FD went on to monopolize the production of scientific, educational, news, documentary, and animated shorts in India, and its films enjoyed guaranteed viewership because the Indian government required mandatory theatrical exhibition of instructional films for close to five decades after India's independence.

Thapa is best remembered by fellow documentarians as "Nehru's favorite cameraman."[8] Between 1948 and 1991 (when India's turn to privatization altered the government's monopolistic film exhibition practices, discussed further), FD sponsored several landscape shorts. Thapa, who was commissioned to make a majority of these shorts, developed what I will discuss further as a certain FD house style of a *catalogue* aesthetic, to display recurrent visual and narrative tropes: specifically, India's technological mastery over its natural resources; nature's national symbolism; and, contrarily, nature's sublime transcendence over human or technological effort. In recording and editing images of India's landscape, Thapa proved himself to be profoundly dedicated to FD's Nehruvian mission and its visual dissemination. At the same time, his grumble about the "disadvantages" of being Pahadi (one of India's mountain people) and so being overassigned FD documentaries about the Himalayas, quoted in this chapter's epigraph, reflects that there is more to his story.

Thapa was a state agent, but he had his disagreements with FD. Recalling a central argument of this book, prioritizations of place over space in film analysis evade the ways in which power, technology, and capital are central to our encounter with the world. Analysis of how a place becomes part of a screen's enframed space, and how the cinematic or mediated image is produced and subsequently resides within the innumerable social spaces of industry, regulation, ideology, memory, consumption, and daily life forces back the horizons of historical analysis to many overlapping sites, whose histories can also be written. Where place in film demands a focus on a location's layered histories, space calls forth an awareness of the principles underlying its definition as place, and an awareness of the institutions and people who participate in the perpetuation of its territorial boundaries. Thapa was one such person.

Thapa, a documentarian and a bureaucrat, appointed regional officer of the Film Censor Board in Bombay during the Emergency years (1975–1977),[9] and FD's chief producer in 1980, was on occasion also the target of bureaucratic caprice. Following Michel Foucault's notion that the body is the smallest biopolitical unit, it is possible to consider how a person can be a subject as well as an agential entity of state power. In his role as a state-employed documentarian and citizen, Thapa was an affective microcosm within whom state power over the spatial imagination of a nation became individualized and idiosyncratic. Begoña Aretxaga and Judith Butler remind us that the psychic lives of individuals are unruly.[10] Policies and nationalist discourses read together with subjective enactments of compliance, resistance, loyalty, and resentment toward state institutions fill in the many shades by which chaotic ideas, thoughts, and images harden into structures of institutionality and power.

At stake in framing the argument in this manner is the excavation of multiple layers of personal, institutional, and sociopolitical history governing FD's landscape shorts. A Lefebvrian analysis of the spatiality of society, state, and capital divulges the processes through which media texts acquire their seemingly objective identity and concreteness. At the same time, attentiveness to a film's aesthetics and to the formal specificities of cinema points out that Lefebvre's dismissal of cinema as a spatio-visual abstraction risks ignoring the medium's textural particularities and productive infrastructures. This chapter attends to all these aspects—Thapa's documentary aesthetics, their production process, the preconditions of the state's mandate to exhibit instructional shorts in India's commercial theaters, the circumstances governing the metric length and style of such shorts, and Thapa's own struggles adapting to a state's bureaucratic regime—in the production of India as a regulated space in FD documentaries on the Himalayas.

A textual analysis of Thapa's shorts opens this chapter despite the unsurprising revelation that their nationalist address and statist sensibility was manufactured by a visual cooptation of regional differences. The analysis of film form is nevertheless a necessary first step in seeing how FD's shorts displayed the precise visual mechanisms by which India's heterogeneity was regularized on the aesthetic realm, in parallel with the government's efforts to regulate the commercial space of film production and exhibition at the institutional level, discussed later. The FD's mandate to produce films about India's physical geography occurred within the parameters of power available to the Indian government as a democratic republic. As we shall see, FD was an institution sustained by a precarious extension of an older, colonial-era legislation. Strictly speaking, colonial state powers should not have been compatible with the new Indian state's constitution as a democratic republic. However, Nehru's desire to reinvent imperial film institutions for peacetime developmentalism and to use them for the promotion of a national consciousness introduced both the conditions of possibility for FD and its limits as an organization. Institutionally, FD would derive its funds and key exhibition venues from the governmental practice of regulating India's commercial film industry and exploiting it as a tax base. If FD's content was responsible for the visual construction of India's geographical imagination of itself, then the state's role in fostering an economic media landscape that could sustain an organization such as FD was concomitantly crucial to the nation's territorialization as a fiscal entity.

Put another way, although not equivalent beneficiaries, both FD and India's commercial film industry were products of post-Independence state policies that subjected commodities to restrictive export and import laws, as formulated by a protectionist state attempting to incorporate its regions into a domestic national market. Within this regime, No Objection Certificates (NOCs) and licenses were required for trading in essential and inessential commodities. Licenses defined the terms of commercial life in India. A maze of licenses, taxes, and regulations over the production and exhibition of commercial films were formative conditions of trade for the nation's new entrepreneurs. Among the state's "graphic artifacts" in the sense defined by anthropologist Matthew Hull,[11] licenses can in this sense be considered a literal and visible trace of how the state produced the nation as a fiscally bound entity during the preglobalization period. Film exhibition licenses and import licenses determined the commercial filmmaker's access to critical resources such as theatrical space and raw film stock, which were also needed by FD's documentarians and guaranteed to them by the I&B Ministry. The I&B Ministry closely monitored FD's acquisition of film stock and their access to theatrical or nontheatrical spaces.

The regime of licenses and supervision over film stock consumption described in this chapter makes the Indian state's mechanisms and its realms of spatial control explicit. Government authorities could grant or deny licenses to run theaters or purchase film stock, and the dynamics of push and pull among the government, its employees, and the nation's entrepreneurs would define the terms of trade and institutional life for India's commercial film industry and FD until the 1990s. Given this centrality of paperwork, the scant attention paid in Indian film histories to the regime of stock regulation and theater licenses is puzzling, unless the neglect is accounted for by the very proliferation of licenses in all aspects of commercial life in post-1947 India. During the License Raj, as it was commonly referred to, licenses for conducting business were commonplace objects, which rendered them nearly invisible by virtue of their ubiquity. Licenses were granted by state authorities, but they were also tradable commodities within the nation's thriving extralegal and black-market economies, which meant that licenses extended state power while also becoming objects through which state authority could be ingeniously circumnavigated. In either case, it was not just the film's content or style that displayed the spatial construction of India. The right to make and exhibit films was contingent on paperwork that was the literal manifestation of abstract state power, and also at the heart of informal and social workarounds to a protectionist state's economic management.

A sociality formed around infrastructural elements—film stock, theatrical and nontheatrical spaces, licenses and certificates—that were central to filmmaking. The "social life of things"[12] as it pertained to filmmaking in India reveals the trajectories of transaction that defined India as a socioeconomic entity and shaped the experiences of those making films or doing business in the country. Borrowing from Georg Simmel's thesis about the production of an object's value through money in the reciprocal realms of exchange between the actuality of objects and subjective desires for them, Arjun Appadurai has consistently made a case for "exploring the conditions under which economic objects circulate in different *regimes of value* in space and time . . . [to permit] a series of glimpses of the ways in which desire and demand, reciprocal sacrifice and power interact."[13] The messy materiality of filmmaking that, prior to India's deregulation, involved permissions, licenses, indents, filed and misfiled bureaucratic records, and appendages to regulation manuals are part of the story about how the idea of India acquired its contours as a concrete fiscal space during the post-Independence period. This is not only because such documents were graphic objects in themselves, but also because they defined the terms of regulatory compliance for India's filmmakers, which simultaneously set the parameters for regulatory avoidance as well.

With this chapter, I add to a growing field of research on FD's films and institutions. Studying the postcolonial state's consolidation of authority through a "*naturalization of diversity*,"[14] Srirupa Roy has delinked the hyphen between nation and state to consider how state institutions like FD imagined a unified India for its people despite the organization's deep structural instabilities, such as a constantly changing leadership and collaboration with nonstate actors. Anuja Jain has expanded on this lack of consensus to posit potential problems with understanding FD in primarily statist terms. Where Roy highlights the developmentalism of FD's documentary vision, Jain shows us the importance of its organizational debates around the purpose of documentary in India. Both interventions have been useful in broadening our understanding of the relationship between state, nation, and visuality.

My analysis is founded on a conceptual shift from the notion of the state as *institution* to the state as *space*. Put simply, state space is the space produced by those strategies for managing territory, capital, and life that sustain and authorize governments. Thinking in terms of state space focuses our attention on the myriad practices through which states acquire a territorial and spatial fix, most recognizably in the form of a nation. It effectively denaturalizes the presumption that states preexist a field of actions, agents, and policies that give them a territorial identity, without negating the existence of legal, socioeconomic, and discursive domains that are conducive to particular state formations. Reconceptualizing the state in terms of spaces rather than institutions and apparatuses (which are, in fact, instances of instrumentalized space for Lefebvre) owes a debt to Michel Foucault, who makes us attend to the permeation and dispersal of power across spaces as much as to its centralization in space; and to Lefebvre and Nicos Poulantzas, who focus on the processes that transform regions into frameworks of power that stabilize and authorize preferred modes of (liberal, democratic, or fascist) statehood.[15] In this sense, states may consolidate their power over territorial spaces not only through their military, propagandistic, and carceral paraphernalia but also by fetishizing or ostracizing particular identities

FIGURE 2.1 N. S. Thapa. Courtesy of
Films Division of India.

The Boy from Lambata

Memoirs of a Combat Cameraman
and Documentary-Maker

N. S. Thapa

FIGURE 2.2 Thapa's memoir.

(for instance, by aligning with a race, class, gender, or sexuality) or normalizing structures of institutionality (by setting the terms of monetary transactions or the distribution of property, boundaries, and natural resources). In post-Independence India, FD was a particular manifestation of the state's attempt to regulate the nation's visual, fiscal, and psychic spaces.

The Boy from Lambata, the memoir published by FD's documentarian Narain Singh Thapa, adds a subjective layer to my broad-strokes analysis of state space in this chapter. It puts pressure on the protocols of an academic argument to account for the stuff of everyday life. A filmmaker and would-be administrator's memoir serves as source material and referential counterpoint to the discussion of FD's landscape documentaries because it tempers my inclination to read FD's film content and institutional structure as a pure manifestation of impersonal statist and ideological forces. Too often the centripetal impulse to frame a life and a period within a systematizing argument reduces complex realities into the cadences of a thesis. Certainly, an impersonality of effect was crucial to how state visuality extended its power over the idea of a nation, grounded in the image of a sovereign and bounded territory that subsumed all its citizens within it. But taking that effect at face value fetishizes the state. When read in conjunction with the memories of an individual and his part in his nation's bureaucracy, the state begins to dissolve into teeming microspaces of people creating and grappling with a tangle of institutional stipulations, organizational cultures, political beliefs, and personal decisions.

THE FILMS DIVISION'S MOUNTAIN PANORAMAS AND TABLEAUS

The Himalayan, Karakoram, and Hindu Kush mountain ranges in northern India extend through the political territories of Pakistan, Afghanistan, India, Bhutan, Nepal, Tibet, and China.[16] This region has witnessed state violence, militant rebellion, and environmental crisis, but through decades of upheaval from the 1950s to the 1990s, India's I&B Ministry produced landscape shorts about the mountain ranges that were remarkably homogeneous in form. Thapa, known as an intrepid filmmaker of the mountains, shot several of these shorts. An oft-repeated incident involves Nehru saving Thapa from slipping into the flooding Brahmaputra River in Dibrugh, Assam, in 1954. Thapa and others recall the prime minister scolding him (*"Apni jaan ka bhi khyal rakho!* Take care of your life too!"), when the documentarian, fiddling with his camera, seemed impervious to the dangers of his environment.[17] In later years,

Thapa recounts Nehru telling him, while aboard an Indian Air Force plane, to "make a film on snows [*sic*] and glaciers of the Himalayas." "Yes Sir, I can and I will," said Thapa,[18] building his career on mountaineering, travelogue, and army films about India's rugged northern border states, including *Coronation in the Himalayas* (1953), *The Hidden Land Bhutan* (1953), *Himachal* (1959), *Kangra and Kulu* (1960), *The Valley of the Gods Kulu* (1961), *Himalayan Heritage* (1962), *Song of the Snows* (1963), *The Silent Sentinels* (1963), *Mountain Vigil* (1963), *Sawal ka Jawab* (1964), *Getting Used to Heights* (1964), *Lahaul and Spiti* (1964), *Everest* (1968), *Himalayan Endeavour* (1983), *Kumaoinis on Kamet* (1983), *The Spirit of Adventure* (1989), and *Fragile Mountains* (1990).

Repeated tropes in all of FD's mountain films—including animated maps reminiscent of British educationals, panoramic shots of the Himalayas, still photographs punctuating moving images, stentorious anglicized voice-overs, and life's struggle for survival at high altitude in narrative arcs moving from obstacles to triumphant conclusions—belied the contentiousness of this territory over decades of political change in India, spanned by Thapa's career. Starting government service under Nehru and going up the ranks by Indira Gandhi's tenure as prime minister, Thapa was still making documentaries when Prime Minister Rajiv Gandhi was assassinated in 1991. During this period, the Congress Party's monopoly on the state government collapsed, coalitional national governments emerged, and the nation exploded into separatists movements. The Indian Emergency of 1975–1977 exposed the fragility of India's democracy, and grassroots movements chipped away at the myth of the state as a secular and apolitical agent harnessing the land's resources for the common good of all Indians, which was a vision substantially propagated by FD documentaries and exemplified by Thapa's *Bhakra Nangal* (1958).[19] Thapa witnessed the Indo-Pakistan and Sino-Indian wars and India's transforming politico-economic priorities. Through it all, Thapa's documentaries fit India's geography into homogeneous tropes of national and humanistic progress, creating what Srirupa Roy calls an "undifferentiated sense of being Indian."[20] Thapa's shorts, which craft state-approved visual essays on India's geography, exemplify the house style of FD documentaries in their generic nature. Whatever else happened politically in these regions, Thapa's shorts soothed with visual panoramas and rhetorical closure.

The neutrality and timelessness of FD's mountain and landscape films can be woven into a historicist narrative if we focus not on the monolithic effect of state power but on the mutable and dispersed fields of its operations. Liberating nature from a circumscribed statist perspective involves formulating an

expansive understanding of the role that visual images play in the state's bureaucratic and technological mediation of its environment. In Thapa's decades
of accumulated footage lies a story of the state's changing stakes in its claims of
sovereignty over a volatile territory. In what follows, I analyze Thapa's shorts as
a precursor to a broader inquiry into FD's operation as a state agency that naturalized a statist vision, to make the state appear territorially and symbolically
coextensive with a land.

Indian Panorama/Bharat ki Jhaanki, *Thapa*

Writing about his experience shooting Himalayan scenery in the 1860s, a scenery "which has never been photographed before," British photographer Samuel
Bourne found the world's highest mountain ranges inspiring in their grandeur,
but for that reason unsuitable for the ideal compositional principles of photography.[21] Colonial photographs of the Himalayas are marked by a desire to
domesticate the overwhelming scale of the ranges within the dimensions of
the picturesque, because their difference from English landscapes provoked
both awe and nostalgia in British photographers and landscape artists.[22] Sash-
wati Talukdar shows in her analysis of British picture postcards of Himalayan
mountain ranges that the sublime affect of the panoramic "was inimical to the
purpose of the hill stations which were set up to create a space for colonial society to enable it to rule more effectively."[23]

In contrast, Thapa's Himalayan films render the mountain ranges in a series
of panoramic aerial shots and photographic stills with slow pans that introduce
movement to their mammoth fixity. Arguably, the panoramic filming of the
Himalayas can be read as being in conscious or unconscious defiance to colonial representational traditions that fragmented their scale. In most of Thapa's
shorts, tilts and pans make the mountain ranges a "centripetal" as well as "centrifugal" space, to borrow Edward Dimendberg's evocative spatial analysis, giving the Himalayas a vertical grandeur and horizontal integrity that anchors the
film's images.[24] The visual panorama's all-encompassing hubris suits the postcolonial Indian state's vision of its environment, because as visual compositions,
panoramas hold out the promise of making visual mastery accessible from a
wider range of viewing positions.[25] Here I am accepting Stephan Oettermann's
thesis that historically the European panoramic form evolved from a democratization of perspective, in that it represented the middle class's response to
aristocratic structures of Baroque theater that were spatially organized to maintain royal viewing boxes at a perfect vanishing point. Panoramas dissolved

FIGURE 2.3 Himalayan panorama in Thapa's *Everest*.

ideal viewing points. In addition to being immersive somatic experiences, panoramas presented a horizon of universally graspable spatial reference points by articulating their vision in relation to several nonexclusive viewing positions. When FD shorts represented the environmental sublime through panoramas, they were visually registering the scale of the Himalayas and democratizing its views at the same time. The visual form of the panorama resembled the political aspiration and hubris of the state to unify an abstract collective into a singular viewing body.[26] Srirupa Roy sees a similar maneuver in the state slogan of "unity in diversity," invoked as the "central idiom" of self-legitimization for the Indian nation wherein incommensurably vast scales of regional, religious, caste, and gender differences and hierarchies were subsumed under an abstractable position of a citizen subject.[27]

Thapa's documentary *Indian Panorama/Bharat ki Jhaanki* (1959), about New Delhi's urban exhibition grounds, is an urban counterpart to his mountain films and follows the same hermeneutic of unifying vast differences under the sign of an ideal citizen. The film was shot on location in Pragati Maidan (translatable as "Field of Progress"), which was a sprawling field constructed by the government as an urban exhibition complex for India's first national exhibition (*Pradarshini*) held in 1958. Staged in the second decade of India's independence, this *Pradarshini* spatially translated the state's first and second *Five-Year*

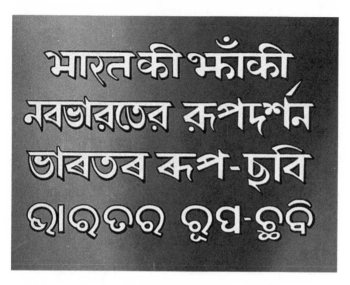

FIGURE 2.4 Title frame from *Bharat ki Jhaanki/Indian Panorama.*

Plans into a spectacle for the consumption and edification of all Indians.[28] The FD commissioned Thapa to shoot the exhibition, with Ezra Mir as producer. The resultant short film was titled *Indian Panorama/Bharat ki Jhaanki.* The Hindi version of title translates as "A Tableau of India" and not as a "Panorama." Different linguistic translations of the same title point to two compatible but nonequivalent visions of the nation. A *jhaanki* is a tableau, and the verb *jhaank* suggests peeking, so that in a collective sense jhaankis may provide a peepshow of tableaus, conveying a totality of space in a manner quite different from the instantaneous wholeness of a panorama. In contrast to the jhaankis, or assemblage of tableaus, panoramas convey vision scaled at 360 degrees to capture an entire horizon in one viewing. Both extend the promise of total vision but differ as a "pattern of organizing visual experience."[29] Jhaankis assume a cumulative experience composed of little scenes, against the panaroma's immediate deliverance of one view to all viewers.

The FD's deployment of both terms—"jhaanki" and "panorama"—in naming this short draws attention to a habitual mode of visual organization that combined a jhaanki's collage aesthetic with the sublime affect of a panorama. In this case, the vernacular glance of a jhaanki fuses with a panorama, the English word for "total vision," to signal a desire to coopt dispersed regional variety into an engagement with universalist categories of nationhood and modernity. It transcends the particular to articulate an abstraction but cannot do so in the

FIGURE 2.5 Entrance to the industrial exhibition of 1958.

absence of the specifics. To use Noa Steimatsky's words, the "minor, regionist key" and the "major, *monumental* one" are perpetually fused in FD's "imaginary reinhabitation" of land through the documentary mode.[30] In this short, for instance, our guide through the Indian panorama is the farmer *Budhe* Thakur ("Old Thakur," where Thakur is a title and a caste name) from Rajasthan, who represents the archetypal rural innocent encountering a bustling urban spectacle. He is the provincial visitor entering New Delhi's urban exhibition site, resplendent in his colorful Rajasthani garb and amusingly startled by abstract sculptures. At the same time, he coopts the desert state to the abstracted position of a national subject by being a caste Hindu (Thakur) who is also symbolic of the new Indian state's investment in the agrarian sector ("the most important man in India—the farmer").

Intermittently following Budhe Thakur, the documentary edits together a peripatetic encounter with the exhibition's displays, traversing buildings named for India's regional states and corporations, sponsored banners, statues, dioramas, food courts, and a Ferris wheel. The film's spotlighted monuments and billboards are easily recognizable as flagship projects as well as enduring problems of India's post-Independence decades. The first building seen on-screen is dedicated to Kashmir's arts and crafts. From here we move to buildings showcasing India's private and state trade corporations (Tata, Coir Board of India, Times of India, Scindia, Small Scale Industries); banners heralding

FIGURE 2.6 Budhe Thakur buys his ticket. (ABOVE) FIGURE 2.7 Budhe Thakur visits the agricultural exhibit. (BELOW)

FIGURE 2.8 Budhe Thakur is pleased by the farmer's display in *Bharat ki Jhaanki*.

India's move "Towards a Socialist Pattern of Society" (a phrase from India's first Five-Year Plan); India's celebration of "The Most Important Man in India—The Farmer" (which pleases Budhe Thakur); buildings for Kerala, West Bengal, Bihar, Himachal, and others; Indian handicrafts and textiles; mock-ups and maps of India's big dam-building projects ("temples of our future" in Nehru's celebrated phrase); India's military industry (*Hathiyar Karkhana*); scientific technology; concluding with the tune of "*Saare Jahan Se Achha, Hindostan Hamara*" (Our India is better than the entire world) that plays at the exhibition's Defence Pavillion. This short's hybrid "minor-monumental" style, similar to FD mountain documentaries, combines a visual accretion of detail with panoramic shots of the nation's natural and industrial horizons, simultaneously deploying *and* transcending regional perspectives to construct a normative universal. Thapa's travelogues and state-visit films follow a similar pattern.

Bhutan: Coronation in the Himalayas, *Thapa*
Made in 1953, Thapa's short on the coronation of Jigme Dorji Wangchuck as the king of Bhutan demonstrates the same dynamic of subsuming the regional under the sign of the national, projected in this case onto natural landscapes rather than industrial exhibition grounds. The documentary about India's neighboring Himalayan state Bhutan combines the cinematic modes of a travelogue

FIGURE 2.9 Thapa introduced as the cameraman in *Bhutan*.

with a state-visit film about India's political officer Mr. Kapoor. The film starts with an invisible third-person narrator familiar from British colonial documentaries. In a plummy English accent, the voice of Berkeley Hill introduces viewers to Thapa, standing with an Eyemo camera on a tripod. "Here is one of FD's cameraman, who was given an assignment to cover the coronation of the ruler of the little-known land of Bhutan." Thapa waves to the viewer on cue. The self-reflexive frame of the film mostly disappears at this point. The now-invisible cameraman navigates us through Bhutan's coronation ceremony. The camera's close attention to regional detail provides a perspective distinct from that of the initial anglicized narrator and the statesman. Because the film isolates the state and technology to one person (Mr. Kapoor) and one object (Thapa's camera), both initially shown on-screen, once they disappear, our attention is effectively deflected away from the integral role that state and technology continue to play in rendering the landscape legible to us. Bhutan's land and people, their clothes, dances, and customs, appear as pure spectacle. Under construction is a seemingly unmediated protonational vantage point observing regional and neighboring difference.

The myth of neutrality belies the technologization of environment. Rosalind Williams has argued that human existence on earth has always been predicated on environmental modification. The only things that have changed over

FIGURE 2.10 Thapa acknowledges the audience in *Bhutan*.

time are the degrees of environmental artificiality, and the meanings attributed to environmental technologization in humanity's scientific quest for fact and in its spiritual quest for truth.[31] British geographical shorts on India characteristically rejected mythic and adventurous depictions of India made popular in commercial films, preferring social scientific discourses acceptable to the discipline's rationalization. The divide between scientific and spiritual discourses of place become unstable as India envisions its own land. Boundaries between science and spiritualism have always been more permeable in modern India, as historian Gyan Prakash argues, not least because Western and empiricist models of knowledge encountered a hermeneutics of suspicion in the subcontinent.[32] When scientific ideas were reinterpreted through a vernacular cultural and religious lens in India, they produced volatile cohabitations between rationalist and mythic visualizations of land.

Western antinomies between the scientific and mythic registers were replaced by something more fluid, malleable, and explosive in India's imagination. "Explosive" because India and Pakistan's independence was only the beginning of several modern reinventions of mythic and nativist Hindu and Islamic claims to land. "Fluid" and "malleable" because, in strong opposition to the politics of intolerance although still writing outside the language of secularism by remaining attuned to the significance of spirituality for the people of the subcontinent, there have been ongoing efforts to reconcile faith with critical inquiry in India. Lata Mani offers a "contemplative cultural critique" that combines notions of the sacred and the political in comprehending humanity's relationship to its environment, reminding us that intolerance and communal politics do not have to be the only ways to assimilate a land to spiritual traditions.[33] The long-standing mutual imbrication of the sacred and the pragmatic in indigenous tradition among the land's *adivasis*, or original inhabitants, politically allied with contemporary feminist and environmental activism, offer another possibility vitiated by a state-based economically rapacious territoriality that was by no means historically inevitable.[34] The subcontinent's partition, state-sponsored industrial development, and the border wars of the 1960s and 1970s worked to politically suppress alternative noncommunitarian and anti-institutional visions of the environment as sacred habitation.[35] In keeping with its period, Thapa's mountain shorts display the influences of empiricist as well as religious epistemes in modern India's cosmogony and cartography. They offer popular science a seat at the exposition of the "enchanted mappings" of India's "geo-body," described in Sumathi Ramaswamy's analysis of India's visualization as mother, woman, and goddess in the nation's cartographic imagination.[36] This cinematic admixture of popular science and spiritualist nationalism is evident in Thapa's documentary *Song of the Snows*.

Song of the Snows, *Thapa*

For the artist a world of beauty, for the pilgrim an incarnation of divinity, for the mountaineer a challenge to his virility.

Kalakar ke liya saundarya ka sansar, shraddran ke liye devaatma ki divvyata ka avtar, parvatarohi ke liye paurush ki lalkar.

NARAIN SINGH THAPA, SONG OF THE SNOWS

Thapa's *Song of the Snows* (1963) introduces the Himalayas with a verse from Kalidasa, the Sanskrit poet who lived circa the fifth century CE. Following the verse, an authoritative voice-over gives us a brief lecture on the condensation and precipitation of water (to an accompaniment of a fast sitar) and the formation of snow (to a *jaltarang*). Fiction, myth, and scientific fact are undifferentiated in their truth-value in this film, unlike in the British geographicals. Thapa reused footage from his mountain films *Himalayan Heritage* (1962) and *The Silent Sentinels* (*Prashanth Prahari*, 1963) for the documentary *Song of the Snows*, which received the President's Gold Medal for best documentary at an event attended by the then-ailing Nehru. Rhetorically, each of the three films uses panoramic long shots of the Himalayas as unifying visuals around an itinerary of smaller film segments.[37] These shorter and differentiated sections (in music and shooting style) consist of a variation of the following themes: the Himalayas as the originary place for sacred Hindu texts, the Vedas and Upanishads; Mount Kailash and Kedarnath as Lord Shiva's abodes; the Himalayas as the place for pilgrimage and inspired literature (particularly Kalidasa's *Meghadutam* and *Kumarasambhavam*); the diversity of people who live on the mountains and valleys (including Ladakhis, Kashmiris, Dogras, and Lahulis, among others); mountain agriculture and produce; types of vegetation; climate; rivers and dams; crafts and dances; and mountaineering. Panning camera movements and changes in music cue topic shifts in these short films that move from one theme to another with rapidity.

What unifies the slideshow format is, in part, its educational intent. While there is a sense of a Hindu *apologetics* in these films,[38] the expository style that treats everything from religion to mythology to cultural practices to science on equal footing lends the films a bullet-point format of unassimilated categories that cannot challenge or displace one another, because they merely exist in relationships of adjacency. (The dilation of the spheres of commodification and religious nationalism would have to await India's globalization, as discussed in chapter 5.) Secularism, as delivered by Thapa until 1991, translates the land into a landscape by borrowing from orders of knowledge that coexist with each other because they are presented as a catalogue of factors, each of equal significance and subservient only to an overarching national developmentalism. The found-footage and compilation style of FD landscape shorts are too haphazard to convey a consistent philosophy of science, territory, technology, or the state, but they reflect popular confluences between a scientific logos and sectarian metaphysics and volatile combinations of ecological and mythological conception of land.[39] The exegetic bullet points structuring the assemblage of images find their mooring in overarching panoramic shots of the Himalayas and in the authority of an omniscient voice-over, which ranges over topics as if they were discrete subsections of a textbook or catalogue, covering the land's physical features, types of people, types of vocation, and so on. The bullet point mode conveys the style that I discuss in this chapter as FD's catalogue aesthetic.

Thapa's FD mountain documentaries may be considered educational films in this sense. Devin Orgeron, Marsha Orgeron, and Dan Streible note that educationals are, at best, an amorphous group of films. Any film, irrespective of its context of production, exhibition or viewership, may be deemed educational in intent.[40] Despite this broad definition, I would argue that educational films carry a distinct relevance to postcolonial nation-states. Under colonialism, imperial commissions to educate and inform Indian or African subjects produced infrastructures such as the Film Advisory Board and the British Colonial Film Unit, which became templates for a postcolonial developmentalist ethos that encouraged the state to imagine media primarily as a technology of instruction for the new adult franchise. The postcolonial state's need to educate its populace in a sentiment of shared territory, history, and civic responsibility meant that educational and instructional films were never restricted to classrooms or to children in India. Rather, they were part of the overall infrastructure and culture of media viewership, as clarified by the system of mandatory theatrical screenings of instructional films in India, discussed below.[41] This is one reason why, in comparison to the disciplinary disaggregation of British geographicals into specific curricular frames, Thapa's FD shorts exhibit a sort of disciplinary delirium. Through their textbook or catalogue aesthetic, the FD geographical films compact information from multiple fields of study into twenty to fifty minutes to address every demographic and age group as a potential citizen-pupil. Thapa's shorts stage an assortment of reused footage drawn from scientific, spiritual, literary, and ethnographic material to construct an expansive vision of India's deserts, rivers, and mountain ranges aimed at the general public.

DISCIPLINARY DELIRIUM AND MIXED MANDATES

For all Indians born before the 1980s, the postcolonial state's expanded educational mandate created an encounter with the state as an inescapable tutor. If Britain saw a proliferation of discussions to formalize the disciplinary use of visual media in classrooms between the 1930s and 1950s, Indians encountered their nation as a mass classroom when commercial theaters screened government-sponsored programming. The pervasiveness of FD shorts was part of their power. They were not viewed in isolation but embedded within a quotidian commercial media world that also brought India's geography to life. Theatrical audiences who viewed FD shorts on Darjeeling were part of the same generation that hummed to the music of *Aradhana* (1969), as Rajesh Khanna lip-synced "*Mere Sapnon ki Rani kab ayegi tu?*" (Queen of my dreams, when will you come?) beside Darjeeling's small-gauge train, with Sharmeela Tagore dimpling inside it. Instructional and romantic registers coexisted on India's theatrical screen that played FD documentaries before the commercial feature, investing the same land with a large repertoire of meanings and a gamut of affective charges. Alongside commercial cinema, the narration and affect of

FIGURE 2.11 Small-gauge train in a documentary on Darjeeling.

FIGURE 2.12 *Aradhana* movie poster representing a scene in Darjeeling.

FD's landscape films contributed to creating the nation's geographical sense of itself. Mapping this affective complexity and the admixture of commercial and public messaging around land imagery in post-Independence India displaces exclusively ideological readings of FD shorts.

As visual scholars note, the modern redefinition of human perception in technological encounters with land occurred across a wide range of professions and avocations, from cinema and medicine to exploration, militarization, and reconnaissance.[42] Aerial imaging technologies are a good example of this, most recently discussed by Caren Kaplan for the technology's uses in war, cartography, and visual culture.[43] In post-Independence India, the bureaucratic branch of the government tasked with producing educational and informational films utilized visual technologies deployed as well in military and commercial endeavors. The FD's instrumentalization of land as landscape was a product of the liberal-administrative branches of a state that supervised, in its complete ensemble, militaristic strategies of governance. Not coincidentally, then, the camera-rifle and aerial cinematography used by Thapa in his mountain films incorporated some of the same hardware used for the visual surveillance of India's border areas. Overlaps are also explicit when we follow the personnel and their professions: Thapa rose up the ranks as a member of the British Army and a combat cameraman. In broader terms, the state that defended its territory militarily also exhibited domestic restraint as a secular democracy, and these two aspects were related in the state's ensemble of strategies that define the spatial parameters of its power. The hybrid aspects of "seeing like a state" can be untangled in Thapa's works when we follow a wider range of his land-related films, including his military and mountaineering films.[44]

Thapa's Military and Mountaineering Films

Thapa was commissioned by FD to make military training and morale-boosting films during the Sino-Indian border conflict, such as *Mountain Vigil*, *Getting Used to Heights*, and *Sawal ka Jawab*. These shorts were made with the assistance of India's Ministry of Defence for a range of audiences, including urban Indians, who provided a key tax base and moral sanction for the war; soldiers in need of encouragement and acclimatization to high altitudes; and the enemies who were the target of "psychological warfare films."[45] For these films, aerial shots were filmed from aircrafts used by the Indian military, such as the BL554 plane in *Mountain Vigil*. Thapa used the air force's cine-gun for several shots in *Harvest of Glory* and *Valour in the Sky* to record the Indian Army and Air Force in the Indo-Pakistan conflict of 1965.[46] Such newsreels quite literally drew audiences into the military's perspective when cameramen got on military flights or rode on tanks and operated cameras that incorporated military technology.[47] *Mountain Vigil* opens with a voice-over speaking about the *jawans* (soldiers) and soliciting the viewer's sympathies for the man who was "alone in the snow, a jawan, our jawan, perhaps your brother, perhaps your son." The seemingly direct address of a familial presence serves as a proxy for a state abstracting the nation as a family. The film's vision reproduces what James Scott calls "seeing like a state," wherein individuals are translated into collectivities in service of the state apparatus.[48]

The low-ranking jawans, shot from afar, are unlikely to have been sons and brothers of the short's presumed spectators. Although FD had regional units and translated some of its shorts into different languages, the anglicized English of the production, the camera's distance from the jawans, and the voice-over's instruction on empathizing with the foot soldier primarily appears to address middlebrow English-speaking urban Indian audiences at a comfortable detachment from the war front.[49] India's middle classes, nascent in the 1960s and 1970s, were important addressees of the FD shorts and central to the assimilation of the Himalayan mountainscapes into a discourse of militarism and the emerging consumer cultures of sports, leisure, and travel. The FD's message in these mountain documentaries was never narrowly nationalistic or militaristic. It additionally mobilized the commercial appeal of India's rugged terrain as a potential holiday venue and presented mountaineering as a serious avocation for India's new middle classes.[50] Prime Minister Nehru, an enthusiastic supporter of mountaineering and a patron of the Himalayan Mountaineering Institute and the Indian Mountaineering Foundation, noted in 1961 that although "trained mountaineering has not been popular in the past . . . the spirit and lure of the Himalayas is spreading now all over India among the young people, and that is a sign and a symbol of the new life and new spirit that is coursing through India's veins."[51] Professional mountaineering associations were reimagining the nation's citizenry as a youthful and resilient body. The 1960s were a decade that saw the mountains reimagined as a bastion of national defense, a challenge to human endeavors, and an idyllic retreat from urban life in both FD's shorts and their cognates in commercial films, such as *Haqeeqat* (Chetan Anand, 1964).

Thapa's award-winning documentary *Everest* (1968) is a good node from which to unravel the interconnected histories of FD bureaucracy, its militarization of land, the nation's commodification of sports and travel, and the aestheticization of the environment. The eighty-minute film recorded the historic

FIGURE 2.13 Title shot from *Everest*.

expedition of the first all-Indian team to scale Mount Everest from the Nepalese side of the Himalayas on May 20, 1965. British, Swiss, and American teams had successfully completed this mission previously, and Tenzing Norgay and his nephew, Nawang Gombu, from Nepal had participated in prior expeditions with international and Indian team members, such as the pioneering British expedition completed by New Zealander Edmund Hillary with Norgay in 1953. But the task had yet to be undertaken by an entirely Indian team. Preparations for the expedition started two years after the Sino-Indian border conflict of 1962, which also coincided with escalating tensions between India and Pakistan (leading up to the war of 1965), making the show of mastery over the Himalayan ranges a matter of deep national anxiety and pride.

The event got extensive coverage in the English-language journal the *Illustrated Weekly of India* (or the *Weekly*), which cast a wide gamut of appeals around the expedition beyond the purely nationalistic ones.[52] An English-language publication with a long print life (from 1880 to 1993), the *Weekly* was an illustrated magazine published by the *Times of India* group that became a central platform and aspirational resource for India's post-Independence middle classes.[53] Over the course of its long career, the *Weekly* saw itself as a journal setting standards for the informed and anglicized middle-class Indian. With its illustrated coverage of India's different regions and people, gently satirical cartoons about politics and everyday life by R. K. Laxman and Mario, opinion pieces, jokes, and modest doses of tabloid sensationalism, the *Weekly* occupied an intermediary space between the statist interpellation of its new citizenry and a distinctly anglicized Indian bourgeois ethos of life. Thapa's *Everest* extends the same range of appeals, which put it at odds with the statist rhetoric of war during the 1960s. Its combinatory affective investment in India's rugged northern borderlands range from calls for military pride and regional unity against cross-border enemies to celebrations of a spirit of sports and adventure, all of which naturalize and personalize a political boundary.

Everest: *The Production*
Everest deploys spatially fluid airborne cameras and camera-guns that give its viewers dematerialized and out-of-body experiences. To borrow Lynn Kirby's phrase, Thapa's use of camera technology made landscape "evanescent" and invited the viewing multitude to experience the exhilaration of a select few climbers who reached the summit.[54] The story of *Everest*'s production, however, is less soaring, although it is matinee worthy for its intrigues. The FD made several attempts to block Thapa's involvement in the film and denied him permission to go on the climb that his film triumphantly claims to document. The aesthetics of the film's completed version and the haphazard production process of the film tell parallel stories of cinema's status as a visual image and regulated object.

The Indian Mountaineering Foundation (IMF) first contacted FD to record India's pioneering attempt to climb the Everest summit on September 1964. It requested Thapa as the filmmaker given his extensive mountaineering experience. The I&B Ministry refused to give him permission and did not seem interested in recording the historic climb. Inaccessible and majestic at 8,848 meters,[55] Mount Everest had long fascinated fliers, filmmakers, and geographers. The pioneering British flight over the summit in 1933, discussed in the previous chapter, had been recorded by four kinds of cameras mounted on planes, yielding footage that would become the source for the British documentary *Wings over Everest* (1934).[56] Recall that footage shot with *Wings* provided visual material reused in the *Secrets* and *Indian Town Studies* series, both of which visually erased the lead film's fascination with technological logistics—the flight's planning and execution, metal casting, and machining—to adopt an invisible authorial position highlighting India's people and topography (see chapter 1). Thapa's *Everest*, however, frequently foregrounds technology as well as technological breakdowns in part because recording the Indian ascent was not a seamless process but ended up requiring partial reshoots.

The climbers Captain H. P. S. Ahluwalia, Gurdial Singh, and C. P. Vohra were amateur filmmakers and, in Thapa's absence, recorded their climb to the Everest summit with one still and three Bolex 16 mm motion picture cameras.[57] They subsequently sent their rushes to FD in the hope of getting assistance in editing and producing the film. The FD's chief advisor (Films), J. S. Bhownagary, informed the I&B Ministry that the footage was "substandard and unsuitable for a full-length documentary."[58] On Defence Secretary H. C. Sarin's request, a second screening of the rushes was organized for an audience comprised of Thapa, members of the Defence Ministry, and the IMF. Although some senior FD staff took umbrage at the circumvention of their authority, evidently all those present at the screening concurred that the footage shot by the mountaineers was visually superlative. Bhownagary apologized for having rejected the footage on the basis of secondhand reports and recruited Thapa at this late stage to direct and edit the film. Thapa agreed on the condition that he be permitted to organize a partial reshoot for continuity and eventually received screen credit as director, second-unit photographer, and editor.

It is unclear why the I&B Ministry blocked Thapa's initial involvement, but he had been reprimanded earlier, and this kind of censuring was not unprecedented at FD. During the filming of the documentary *Song of the Snows* (1963) in Ladakh, Himachal Pradesh, and Kumaon, Thapa used his long-standing contacts with the Defence Ministry to get aerial shots by riding on an Indian Air Force supply plane to Ladakh. The FD vetoed the use of footage captured from this flight, and Thapa was threatened with "disciplinary action . . . for flying by air without permission."[59] The filmmaker then invoked his clout with Nehru's office and successfully included the suppressed footage in a short that went on to win the Presidential Gold Medal for best documentary. The *Song of the Snows* episode reveals a typical wrangle between the state's cast of characters, with FD bosses bristling over a subordinate's connection with other state bodies, a network of permissions almost derailing a film's production, and strategic high-ranking contacts stepping in to upend another state agency's official veto. A similar story may have repeated itself with *Everest*. What we know is that when the I&B Ministry denied Thapa's involvement with *Everest*, it was the Defence Ministry that brought him back in.

Thapa crafted his documentary partially from footage shot during the expedition by the climbers who were amateur cameramen, and in good measure from a staged reshoot that he organized in Darjeeling at the height of six thousand to seven thousand meters. To state the obvious, though, Darjeeling is not Mount Everest. Reshooting India's first ascent to the Everest in Darjeeling cut to the roots of the documentary's evidentiary claim.[60] Ironically, Thapa's reshoot was in pursuit of bringing a greater measure of truth and authenticity to the material because the amateur footage did not contain sufficient images to replicate the exact chronology and experiential arc of the original expedition.

Thapa combined the amateur material with restaged footage to craft a finished product within the recognizable lexicon of an FD landscape documentary. The final film reuses preshot stills and footage with restaged moving images, animated maps, postsync sound effects, and a voice-over. What is interesting about the finished film is that it retains key gaps from the original footage, as discussed further. The documentary's cut-and-paste format foregrounds the strategic nature of creative and technical decisions in all filmmaking. It also makes the film less technically and ideologically seamless than the *Indian Town Studies* of Gaumont British Instructional (GBI).

Everest: *The Film*
Everest was first screened on May 15, 1968, for Prime Minister Indira Gandhi in Vigyan Bhavan, which was the Indian government's premier convention center. It begins with pans, zooms, and still images of the Himalayan ranges, alongside stills of the mountaineers and their base camp. An authoritative voice-over introduces us to the expedition and to each team member. The voice-over becomes the primary device to weave together disparate footage, accompanied by rudimentary animated maps that are inserted to track the mountaineers' path to the summit. Unlike the frictionless arrows that move from one location to the other in GBI's *Indian Town Studies*, material transitions between different kinds of footage and spatial shifts from one locale to the other do not appear seamless in Thapa's film. Influenced by the British Documentary Film Movement, FD directors frequently quoted (and misquoted) John Grierson's definition of documentary as "the creative treatment of actuality."[61] The ambivalence of this aspect of documentary cinema, discussed by scholars Brian Winston and Jack Ellis,[62] was not lost on Thapa, who became more keenly aware of it after he was promoted to a supervisory position within FD. If "creativity depended on the perception of individual directors, how could one supervise it?," he notes. Clearly, the truth claims of an FD documentary were filtered through layers of institutional sponsorship, permissions, and supervision.[63] In the case of *Everest*, still and moving actuality footage shot during the original climb were collated with restaged footage to convey the climbers' team spirit and their struggle against all odds. But having missed out on the actual climb, Thapa's documentary contains ellipses that the final film does not always cover up.

Thapa does not substitute all the missing footage with reshoots, and the most significant omissions are of the climactic images of mountaineers reaching the summit. This culminating event comes to us in the form of staccato stills rather than moving images, because the 16 mm motion picture camera used

FIGURE 2.14 A film still from *Everest* conveys the moment when climbers reach the Everest summit.

by the amateur filmmakers froze at the summit despite being coated with antifreeze treatment. Thapa clearly drew the line at restaging summit shots in a second location. By retaining this gap, Thapa allows nature to make incursions into his cinematic image so that the halting surface of the film becomes a testimonial to technology's shortcomings when confronted with an unforgiving land. The sequence foregrounds art's compensatory mechanisms in capturing the environmental sublime, and the technique works because the disjuncture between moving and still images highlights the climbers' arrival at the summit as an experientially distinct moment, seized upon through a different format of film that halts the narrative.

The film's music and voice-over narration are similarly arrested a few times, although overall the documentary's sound design works unevenly. On the one hand, music and a dubbed soundtrack create a uniformity to surmount perceptual breaks between different kinds of footage. On the other, the film uses devices that are abrupt in their effect if not in their intention and expose gaps in footage through amateur and low-tech deployments of experimental techniques. One such occasion is the use of postsynchronized recordings of harsh, shallow breaths and grunts to convey the climbers' labor. The quality of intimate and jagged breathing is comparable, to the ears of contemporary viewers, to sound effects from exploitation, horror, and pornographic films.[64]

FIGURE 2.15 Music credits from *Everest*.

Within the film, it is meant to underscore the land's turgidity and its unyielding indifference to humanity, making the mountaineers all the more heroic for the overwhelming inequality of the encounter.

The disjunctive visual encounters with land staged by the film's (re)combination of actuality footage and sound effect is reinforced by the background music, which is composed by the popular duo Shankar-Jaikishan. Shankar-Jaikishan typically scored music for popular Hindi films and were particularly well known at the time for their scores composed for commercial films with extensive outdoor and travel sequences, such as *Hariyali aur Rasta* (1962), *Sangam* (1964), *Love in Tokyo* (1966), *Evening in Paris* (1967), *Around the World* (1967), and more. Their music for *Everest*, occasionally quiet, changes with topic shifts and repeats a spiraling crescendo akin to Bombay cinema's romantic epics, particularly at moments that are critical to the climb. Although not FD's typical score, the music would not have sounded unusual to film audiences seeing this documentary theatrically. But the theatricality of the music is combined and countered by the omniscient documentary voice-over and amateur sound mixing, which unexpectedly includes a range of vernacular Indian accents. Nearing the summit, we hear All India Radio broadcasts providing weather reports dedicated to India's climbers on Everest. Climbers discuss its implications in a range of regionally inflected accents, supplanting the anglicized

FIGURE 2.16 Everest base camp with mountaineers, Sherpas, and the Indian flag.

English of the voice-over with an assortment of Indian Englishes. Overall, *Everest* the film has an unevenness that allows it to evade seamless political messaging. Until the film's concluding stills, its nationalism remains largely subliminal given the film's focus on an arduous ascent. Near the film's end, the climbers plant a tricolor flag on the summit and symbolically stake a claim for India's territorial supremacy in the year of an Indo-Pakistan war.

Everest: The Human Landscape

Thapa's military and mountaineering films for FD affirmed India's technological triumph over its natural and political boundaries, but incidents of technological breakdown and human failure retain their place in these spectacles of accomplishment. In *Everest*, catastrophes performatively demonstrate the challenges posed by the environment to humans and to technology.[65] Images of India's mountain ranges have always been predicated on the functionality of cameras in frigid temperatures, and on the assistance of porters who carry the photographic and film equipment into inhospitable land. What is of interest is the extent to which these realities—laboring crews assisting filmmakers and the weather imposing formidable challenges on underfunded expeditions—are acknowledged or ignored in the cinematic and extracinematic accounts of the process. These are moments when the script of a unified ideology, shared political platform, easy cooperation, and unproblematic state support break down.

Thapa's struggle to film at a high altitude forms key dramatic moments in his memoir, as in this account of shooting footage for *Everest* at six thousand meters at Fray's Peak, which was named for a mountaineer buried there after a fatal fall during his descent with Tenzing Norgay: "The camera battery had almost frozen due to cold and the camera was running at a speed of 8 frames per second instead of [the] normal 24 frames. I had to pan the camera at slow speed and managed to get a couple of excellent panoramic shots before the battery collapsed."[66]

Thapa's combination of still and moving images in the film retains the interruptions and varying formats involved in filming the documentary, and through its visual fragmentation *Everest* conveys (intentionally or unintentionally) the difficulties of filming at high altitude, the vulnerability of technology, and the superiority of nature. Certainly, there is a politics to showing the diminution of humanity before nature. If the sublime scale of the environment is politicized when a national lens lays a visual claim to its horizon (as with Thapa's military and mountaineering shorts) it is also galvanized, albeit differently, when nature is treated as the leveler of humanity's technological control and social hierarchies (as in *Everest*).

This is important to a film that tries to incorporate (class-based and regional) difference to present a unified national front. Thapa's documentary goes to some lengths to note the partnership that the mountains forge between urban climbers and local Sherpas, who carry the mountaineering and camera equipment for the group tackling the formidable summit as a team. The Sherpas are an ethnic group originally from Nepal, several of whom were (and continue to be) employed by visiting mountaineers and tourists as guides, assistants, or laborers on climbs because of their acclimatization to the mountains. Their participation is frequently taken for granted and at worst severely exploited. *Everest* offers a vision of integration in the face of this reality. The camera pans over the faces of smiling Sherpas after the base camp is set up, and the voice-over notes that there is "no master-servant relationship here. . . . You must win the affection of the Sherpas." Sherpas, who carried the food, the ladders, and the bulk of the camera equipment for the film, were crucial to the success of the mission. Samuel Bourne's accounts of the relative merits of his "coolies" and the beatings he dispensed to discipline them while photographing the Himalayas betray the extent to which the effaced and abused labors of those guiding him to a location and carrying his equipment were indispensable to these shoots.[67] Allowing local labor and inhabitants some agency and subjectivity potentially stretches the frame of Thapa's camera in that it draws the eye to information outside the voice-over's ambit.

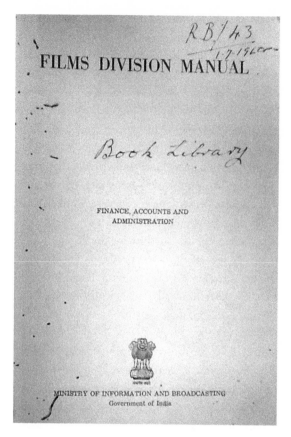

FIGURE 2.17 *Films Division Manual.*

Satyajit Ray's film *Kanchanjungha* (1962) is a good illustration of a film in which this dynamic is used deliberately to disrupt the frame of the narrative and the fantasies projected onto the place. Ray's feature adheres closely to the classically realist principles of a narrative that is set in a unified time within the circumscribed location of Darjeeling. Over the course of a day, Ray's film plays out a subtle bourgeois drama while a grimy Lepcha boy lurks along the margins of the action and the film frame. The local boy watches, hums, and occasionally follows characters who meander around the mountainous paths of the popular colonial-era hill station. By creating this character, Ray decenters the film's fictional core. The boy is granted an observational and nonverbal (musical) presence that disconcerts our focus on an extended bourgeois family on a holiday, whose relationships we begin to see as repressed, narcissistic, and alienated from the environment. Given Ray's primary focus on the anglicized dramatic center, the film's radicalism lies in foregrounding the narrative's own perspectival limitations with a view from the margins.[68] Although Thapa's shorts are not self-reflexive and the visual inclusion of Sherpas does not provoke an auto-critical reading of the limits of the documentary's frame on topography and locality, the film's impulse to discuss the Sherpa's cooperation hints at hidden layers of friction that Thapa faced while shooting on location.

FD cameramen who were embedded within travel expeditions or military forces were pulled into fraught encounters between state agents and local inhabitants when their leveling nationalist rhetoric abutted against the human tendency to empathize with people in the singular rather than the collective. Writing about the experience of filming India's big dams, including the Bhakra Nangal, Hirakud, and Damodar Valley projects, Thapa is critical in his memoir about the condition of the *adivasis* (indigenous or original inhabitants) forcibly and violently displaced by dam construction without compensation:

> I was happy to film their old customs and traditions of weekly market days and tribal dances. However I was shocked at the way our aborigines were being treated by so called civilized Indians, as mere anthropological oddities, segregated in their forest dwelling . . .
>
> The Films Division appreciated my work. But what was released in the News Review was only what the authorities considered to be the positive side of tribal life and development. . . . Unless we listen to the voice of reason, blood will keep flowing down the Brahmaputra and Godavari rivers.[69]

Thapa was no radical. He was complicit in the state's visualization of the adivasis as exotic people whose disappearing customs could be recorded as a symbol of their authenticity. But he was also negotiating between his commitments as a state agent and his frustrations with state mandates, which occasionally cause his personal writings to veer between a doctrinaire support for FD and an awareness of the state's power and authority as facilitated through him. He faced the challenge of satisfying FD's bureaucratic demands while grappling with his own sympathies as a Kumaoni. Thapa was an FD employee but also a native of the mountains, an ex-military officer and a mountaineering enthusiast. As we shall see in more detail further on, each of these identities brought its own set of personal preoccupations for Thapa when he sought government approval for funds to shoot and edit location footage. The volatile hyphenate of India's regional-national nexus celebrated in Thapa's documentaries seems ready to implode in the smaller scale of Thapa's personal experiences. On the one hand, the state's institutional conflicts conditioned Thapa's career. Panoramic shots and access to aerial vantage points betrayed a colonial military training that acculturated Thapa to the technologies and habits of imperial adventure and nationalist surveillance. On the other hand, his access to such images was enabled by his acquaintance with military personnel and mountaineers, whose company put him at odds with the I&B Ministry when the ministry did not wish to cooperate with the Ministry of Defence or the Mountaineering Foundation.

SOCIAL SPACE AND THE TECHNOMATERIALITY OF FILM STOCK

The aesthetic form of Thapa's landscape shorts also bespeaks film's function as a technomaterial object in India, because its look was defined in part by the quality and quantity of film stock (that is, the unexposed analog base used for recording images in photochemical film) available to him. The 1960s and 1970s were decades of severe governmental rationalizations of commodities, and the availability of film stock was a contentious issue in India during these years. Without veering into technomaterial determinism, an account of infrastructural conditions clarifies the material circumstances under which Thapa created his vision of India's landscape. The practice of rationing raw film stock started in India in 1943, when the British India government ostensibly wanted to conserve stock for the state's wartime film productions.[70] After Independence, the Indian government continued to exercise close oversight over raw stock usage as the product was largely imported into the country against the expenditure of precious foreign exchange reserves. In 1960, a public sector company under the Department of Heavy Industry called Hindustan Photo Film (HPF) was established in Ooty, India, to indigenously manufacture black-and-white positives, sound negatives, and color positives by 1968. Although this company eventually met the domestic film industry's demand for black-and-white raw stock, color stock was largely imported into India.[71] With the norm of production shifting to color films during the regime of stock regulations in the 1960s, filmmakers were in fierce competition for access to the limited supplies of raw material and foreign exchange released by the state.

Raw Stock Shortages and Regulations

The state's control over film stock took several forms. Prior to the 1950s, raw film stock was on the Open General License (OGL) list, which was a list that included all commodities permitted for import without a license, as long as importers could prove that they were the actual users of the product and provide an assurance that there was no local substitute for the product available domestically. By the late 1950s, the government threatened to remove raw film stock from the OGL list and faced predictably strong objections from the film industry.[72] Raw film stock was eventually removed from the OGL in 1963 and "canalized" through the Indian Motion Picture Export Corporation (IMPEC), which meant that the public body was tasked with regulating the import and export of films as well as the importation of film stock.[73] The identity and form of these canalizing institutions would change over the years, with the Film Finance Corporation and the National Film Development Corporation taking over IMPEC's role.[74] But in all cases, governmental policies controlling film stock through import restrictions and export obligations had an impact on the power balance within India's film industry and defined the fiscal boundaries of national trade. Decades of state control over raw film stock in India are best understood not as a direct exercise of state power over an industrial product but as a period of dense interaction between a range of governmental and industrial bodies that variably resisted as well as profited from import restrictions.

For instance, in 1957, in order to avoid the removal of film stock from the OGL and to respond to the "government's move for economy and regulation in the use of raw film," the film industry led by the Film Federation of India set up regional committees in Delhi, Calcutta, Bombay, and Madras to "scrutinize all applications for raw film to make motion pictures."[75] As a bid by the industry to exert some control over the regulatory system, this committee was nominated by the film industry with the purpose of reviewing every applicant's credentials, in order to provide a list of recommended buyers to authorized importers. Needless to say, a committee selected from among members of the industry could not be expected to be entirely neutral on the matter of recommendations. One factor that was supposed to figure into the prioritization of some filmmakers over others was their proven ability to stay within a shooting ratio of 5:1. Shooting ratios defined the ratio between the total amount of film used on a shoot against the footage included in the final cut of a film. The Indian state had determined that every five feet of film shot had to yield a minimum of one foot of usable material.[76] (There is no precise norm, but shooting ratios are more typically in the range of 10:1 and 16:1 for feature films, and significantly greater for documentaries because documentarians do not always know what material will be used in the final product ahead of a shoot.) The Indian government granted raw stock piecemeal to commercial filmmakers depending on whether or not they kept to a stipulated shooting ratio of 5:1. Film processing laboratories came up trumps in this paradigm and became part of a thriving underground economy in the circulation of stock in India. This is because a film laboratory's certification of the quantity of exposed film was the key document that proved whether ratios between issued stock and exposed stock were within stipulated limits. Control over this highly desirable commodity transformed film laboratories into powerhouses in the commercial film industry.

Sohrab Irani, who served as chairman and managing director of Chetan Anand, Dev Anand, and Vijay Anand's company, Himalaya Films, in the 1980s, remembers that laboratories issued a "consumption certificate," or a certificate proving that producers were demonstrably within the minimal stock wastage ratio of 5:1. Based on this, producers could reapply to the regional committee, referred to as the "Steering Committee" by Irani, to get additional raw stock to shoot the next schedule of their film.[77] As Irani confirms, producers were never given the raw stock needed for a film "in one go," so that film laboratories could effectively hold film producers hostage with their power to falsify certificates, refuse to return film negatives, or prevent final release of the film print, making the sale of stock "a big racket" in the industry.[78] Since no one was guaranteed the entire quantity of stock prior to a film's shooting, the completion of a film became entirely contingent on acquiring consumption certificates, which invested lab consumption certificates with the equivalent of monetary value. To tell this story as a chain of dependencies and conditionalities: stock regulations extended state control over film stock; control over stock was based on proof of rationalized usage by film producers; this proof was contingent on lab consumption certificates; consequently, lab certificates became hot tradable commodities in a shadow market.

The requirement of a certificate from the laboratory to demonstrate raw film use added new avenues of corruption to the well-recognized problem of a thriving black market in raw film stock and silver recovered during the chemical wash while processing film.[79] For commercial films, the significance of lab certificates for stock translated into a preference for films that skewed toward formulaic productions of big budget blockbusters with known producers, who had significant influence or "pull" in the Steering Committee and could guarantee returns (discussed further in chapter 5). Unlike commercial film producers, as state employees FD cameramen had access to their own laboratories and were in a less precarious position regarding *access* to stock. Nevertheless they were hostage to laboratory certificates to demonstrate appropriate stock ratio and *usage*, which was closely monitored by the FD bureaucracy.

Peter Sutoris, in his reconstruction of the constraints involved in the production process of FD documentaries, suggests that the ratio was even more stringent for documentaries (at a 4.07:1 ratio).[80] Despite the tedium of bureaucratic details, the filmmakers' procedures for reporting on stock usage deserves attention because they demonstrate the actual working conditions of FD cameramen. I present a breakdown of some of these procedures because they reveal the range of rationalities that defined the state's relationship with the nation's (commercial and state) filmmakers as a whole, defining rationalities here as the modes by which the state was organizing its industries and managing their responses. This may be a better way to think of FD's and Thapa's landscape shorts, rather than bracketing them apart as state-controlled national propaganda.

The first of these deliberative rationalities becomes legible in the contentious debates between the state, state-employed filmmakers, and commercial filmmakers over the actual length and usage of film stock. The second relates to the procedures for procuring raw stock during the Indian state's License Raj. Both are discussed below, but as an aside, the difficulty in accessing the conditions under which FD filmmakers made their films points to the arbitrariness of document preservation in India's state archives and the commercial film industry. The Indian state's decades-long monopoly over documentaries and "useful cinema"[81] creates an archival asymmetry in present-day India: a country with poorly preserved commercial films is developing a comparatively rich archive of official shorts, state-funded films, and documentaries. Even as FD's films become easier to access and view, however, the library of physical documents accompanying them remains unevenly preserved because of inconsistent state and private interest in the retention and care of physical records. In recent years, researchers such as Sutoris, Iyesha Geeth Abbas, and Ritika Kaushik have worked to systematize and digitize some of these paper trails and records with the cooperation of FD, but in the absence of a consistent institutional will toward preservation, it is an interrupted process.

This is not offered as a lament about the archive's neglect but to underscore a dissonance between state demands for paperwork at a given historical moment and the irregularity of surviving paper trails over time. As much of the documentation is incomplete or incompletely systematized, it must be assumed that paperwork critical to its own moment had little longevity because the indents and forms prevalent in the 1960s and 1970s addressed needs entirely endemic to strategies of managing film and commerce within that particular period. It also means that defunct records are very useful chronicles of the state's past priorities.

FD's Antiwaste Policies and Its Catalogue Aesthetic

Peter Sutoris's book on FD offers an account of the institutional roadblocks to the approval of finances, raw stock, content, and individual authorship within FD. However, as opposed to FD's more distinguishable stylistic "outliers"[82] who are the focus of Sutoris's attention, Thapa's landscape shorts fit a generic FD house style. This style more palpably reveals the ways in which FD's film form was regulated through the policies and practices governing stock usage, film length, desirable visuals and narratives, because of the generic interchangeability of one landscape or mountain film with other films of its kind (often in literal ways, given shared footage).

The 1960 *Films Division Manual* (which FD directors referred to as their "bible," according to Sutoris[83]) outlines the extensive procedures that newsreel producers and documentarians had to follow to access raw film stock (Fig. 2.17). Cameramen for newsreels and documentaries were required to submit a series of forms, registry entries, and statements to demonstrate their legitimate use of raw stock for each film in adherence with the agency's stringent measures against wastage. A brief summary of these procedures conveys the reams of paperwork that accumulated for each film made under the FD umbrella, given governmental oversight over raw film stock.[84] According to the manual, in order to make a newsreel, cameramen had to take an "indent" (order for raw film stock) to the FD Raw Stock Accounting Section, signed by the associate chief producer (Newsreels) or the ACP(N). The raw film stock received was accounted for by the ACP(N) in Form RA-5 in the Raw Stock Register. Form RA-6 was then used to account for the raw stock issued to each cameraman, with columns for type of raw stock, laboratory supervisor comments, and the cameraman's comments. The exposed film went to laboratory supervisors with requisitions for processing, and laboratory supervisors filled in Form RA-10 showing the quantity of exposed film received. Based on this, the Raw Stock Accounting Section calculated the percentage of wastage to make sure it conformed to standards. This was reported back to the ACP(N), who kept a check on the use-to-wastage ratio of individual cameramen and reviewed the coverage of material received from cameramen on a weekly basis to examine whether it was "technically good and whether any raw film is wasted by covering unnecessary or unimportant items."[85] The ACP(N) could write a circular "to serve as a guide and case law" to "reduce future wastage of raw film" for all cameramen. In the first weeks of January, April, June, and October every year, ACP(N)s prepared a statement indicating each cameraman's ratio of usage.[86] Oversight of the content of finished material lay with the FAB and the I&B Ministry, but supervision of stock usage during production primarily fell on the ACP(N), who compared indents against laboratory certificates to determine use-to-waste ratios.

The state's excessive bureaucratic monitoring to ensure adherence to its antiwaste policy was therefore at least partially responsible for what I have called the disciplinary delirium of FD's landscape films and for a bullet-pointed catalogue aesthetic of the era. In the post-Independence context, the tenor of statist nationalism in Thapa's landscape films is unsurprising. Less explicable is the visual language of his landscape films that repeatedly reuse and recombine old footage with new shots that are crammed into fast edits of close-up, medium, and panoramic shots, all edited together with rapid-fire facts about India's topography, ethnography, climate, mythology, and history. The antiwaste policy of making every foot of film stock count, alongside demands for a quick turnover of films from each FD filmmaker,[87] meant that someone like Thapa had to compress a geographical film's educational and ideological content within available authorized film stock in a continuous stream of films, producing the effect of a sort of bureaucratic and disciplinary delirium. This visual syntax is shared by several FD nonfiction films and mimics the bullet-point structure of a classroom lecture or of that era's National Council of Educational Research and Training (NCERT) geography textbooks. In addition to the informational and secular-nationalist significance of this mode of address, arguably the rapid topic shifts, reused footage, and collage aesthetic of Thapa's landscape films can be explained by FD's antiwaste policy and an industrial incentivization for reusing old or stock footage.

Everest: The Final Hurdle

Thapa's account of getting raw stock and financial resources to reshoot and edit his documentary Everest conveys the challenges inherent in procedures that, although mostly just tedious formalities, could on occasion be used by the I&B Ministry in obstructionist ways to discourage or delay a film's production. The internal opposition in FD to Thapa's involvement in the Everest film has already been described. After Thapa was approved for the project following the intervention of the Defence Ministry, FD demanded that he find "foreign exchange for the purchase of 35 mm Eastman color raw stock for the additional shooting."[88] This was an unusual request even by the standards of an organization that routinely monitored filmmakers' expenses on raw film stock. Whereas the need for foreign exchange was a perennial hurdle for commercial filmmakers,[89] individual

FD cameramen were typically not expected to produce foreign exchange to purchase raw film stock to make a commissioned film. However, in practice, it becomes evident here that state-sponsored documentaries *could* be denied access to foreign exchange for color film stock. Thapa writes that it was eventually the Defence Ministry again that stepped in to approve requisite funds for his project.

The credibility of Thapa's personal memoir in this episode cannot be taken at face value. But what is obvious is that the Indian "state" involved in FD productions was not (and within any liberal democracy, cannot be) identifiable with a singular organization or entity. The egos of several male bureaucrats in FD, the I&B Ministry, and the Defence Ministry were inflamed over one important film dealing with India's first ascent to the Everest summit. If FD cameramen faced potentially thwarted productions when a commissioning state agency refused to back their request for raw film stock, the crisis was chronic for commercial filmmakers who had no state support. A technomaterial history of post-Independence Indian cinema would show that commercial and governmental film sectors in India felt the state's presence in their work through its strict oversight on the availability of raw film stock, which was in high demand and limited supply. India's regulatory apparatus and bureaucratic caprice abutted with individual adherence and workarounds to such rules in influencing the look of FD films.

NO OBJECTION CERTIFICATES AS SOCIOSPATIAL OBJECTS

Thapa's landscape films, like other FD films, were screened in theatrical and non-theatrical settings. Financially, however, these films could be subsidized by the state because a majority of them enjoyed guaranteed theatrical exhibition preceding the main feature films in India's commercial theaters, and FD passed on the rental cost of their films to commercial theater owners. Historical accounts of documentary in India note that the way for this mandate was paved by Rule 44A of the Defence of India Act, which had been in force since May 15, 1943. As a wartime measure, the rule made it mandatory for India's film exhibitors to show a maximum of two thousand feet of film approved by the central government at each commercial film screening, and pay for the film's rental costs.[90] This rule was set to expire in September 1946. With the end of World War II and the imminent departure of the colonial government in sight, the act appeared blatantly coercive and irrelevant, as exceptional conditions of combat could no longer justify compulsory screenings of propagandizing newsreels. However, after the briefest of intervals, the spirit behind this ruling was reintroduced by the Government of India in 1949 despite strong resistance from India's commercial film industry, because of a conviction shared by Prime Minister Jawaharlal Nehru, Home Minister Sardar Vallabhbhai Patel, officials of the new I&B Ministry, and key nonstate stakeholders, that newsreels and short films were essential in educating and modernizing the citizens of a new country who needed to be inculcated with a sense of a shared past and future.[91]

Historical accounts of this period move too quickly from Rule 44A of the Defence of India Act to the introduction of compulsory theatrical screenings of documentaries and newsreels in independent India, imputing a continuity and neglecting subtle but necessary differences in the new policy's political frame. Rule 44A was a crucial precedent, but the new legislation also drew on a clause in India's Cinematograph Act to justify a state mandate that could have been (and, in the 1990s, was) challenged in the courts as undemocratic. The democratic Indian state asserted its monopoly over scientific films, newsreels, documentaries, and shorts until 1996 through a presumption of obligation from the commercial film industry rather than through direct coercion, to leave room to defend the rule's constitutionality. To this end, the exhibition of newsreels and documentary shorts in independent India was also made possible by the licensing regulation of the Indian Cinematograph Act of 1918, maintained in the subsequent act of 1952 and its modification in 1959.

The substance of the licensing regulation stated that to operate a commercial film exhibition site, a person needed to get a license from a licensing authority (LA) whose powers were typically vested in the region's district magistrate or chief commissioner of police, unless otherwise notified in the official gazette. The LA could not grant a license unless it was satisfied that the applicant met various stipulated conditions. In addition to the building site's safety, the Cinematograph Act (of 1918 and 1952) included this conditionality: "The Central Government may, from time to time, issue directions to licensees generally or to any licensee in particular for the purpose of regulating the exhibition of any film or class of films, so that scientific films, films intended for educational purposes, films dealing with news and current events, documentary films or indigenous films secure an adequate opportunity of being exhibited, and where any such directions have been issued those directions shall be deemed to be additional conditions and restrictions subject to which the license has been granted."[92] The Indian state used the central government's ability to demand the screening of news, documentary, and educational films from "time to time" to insert "a clause in the license issued to each exhibitor making it incumbent on him to include at least one thousand feet of 'approved' film in each show."[93]

The state governments were under instruction from the central government to include this clause as a condition of giving licenses to film exhibitors.

As middle ground between the injunctions of a colonial state issuing wartime regulations and the bureaucratic requirements of a democratic government during peace time, the language of this clause appears as a hybrid of Rule 44A of the Defence of India Act 1943 and the prior Cinematograph Act. Semantically, Rule 44A dealt with the "Control of Cinematograph Exhibitions," whereas the Cinematograph Act referred to the "Regulation of Exhibitions by Means of Cinematographs."[94] Rule 44A defined an "approved film" as "a cinematograph film approved for the purpose of this rule by the central government," and exhibitors found in noncompliance were "punishable with imprisonment" for a year, or a fine, or both.[95] The Cinematograph Act clause, in some distinction, restricted the licensing authorities to grant licenses only to those exhibitors who screened a percentage of approved films. This was a softer touch. The clause was continuous with an extension of state power over the nation through the Indian government's License Raj, wherein a maze of licenses put the individual citizen and entrepreneur under the state's gaze at all times. In order to get a license for film exhibition, exhibitors needed to get a series of "No Objection Certificates" (NOCs) from various agencies to demonstrate that they met health, fire, and safety requirements. One such NOC was contingent on their proving that exhibitors rented and screened a percentage of nonfiction films. Technically, this wasn't the exact equivalent of the state coercing theaters *to* show something, although that was effectively the intent and result. The state was mandating instructional screenings as a condition of acquiring commercial film exhibition licenses, but getting a license was a matter of volition for any citizen.

In theory and practice, any commercial producer could have competed with FD as a producer of nonfiction films. The state remained open to this challenge.[96] The *Patil Committee Report* of 1951 discussed the precariousness of the state's stipulation to show educational films in theaters:

> The Constitution empowers the Central Government only to sanction films for exhibition. It is a moot point whether this power would include the authority to issue directions to licensees for the compulsory exhibition of certain categories of films.
>
> ... The validity of such a clause or order has not so far been tested in a court of law. We are ourselves doubtful if such an obligation can be imposed under a license issued under the Indian Cinematograph Act, having regard to the limited constitutional sanction of that Act. We have

found the industry generally critical but submissive to this obligation. Nevertheless, Government might, in their own interest, like to put the position beyond legal or constitutional challenge.[97]

The FD became a monopolistic agency by anticipating a demand in the market created by the state's clause and then inscribing itself at both the supply and demand ends of the short films sector.[98] The films of the FD, a government organization, automatically met the requirements of any licensing authorities, whereas competing producers lacked this preordained stamp of approval.

The end of FD's monopoly over documentaries and newsreels attests to the dubious nature of the state's compulsion that is better described as an *expectation* of the commercial film industry's submission to state monopoly that the central government got away with until 1993. That year, film exhibitors from India's A-plus metros, such as Delhi, Kolkata, Mumbai, Chennai, Bhopal, and Hyderabad, filed writ petitions with their respective high courts protesting the requirement for mandatory screenings as a violation of their fundamental right to free speech and expression under Article 19 (1) of the Constitution. Exhibitors also contested the rental fee for "approved films" charged by FD.[99] This fee had served as income for FD's film productions. All petitions were consolidated and transferred to the Delhi High Court, and in 1995 the high court deemed the 1 percent fee unconstitutional.[100] The FD retaliated with the Union of India, the State of West Bengal, and the State of Uttar Pradesh filing an appeal against the Delhi High Court judgment at the Supreme Court of India. In 1999, the Supreme Court upheld the practice of renting and screening approved films but observed that this did not enshrine FD's monopoly.[101]

By this time, the cracks in the system were showing. The FD's decades-long stronghold on documentaries was shaken, as was the government's insistence on the mandatory screening of state-produced documentaries. Two private organizations—Indovision Media, headquartered in Lucknow, and India Infotainment Media Corporation in Mumbai—moved into the space left by the temporary disabling of FD.[102] In 2013, they quoted this Supreme Court ruling on their website: "None of the provisions make it mandatory for the exhibitors to procure such films only from the FD."[103] Prior to the appearance of these competitors, a vast network of unofficial and self-proclaimed licensing authorities had already introduced several levels of corruption into the system, in any case. NOCs could also be authorized with bribes or procured by exhibitors who rented approved films without screening them, since local authorities policed actual screenings only irregularly. After the attrition of its mandate to be the primary documentary producing institution for the nation, FD has in recent years redefined itself as a sponsor of festivals (such as the Mumbai International Film Festival), an archival and exhibition space, and a valuable film resource.[104]

Linking the Indian state's surveillance of raw film stock usage to the productive conditions as well as formal affiliations of FD's mountain shorts allows us to see how film's regulation as a commodity and film's depiction of land as landscape consolidated state power in post-Independence India. In making this historical case, I have implicitly accepted Michel Foucault's thesis that the liberal state's authority derives from a dispersal of its power over a range of microspaces.[105] In his historiographies of the penal, clinical, surveillance, and sexual regulatory systems of liberal governments, Foucault shows that the state is not merely "a delimitable domain of political power," to use Wendy Brown's expression.[106] Rather, state power manifests itself in the interactions between policies, technologies, discourses, and bodies, extending the ambit of its power beyond governmental institutions to the management of life and the "conduct of conduct" itself.[107] Unlike Lefebvre, Foucault does not accept the state as a framework of power external to state apparatuses (such as legal and judicial systems, the media, and so forth). Whereas for Foucault state power is actualized in and through its discourses, practices, and constituent lives, Lefebvre conceives of the state as a *framework* that is not fully subsumed under its practices. My approach to FD as an institution actualizing state power is closer to Lefebvre's theorization of state space than to Foucault's in this sense, although it has also been indebted to Foucault's work.

Lefebvre suggests that states survive in their particular form to the extent that they are able to manage territory, capital, and life within spatially scalar frameworks that sustain their modes of governance, while coinciding those frameworks with the authority to partition socioeconomic space in the first instance. Consequently, the use of statutes to partition socioeconomic space constitutes the first order of a state's framework, and positions the state *as* framework.[108] In the case of FD, we have seen that the institution was created because the new Indian state invested in educational films as a means of tutoring a diverse population in the lessons of citizenry. Financially, the state sustained this model of mandated films through a system of licenses, regulations, and taxes on commercial filmmakers and theaters. Regulations that governed India as an economic territory and adjudicated over film as a material object thus provided the political and institutional framework within which FD issued its nationalistic vision of India. Classificatory aspects of the state begin to appear apolitical or neutral when they are taken at face value, making spatial histories a critical imperative.

These grand theories of statist and discursive spaces nevertheless leave something to be desired. Documentarian Thapa's memories of filming India's northern terrain and the visual and aural texture of his shorts remind us that a celebrated government employee's commitments and the aesthetics of his films corresponded only imperfectly with statist visions. Material and visual regulations of the nation as a territorial space were ever discontinuous, even in the most regulated years of the Indian film history.

PART II

AFFECTIVE SPACES

3

SUBLIME:
IMMANENCE AND TRANSCENDENCE
IN JEAN RENOIR'S INDIA

My third argument for a spatial film historiography rests on the revelation that putative differences between a film's location and its assumed viewership are frequently used as triggers to explore the singularities of a place and, contrarily, the universals of the human condition. A historiography alert to this bifurcating hermeneutic shows the dual imperatives of ethnography and metaphysics in location-based filming, to lay bare the links between a film's politics and its aesthetics.

I went to India and I was convinced. The word convinced is weak. I was over-whelmed. It's an extraordinary country, with extraordinary people, and I'll tell you right away that it's the least mysterious country in the world. For a French-man, India is very easy to understand.

JEAN RENOIR, RENOIR ON RENOIR

India figures only as a setting, but more as a moral than a geographical setting. Its silent presence, to which the protagonists pay only half-conscious attention, acts on their minds as a magnetic field influences the needle of a compass.

ANDRÉ BAZIN, JEAN RENOIR

We may all disagree with a work of art, and yet acknowledge it as great; as providing us with insights every time we approach it—even if it be removed from us in space, time, ideology, established knowledge and its structures, the ethics of our life and times.

KUMAR SHAHANI, "FILM AS CONTEMPORARY ART"

Like rivers, and like Renoir's film that evokes a sense of liquid eternity, there is an endlessness to the stories that flow and ebb from *The River*'s location shoot in India between 1949 and 1951.[1] The film's slipstream of characters, images, and stories yields a history of how the West has related to the East, art to reality, objects to symbols, and people to places in the process of filming on location. To use Renoir's preferred word, shooting in India "initiated" several significant events.[2] By Renoir's own admission, filming in India renewed his faith in hu-manity and his enthusiasm for filmmaking after difficult years of working with Hollywood studios. *The River*'s success at the Venice Film Festival (where in 1951 it shared the International Prize with Robert Bresson's *Diary of a Coun-try Priest* and Billy Wilder's *Ace in the Hole*) marked the end of Renoir's exile from Europe. European directors as different as Fritz Lang, James Ivory, and

Louis Malle were enticed to consider India as a filming location because of the success of *The River*.[3] The film introduced Technicolor to Renoir and to India and went on to influence how American directors Martin Scorsese and Wes Anderson would think about color and about the Indian subcontinent. Famously, Satyajit Ray met Renoir during this period, initiating a friendship that would give Ray the encouragement of a globally celebrated master to pursue his own creative vision in cinema. For his own productions, Ray would eventually partner with friends from *The River*'s crew, particularly art director Bansi Chandragupta, camera operator Ramananda Sen Gupta, and Subrata Mitra (uncredited in *The River*).[4] Infamously, Renoir would recommend sound engineer Hari Dasgupta to Roberto Rossellini when the Italian filmmaker shot *India Matri Bhumi* (1959) in the country, setting the stage for Rossellini's elopement with Dasgupta's wife, Sonali.

The film's afterlife is sustained by an equally scattered range of responses to it, from André Bazin's defensive praise of the film, Ray's disappointment over its neglect of Indian characters and realities, Kumar Shahani's fleeting embarrassment on Renoir's behalf, and Renoir's own lasting attachment to India. *The River*'s itineraries of influence and equivocal responses reveal the significance and divisiveness of a celebrated classic of world cinema,[5] which is formally intriguing and politically questionable. Debates over the film's politics may be characterized as debates over India's relevance or irrelevance to the film, and broader concerns about the cinematic use of politically and economically vulnerable populations and territories as ambience in location-based films. Contemporaries questioned Renoir's insistence that he would "rather abandon the idea" for the film than "shoot on sets in Hollywood" despite the inconveniences and ethical dilemmas of filming in a region immediately after its decolonization and bloody partition.[6] As Satyajit Ray noted wryly, "I couldn't help feeling that it was overdoing it a bit, coming all the way from California merely to get the topography right."[7]

Despite Renoir's proclamation that he broke with the visual cliché of India as a land of "charging cavalries, tiger hunts, elephants and maharajas" perpetuated by Hollywood and European films,[8] *The River* participates in the longstanding trope of making the world a stage for the Western protagonist's theater of emotions, reviving criticisms of the habitual subordination of a feature film's environment to its fictional narrative, and Euro-American cinema's investment of agency in a film's white protagonists at the expense of its supporting and background actors of color. *The River*'s orientalism opens (rather than forecloses) my analysis because the film's use of India as a visual canvas is one part of a varied and profuse history of personal revelations, artistic ambitions, and political contentions generated during a landmark foreign location shoot that disperses the meanings of a filmed location across a range of interactions.[9] The multiple registrations of India as location do not absolve *The River* of its orientalism, which is as evident on-screen as it is in off-screen remarks, such as in Renoir's elaboration of "the Hindu soul" or in Bazin's description of Bogey's "little native friend" who is "as mysterious and taciturn as a bronze statue."[10] But the film crew's experiences of shooting in India push us to discern the film's rich discursive and material contexts while also opening up to the reciprocal influences and associations that were generated during the film's production and pre-production process. One such story is of Renoir's willingness to make himself vulnerable to the tutelage of a country that tested the limits of his knowledge and comfort. Echoing Octave's dialogue from *Rules of Game* (*La règle de jeu*, 1939) to convey the sentiment that India taught him the value of patience and detachment at a time when he was distressed by European politics and embittered by Hollywood studios, Renoir noted that the experience "brought me a certain understanding of life . . . India may have taught me that everyone has his reasons."[11] Renoir allowed his personal narrative about India to reflect the arc of experiences encountered by his characters in *The River*, who learn not to quarrel with things but to consent.

I hold this historical and extracinematic material in some tension with the cinematic text's construction of India because doing so allows us to analytically disaggregate the textually inscribed India from the encounters generated in the place. These encounters, recorded in interviews, memoirs, and circulated publicity, provide material density to the film's production on-site in Barrackpur, in the North 24 Parganas District of Calcutta (now Kolkata), West Bengal. While these accounts are as instrumental as the cinematic text in producing discursive truths about India, they possess distinct affective and narrative registers. They frequently reinforce the film's portrayal of India, and yet possess their own autonomy as events (and accounts of events) surrounding the film and its production. They refract the film's text through a wider notion of the spatial encounters generated by the film and its location. This is because if *The River*'s images archive India, the film's production process archives the experience of a Euro-American film crew encountering India and crews of different nations working with each other. In effect, the film and filmmaking process encompass a range of affective responses to the location. In distinction from the previous two chapters, which examined the rationalist impulses powering India's visualization as an object of imperial (British) disciplinary instruction

FIGURE 3.1. Renoir on location for *The River*. Courtesy of USC Archives of the Cinematic Arts.

and nationalist (Indian) regulatory management, this chapter and the next will look at (Euro-American and Indian) art and commercial feature films, which portray India as a place of affective encounter and experience. These chapters follow vectors outside statist institutionalizations of India as a filmed space to look at another kind of film, in which India is presented as a place that engenders personal and metaphysical revelations about the nature of self, mortality, and existence. They present India as a sublime place.

REVERSE ETHNOGRAPHIES AND COMPARATIVE SUBLIMITIES

Fiction films shot in foreign locations are frequently accompanied by geographical and ethnographic descriptions of the place and its people in the film's publicity material and, correspondingly, by an ethnographic gaze embedded within the cinematic text, both of which can combine to identify the filmed space as exotic or strange to its assumed audiences. Filming *The River* in India prompted several narratives of personal and professional experience. Melvina McEldowney, publicist to Hollywood star Esther Williams and wife of *The River*'s producer Kenneth McEldowney, advertised the film in the United States with the following sensational statement: "Making the first Technicolor picture in India gives one a deep appreciation of how old Cris [*sic*] Columbus must have felt when he sailed forth on unknown waters."[12] Such statements invite a sort of reverse ethnography,[13] tempting researchers to turn the critical lens back on those who claimed for themselves the position of pioneers while relegating others to anonymous alterity and novelty ("ol' Cris Columbus" sailing into "unknown waters"). In addition to disrupting imperious statements by making the presumed transparency of ethnographic othering visible as a product of politico-economic history, a reverse ethnography that reads the poetic vein of *The River*'s fiction in relation to the ethnographic tones of its production files generates a more capacious sense of the film as a document of India. *The River*'s production files also offer glimpses into a nation that rarely documented or preserved any record of its own filmmaking practices, so that any documentation provides welcome detail and relieves the dearth of historical information in the film's text.

In the same breath, it must be admitted that the ethnographic mode does not exhaust the ways in which India is produced as a place by *The River*'s cinematic and extracinematic texts. As film theorist André Bazin implied by calling the film's India more "a moral" than "a geographical setting," *The River* uses India as a place to stage encounters with the sublime. In the film, the Hooghly River (a tributary of the Ganges) in Bengal is metonymic not only for India's topography but, more crucially, for life's eternal rhythms.[14] Despite Renoir's claim that India was not in the least mysterious to him, the film's location operates as a geographical site as well as the bearer of transcendental truths.

As a film and production event, *The River* shows the metaphysical and ethnographic impulses of location filming. India is narrated as full of immanent *and* transcendent meaning, as mundane yet metaphysical, real but providing intimations of a sublime that exceeds the kind of geographical imagination mapped earlier. If this hermeneutic binds the text to familiar tropes of orientalism, it also unbinds other stories of encounter in and around the film. Colloquially, the term "sublime" indicates "the effect of grandeur in speech and poetry; for a sense of the divine; for the contrast between the limitations of human perception and the overwhelming majesty of nature."[15] As an aesthetic term, it has expressed to different ends the struggle (and professed failure) of representational forms ranging from art to language to architecture and poetry, in confronting *and* eliciting ineffable sensations of terror and wonder, or revulsion and awe, in the face of the vast unknowns of nature, death, and divinity (or the void left in absence of the divine). After Edmund Burke's eighteenth-century treatise on the sublime in particular,[16] the term has described an admixture of awe and terror, pleasure and pain, the subjective state elicited by something external to the self, the thing so wondrous that it crosses over into the monstrous. For the purposes of my discussion, the vast Western philosophical traditions of the sublime (traceable through Longinus, Burke, Kant, Hegel, Derrida, and Lyotard)[17] are less relevant than the dual concepts of the *oriental sublime* and the *cinematic sublime*, both of which are operational in *The River*. As I will argue, both are deployed to convey a sense of an encounter with the Other (manifested, variously, in the form of strangers, adulthood, love, and death) in India, with a charge of sentiments that transcend the geographical boundaries of place.

The oriental sublime emerged during the eighteenth and nineteenth centuries in the literature, art, and history of German Idealism and British Romanticism that cast the Orient as a mysterious and inexplicable Other. To quote Vijay Mishra, "Whereas the beautiful is about the West and history, about principles of order, the sublime is a threat to the imagination, a subversive impulse with the sole aim of disturbing or doing violence to the intellect."[18] In distinction, the "cinematic sublime" is my phrase for a concept described by early film theorists who found in photography and film technological inventions that could unlock the profound possibilities of human control over time, movement, and space, while simultaneously exposing the untamable margin of the real.[19] For André Bazin, "cinema is an idealistic phenomena" when it bases itself on the unattainable myth of reproducing reality;[20] it is unattainable because its absolute realization involves cinema's disappearance. For cinema to be cinema in whatever form conceived, there must linger some residue of difference between reality and its representation. Consequently, estrangement is part of all cinematic perception, particularly when the camera encounters reality as something that is documentable but fundamentally unknowable in any complete sense. As Michael Renov argues using the voice of Emmanuel Levinas, allowing the subject in front of a documentary camera a selfhood that exceeds the authoritative grid of complete visual or narrative comprehension can constitute an ethic of acknowledging the "infinity" of the Other, against the calculable "totality" of the knowable.[21] To be unfathomable then becomes not merely the blighted destiny of humanity's darker races or of the female sex but of reality itself.

Perhaps I overreach myself in calling such occasions—when cinema's technological "reach" seeks to "exceed its grasp" by trying to capture what is ultimately unknowable[22]—an aspect of the cinematic sublime. But for cinema, following Bazin, what lies beyond the limits of its technological artifice *is* the threat of its disappearance into reality. I use "reality" here to refer to the profilmic realm, expanding to its accumulation of organic and inorganic beings and infinitely to all existence. So a technological medium's effort to reach for the Other (which stands for all that is outside the self, for reality, infinity, and thence to oblivion) is imbued with a sense of the sublime. Whereas the orientalist sublime encounters or projects the Orient as fascinating and potentially horrific, the cinematic sublime stems from an acknowledgment that all reality exists far in excess of its technological reproducibility and must be framed or tamed in some manner along the razor's edge of its impossibility. Modalities of such (cinematic and philosophical) limit-texts are precisely what are in question for a theorist such as Bazin, and perhaps also for a philosopher such as Levinas. In other words, the cinematic aspiration to grasp reality alongside acknowledging the inherent impossibility of such an ambition can potentially transform the discriminatory index of the oriental sublime into an egalitarian index of self-abnegating knowledge or epistemic humility. Whether this happens in *The River* or not is what I will be debating, but in weaving between the film's text and its pre- and post-production contexts, I hold on to the possibility that encounters with strangeness *can* be genuinely transformational and break entrenched perspectives through considerations of alternative ways of thinking and being.

Encounters with strangeness can put us in the realm of a "brokered sociality" discussed by Judith Butler (following Klien, Levinas, and Derrida in ideas that hold an affinity with vocabularies of neo-Vedantism that Renoir would acquire in India, as we shall see).[23] The space of encounter holds the potential to make one's self vulnerable through realizations that "in the world of others, in a space and time" outside the self, our body "not only exists in the vector of these relations, but as this very vector ... the body does not belong to itself."[24] The idea of making the Self vulnerable to the Other runs through *The River*'s cinematic text and, in a more tenuous vein, through its production contexts. Tropes of encounter appear repeatedly in Renoir's and his crew's accounts of filming in India. While there is no way to objectively differentiate between the function of this rhetoric as a publicity gambit against its expression of transformative potentialities, holding up the film's visual and narrative mechanisms in relation to its extracinematic material reveals the centrality of strangeness and alienation as a primary affect to the film and its filming process.

I pursue these ideas—of the film's liminality between the ethnographic and metaphysical registers, and of its suspension between the affective realms of the representable and the ineffable—with extended discussions of three key elements in the film: specifically the *rangoli*, or pattern drawn on the thresholds of Indian homes; the South Indian Bharatanatyam dance form; and the Hooghly River. *The River* uses particular details drawn from India's cultural realm (the dance, the rangoli), topographic realm (the river, the village), and typographic realm (the "river people," in Harriet's words) to identify and signify India as a land while also transforming those very elements into the basis of a moral vision. The rangoli, the Bharatanatyam, and the river all serve as documentations of "things," events and landscapes or waterscapes that define India, while also becoming occasions for a metaphysical meditation on strangeness, exile, and loss in the film. The rangoli, the Bharatanatyam, and the river can thus be understood in relation to the dialectic between the documentary and poetic impulses of this film, which endow the film's ethnographic representations with a metaphysical significance.

Subsequent films that venture into a similarly liminal territory clarify Renoir's poetics and politics by comparison. Roberto Rossellini's *India Matri Bhumi*; Ray's *Pather Panchali* (*Song of the Little Road*, 1955), *Aparajito* (*The Unvanquished*, 1956), and *Apur Sansar* (*The World of Apu*, 1959); and Ritwik Ghatak's *Titas Ekti Nadir Naam* (*A River Called Titas*, 1973) are all films in which India's land and water are at the center of a cinematic vision.[25] These filmmakers share something with Renoir, either by way of direct contact with the man and in acknowledging his artistic influence (as with Ray and Rossellini), or by way of employing some of Renoir's production crew (as with Ray and Ghatak, who worked with cinematographer Ramanand Sengupta). All launch their own interrogations into the filmic medium's ability to tackle mundane and metaphysical themes through a focus on land while engaging, subverting, or completely ignoring Renoir's precedent. Despite his disapproval of *The River*, for instance, Ray displays an affinity for testing and blurring boundaries between documentary and fiction and for the related ambition of using aesthetics as a means to probe the human condition, much like Renoir. For these reasons, my reverse historical ethnography of *The River*'s production context is followed, in this chapter, by a reading of comparative cinematic sublimities that permit Renoir's vision of India to stand out in relief. This analysis delves into films that represent proximate quests into cinema's ability to document a location while also transcending it, by making place (in this instance, India) into an affective, moral, and existential realm as much as a geographic or ethnographic terrain.

THE STAKES OF UNIVERSALS AND PARTICULARS

Renoir's film opens with the adult Harriet claiming, "First love must be the same any place, and it might have been in America, England, New Zealand or Timbuktu. . . . But the flavor of my story would have been different in each, and the flavor of the people who live by the river would have been different."

The pivot of a qualifying "but" in this passage indicates that the universalist premise of experience hinges on negotiating with the particularity of place, in what can be recognized as an ambition to make generalizable truth-claims (in this case, about the nature of first love) compatible with the lived particularity and visceral singularity of location (claimed by the narrative and cinematography of this film). Negotiations between the particular and the universal affiliate *The River* with two kinds of discourses. First, India as a place of self-discovery and spiritual revelation for the Western protagonist resembles a well-worn orientalist trope. Filming India as a place combining everyday chaos with profound spiritual truths of self-discovery for the traveling Western subject is orientalist in the Saidian sense of being "an idea that has a history and a tradition of thought, and vocabulary" recurrent across a swath of Western popular culture.[26] If such a representational framework binds the film to a history of orientalism, it also potentially unbinds it from such orientalism with the mutuality of an encounter.

There are political risks to reading *The River* through the optics of encounter.[27] Edward Said entered similarly treacherous ground when he discussed Joseph Conrad's *Heart of Darkness* and Rudyard Kipling's *Kim* as generative texts that offer aesthetic pleasures and insights despite accepting imperialism as the order of the places where their fiction is located. *The River*, which focuses on the transience and fragility of a garden community of English expatriates in colonial India, creates a complex sense of temporality, but it also falls within a large range of texts that make the East part of a narrative and moral canvas subordinated to the preoccupations of Western protagonists. Said finds a modulated pitch for his argument that lies somewhere between his anger at affiliations between orientalism and canonized Western literature (which go unacknowledged in Western literary criticism) and his rejection of the postcolonial critic's "rhetoric of blame" against such literature.[28] The latter, in his view, is "neither intellectually nor morally sufficient" in its dismissal of Eurocentric and orientalist texts because it fails to grasp the historical complexity and complicity between a work's aesthetic influence and its multiple contexts.[29] Said's position is one of critical cosmopolitanism in that he narrates empire as a regime of domination *and* exchange, to better understand orientalism's mechanisms, its terrain of contestations, and its continuing legacies. His politicization of Western classics of world literature neither reduces them to doctrinaire tracts nor flattens his own analysis to a polemic.[30]

This form of analysis serves as my model for more reasons than one. Said illuminates the spatial density of exchanges embedded within orientalist texts to foreground histories that lie in suppressed and ignored corners of a text. By doing so, he shows that anticolonial criticism was not merely antecedent to the age of empire but also synchronous with it. Said also makes history personal. He unravels fiction's personalized dramatization of historical context—a history quickened in Kim's adolescent enthusiasm for the Great Game, in Marlowe's obsessive quest for Kurtz, in Fanny's familial relationship with the Bertrams—by a parallel critical traversal. Said's readings unearth the political-global implications of a novel's intimate and affective registers to show how the "emphases, inflections, deliberate inclusions and exclusions" of dominant imperial worldviews are sustained in the minutiae of emotions felt by fictional characters.[31] As an adolescent coming-of-age narrative, The River also presents a place and a time in intensely personal and melodramatic terms, and the text's political orientations are elusive because affect is compacted into deeply subjective registers. It is not surprising, then, that the film elicits reciprocally personal responses from filmmakers, scholars, and audiences who either celebrate the film for Renoir's personal vision and innovative style, reject it on grounds of its orientalism, or remain ambivalent about it.

The challenge in writing a historiography of The River, which comes to us across a political divide of contested interpretations, is to be neither dismissive of the principles of humanism and love embraced by Renoir and Bazin in relation to this film, nor dead to the geopolitical asymmetries of their well-intentioned sentiments. This is a challenge worth accepting because it forces film historians to look beyond their own aesthetic preferences and geopolitical commitments to perceive the complexity of transforming a location into filmed space with the same detached compassion that Bazin urged us to perceive in Renoir's lens. In the language of contemporary literary and art criticism, adopting such an attitude can be aligned with the historicization of affect, which brings out the social function of feelings.[32] The historicization of affect is particularly useful when approaching a classic but contested film: it allows us to plumb the complex range of feelings elicited by a text that is potentially antithetical to contemporary sympathies but that nevertheless seeps into our ways of imagining, comprehending, and framing art and the world, producing the varied responses of admiration, rejection, embarrassment, and acceptance of the text over the years.[33]

In other words, in addition to Bazin's analysis and Renoir's intention in his film, we must give weight to Ray's and Shahani's uncertainty about The River, which will be a familiar emotion to many viewers approaching any twentieth-century Euro-American classic of cinema and literature that is a product of its period's blind spots and social hierarchies. Frequently bracketed out of the study of film aesthetics and film history because they are slotted into categories of ideology critique, identity politics, or cultural studies, such critical responses provide a methodological direction for a "situated knowledge" of film art.[34] The stakes of producing a situated knowledge of *The River* lie in showing how its message of universality had place- and time-specific motivations and implications, involving several people and their systems of sociality, sympathy, acclaim, and production. At the broadest horizon of its critical acclaim, Renoir's quest for universal themes through a depiction of the particulars of life in India can be recognized as a historical impulse shared by other postwar filmmakers, who were celebrated in what film historian David Bordwell calls the "international film ideology" of European film festivals of the 1950s.[35] Discussing the birth of an international movie culture around film festivals during this decade, Bordwell points out that the global recognition received by a select group of male filmmakers (such as Vittorio De Sica, Akira Kurosawa, and Satyajit Ray) above other directors from their nations was in significant part because they were seen as humanists, although this critical lens often suppressed other tendencies in their work. Their work satisfied a postwar need to see in cinema, once again, the promise of a unified humanity.

Renoir's shift from being a "pagan" to a "mystic" in *The River* was part of an evolution in the artist's need to seek cinema's apposite goal in confronting the world after its recent history of carnage.[36] This was a poignant quest as filmmakers and critics sought redeeming human connections after witnessing mass displacements and a large-scale redrawing of the world's political boundaries at a high human cost over two world wars. However, if their humanism was an act of courage in the face of ugly political fractiousness, the postwar years also proved that their worldview was too easily coopted by regimes that suppressed difference in the name of universality to offer an uninterrogated alternative. Critical ambivalence toward *The River* can be understood as a larger ambivalence toward Renoir's strain of humanism. A contemporary reassessment of the director's well-meaning insistence to shoot in India must begin with an acknowledgment that any set of responses focused on classics of Euro-American cinema that use non-Western locations as backdrop will provoke opposing aesthetic and political sympathies. The recognition of insurmountable difference in this world's historical and political experiences has to presage any "critical border thinking" that engages insights from both sides of such debates.[37]

The River's opening credit sequence is accompanied by the visual of a rangoli drawn by female hands on a mud floor. Harriet's voice-over explains that rangolis are traditional patterns made with a paste of rice flour and water by Indian women to invite guests across the threshold of their homes. The sequence sets out the affective terms of the film: namely, that it will follow the nostalgic register of an adult Harriet recounting her adolescence in India, and Indians will not be the film's only assumed audience because (much like this text) they are not the ones who need a gloss on the meanings of rangoli, or the festival of light Diwali, or worship of the fierce goddess Kali, and so on. Recalling "thing theory" elaborated by Bill Brown and others in his wake, an object is what we look through because of its functionality in our lives. We confront its *thingness* when it breaks down or steps out of its functionality, to realize its temporality before and after its object-function.[38] The film's opening image presents the rangoli as several things: it is a visual document of a woman's hand drawing a pattern; it is an Indian symbol of invitation; it is also, therefore, an icon of foreignness to Euro-American viewers. Foreignness is the unbridgeable gap between the animation of an object for one culture and its opacity as a thing for another culture, necessitating its explanation.[39] Such markers of foreignness are repeatedly produced in the film's voice-over, placing some (Western) viewers as the text's addressees and others (its Indian viewers) in the more complicated position of insider to the text's *meaning* but outsider to the text's *address*.

A similar duality is replicated in the film's publicity, revealing its ethnographic texture. Here is Melvina McEldowney again, writing to Hedda Hopper with material to circulate about shooting in India as she describes the ceremony for auspicious inaugurations: "We attended one of these [*muhurat*] ceremonies at a Calcutta studio the other day. The producer, director, cast, crew, friends, and the press go to a temple in the early morning, place the script on an altar, ask of the Gods a successful picture, receive a red dot on the forehead, then go to the studio. There they place garlands of flower around everyone and everything including the camera, and other equipment, break a coconut (instead of a bottle of champagne) and the actors kiss the feet of the producer and director!"[40] The red dot, the garlanded camera, the coconut, and the kissed feet are played up for their absurdity, making the account one of many instances in which India and Indians are locationally positioned outside the address of the film and its publicity. The Indian habit of simultaneously propitiating gods and technology at a film's inauguration is marked as premodern, much as the

FIGURE 3.2 Female hands draw a rangoli in *The River*.

FIGURE 3.3 Garlanding the
camera at *The River*'s *muhurat*.
Courtesy of USC Archives of
the Cinematic Arts.

film's text portrays a pastoral and almost preindustrial India. But there are crucial differences between the ethnographic material generated for the film's publicity and the ethnographic gaze of the film's text. Accompanied by Harriet's voice-over, the film's documentary sequences acquire a near-poetic and lyrical tone (in comparison to McEldowney's own absurdist one).

The documentary shots incorporated into *The River* were partially motivated by the contingencies of filming in India. Working within the constraints of time, cost, and equipment, Renoir shot many of *The River*'s sequences in one take, which meant that he did not have reams of extra footage to give him a sufficient margin of error while editing the film's final cut. He made up for this by shooting documentary sequences on location, with the intention of inserting them into the film if needed. Of necessity, these documentary sequences were shot on available nonblimped cameras that could not record clean ambient sound because they were not soundproofed from camera noise. The blimped cameras (so-called because a soundproof housing or blimp surrounded them), which had been aboard ships and planes diverted to French Indochina to unload military cargo, were delayed in their arrival to India. When on his return to the United States Renoir screened an early black-and-white edit of *The River* to preview audiences at the Hal Roach studios in Los Angeles, he found audiences responding enthusiastically to the film's silent documentary sequences. This was despite the fact that the film lacked gradational values because the black-and-white version was printed from a single color of the Technicolor separation negatives, given the expense of editing on Technicolor.[41] Seeing how the place asserted itself despite this version's silent and degraded technological reproduction, Renoir reedited the film to incorporate more documentary sequences for his final cut. As Christopher Faulkner writes, Renoir "diminished the manifest storyline with each successive montage" and "interpolated documentary footage" into the fiction until, in Renoir's words, "the extraordinary ambience of place imposed itself on us little by little and became a new element in the story, probably the most important."[42] Renoir decided that the silent sequences would be "seminarrated" by Harriet to give the film's hybrid format of documentary and fiction some textual coherence.[43]

Consequently, while our visual encounter with the film's documentary sequences is direct, our narrative encounter is mediated through Harriet. We might call her our oral ethnographer. Speaking as an adult reliving her first love, Harriet speaks wistfully, creatively, and as something of a fabulist, which casts the film's documentary sequences in the same perceptual frame as the film's fictional artifice. The adult Harriet frequently adopts a tone of indulgent and affectionate distance from her younger self because she has the benefit of retrospective wisdom that infuses her documentary gaze with more romance than realism. Renoir treats the documentary segments as the most lyrical parts of the film, recalling Bill Nichols's description of documentary in the poetic mode.[44] Renoir's experimentation with a hybrid fiction-plus-documentary format to represent Indian landscape prefigures Rossellini, who would start his film *India Matri Bhumi* with a mock newsreel style of narration only to rapidly shift into what may be called a mode of realist fable. Renoir does not decenter the omniscience of his film's unseen narrator as much as Rossellini does, but he does puncture the orientalist fantasies of Hollywood, British, and German commercial films about India just as he upends the pseudo scientific ethnographies of British instructional shorts (discussed in chapter 1).

In *The River*, visuals of the river are accompanied by Harriet intoning dreamily, "The river runs, the round world spins. Dawn and lamplight, midnight, noon. Sun follows day; night, stars and moon. The day ends, the end begins." She remembers feeling "alive" and "curiously powerful" composing a poem about the river for Captain John, and her poem accompanies a drifting visual sequence in which boats pass by a static camera, followed by slight camera movements that glide over static "river people," evoking the gently kinetic visual imagery of early travelogues.[45] The sequence is echoed in Satyajit Ray's *Aparajito,* the second film of the *Apu* trilogy, in which a young Apu wanders past the banks of the river Ganga, hopping from step to step and leaning over the parapets. Although shot and set in Banaras, Uttar Pradesh, Ray's shots share patterns of image and movement with Renoir's river sequence: both use, to varying degrees, the lateral movements of people and the camera in imitation of a flowing river; both feature nonactors; both are evocative of a rhythm of life by the river and, in that sense, provide a hiatus from the tautness of dramatic storytelling. In both, shot durations appear to be almost the same as the duration of action, and camera movements define the sequence's pacing as much as the edits.

Despite this shared neorealist sensibility, there are differences. Unlike Harriet, Apu is not an aural presence but a corporeal one. The camera appears to take his perspective rather than an omniscient view as in Harriet's narrative, which is reinforced by the fact that Apu begins by first seeing his father reading scriptures by the banks. If the camera alights on people when Harriet describes them in composing a poem about the river to woo Captain John, Apu is seen as simply whiling away his morning as his father works. Where Harriet's excitement over her inspired verse competes with her fascination for the river's rhythms and lives, a childish curiosity mingles with boredom in Apu's wander-

FIGURE 3.4 Lobby card of boats floating by in *The River*. Courtesy of USC Archives of the Cinematic Arts. (ABOVE) FIGURE 3.5 Apu by the riverbank in *Aparajito*. (BELOW)

ings, bringing the camera affiliated with his perspective closer to Bazin's notion of an "impassive lens."[46]

This is not to say that *Aparajito* offers a better or more authentic experience of the Ganges and its tributaries than *The River*. Both sequences use glimpses of the mundane to offer us a sense of cinema's ability to capture rhythms beyond those of a dramatic narrative. But the sequences have different intents. Renoir's gaze is deliberately that of an outsider. The gaze, mediated through Harriet, is a romantic one. Ray's camera does not so much idealize its environment as observe it in its idiosyncratic detail, with the wandering and distracted attention of a casual note taker. It is an act of flânerie rather than one of romantic idealization. More interestingly, Ray's vision is a secular one. Spirituality doesn't infuse Ray's perspective so much as stand outside it, manifesting itself in discrete religious practices that are open to detached observation and, later in Ray's career, to social critique (as in *Devi* [1960]). *The River*, however, uses an idiom of the secular to reach toward a sense of the sacred. Events and objects lead people to encounters that offer a sublime understanding of the connectivity between the material, the mortal, and the subtle universe.

A sacralization of objects is intrinsic to the visual lexicon of *The River*, as witnessed in the reappearance of the film's opening rangoli. The rangoli as ethnographic object returns in the middle of the film, embedded within the film's most experimental sections of a story within a story, when Harriet invokes as her muse Saraswathi (the Hindu Goddess of learning) to win over Captain John with fables about Lord Krishna. The fable fills the screen as Harriet invents a story of an Indian girl whose father compels her to marry a man of his choice. The film's opening shot of a rangoli returns as part of the girl's forced marriage to an unwelcome groom, and a truth about the rangoli now lays exposed. It is not just an invitation to guests. It is an invitation to *all* guests, including those who are unknown, unwanted, and feared. Jacques Derrida, with characteristic lexical-philosophical play, argues that the concept of "invitation" holds within it a trace of the word "visitation." Elaborated with his neologism "hostipitality," Derrida implies that every act of hospitality embeds within it a sense of hostility. His point is that hospitality means nothing if it is extended only to those we expect or invite willingly. The ways in which the arrival of the *un*invited tests the host defines the true limits and logical aporias of hospitality.[47] In *The River*, uninvited guests include not only the groom in Harriet's story but also a traumatized US war veteran, sexual awareness, adulthood, the end of innocence, and, least welcome of all, death. The ways in which we cope with aging, human frailty, and mortality are the true tests of our selves because they represent something radically other than what we are now. Feelings of estrangement and the figure of a stranger are central to *The River*'s theme and style.

Renoir wanted his film to be from the point of view of an outsider, noting, "I had to see India through the eyes of a Westerner if I didn't want to make some horrible mistake."[48] *The River* shows us a world of displaced people. The orientalisms of Renoir's perspective are leavened by this self-consciousness manifest at the level of film content and style. In adapting a novella by Rumer Godden, herself a white British author who resided in India for much of her life,[49] Renoir populates his film with expatriates and misfits who are out of sorts in their domestic space. Characters constantly recognize their status as strangers, their quests as illusory, and the place as indifferent if not hostile to them. Captain John cries to Melanie, "I'm a stranger. You know what that means? A stranger," speaking to a tribe of people (including the biracial Melanie and the child-woman Harriet) who do not know where they belong. For the film's characters, as for Renoir, whose self-narrative follows their arc, transformation comes from a confrontation with sublime moments of radical strangeness, a realization that everyone is Other because home, in the receding horizon of "the big river, the whole world, everything" as telescoped by Harriet, remains detached from human fate and feeling. The universe does not care for Captain John's love or Bogey's death. It merely exists, even when imbued with the intensity of youthful traumas, as in Harriet's vision.

WHEN A GODDESS DANCES

In Harriet's fable narrated to Captain John and Valerie, the bride-to-be (played by Radha Sri Ram, who is Melanie in the film) consents to marry a stranger. Her consent is followed by the revelation that the man of her father's choice is none other than her true love. This vision transforms the couple into Krishna and Radha, god and goddess in the Hindu pantheon. "The love of a god made her a goddess," says Harriet, as Sri Ram performs a Bharatanatyam dance, and then Harriet's narration falls silent, making room for a performance by a dancer who is transformed into a personification of an Indian goddess. The dance is fantastical to an American audience for its departure from the space-time unity of the story. It is also surreal for Indian audiences because of the dissonance of seeing a South Indian dance accompanied by southern India's classical Carnatic music presented as an archetype of pure dance in West Bengal. To an Indian ear and eye, *The River* does not cohere geographically because it combines the music of Tamil Nadu's Kalakshetra with the story of a Bengali village.

FIGURE 3.6, 3.7, AND 3.8 Radha's dance in *The River*.

Renoir's betrayal of geographic logic to create Harriet's fantasy of eternal love highlights a friction between film's documentary realism and its stylization, pointing to the film's artistic ambitions *and* its blind spots. To begin with an enumeration of its shortcomings, the dance obliterates India's regional and historical particularities into an orientalist cultural generality. Moreover, dance as an expression of transformative joy in a woman who unhappily succumbs to paternal demands feels like the projection of patriarchal fantasy. The film's timing also makes this wistful fable suspect. Released during India's post-Independence period of student riots and peasant insurgency movements, and produced soon after Bengal's 1947 partition along communal lines, *The River* chooses to emphasize the role of "consent" in Hindu philosophy. "Everyone tranquil in the security of their faith" intones Harriet, in what sounds like tragically willful ignorance. The story of an Indian girl's actualization of a romantic dream through her quiet consent to her father's will is a metaphoric rewriting of a territory's history of trauma and active resistance as one of passive fatalism.

At the same time, the woman's/Melanie's dance as pure movement transforms her body into an intersection of multiple forces that surpass the immediate narrative preoccupations of the film. Renoir's betrayal of geography's aural logic creates a moment in the film in which a figure's choreographed movements relax the film's narrative logic. This does not mitigate the film's ideological shortcomings, but it does point to something interesting in terms of the film's form, hitherto governed by a gentle humanism, but now suddenly ruptured by a performative spectacle of theism. To hover briefly over those two words ("humanism" and "theism"), the theistic presentation of the dance sequence initiates a more complex mode of viewing than the film's overall humanism. In the sequence, Harriet's voice-over ceases and a dance performance fills the space. The Bharatanatyam performance is shot frontally in documentary mode with a static camera, and for the duration that the village girl is transformed into "Lady Radha" she is not embedded within the visual lexicon of the film's fictional universe but becomes part of its documentary images. Though an ideologically problematic move in its flattening generalization, the Bharatanatyam sequence is unusual in creating a tableau of opaque formalism that doesn't entirely coincide with the film's ethnographic assumptions of a culture's transparency. The looser structure of this section creates a digression that allows Carnatic music to acoustically enter West Bengal and enables an affective logic through which characters' emotions are harnessed to transform them into divinities unbound by culture or region. I return to the film's soundscape later, but notable at this point are the ways in which the dance sequence makes explicit an instability that accompanies the modes of realism and stylization in much of *The River*, wherein each modality keeps collapsing into the other.

The parenthetical dance sequence shows how objects and people in Renoir's film are repeatedly routed from the realm of the ordinary to the realm of the sublime through their spatial placement within a frame, or by their movement in relation to the frame and other figures, before they return to becoming a mere object among other objects, embedded once again in the mundane details of the film's narrative. In the visual locution of this dance sequence, a familiar figure from the narrative world (Melanie) visually represents the everywoman of Harriet's fable (the Indian girl) and is shot in the frontal style of an ethnographically documented performance (as a dancer) to illustrate a cosmic story about eternity (as a goddess). The imagined dance is embedded in Harriet's inept and youthful attempt to seduce Captain John by explaining a culture alien to him, but it also describes a transformative moment in a fable about the cycle of life, procreation, and regeneration that affiliates it with something more elemental. Renoir's films often display similar locutions and layered animations of filmed objects, where some *thing* firmly rooted within the concrete details of a scene begins to operate on a metaphoric and symbolic level, as in the rabbit hunt sequence or with Dario's elaborate automatons and mechanical toys in *Rules of the Game*. To a greater extent here, given the unfamiliarity of the Bharatanatyam dance to its Western audiences and the incongruity of its cultural placement to Indian ones, the dancing body in *The River* comes unhinged from narrative and ideological meanings to point to a kind of sublime abstraction that is characteristic of Renoir's cinematic realism.

CROSSCURRENTS OF SUBLIME IN *THE RIVER*

Combining concrete detail with abstract meanings, or what we may term the "concrete abstraction of reality," signals the ways in which Renoir's cinematic vision in *The River* in particular corresponded with Bazin's theory of cinema. André Bazin notes that Renoir's camera is "at once idealized and concretized."[50] (As an aside, social theorist Henri Lefebvre extends Marx's analysis of things that become *non*-things through exchange value as being paradoxically concrete and abstract or concrete abstractions.[51] The resonances and deviations between Lefebvre's and Bazin's ideas are taken up in this book's conclusion.) As Prakash Younger argues with reference to Eric Rohmer's comments on the dialogic, exploratory, and nonassertoric nature of Bazin's writings, "what Bazin means by reality in a given context only emerges when a film is *re-experienced* through the act of reading his writing."[52] Reentering *The River* through a Bazinian lens shows how, for the theorist, as also for Renoir, there was no intrinsic contradiction between cinematic realism and the cinematic manipulation of reality. With his well-known division of film directors into the two oppositional camps of those "who put their faith in the image and those who put their faith in reality,"[53] Bazin identifies the manipulation of *images* rather than a selective treatment of reality as a betrayal of the camera's ontological nature, because the former camp of filmmakers left little margin for the medium to express its own plastic relationship to the real. For Bazin, Renoir's staged choreography of movement within different planes of a shot served as an initial elaboration of the filmmaker's ability to use cinema's plasticity to selectively organize and convey the lived density of reality.

Discussing depth staging in the films of Renoir, Orson Welles, and William Wyler, Bazin calls their screen a "dramatic checkerboard" because such filming demanded a firm control over the profilmic in order to orchestrate dramatic action, while also giving viewers the freedom to let their eyes wander over the enframed action in a manner approximating to our visual experience of reality.[54] Tom Conley memorably calls this aspect of Renoir's filmmaking his "cartographies in deep focus."[55] Unlike most of Renoir's films, *The River* has more edits and static shots than mobile shots, in part because Renoir had limited access to lighting equipment in India and could not light large areas at any given time.[56] Nevertheless, he composes several shots in depth to produce a montage internal to the frame. The spatial organization and movement in such scenes emphasize watching, waiting, and emotional yearning without ever deviating from each character's rootedness within their environment or their placement relational to other figures. For instance, at the beginning of the chase in the mangrove sequence, Valerie crouches near the broken wall in the foreground, watching Harriet in the midground, who looks at Captain John as he begins to follow Melanie, who is fleeing into thickets in the background. By giving the sequence spatial continuity and organizing it around a relay of gazes, Renoir telescopes action across different spatial planes in the film. In the frame that begins the chase, dramatic lines of tension are created between people and objects through spatial choreography rather than facial close-ups, which would have been classical Hollywood cinema's preferred framing. The figures are one among many elements in the frame, which simultaneously diminishes them in relation to their environment and imbues the environment with the tension of their emotions.

In order to animate the meanings of people and objects in fluid ways—in relation to each other, to their environment, to the frame, and their own phe-

FIGURE 3.9 A chase in the mangroves in *The River*.

nomenal nature—Renoir's production process gives precedence to profilmic elements rather than to the narrative or recorded image. This is implicit in the process through which Renoir found locations for filming. According to Ray, Renoir scoured places for their "*couleur locale*" to find areas that corresponded best to his notion of a quintessential Indian landscape.[57] Renoir talks of spending a fortune on cans of green paint to make the halftints of Bengal's vegetation into tropical monochromes. Claude Renoir, Jean's nephew and the film's director of photography, walked around Barrackpore dousing grass with bright green paint to abstract a commonplace object into a luminous vision of pure color.[58] Although it was common practice to stage settings in order to transform real places into filming locations, in Renoir's case the efforts were distinguished by a strong antipathy to any "laboratory effects" or "special filters or re-touching."[59] Renoir found that the manipulation of profilmic reality accentuated cinema's receptivity to its environment's affective qualities by loosening up, rather than prescribing, possible relationships between the film's spectator and the filmed space.

This approach of minimizing post-production work while staging the profilmic to enhance a location's given qualities had an affinity with the cinematic realism of Satyajit Ray's films, whose frequent cinematographer, Subrata Mitra, did uncredited work on *The River*.[60] Under Mitra's guidance, Ray developed a method of bouncing daylight with mirrors to get a realistic effect. Like Renoir, Ray believed that the manipulation and framing of reality in a manner that heightens nature's drama allowed for a more authentic dialogue between the environment and its visual reproduction because it was not tampering with the surface of the image. Renoir understood this as an alertness of the camera to the "poetry" of reality, implicit in his equation of the "documentary side" of *The River* with the film's "poetic side."[61] This meant that the things that visually document India in Renoir's film, the ethnographic India if you will—such as the rangoli, the Bharatanatyam, the Peepul Tree, the snake, the kite-flying, the river, and much else—constantly traverse the space between their object or thing status and their incarnation of a greater meaning. While this is a familiar trope of the oriental sublime in the Western imagination, wherein the Orient is a real place as well as an unmappable and incomprehensible territory that exceeds the grasp of rational intelligibility, the trope is complicated in a film that reaches as well for a cinematic sublime, best elaborated in Bazin's defense of Renoir.

BAZIN AND *THE RIVER*

The idea of retaining the camera's vulnerability to its environment while treating reality itself as a canvas is conveyed by Renoir when he says, "*The River*, which looks like one of the most contrived of all my films, is in fact the one nearest to Nature."[62] Not surprisingly, the sentiment echoes Bazin's paradoxical formulation of *The River* as a "precisely controlled" film in which "the screen no longer exists; there is nothing but reality."[63] On the one hand, according to Bazin, "not a frame of *The River*" conveys the "uncertain and involuntary poetry of the machine," implying that Renoir maintains complete command of his spatial design despite a camera's compulsion to record whatever is set in front of it.[64] On the other hand, Bazin insists that Renoir is "interested only in showing things precisely as they are."[65] This oxymoronic formulation (contrived and natural, controlled and authentic, in binaries that echo Leo Braudy's arguments about Renoir's equal attraction to nature and theater) makes sense in light of Tom Gunning's and Daniel Morgan's work delinking Bazin's theory of realism from the semiotic notion of the index, to create a different sightline for the range of aesthetics that Bazin found illustrative of realism.[66] Morgan underscores Bazin's argument that the photographic film "actually contributes something to the order of natural creation instead of providing a substitute for it."[67] In other words, for Bazin the photographic image could add or "transfer" something to reality because it freed objects from the "temporal contingencies" of the world. By subjecting reality to the temporal and spatial rules of its mechanical medium, photography and film enabled "the possibility of forming relations to objects . . . that are not possible with respect to objects in the world."[68] Gunning further reminds us that Bazin's theory is not founded on the logic of a semiotic system but on the instabilities of an aesthetic world that comes into being with "spectatorial involvement" in moving images.[69] This makes questions of embodied affect and the spectatorial relationship to filmed space more central to cinema's ontology than is permitted by an exclusive attention to cinema's indexical, or indeed to its photographic, nature.[70]

Gunning's and Morgan's readings—which draw attention to the significance, in Bazin's work, of the affective relations enabled by cinema between spectators and the world and the essential difference between the photographic image and reality—focus on Bazin's realism, but they also pave the way to interpreting Bazin's enigmatic use of the words "truth" and "love." If realism designates a range of styles unified by their orientation toward the ontology of the image in Bazin,[71] love and truth are equally nonprescriptive qualities that are both subjective (describing what we feel and know) and objective (what is in the world). Inferentially, in Bazin's reading of Renoir, truth and love have an affinity with the Romantic belief in the experiential or emotional ability of art to access and make perceptible what is hidden in reality, although such a characterization is insufficiently specific to cinema and insufficiently nuanced to reflect Bazin's more elliptical argument, which is worth rehearsing briefly.

Referring to *The Rules of the Game,* Bazin declares that "henceforth the screen will no longer offer us a sense of reality, but will deliver it to us in the manner of a cipher grid moving across a coded document."[72] For Bazin, the screen in Renoir (similar to the canvas of Impressionist painters Manet, Degas, and Pierre-August Renoir) is a "cipher grid" for reality *not* because it replicates the world but because it "masks out what lies outside" the screen. Thus cinema realizes its ontological realism by exploiting its "discordance with reality."[73] Bazin suggests that the screen has the potential to show what lies beyond both the representational frame and brute reality by its very ability to mask or interrupt reality's continuum. By "departing from reality" and "interrupting the continuum of reality," the frame begins to suggest "what lay beyond it."[74] But what is beyond the frame if not more of the same? How does the difference between what is seen and unseen on the screen go *beyond* something that is merely enumerative if, as Bazin notes, "reality is not to be taken quantitatively"?[75] Never fully named because it identifies an impossible realm, or what I am referring to as the "cinematic sublime," this alchemy is created by a precarious interaction between the objective world, the subjective sensibility of the artist, and the inhuman machine lens of the camera, in a mediated process that collectively enables affective proximities between the world and the spectator *other* than what are possible in mere encounters with reality.[76]

The River, for Bazin, is successful in putting the spectator in proximity with such a perception of the world for a few reasons. First, because Bazin dissociates both "raw documentary reality" and "truth" from the psychological verisimilitude prioritized in narrative cinema, he can argue that *The River*'s "indifference to dramatic scaffolding" and "barely sketched out" characters allow avenues for realism. In his view, the film offers "merely an intimate and indiscreet way for us to live with [the characters]."[77] Consequently, despite Bazin's recognition that *The River* has a "superficial, overly optimistic, and implicitly imperial" story, he finds Renoir standing close to "the false perspective of Protestant, imperialism bourgeoisie" to "render the mute, diffuse, and inexhaustible light of *The River*."[78] This light comes from the gap between cinema's technological proximity to reality and its eternal machinic difference from it, wherein lies the medium's potential to reveal something more than the merely real or the merely representational, something in the order of (in Bazin's invocation) an "ethical" or "moral truth" that transcends the contingencies of any reality or sociological document, and the particularities of any fictional narrative.[79]

Second, when Bazin writes that "it is through Renoir's love, his sensibility, his intimacy with objects, animals and people, that his moral vision confronts us so strikingly,"[80] he displays his faith (or belief[81]) not only in Renoir but also in cinema's ability to reach for something ineffable as it records objects and people in their concrete materiality. Filmmakers who understand that the camera can allow places and things to retain their own particularity and texture despite being subordinated to a story begin to realize the phenomenology of automatism, which exhibits a kind of compassion to the world by abjuring intrinsic bias. Bazin seems to be saying that certain artistic deployments of the medium's potential to film with an impassionate eye toward all creatures, places, and objects in the camera's profilmic range allows an egalitarianism of affect to enter the frame, irrespective of the film's narrative mechanisms. Bazin finds that *The River*'s camera and cinematography extends this form of impartial love to its subjects and environments. While this affect may not describe the terrors implicit in the sublime, its elusiveness and reach to all beings is sublime in resisting prosaic description (turning Bazin to metaphoric and figurative speech).

At this point, we can agree with Bazin that Renoir's camera is "at once idealized and concretized" in *The River*,[82] so that elements that ostensibly document

India repeatedly become incarnations of truths about the human and cosmic world as the film transforms realism into a poetic abstraction.[83] Does this disrupt the orientalization of India as a location, or does it promote it? Bazin's admiration of the film was underwritten by a sense that Renoir's "ethic of realism" in *The River* was enabled by fragile and hard-won intersections between the disparate entities of India's profilmic reality, the director's artistic vision, and the film's spectatorial affect.[84] The artistry of location cinematography was at the heart of this realist ethic. Recalling the Bazinian sense that the camera conveys the plenitude of reality by casting an arbitrary mask or frame on reality, we can define a locational camera as one that requires the camera to enter an environment and make itself vulnerable to truths that exceed its frame. The locational camera is not only a part of its environment but also always *apart* from it. It is an intruder in a space that it must partially mask in order to record. The locational camera enters an alien environment that existed before, after, and beyond its presence to stage an encounter akin to the meeting of strangers. This coming together entails—for Bazin as much as for Renoir—what Philip Watts has called a "shock" of confrontation allied with "our encounter with others, and to the ways in which we live together."[85]

The estrangement and shock of confronting others and otherness, and the necessity to live with that shock, were central to Renoir's autobiography of exile and to India's post-Partition reality. These sensations of shock and estrangement manifest in *The River* as a universal condition, although they are created in relation to the concrete materialities of a location. A brief example of this is the sequence following Bogey's death, when his coffin is carried over a village bridge to the funeral grounds. As Satyajit Ray recalls in his notes on Renoir's shoot (which would serve as a sort of master class on location filming for Ray), Renoir reconstructed a replica of the real bamboo bridge and built an obstruction on it, in order to film the same sequence twice. Renoir wanted to make the shot of the funeral cortège more interesting.[86] When the procession passes over the real bridge, Renoir cuts to close-ups (shot on the mock-up of the bridge) as each family member looks down to mind their step. With this minor manipulation of a location shot, Renoir accentuates the enormity of the loss of a child by suddenly isolating the grief against an unconscious, minute, and utterly human gesture of the family pausing, each person for no more than an instant, to avoid an obstacle on the ground. It is a small gesture. But it makes the bereavement of an alien family in an alien land entirely relatable and mundane. The characters are fleetingly pulled out of a profound personal grief by an unrelated distraction, becoming every man or every woman who has struggled to balance life's minor irritants with its debilitating sorrows. The reconstructed bridge is a slight directorial touch, but it expresses the ways in which Renoir, a man exiled from his home in Europe and alienated from his work in Hollywood, could transform a location through interplays between the camera and the profilmic to realize his "desire to reach out and touch my fellow creatures throughout the world."[87]

My larger point here is that *The River*'s claim to (universal) experiential truths parallels (particular) personal and historical events. To say this is not to dull the film's meditations on so-called universal themes such as adolescence, adulthood, love, loss, and regeneration but to produce a situated knowledge of Renoir's film that retrieves a sense of specificity for India *and* for Renoir. To use Donna Haraway's phrase again, situated knowledge in this instance shows us that any art's universal message and appeal comes through an aesthetic and a sensibility that has place- and time-specific roots, involving localizable systems of sociality, sympathy, and acclaim. Two kinds of historical interventions can extend a situated knowledge of *The River*. The first involves conducting a reverse ethnography of the film's production process. The second involves situating *The River*'s depiction of India in a comparative context of *other* films that use India as a location for sublime encounters. A comparative reading interrupts assumptions of India as a conveyer of eternal truths because it shows that pieties about place are crucially about the historical production of a perspective and aesthetic, rather than about truths transhistorically immanent in the place itself. This is, once again, my turn to the rival geographies of India's landscapes and riverscapes. Similar to *The River*, the comparative films under analysis in this chapter abjure rationalist and empiricist perspectives of India to find intimations of the sublime in the land.

In thinking of *The River* against a canvas of other films that use Indian locations to meditate on unanswerable questions, I address how locations have animated artistic and auteurist preoccupations with cinema's abilities (and shortcomings) in confronting humanity's mortal and limited consciousness in the face of an unfathomably large universe. Here I invoke the cinematic sublime again to describe those aspects of cinema as a form that have pushed it, historically and philosophically, to grapple with unknowable truths about life and death with no more than the frail mechanical tools of its medium. I would argue that an interest in the cinematic sublime is precisely what drew Bazin, Ray, and later Shahani, Scorsese, and Anderson into the ambit of Renoir's film. What follows is a spatial film historiography that offers, by turns, a reverse ethnography of the film's production on location and a reading of the film within a comparative matrix of other films that transform India into a place that elicits unsettling confrontations with human finitude and transience.

A REVERSE ETHNOGRAPHY OF *THE RIVER*

Differing from Ray's criticism that there is not enough India in *The River*, some critics felt that there was too much of it. They felt that the story was "constantly interrupted by sumptuous excursions to the bazaars, by native dancing, by crowded river scenes" to distract the film away from its plot.[88] Despite differences of opinion over India's marginality or centrality to *The River*, accounts of the film's production (and Renoir's own accounts of the experience) indicate that visiting Bengal and traveling in India were pivotal experiences for the French director. Rumer Godden, who grew up in a household not unlike Harriet's Big House in the East Pakistan (Bangladesh) region, found that "Jean came under the influence of India very, very much, and lost a little bit of the balance he should have had."[89] India's influence on the director was both tactile and spiritual, mediated by new acquaintances and friends that Renoir and his wife, Dido, made during their sojourn to India. Renoir immersed himself in classical Hindustani and Carnatic music, attended Bharatanatyam and Kathakali dance performances, and after the film's completion, stayed at the residence of Radha Sri Ram (Melanie in the film) in Adyar, Madras (now Chennai), eating home-cooked South Indian vegetarian food and marveling at its flavors.[90]

Renoir came to India seeking an alternative to Hollywood with a proclaimed openness to the location's ability to transform his film. So perhaps there was a degree of self-fulfillment to the ways in which India opened him up to new tastes, sounds, socialties, and beliefs.[91] After leaving France for the United States following the German occupation of France and the critical failure of *Rules of the Game,* the director found himself chafing under Hollywood's system of stars and studio control.[92] With *The Southerner* (1945), his first independently produced film in the United States, Renoir made a break from the studio system and avowed a preference for "adventurers" over "organization" in film finance.[93] Kenneth McEldowney, eventually *The River*'s producer, was at this time a Beverly Hills florist and real estate agent in Los Angeles, California. On a dare from his wife, Melvina (the MGM publicist), McEldowney decided to produce a film to prove to her that he could improve on standard MGM fare.[94] McEldowney tried to get an option on Rumer Godden's novella, only to find that Renoir had already acquired it. This began a collaboration between a first-time producer and an acclaimed European filmmaker looking for avenues outside

Hollywood. Among the film's financiers contracted by McEldowney were the Maharajas of Baroda and Lindi in India.[95] McEldowney also discussed financial support from the Reserve Bank of India and acquired the Maharaja of Gwalior's mansion in West Bengal (later to become a children's orphanage) as the set for the Big House.[96] Permission to shoot in India was contingent on 75 percent of the crew being Indian citizens,[97] at a time when citizenship was a new experience for Indians. For Indian film technicians, crew, and craftsmen, this opened up a rare opportunity for below-the-line work[98] on an international film.

A motley crew—including the film's technicians, who lived all over Calcutta, and Radha Sri Ram (Melanie in the film), whose strict vegetarianism demanded a purified Brahmanic kitchen—departed for the shoot by joining the film's largely European cast at the Great Eastern Hotel on Bentinck Street, Calcutta, where the foreign nationals stayed. This crowd was more diverse than anything seen in the frames of the film they produced, and the place's environment more chaotic. For Renoir, shooting in India opened up an opportunity to be free of Hollywood studio managers who were focused on the company's bottom line and actively interfered in his directorial efforts. At the same time, filming in India raised obstacles of an entirely different nature for the filmmaker. India lacked the infrastructure to support large-scale foreign film productions at the time. Mobile electrical equipment, generators, and arc-light projectors had to be imported from Britain, and this equipment was delayed by the requisitioning of ships to Indochina. Even with the arrival of equipment, there was only enough power on-site to light up small areas, forcing Renoir to conceptualize the film in terms of static rather than mobile shots with the camera moving in and out of an image rather than laterally.[99] In producer McEldowney's words, "Taking a film company on location to India is something like doing a juggling act while walking a tight rope in high wind."[100]

India's Infrastructural Challenges

The infrastructural problems that Renoir faced shooting in India were compounded by communal tensions in West Bengal. Not only did the film's electrical department have to find ways to make their AC power plugs compatible with India's DC sockets, they also had to figure out how a predominantly Muslim electrical crew could work on the grounds of Hindu property owners on whose land stood their two electrical generators.[101] The presence of two million refugees in Calcutta, ongoing communal rioting, and a violent episode of students who stopped the film's shoot because of rumored impropriety caused the crew to get police protection.[102] The crew was also vulnerable to sickness, and Renoir's nephew, Claude, the film's cinematographer, contracted typhoid while in India.[103] If India's historical context is effaced at the level of film text, it was nevertheless a daily reality for the film's production crew and well documented in the production files, providing grist for the publicity mills and confirming India's hinterland status.

In terms of filmmaking, the lack of production facilities meant that at the end of a day's filming, the footage was flown from Bengal to Britain to be developed at the London Technicolor office.[104] Renoir and art director Eugène Lourié viewed the film's rushes about ten days after the shoot with "some of the sequences lost or ruined," and received cryptic telegrams about the quality of the color prints from Carl Koch in London.[105] Given a lack of screening facilities and the monitoring of film content imported into India, Renoir and Lourié had to view the film's rushes with the Calcutta customs officer who invited "his entire family . . . his wife, his children, his cousins and his aunt to a small screening room."[106] Unintentionally, this would have been the film's first test audience. Indian voices are largely silent in the film, but we can conjure up a din of the unrecorded conversations in Bengali that must have taken place between this officer's family members when the film's rushes were screened.

India's fiscal condition was also unstable after its independence. Whereas the Euro-American film crew benefited greatly from the country's inexpensive labor and human resources, repeated devaluations of the Indian rupee led to revised contracts for the crew and constant rebudgeting for the producer.[107] Additionally, Indians lacked Hollywood's streamlined production practices and safety protocols. Lourié constructed a mock village on location because Renoir had some difficulties in finding the perfect village for his film. Real huts were fire hazards, and those situated by the river were surrounded by overgrown vegetation that was an obstruction to natural or artificial light sources.[108] To Lourié's surprise, Indian laborers accustomed to working with brick and teakwood rather than plastic and synthetic materials built a real village street rather than a simulation, blurring the line between reality and its simulation. While *The River* includes documentary shots and some actual locations, several places in the film were constructed sets rather than preexistent sites. After Renoir left India, these sets were assimilated with the land as actual habitations for local populations. The fictionality of the film's set was but a brief interregnum in the habits of life within a region that was not set up for film production.

Whereas Renoir had decried Hollywood's intractability, he tolerated these delays and frustrations because he treated India as a moral and life lesson. Obstacles faced in the country were integral to Renoir's account of how India taught him to have more patience.[109] In his first interview with *Cahier du Cinéma* after the film's release, Renoir remarked that "the theme of acceptance" was his own, but "India could not have helped but develop it" because of the "Hindu metaphysics" that the "world is one."[110] Renoir's reference here is most likely to Advaita philosophy, introduced to him by Radha Sri Ram. Advaitism, the nondualistic philosophy of the Vedantic Upanishads, was reinterpreted and popularized by Adi Shankara (c. 788–820 CE). According to Advaitism, there is merely a perceived or epistemological difference rather than a metaphysical difference between the ultimate reality or basis of all being (the *brahman*)[111] and the individual soul or self (the *aatman*). Different schools of interpretation within Advaitism share in common the belief that liberation, or *moksha*, lies in realizing the indivisibility of the multitudinous phenomenal world of *things* when we apprehend the presence of the brahman within the multiplicity of organic and inorganic matter.[112] The lure of things (including the distraction of one's own self) is thus to be recognized as illusory and part of a clutter of materiality that hides the oneness of being. Shankara's teachings were central to the neo-Vedantic renaissance in India during the late nineteenth and early twentieth centuries, particularly in the Vedanta movement led by Swami Vivekananda (1863–1902) and the Self-Realization Fellowship developed by Paramahamsa Yogananda (1893–1952).

The global popularity of these movements and the lecture tours conducted by the two spiritual leaders in the United States created a context for significant "interculturation" between neo-Vedantic Hinduism and American Theosophy.[113] Renoir and his wife, Dido, were introduced to Theosophy through their friendship with Sri Ram,[114] whose father was president of the Theosophical Society in Adyar, Madras, the international headquarters of Theosophy established by the movement's cofounders, Madame Blavatsky and Colonel Olcott. Without losing the present discussion in the thickets of Theosophical and neo-Vedantic philosophies, a brief detour through their relevance to *The River*'s cinematic vision clarifies the film's artistic and philosophical affiliations.

Renoir, Radha Sri Ram, and Neo-Vedantism

Neo-Vedantism would have appealed to a filmmaker drawn to the French literary movement of *unanimisme* associated with the works of poet Jules Romains in the early 1900s. Unanimisme, which treated individuals as constituents of a collective or transcendent consciousness, was a movement in French literature and poetry that conceptualized characters with less recourse to individual psychology than to group patterns, historical events, decentralized communities, and social tableaus of crowds and city blocks. In discussing Renoir's film *The Crime of Mr. Lange* (1935), Bazin uses a graphic diagram of a courtyard that serves as the film's central location to illustrate how it becomes a "chance product of urban geography, in an almost *unanimiste* sense."[115] Bazin persuasively argues that the courtyard "synthesizes the whole spatial structure of the film" as a set specifically built for the film with a circularity inscribed in the concentric patterns of the courtyard's tiles, which is a pattern picked up by the camera movement that provides viewers with a 360-degree pan following the motion of a character pursuing his murder victim. In this sequence, Bazin finds that the psychological and dramatic motivation of a character and the lives of the people arrayed around the courtyard fuse into "pure spatial expression."[116]

The River's mise-en-scène shares similar moments of pure spatial expression (such as in the dance, or the chase through the mangrove discussed earlier), but a waterscape is itself a spatial trope that repeats across a range of Renoir's films (particularly *The Whirlpool of Fate* or *The Girl of the Water/Le Fille de l'eau* [1924], *Boudu Saved from Drowning* [1932], *A Day in the Country* [1936], *Swamp Water* [1941], *The Woman on the Beach* [1947], and *The Southerner* [1945]). In *The River*, the waterscape conveys with tactile immediacy the many lives that are bound to rivers and caught in rhythms of community and nature that are larger than individual lives. Perhaps Renoir was drawn to *unanimiste* and Theosophical teachings about the illusory nature of subject-object dualism because they spoke to his search for a cinema that hinted at possible interconnections between object forms and subjective as well as communal meanings. Historically, Theosophical ideas about the evidence of a greater plane of existence beyond the mortal object world drew on such practices as the Kabbala, Freemasonry, mesmerism, and occultism.[117] All forms of spiritism found fertile ground in late Victorian England, and Theosophy in particular spread among Europeans, Anglo-Indians, and the local elite of colonial India in part because "the otherworldliness of the occult offered alternative possibilities for imagining colonial relations outside a hierarchical framework, without succumbing entirely to the next logical step of miscegenation."[118]

As Gauri Viswanathan argues, Western initiates and Eastern guides came together under the aegis of the Theosophical Society to commune with the spirit world in interactions across racial lines less tolerated at the extremes of British imperial administration and Indian nationalist resistance. If the communion of spiritism was more adventurous than exclusionary colonial policies, it was also a safe alternative that held at bay the fear of "racial 'degeneration' caused by sexual contact."[119] The desire to transcend the hierarchies and divisions of society to seek oneness of spirit amid the atomization of matter permeates the philosophies that Renoir was drawn to during the making of *The River*. Their force works within the film as a potential source of reconciliation for characters faced with personal and historical traumas. At the same time, these philosophies portend a political conservatism in that the union of spirit implicitly obviates the union of racially mixed bodies, which *The River* partially addresses but finally dodges with the character of Melanie, who makes racially safe choices.

In *The River*, Sri Ram's Melanie personifies both the possibility of a spiritually unified humanity as the film's sagely presence and the embodiment of racial miscegenation. Alongside her father, Mr. John (Arthur Shields), who speaks of "digestivism," Melanie is a proponent of "consent," espousing a personal philosophy that accommodates humans to a universe indifferent to the individual's fate. Understanding her place in this universe involves, for Melanie, coming to terms with her own racially mixed heritage. Melanie's discomfort with her Anglo-Indian status is shown to be a hard-won realization over the course of the film's narrative, but Sri Ram's amateur acting produces a curious effect. While her character Melanie's self-interrogation in the film remains ineffective as a dramatic crisis, Sri Ram's amateurish delivery of lines disturbs the film's fictional universe and, perhaps unwittingly, underscores the affect of alienation and vulnerability central to the film's themes.[120] Additionally, Sri Ram's significance to the film is revealed not only in relation to her character Melanie but also in the context of her extracinematic relationship to Renoir as his unofficial guru, or spiritual guide, in India.

In Godden's novella on which this film is based, there is no "Melanie." Renoir created the character with Godden's collaboration in response to criticisms about the lack of Indians in the film. When Renoir met Sri Ram, he thought the camera was particularly susceptible to her charms, calling her a "screen animal"[121] who "makes me think of a young Nazimova."[122] I find this claim largely unsupported by Sri Ram's performance in the film. Renoir's fascination with her feels like misplaced ardor until it is seen in terms of his interest in a certain way of life and embodied belief represented not only in the character of Melanie but more centrally by the person Sri Ram. Katherine Golsan makes a close study of the contrasts between the film and early drafts of the script titled "East of Eden," which was revised as "Big River."[123] In these earlier drafts, Golsan shows, Captain John was closer to the book's version of his character as a bitter, misanthropic, and alcoholic war veteran who despises Western culture and the United States. In the draft, Mr. John has two daughters: the white Valerie and the Eurasian Melanie. Melanie marries Captain John,

FIGURE 3.10 Publicity image of
Radha Sri Ram (later Bernier)
in *The River*. Courtesy of USC
Archives of the Cinematic Arts.

winning him over with her devotion and selflessness. She brings a restorative
humanity to Captain John, while Captain John legitimates Melanie's precarious racial and social status through marriage. Golsan points out that this draft
altered profoundly after Renoir met Sri Ram and decided to cast her as Melanie despite her lack of acting experience. Accounts of Renoir's meeting with
Sri Ram rehearse the transformative moment when he first saw her perform a
Bharatanatyam dance.[124]

Sri Ram's aunt was Rukmini Devi Arundale, a well-known Theosophist,
animal rights activist, and high-caste Hindu woman who appropriated a
dance form practiced by Devadasis into the Brahmanical tradition, giving it
the modern bourgeois respectability that it enjoys today.[125] Sri Ram's performance of the dance so impressed Renoir that he wished to incorporate it into
his film. Sri Ram's absorption into the film paralleled the ways in which the
film's background began to assert itself more vigorously into the film's narrative and visual schemes, with each successive draft and edit of *The River*. As
Golsan rightly notes, the presentation of Sri Ram's dance sequence through
the optics of a documentary testify to the increasing autonomy of place over

narrative.[126] Renoir hoped to shoot a second film with Sri Ram, and while that never materialized, his fascination with her would become an inextricable part of his involvement with India. Talking about the Hindu caste system with *Cahier*, Renoir describes Sri Ram as someone in touch with her traditions.[127] He admires the idea of a living tradition: "The Hindu caste system is a bit like a hereditary union... you belong to it for four thousand years.... You can escape it only by death or resurrection."[128] Renoir's writings evince a nostalgia for an era of wholeness, belief, and continuity. The filmmaker expresses this when he talks of Bazin in his introduction to Bazin's book on Renoir's films: "I loved him [Bazin] because he belonged to the Middle Ages. I have a passion for the Middle Ages, just as I have a distrust for the Renaissance... which laid the foundation of industrial society."[129] A similar sense of nostalgia is central as well to Renoir's book on his father, the Impressionist painter Pierre-Auguste Renoir. Based on conversations between father and son that took place when Jean was injured on the Bavarian war front in 1915, and Pierre-Auguste severely incapacitated with rheumatoid arthritis (though still making art), the memoir *Renoir, My Father* opens with vivid evocations of the artist's life before "civilization had evolved from the work of the hand to that of the brain."[130] In response to the civilizational rupture indexed to World War I by the son, and idiosyncratically linked to the "invention of the tube" (in reference to infrastructural metal pipes that geographically connected countryside to cities by delivery systems of water and gas during the 1800s) by his father,[131] both men shared an aesthetic and emotional investment in art's capacity to redress the bewildering historical break of industrialization.

Renoir belonged to the generation of European artists and theorists confronting Western modernity not as a trajectory of progress promised by the Enlightenment but as the horror of "living on the brink of catastrophe," with its tools of advancement turned into grotesque instruments of "industrial warfare and mass death."[132] Recuperating, in Benjaminian terms, the memory of auratic art that could reveal an object's material affiliations to its origins, the son celebrates his father's ability to perceive in things their "intrinsic value."[133] For Renoir, this refers to his father's belief that objects become more meaningful when they, painted or artistically rendered, convey the circumstances of their creation and creator rather than their attributed value, to show their "pettiness as much as grandeur of creation."[134] Such themes—of nostalgia for a sense of continuity with origins, estrangement as historical inevitability, art as a response to the shock of historical rupture and imbued with the potential to unify a fragmented reality, and creativity as conveying the totality of experience ranging from the ephemeral to the grandiose—are repeated tropes in Renoir's writings and his films.

Miriam Hansen discusses similar themes in Siegfried Kracauer's writings on film and photography. For Kracauer, photographic media reflected the alienation of modern society, but it was equally possessed with the ability to play with "pieces of disjointed nature" to create radical perceptual insights.[135] Cinema's ability to defamiliarize the everyday and freeze a moment in a manner that could arouse our "awareness of a history that does not include us" was part of a roster of possibilities for a medium that, according to Kracauer, redeemed a material reality otherwise lost to the abstractions of commodity form.[136] Read in the context of Renoir's nostalgia for a preindustrial era, *The River* is its director's attempt to create a film language that could retrieve (with the tools of industrial technology) meaning from a world rapidly depleted by the banalities of commercialism and overdetermined by the ideologies of political doctrine. Filming in India held the promise of restoring Renoir's faith in the filmmaking process, because to him, the place itself seemed to possess a regenerative sense of continuity with its past.

The significance of Renoir's Indian journey to the evolution of his own thinking is clarified by the fact that, by his own admission, he finally felt ready to write his long-planned book about his father after he returned home to Lenora Drive in Beverly Hills, California, following the filming of *The River*: "Now I know that great men have no other function in life than to help us to see beyond appearances: to relieve ourselves of some of the burden of matter—to 'unburden' ourselves, as the Hindus would say."[137] A metaphysics of liberation based on recognizing the interconnectedness of all things despite their material atomization and transience, as taught by Theosophy and neo-Vedantism, resonated with Renoir's historical experience of exile, separation, and loss. Shanay Jhaveri accurately describes *The River* as a film that "re-creates the nostalgia of indivisibility, but also foregrounds the necessity of separation."[138] *The Rules of the Game* and *The River*, two stylistically distinct films that bookend Renoir's departure from France and the beginning of his return, are similar in their striving for a film language that conveys the director's confrontation with the paradigms of faith and reason that he felt the world to be historically astride. In Renoir's terms, he was caught between the enchantment of the Middle Ages and the disenchantment of the twentieth century. In *The River*, Renoir makes India the threshold space for this oscillation.

And so a dialectics returns. India became the occasion for reconciling Renoir's personal struggles, but a purely philosophical or abstract engagement with India denies its own contextual and material density and misreads the nature of global history. Registering the sensory experiences of shock and alienation as a specifically twentieth-century phenomenon indexed to the two world wars and the European Holocaust is a Eurocentric narrative that ignores the fact that Enlightenment's legacy of modernization visited a much longer history of devastation upon the rest of the world. Predating the two world wars by centuries were slavery and colonial policies of deindustrialization, pauperization, repression, and death that funneled resources from territories constituting present-day South and Southeast Asian, Middle Eastern, and African nations to a rapaciously industrializing Europe. India was among the regions that experienced a violent severing from its own history and tradition as a precondition of its induction into an imperially connected modern world. By placing Sri Ram's philosophical and cultural pursuits—and by extension, India—in the context of a pure and unbroken tradition, Renoir neglected several historically contingent events such as Theosophy's popularization of neo-Vedantic beliefs, the politics of caste in the propagation of Bharatanatyam, and imperialism's complex interconnections that made neo-Vedantic metaphysics accessible for wider international adoption in the first place. My point is that Renoir's initiation to India was channeled through a particular echelon of India's class, caste, and culture that can be identified with elite Tamil Brahmanical and Theosophist social circles within which Sri Ram and European expatriates moved. The places and people Renoir encountered and experienced as part of India's unbroken tradition and past were defined by his particular itinerary through India, which provided him with a socially and historically circumscribed set of cues and hosts to translate the place onto film.

A RETURN TO THE ORIENTAL AND CINEMATIC SUBLIME

The River evacuates India of its historicity, but temporality remains crucial to the film's spatial design. Interplay between the film's missing historical index and its complex use of temporality returns us to internally destabilizing interactions between the film's use of the oriental sublime (with its tendency to dehistoricize the east) and the cinematic sublime (founded on the medium's ontological proximity and plastic control over reality, when these abilities are used to convey reality's fundamentally ungraspable nature). This instability is visible in the film's use of an adolescent perspective, its use of color and sound, and its temporally charged spatial design.

FIGURE 3.11 A summer of first love for three girls, as shown in *The River* lobby card. Courtesy of USC Archives of the Cinematic Arts.

In Godden's 1946 novella from which the film is adapted, a beautiful English girl called Bea, who is on the brink of womanhood, explains to her sister why she is sobbing into her pillow in the middle of the night:

"Because *it* is going," said Bea in another rush.

"It? What 'it' Bea?"

"It is all going so quickly," said Bea. "Too quickly. It is going far too fast."

"Mmm," said Harriet, beginning to understand.

"Much too quickly and too fast," cried Bea. "It is all changing, and I don't w-want it to change."[139]

Renoir and Godden's adaptation (constantly revised during the shoot) eliminates Bea's character but assimilates her experiences into the character of Valerie, the attractive daughter of a jute factory owner in the West Bengal village where the story is set.[140] In the film, Valerie says something similar to Captain John when he kisses her (her first kiss). She cries, "*It* is going. . . . All of us happy, and you with us here. I didn't want it to change, but it's changed. I didn't want it to end, and it's gone. It was like something in a dream. Now you've made it real. . . . I didn't want to be real." The tumult of Valerie, Harriet, and Melanie's transition to adulthood becomes real when Captain John's kiss forces Valerie (and the two girls who witness the kiss) to confront their new desires and its confusions. The kiss brings into the open certain truths about their passage into adulthood, marking the end of their innocence. Valerie, Melanie, and Harriet's inarticulacy and confusion around their sexuality and identity—the experience of adolescence—are stylistically echoed in the aural and visual display of India as foreign space.

The Time of Adolescence

By making Harriet our émigré narrator recalling a lost adolescence, Renoir disables a one-on-one correspondence between India and its nostalgic abstraction because Harriet's narration is the scrim of a fallible character. Experiential truths about adolescence are presented to the audience through Harriet's memories, but those memories are not the only element conveying the place to us in cinematic terms. Two other girls also live through their first summer of love, and their growing awareness of themselves and of Captain John[141] is rendered through their characterization, dialogue, and, most vividly, the film's visual and sound design. To create *The River*'s soundtrack, Renoir drew from classical Hindustani and Carnatic music and interwove ambient sounds from the riverbank with a range of instrumentalizations. The film is divided musically between North Indian classical music that is used in its first half, and the Carnatic Bhairavi *ragam* in the latter half. A *raga* or *ragam* (the word's northern and southern Indian usage, respectively) is a melody constructed with several musical notes, which may be associated with the time of day, season, or mood. Renoir wanted to use the contrapuntality of Indian classical music's "polyrhythmic pattern" to correspond with the film's dramatic moods. So while he uses music to mark leitmotifs (for instance, by repeating notes to signify river music or cobra music) and to signal interludes (around festivals), a fluidity of musical style allows him to borrow any Indian raga to underscore the dominant emotion of the film.[142] Local Bengali folk music mixes with classical notes from India's northern and southern regions because Renoir's concern is with the film's affective tones rather than with regional fidelity. Memorable examples include an exuberant orchestration for the kite dance and the scoring of Bogey's funeral sequence.

This idiosyncratic use of Indian classical music is carried through in the film's use of color. Renoir appears to have had a few different motivations behind the film's color palette. He wanted Bengal's green grass to look greener, blue skies bluer, and red saris redder to exaggerate the tropical feel of India in Technicolor.

He appreciated Bengal's "tropical vegetation" as opposed to the "myriad blended tints" of the French countryside because he felt that the former had a "limited range of colors" that were "neither too vivid nor mixed," and could be well exploited by the stark color variations of the Technicolor camera.[143] Comparing Bengal's colors to a Dufy or Matisse painting, Renoir was keen to highlight the natural extremes of its color palette by removing halftints and heightening the environment's vividness, by framing shots with color contrasts or by repainting nature rather than retouching the image. A careful arrangement of colors in quotidian elements—in exterior shots of trees and boats, and in the interiors of "house, curtains, furniture, clothing"[144]—lends the external world a psychological interiority in that the images burn with the brightness of Harriet's memories.[145] Just as Harriet's slight story of her first crush delivers the darker elements of unrequited love, accidental death, attempted suicide, a battle-scarred psyche, and an amputated body in this film, the film's colors and sounds make the everyday objects of life throb with the feverish sensations of adolescent tumult.

In distinction to Hollywood and Indian films shot in color during this period—such as the epics *Aan* (Mehboob Khan, 1951), shot in Gevacolor; MGM's *Quo Vadis* (Mervyn LeRoy, 1951), shot in Technicolor; and *Jhansi ki Raani* (Sohrab Modi, 1953), also shot in Technicolor—*The River* is careful to depart from color as a code for fantasy, myth, or historical epic. In this aspect, it also contrasts with *Black Narcissus* (Powell and Pressburger, 1947), an earlier cinematic adaptation of Rumer Godden's novel shot in Technicolor entirely in England although set in India, which Godden disliked intensely because it transformed what she perceived to be a realistic story into stylized psychological horror.[146] Claude Renoir's priorities were different in *The River*. In his words, "The most important problem before technicians who want to transpose color onto a screen is the ability to see and to grasp the colours which surround them in the first place."[147] Claude Renoir's brief to his technicians was to use color to intensify the objects that were already present in their actual environment.

In *The River*, a disconnection between Harriet's placid voice-over and the vividness of color and music transports us to the affective disorientations of adolescence. With their use of color, the Renoirs capture a stage of life when things are felt before they are understood, lending emotions an inarticulacy that makes them more intense. The film conveys the essential strangeness of adolescence by the sights and sounds of a foreign land rather than by what Bazin calls "psychological verisimilitude."[148] One of the most interesting ways in which *The River* organizes the spectatorial encounter with the film's environment while also thematizing the girls' growing awareness of their sexuality is through the spatial design of vicarity. Not only does Harriet narrate the summer as if it had happened to another person (that is, to her at another time), but many of her experiences are shown to be vicarious. "It was my first kiss, but received by another. I couldn't bear it," she says. If the film's colors and sounds give the place an affective immediacy, the visual pattern of vicarity lends it distance. With Harriet's presence inside and outside her narrative, we watch her India with the same duality, accompanied by a formal reflexivity toward the act of our looking. Stylistically, this spatial design of refracted gazes combine with Harriet's perspective to transform a minor story about a young girl experiencing the out-of-place and strange-in-body feelings of puberty into an artistic reflection on estrangement and exile. A young girl is at odds with her body and unfamiliar with the sudden volatility of her emotions, much as a sensibility is at odds with its environment. The environment that is cinematically and narratively marked as foreign echoes the uneasiness of Harriet's adolescence when she says, "I hate bodies!" *The River*, in this way, becomes a girl's coming-of-age film, a postimperial film, as well as a postwar film seeking a sense of reconciliation.

The Temporality of Enclosed and Outside Spaces

Time is spatialized in *The River*. Exterior spaces (such as the river, the Peepul Tree, the boats, the river people) glow with a sense of universal temporality, whereas enclosed spaces (of the Big House, Melanie's house, the enclosed garden and gazebo) are vulnerable to the fatalities of human time. Although not neatly binaristic, external spaces are more closely identified with India and appear cyclical and impersonal. Internal spaces are more likely to be changeable human worlds constructed by displaced Europeans. Rather than posing a stark contrast, the film creates a layered patterning of time through this temporalization of space. The film's progression depends on an outside slowly encroaching upon the inside. Boundary attritions are thus a key part of the film's structure and theme. Harriet's carefully constructed fictional and private worlds—her stories, her poems, her diary, and her room under the stairs—are fragile and vulnerable to invasion. In this scheme, a clearing amid mangroves is the perfect site for slippages between one kind of space/time and the other, as an exterior location that extends yet disrupts the intimate world of the film's protagonists. It is in this liminal space that a private kiss is viewed by two others, bringing the reality of adulthood into the lives of three girls and, at the same time, disrupting the idyllic playground of a miniature pastoral England in West Bengal.

The River has been criticized for lacking historical consciousness, but the film's sensory re-creation of adolescence, its multitemporal spaces, and nostalgic reminiscence allow for a more complex patterning of time than is permitted in such readings. On the one hand, *The River* does succumb to the orientalist trope of making India a land of cyclical time that serves as a spiritual corrective to Western expectations of linear time.[149] Harriet's lesson lies in adapting her own traumatic experiences to a sense of life's eternal rhythms. "Bother yesterday," says Valerie. "This is today," says Melanie. The three girls name their present—of the baby, the house, and the river—in a chant that negates the possibility of tomorrows and yesterdays, of memory and progression. On the other hand, such incantations of an eternal present are belied by Harriet's voice-over, which is predicated on the distance of age and the presumption of change. The film's visual register replicates a similarly unstable sense of time, with documentary sequences showing us an Indian river where boys awaken and men cook, bathe, and stack jute in the present continuous, while the images themselves are embedded within Harriet's recursive narrative. Recalling Bill Nichols's articulation of the variably authenticated worlds of documentary and fiction, the documentary segments speak their truths in expository tones while the fictionalized segments utilize a range of narrative devices.[150] With this duality of presentation, *The River* yields to an ambiguous sense of time: India symbolizes eternal rhythms, but the film's variously temporalized interior and exterior spaces disorient any sense of a placid eternity.

Thus elements of the oriental sublime (of an eternal India) and the cinematic sublime (of a reality that exceeds and threatens its mechanical capture and recollection) coexist in *The River*. Other films, although stylistically different, have also used India as a location to confront the challenges posed by reality to cinema's mimetic and representational finitude. Other films have explored the cinematic sublime by making India the topographical surface for such an exploration, and they are worth recalling in order to situate *The River* alongside a comparative cinematic framework. The following analysis of *The River*'s India through a comparative matrix of other films (specifically *India Matri Bhumi* and *Titas Ekti Nadir Naam*) replicates my prior intent of disrupting a location's objectification through a reverse ethnography of the film's own production process. A comparative range of sublime Indias reveals that the portrayal of a place as a simultaneously ethnographic and sublime, or immanent and transcendent location, is not so much an aspect of the place as the production of a perspective and projection of a desire on it.

India Matri Bhumi, released eight years after *The River*, is remarkable for experimenting with a hybridized form of documentary realism and fiction that invites ethnographic subjects into the realm of narrative subjectivity. Rossellini's India starts in the ethnographic mode and without warning moves into fictional dramatizations (similar to *The River*), although the fiction remains embedded in a documentary aesthetic. As director of *Paisan* (Italy, 1946), Rossellini uses what Bazin called an aesthetic of "amalgamation" between fictional and nonfictional elements.[151] Rossellini, who employed some of Renoir's Indian crew on his shoot in India, trod the experimental ground of mixing documentary and fiction in a range of his films, including *India*. The film oscillates between abstract and concrete uses of visual detail and between ethnographic and metaphysical registers of expression.

Invited by India's first prime minister, Jawaharlal Nehru, to make a film about India, Rossellini turned out a film possessed by the unstable alchemy of nonfiction and dramatization. The film opens with a conventionally omniscient narrator expounding on India as a land of immense crowds. The rapid-fire voice-over soon exceeds its mandate of sober exposition and goes into "hyperbolic all-embracing catalogues," as Jonathan Rosenbaum notes.[152] In addition to the usual roundup of India's religions and castes, the narrator tells us what Indian crowds enjoy ("merry-go-rounds, pinwheels, street musicians, balloons, toys") and, more oddly, offers a catalogue of Indian gestures (they "carry, bring, bring back, lift, load, support, shift, transport, transfer and move. They walk, ruminate, sleep, dream, build, work").[153] This is our first clue that the film is interested in looking at the indistinguishable minutiae of all human life while also seeking a texture of the visual particularities of India. Ethnographic observations collapse under a welter of microdescriptions that do not add up to an objectification of a people because of the descriptions' heterogeneous and mundane quality. From references to India's 580,000 villages, the voice-over moves to the hardworking elephants of Karapura (in Mysore, Karnataka) and shifts imperceptibly into the first-person pronoun so that we suddenly occupy the subjectivity of a *mahout* or elephant trainer. "We mahouts, the elephants' masters, get no rest at all during the day."

Rossellini shot in actual locations with nonactors. As the title at the film's opening states, "The actors, all nonprofessional, were cast in the same location where the action takes place." Rather than providing a definitive explanatory framework of the meaning of India or of Indian social customs (despite the film's opening promise), the film uses an omnibus narrative to play with our expectations of documentary and fiction by providing vignettes of the homes and the lives of four men. Collectively, these vignettes raise questions that transcend each of their individual lives. The four fictional sections cover four geographical parts of India (north, south, east, and west); men at four stages of their lives (a young man of marriageable age, a middle-aged man with a wife and child, an aged man, and a dead man); and men engaged in four kinds of transactions with their natural and animal environments (an elephant keeper, a dam builder, a forest dweller, and a monkey trainer).

This division replicates the Vedic Hindu notion of the four *ashramas*, or stages of life (assuming a masculine subject), which move from the first stage of *brahmcharya* (as a student and unmarried man) to the second stage of *grihastha* (a householder), the third stage of *vanaprastha* (literally, a forest dweller or retired man), and the final stage of *sanyasa* (renunciation). Each stage prescribes essential life lessons and behaviors. The sublime enters the film on the back of this implicitly metaphysical film structure, with details of locations as well as quotidian realities of individual characters grounding visual images on-screen. Rossellini concretizes particular lives in a way that undermines the omniscient narrator's reductive account, while simultaneously intimating the universality of experience, albeit through a masculine subject and consciousness.

For instance, in the film's second section, a man called Devi is reassigned from his worksite and home near Hirakud dam in Orissa (Odisha) to a new location. Constructed across the Mahanadi River in Northwest India, Hirakud was the first Multipurpose River Valley Project championed by Nehru and hailed as a technological marvel in India's nationalist political discourse. Rossellini brings affective shades of ambivalence, criticism, and regret into the architecture of the dam as Devi tours its vast infrastructure one last time before his departure. We witness his pride at being part of the mammoth construction, his acknowledgment of the human cost of building it, the number of villages submerged, the rehabilitation of Partition refugees as human labor for national industrialization, and the personal significance of a dam as a place of residence and worksite despite the impersonality of the administrative machinery that relocates its workers and residents. Against the institutional memorialization of buildings and dams, Devi scratches out a memorial with chalk on a rock, "I, Devi Chakravarti, and my wife found asylum here when we were thrown out of East Bengal due to the separation with Pakistan." A refugee from East Bengal who found work in India's big dam-building projects, Devi is now a twice-displaced man.

In counterposing the chalked-in scribble of a refugee worker against the cement-and-steel construction of a state-sponsored structure, this sequence literally defaces the dam as a triumphant monument of nationalism (cele-brated, for instance, in N. S. Thapa's Films Division documentary *Bhakra Nangal* [1958]) and reinscribes it with the graffiti of one man's life and experiences. It dissolves an abstracted icon of national progress into the micronarratives of men and women who worked to build the nation's concrete infrastructures, who have been co-opted by statist propaganda. A one-on-one comparison is unfair, but Rossellini's *India* draws attention to the fact that Renoir also filmed his story on the banks of the Hooghly River, which was the site of the Damodar Valley Corporation initiated by the Indian Planning Commission's Multipur-pose River Valley project during the film's shooting. Certainly, the Hooghly's immediate realities were not relevant to the fictional world of *The River*, and accounting for dam building in the film's fictional world would have made it an entirely different film. Nevertheless, holding the Hooghly River as an example of eternal and impassive nature, absent its technologization and change, required a deliberate masking of certain realities of which the film's production crew must have been aware. Rossellini permits the realpolitik of India to enter his cinematic vision, and in so doing he ruptures the oriental sublime while at the same time reaching for the cinematic sublime. Similarly other filmmakers, such as the director Ritwik Ghatak, would capture India's land- and waterscapes using the optics of history and myth to allegorize the environment, while also using that allegorical vision to cast a sharper eye on the land's history.

REAL AND SUBLIME INDIAS IN GHATAK'S *TITAS EKTI NADIR NAAM*

Ritwik Ghatak offers a counterpoint to Renoir in his use of India's topogra-phy as a concrete abstraction. "Concrete abstraction" is a phrase I have used to synoptically convey Bazin's thesis that Renoir's camera is "at once idealized and concretized" because it realizes "the very ontology of the cinematographic tale" by giving viewers something "imaginary on the screen" without depart-ing either from "the spatial density of something real" nor diverging from "the concrete reality of the moment."[154] Similar to Renoir in his incidental use of dramatic scaffolding as a formal pretext to live "intimately and indiscreetly" with characters, Ghatak uses lives alongside India's rivers to confront sublime questions of eternity and impermanence, loss and the human spirit. Again like Renoir, Ghatak explores these larger questions while embedding his camera in the density of the real. However, Ghatak uses the spectatorial encounter with environment to create affective engagements with India's history, and in this he presents a contrast to Renoir. I analyze a death sequence from Ghatak's *Titas*

Ekti Nadir Naam (henceforth *Titas*), a film made on the filmmaker's return to Bangladesh near the end of his life after a long exile from the region, to show how (much like Renoir) Ghatak shot on location to mask, stage, and scrutinize cinema's relationship to reality, thus exploring aspects of what I have referred to as the cinematic sublime. At the same time, each image averts the orientalist sublime gaze by conferring a depth of history to the land itself.

Both Renoir and Ghatak upheld certain universal principles that influenced their cinematic vision. The historical foundations of their universalisms diverged, and whereas Renoir's universalism may have drawn on European secular humanism, the French poetic movement of unanimisme and the Indian school of Theosophy discussed previously, Ghatak's visual sensibility was defined by the challenge of reconciling Jungian theories of a collective unconscious and "collective memory" with his political affiliations with historical materialism. In his brief review of the "material aesthetics" of Kracauer's *Theory of Film*, Ghatak wishes that Kracauer dwelt more deeply on film as a "psychic study of social history."[155] The effort to imagine historical change as a psychic imperative manifests itself in Ghatak's frames, which compose reality to highlight the allegorical or archetypal elements of a filmed space without giving up on what Bhaskar Sarkar has aptly called an "unrelenting engagement with history."[156] The death sequence of madman Kishore and his bride Rajar Jhi in *Titas* serves as a good illustration of his cinema as a "psychic study" of history.

Set in a little fishing village called Gokannaghat, the film opens with the *maghmandal* ritual to usher in the winter season, but viewers receive no exposition of the ritual. Similar to *The River*, here too a young girl, Basanti, is asked to draw a rangoli or *alpana* by her mother. Basanti has two potential suitors, Kishore and Subol, who are to take their boats to a neighboring village for trade. Events move quickly as Kishore, visiting the new village, is married to Rajar Jhi on the insistence of the elders. As their boat returns in the darkness of night, bandits abduct Rajar Jhi. The trauma of this event causes Kishore to lose his sanity. After a fast-moving plot compressed into the opening sequence, the film progresses at a more leisurely pace to follow the interwoven textures of the lives of women, children, and men who work as fisher folk and merchants sustained by the river Titas. The film draws out their lives and routines that slowly transform as their village succumbs to impoverishment, moneylenders, and a receding river. The landscape changes from a rain-splattered lushness that is physically registered on the camera lens when it is blurred by raindrops and half submerged under river water, into an arid desert with destitute refugees. In the film's final sequence, a dying Basanti claws the sands for water and seeks (in the words of a character) "the last drop without which our soul cannot depart." The fierce will to survive despite privation is etched into Ghatak's visualization of characters and landscape.[157] Ghatak knew from his own life that was torn asunder by Bengal's Partition that India does not promise unchanging rhythms. The river Ganga, a mighty mass of tributaries and distributaries, was parceled out between the political realms of West Bengal in India and Bangladesh (which was part of East Pakistan until 1971, just two year's prior to the release of *Titas*). In Ghatak's films, landscapes and riverscapes are as riven as people. This is displayed in a death sequence that occurs about halfway through the film.

The abducted bride, Rajar Jhi, returns unknowingly to her husband's village with her son. Through chance encounters, she is drawn to the village madman, who is in fact her husband, Kishore. The audience recognizes their relationship, but because Rajar Jhi and Kishore do not know each other by face (they scarcely saw each other on their wedding night), their mutual attraction possesses the mystery of a perverse possibility rather than the certitude of matrimony's social sanction. During the spring festival of Holi, Rajar Jhi helps Kishore's parents bathe him in the river. Village women crowd together in the frame's foreground, gossiping about the inappropriate intimacies between the village lunatic and an outsider who may be an unwed mother. With the unpredictability of madness, Kishore lifts Rajar Jhi into his arms and causes her to faint in a way reminiscent of their first encounter. An extreme long shot shows their two lone figures framed through a shack by the riverbank, as dark shapes of men carrying sticks close in on Kishore's figure. The long shot is held as we see the mob attack Kishore and then disperse in a hurry, visualizing a culpable, homicidal, and anonymous public in silhouette. The frame now shifts in direction and proximity, taking us close to the two figures lying prone on the beach. Rajar Jhi gains consciousness and drags her body, clawing at the ground (much as Basanti will at the film's conclusion) to reach the river and drench her sari's border. As she wrings out its water on Kishore's lips, he awakens briefly to name her as his wife in a flash of possible recognition. Their wedding song plays on the soundtrack and stops abruptly with his death. In pain, Rajar Jhi rolls away from her husband, changing direction to lie in the river waters to die. The fatal sequence ends on an indelible close-up of Rajar Jhi's head, as her hair laps gently back and forth in the water.

The melodramatic sequence conveys a couple's desperation for union and its preordained fatality through figural gestures and movements of rolling and clawing bodies rarely seen on-screen. In a film made after India's Partition, it is possible to treat this sequence as a visualization of a land that cannot be uni-

FIGURE 3.12 Rajar Jhi dies, as her hair laps in the water, in *Titas*.

fied because it is split by angry mobs and unforgiving destinies. The river itself dries up to become a territory that the village farmers will fight to claim from the fisher folk. But to see only its political symbolism is to not recognize several formal, mythic, and psychic levels at which these figures also operate in relation to their environment. Formally, as Sarkar argues in his analysis of *Megha Dhaka Tara*, Ghatak eschews "any naturalized sense of spatial relations" so that we are confronted with the filmmaker's "absolute refusal to resolve spatially, and thus to domesticate, contradictions that have no easy resolutions."[158] The grasping, crawling, and turning of prone figures are desperate and elemental acts that linger with the discomfort of withheld catharsis over the remainder of the film. The sequence also strikes a strong mythic note with the immersion of Rajar Jhi in the river. Imitating the immersion of the goddess's idol in the river during Durga Puja, Rajar Jhi (soon to reappear after her death as the goddess Bhagavati) becomes one of the film's feminine archetypes of mother, protector, and devourer. Her body's partial immersion in the river additionally aligns Rajar Jhi with the river Titas itself, and with the film's overarching theme of impermanence and loss. As a man tells the young Basanti at the film's opening, "It all comes and then disappears again. There's a spark of life. And suddenly it's not there. It all becomes untraceable . . . this ever-flowing river Titas may become bone dry tomorrow. It may not even have the last drop without which our soul cannot depart."

FIGURE 3.13 A river that is simultaneously abstract and concrete in *Titas*.

The film begins with an image of Titas that is both naturalistic and abstract, curved like a horseshoe, with its wide banks reclaiming the water for sand. In stark contrast to the river Hooghly in Renoir's film, Titas is a transient and unreliable river for Ghatak. It is the resulting human suffering and loss that feel eternal. India's history taught Ghatak these truths, which he captured in cinematic form by drawing on the concrete as well as abstract or "epic" dimensions of the land around him.[159] So it was that Ghatak disagreed with Kracauer on the notion of camera reality. According to Ghatak, "All ripples on the leaves, all puddles reflecting invisible house facades and a piece of sky, all these transient things are included in the complex of reactions born out of the social unconscious."[160] The Kracauer of *From Caligari to Hitler* may have agreed with Ghatak regarding film art as a realization of the social unconscious.[161] But for Ghatak, unlike for Kracauer, cinema was *not* what Hansen has called "the matrix of a specifically modern episteme."[162] Despite his commitment to cinema's Marxist and specifically Brechtian mission of disrupting art's subjection to capitalist commodification through breaking the spectator's alienation from reality, Ghatak drew on what he understood as the palpable presence of both myth and history in contemporary India to produce art as revolutionary praxis. Against imagining India's land in the image of an unchanging, spiritual, and premodern other (which characterizes India's land's portrayal in a majority of European and Hollywood films), or in the nationalistic image of a modern and developmental territory (as in a majority of India's commercial or FD films), Ghatak called on folk, mythic, and epic registers to stage impassioned confrontations with India's crisis-ridden present in sensory and affective terms.

Ghatak's experimentation with cinema was marked by eclectic influences, ranging from Sergei Eisenstein, Vsevolod Pudovkin, Luis Buñuel, Federico Fellini, Rabindranath Tagore, and Bertolt Brecht to a profusion of Indian epics, myths, and classical and folk art.[163] In his words, "Film is not a form, it has forms . . . one should approach it from the point of view of the emotions aroused and the intellects sharpened by one's end product: the result that accrues, after all, you create 'for' the people. This is why all the forms, from utter naturalism to extreme expressionism, seem to me to be totally valid."[164]

With this statement, Ghatak disinvests himself from the question of cinema's ontological proximity to any particular form or style but reinvests value in the encounters that cameras can stage between viewers and the world. Bazin may have disagreed with Ghatak's statement (his acceptance of expressionism, for one), but we can perceive an overlapping interest in the phenomenology of the image. Bazin's concept of realism was pliable in adjudicating which particular filmmaking style used the camera's ontological proximity to reality.[165] For Bazin, the question of cinematic realism rested on how an image acknowledged its basis in reality and brought this intimacy to the viewer's attention.[166] It is speculative to imagine how Bazin would have assessed Ghatak's style, but the filmmaker's interest in spectatorial affect and his use of cinematic techniques to perceive mythic and historical traces in physical reality resulted in a body of work profoundly engaged with the kinds of "idealized and concretized" realities described by Bazin.

One sequence from *Titas* bears comparison to Renoir's *The River* in this regard. After her death, Rajar Jhi transforms from a character in the film to a figure that exists outside the bounds of narrative, much like Melanie's transformation from Harriet's friend to a dancing goddess. During her tragic life, those who shelter Rajar Jhi refer to her as Bhagavati, the divine mother who manifests as the goddesses Durga, Kali, Lakshmi, and Saraswathi in Hindu mythology. In dying, Rajar Jhi enters the realm of female folklore, which maintains that dead mothers can transmogrify into powerful devouring spirits. Rajar Jhi begins to appear to her son as an ornate, mute, beautiful, and terrifying Durga. Evoking the river that turns unresponsive and demonic when it arbitrarily withdraws its bounty from humanity, this new incarnation of Rajar Jhi braids together myth and folklore to respond to Bengal's contemporary realities of

FIGURE 3.14 Rajar Jhi manifests as Durga in *Titas*.

famine and Partition that had marked the land as a terrain of death and starvation rather than of fertile sustenance.

Explaining the repeated use of the Mother Goddess image in Ghatak's films, Ghatak's student Kumar Shahani talks about a similar moment in a dance sequence of his own film, *Tarang* (1984). "As a dancer depicting Radha's love for Krishna may include the maternal love of Yashodhara or the heroism of Draupadi, Janaki in *Tarang* alludes to many mother goddesses—Durga, Radha, Sita, Urvashi—and is therefore free of the encapsulating meaning contained by the 'name,' freed in a way by the contemporary cosmos of the commodity *form*."[167]

In conversation with film scholar Ashish Rajadhaksha, Shahani is noting that directors such as Bresson and Ghatak articulate a film language that breaks away from reality's ossification by variously exposing the processes through which actors, actions, dialogues, and situations are flattened into commodities within a commercialized system of signification. In order to reverse this process, Bresson shaves off layers of meaning from the actor until s/he is freed to be a pure "model" of an idea. Ghatak uses folk and expressionist archetypes to create essayistic techniques within fiction. And Shahani explores the lyric and epic forms to create a dialogue with history. Each opens up the narrative function of the actor to an alternative network of meanings. For Ghatak and Shahani, using the idiom of traditional classical Indian dance forms meant drawing on

Indian dances' performative mode of making dancers allusive impersonators who channel multiple personas during a solo performance. This is typical of dance forms such as Kathak, Bharatanatyam, Odissi, and so on, against the Western balletic tradition of attributing a fixed role or character to a dancer.

In *The River*, Radha/Melanie's dance is presented in an anthropological mode that is absent of a historical or mythopoetic resonance in relation to its context in India, which potentially makes the dance feel like a spectacle of difference. Extratextually, the film's posters and publicity used Sri Ram's dancing figure against the backdrop of the river to enhance the exotic value of the dance for its Western viewers. In distinction to this, the transformation of Rajar Jhi into Bhagavati claims the film's present for ancient forces, and brings to the film's surface a mythic sensibility that runs beneath most of the film. Rajar Jhi's transmogrification unsettles Brahmanic orthodoxy's control over the ritualized meaning of divine deities, while also countering Indian secular nationalism's effacement of the region's mythic histories.[168] Ghatak's use of the Mother Goddess archetype is thus an essayistic technique that writes back to the past against the grain of India's present, which was ushering in a triumphalist secular democracy linked to violent partitions, politically fragmented land masses, and divided water bodies.

Ghatak filmed a place to exhume its past. And so a film like *Titas*, although not a historical film but instead focused on the lives of people living by the river, becomes redolent with the territory's histories. *The River* is not a historical film either, and it too does something interesting with temporality. It spatializes time across the dual registers of eternity and transience in a manner that lends self-reflexivity to its narrative. At the same time, in Renoir's film an India aligned with the eternal rhythms of Ganga's Hooghly River serves to stage and reconcile a crisis in postwar European and Eurasian consciousness. *Titas*, on the other hand, raises questions about the nature of memory and history without transforming the filmed place, India, into a moral canvas. The humans and the land absorb and reflect back the interrogation equally.[169]

Renoir's use of India as the location for *The River* is a test case for two strains in Bazin's theory of location cinematography. First, the notion that "a fragment of concrete reality is itself multiple and full of ambiguity," so that films that treat reality (rather than the film image or frame) as the smallest unit of filmmaking can allow the profilmic to transform their narrative by providing "the entire surface of the scene" with "an equally concrete density" to that of the world.[170] And second, that this kind of filmmaking has the potential to show viewers a situation's affective and, in Bazin's phrase, its "moral truth."[171] In my analysis, I have found that the impossible realm of cinema, or the cinematic sublime, successfully manifests itself in *The River* when the camera, color scheme, spatial design, attenuated character development, and narrative logic become pretexts for raising questions about the self and environment that complement but also exceed a story of an adolescent girl's first crush. I have also noted that the film exemplifies the oriental sublime on those occasions when it subordinates India's territory and historicity to the concerns of Western protagonists, depriving the place a sense of its own significance and density. In this, the film betrays an obligation to the Bazinian "ethic of realism" that goes beyond a merely representational relationship with the profilmic to something closer to an ethic of equivalence.[172]

When cinema stages truth-claims about the universality of human experience on geopolitically "different" locations, it exposes the fallacies of its own universalisms. But the attempt neither invalidates cinema's ambition to interrogate the human condition nor the critical struggle to find cinema's apposite goal in confronting the world in all its variation and cussedness. I have used this principle to assess the aesthetics and politics of *The River*, which is not interested in geopolitical critique but does make the choice of using India's landscape as an affective trope and cinematographic palette to generate meanings. This choice makes it fair game for an assessment about its assumptions regarding India. If *The River*'s images document a location, its film's production process documents the experience of encountering that location. The stakes of the film's hierarchized spatiality become clearer when the ethnographic lens is turned toward the film's own production process, and secondarily when the film itself is placed in proximate comparative contexts. I have placed *The River* in relation to other films that use an amalgam of fictional and nonfictional modes to represent India as a place that can activate the cinematic medium's particularizing and abstracting tendencies. These comparisons show that reaching for abstractions in cinema need not come at the cost of abandoning the thick particularities of other histories, other places, other subjectivities, and other realities. I have noted that India serves as a pretext for realizing the cinematic sublime in *The River*, defining the cinematic sublime as the medium's techniques to extend its technological prowess in capturing or reproducing reality while acceding to reality's fundamentally uncapturable vastness. This is a valid ambition, but it becomes complicit with an orientalist sublime when filmed places such as India are allowed to escape their function as a topographical foil primarily by becoming an instigator of metaphysical abstractions for others.

4

RESIDUAL:
LUCKNOW AND THE *HAVELI*
AS CINEMATIC TOPOI

Film brings its own rules of temporality with its ability to manipulate time, but it endows the abstractions of time with the concrete parameters of an image. This aspect of film launches my fourth argument for a spatial film historiography, to trace the disjunctions between the ruination, disappearance, and variable material fates of real places against their immortalization in photography and film. As modern visual technologies transformed cities and built environments into globally circulated images parallel to the expansion of imperial and anticolonial nationalisms, any place could be the object of sensory consumption for some even as it became a prison house of time for others. Uneven temporalizations of place reveal visual modernity to be an affectively and geopolitically heterogeneous phenomenon.

India with all her infinite charm and variety began to grow upon me more and more, and yet the more I saw of her, the more I realized how very difficult it was for me or for anyone else to grasp the ideas she had embodied. . . . She was like some ancient palimpsest on which layer upon layer of thought and reverie had been inscribed, and yet no succeeding layer had completely hidden or erased what had been written previously.

JAWAHARLAL NEHRU, *THE DISCOVERY OF INDIA*

I set it in India so that its improbability might be bearable.

JORGE LUIS BORGES, *COLLECTED FICTIONS*

India is improbable. This trope is rehearsed in appraisals of the country as a land of contradictions, strung between the extremes of poverty and wealth, spirituality and materialism, tradition and modernity, unity and diversity. The assumption that India is an improbable place underlies the frequent incredulity expressed over its ability to adhere as a nation, such as when Ramachandra Guha considers "why India survives" despite secessionisms, extremisms, and a pointillist appearance as a "multi-lingual, multi-religious, multi-ethnic political and economic community."[1] Questions on how to think of India in relation to Western Enlightenment constructs of liberalism, democracy, and nationhood while dismantling the derivative nature of such formulations motivate subaltern historiographies and postcolonial theories.[2] As they show, the casting of a place such as India at the crosshairs of tradition and modernity misreads a symptom for the problem, which is that templates of modernity drawn from Western experiences do not adequately describe socioeconomic "transition narratives" the world over.[3]

The accounts of feudalism in precolonial India given by historians D. D. Kosambi and K. S. Shelvankar are case in point. The historians argue that European land- and labor-based manorial feudalism was different from the loose agglomerate of military aristocracy functioning nominally under the sovereignty of the Mughal emperor, prior to the East India Company's territorial acquisitions over the subcontinent by the late eighteenth century.[4] Feudalism in India neither started nor ended at a time, or in a form, recognizable within Western periodizations and categories. Arguably, as a system of fealty to a ruler, feudalism was strengthened by British India's policies of indirect rule such as the "Doctrine of Paramountcy," which contractually shored up the reign of Indian princes in return for their acceptance of British sovereignty. In more than a third of India's territories, which were designated as princely states by the British, modernization under the colonial administration was underwritten by the continuation of dynastic and patriarchal princely rule. In these instances, colonial modernization entrenched feudal practices rather than supplanting them. Consequently, when the Indian nation-state was constitutionally defined between 1947 and 1949, the accession of princely states became critical to the formation of a democratic union.[5] With the exception of Kashmir, the accession's role in territorially integrating a colonial India split between British Indian provinces and princely states was largely considered a success,[6] officially marking a transition from disaggregated feudal political structures to an integrated secular democratic union under the new nation's home minister, Sardar Vallabhbhai Patel.

However, the nation's secular and democratic legalities did not expel the social weight or moral authority of feudal structures but instead reformed and reanimated them under colonial and national modernity. In this chapter, I consider a particular aesthetic and affective manifestation of feudal and precolonial India in its postcolonial cinematic texts to write about this uneasy historical transition. My focus will be on the ambivalence surrounding the inclusion of vernacular architectural forms and visual representations of India's feudal cities, particularly in commercial Hindi-Urdu films that use ruins, reconstructed cityscapes, and iconic precolonial Indian architectures as cinematic backdrops. Scholars such as John David Rhodes, Noa Stiematsky, Pamela Robertson Wojcik, Vanessa Schwarz, and Edward Dimendberg have shown how architectural and urban design in film can be understood as a portal into cinema's involvement with the social and spatial politics of a period, economy, or nation.[7] Interrogating what we look at when we watch "spectacles of property" on-screen, Rhodes finds material traces of "racial and geographical apartheid" in the filmic adaptation of Harper Lee's *To Kill a Mockingbird* in 1962.[8] Rhodes's historical sleuthing reveals that houses that ostensibly represented Monroeville, Alabama, on-screen were in fact relocated to Universal studios from Los Angeles's Chavez Ravine, which was populated by working-class Latino communities until they were displaced by the construction of Dodger Stadium. Similarly, Dimendberg, assessing film noir's emergence during the "unprecedented architectural destruction" associated with the US federal housing program's infrastructural rebuilding of postwar America, demonstrates how the genre's mobilization of urban decay and redevelopment produces "nonsynchronous" modes of visual perception.[9] Dimendberg finds in noir a history that (in Bloch's words) is not marching forward but rather appearing as *"a polyrhythmic and multi-spatial entity, with enough unmastered"* of the past and future to expose the present as a period of tumultuous socioeconomic and architectural change, and thus as an amalgam of multiple times and spaces.[10] The LA noir's visual patterning around the verticality of skyscrapers and horizontal expansion of freeways further accentuates dualities in the noir camera's spatialization of perspectives.

Of interest in these cases are the ways in which the scholars understand film not only as a historical object but also as a spatiotemporal form that provides a material and affective account of the histories of changing architecture, geography, and urban structures. Following how cinema processes its built environment at a range of expressive registers, these spatial film historiographies catch social transformations in medias res. They write about histories unfolding in cinematic, urban, and studio spaces to convey the historical production of space at multiple and mutually implicated scales. Aligned with these studies, I chart the contradictory emotional claims of a (feudal) past and a (democratic) future upon post-Independence India, after modernization visited the subcontinent in the form of sudden and violent colonization. My narrative starts with the British destruction of the North Indian city of Lucknow following the Indian Revolt of 1857. This key event brought Crown rule and administrative imperialism to India, but it also released the city of Lucknow into local and global imagination as an idea and a memory. Lucknow and its architectural forms, such as the *haveli* (a vernacular style of precolonial mansion mostly prevalent in northern India), would be recorded and represented in colonial British and American photographs and films. In post-Independence Hindi-Urdu cinema, the site of rebellion would be transformed into an iconic symbol of India's feudal past.[11]

I focus on visual recordings and reproductions of actual ruins and the imagined reinhabitation of precolonial architectural forms as a way of thinking about the experience of postcolonial India's temporal asynchronicity, an asynchronicity that settled into the mise-en-scène of popular Indian films. In this discussion, moving images of a ruined city and a built form function not only as representations of architectural objects but also as visual motifs and historical optics. The scholars Julia Hell and Andreas Schönle recently called for an "ontology of ruins" in an anthology rich with allusions to Walter Benjamin's writings on the urban ruins of the nineteenth-century Parisian Arcades. Hell and Schönle contend in an argument not without its irony that ruins have been modernity's enduring image (can things endure as wreckage?), because "only in a secularized world do ruins become objects deemed suitable for study or contemplation."[12] In other words, while landscapes pitted with destroyed structures were nothing new, a new perceptual awareness of them *as* ruins defined the modern. Modernity constitutes itself through a self-conscious demarcation from antiquity as a condition of its existence. So ruins served as an apt metaphor for modernity's emergence as the deliberate project of finding a place in history. In material terms, ruins identify society's utopian drive to incessantly tear down and rebuild environments, which marks industrial modernity's dependence on the capitalist imperative toward inbuilt obsolescence. Capitalist modernity asserts itself via the self-justifying claim to novelty made by ceaselessly measuring its progress against an imagined and slower past. Ruins of the past begin to serve as a demarcation of difference for the present.

RUIN AS OBJECT AND OPTIC

A ruin's designation as a trace of what is past is thus predicated on the collective "awareness of historical discontinuities" at the literal and tropic level.[13] In other words, a spatial and architectural engagement with questions of temporality has been central to the production of modernity.[14] Ruins, as structures from the past in the present, literalize this self-conscious spatial encounter with time through which modernity defines itself. It is this perceptual aspect of the ruin—as an edifice that can incite the shock of awareness about an eternal (infernal) dialectic between past and present—that allows Benjamin to transform architecture into an optic for modernity's history.[15] Benjamin presents a theoretically galvanized concept of the ruin as a structure incessantly tugged by divergent temporalities.[16]

The temporally ambivalent perceptual charge of a ruin also makes it relevant to the visual culture of places that find themselves stuck in time, or erased by it, when they are pushed out of a temporal narrative of progress. Places that have been subject to extreme violence and received neither reparation nor representation within their nation's polity or capitalist machinery have often been represented through the aesthetics of ruin. This is partly because such places are literally ruined and in a state of dilapidation, with shuttered and abandoned buildings that are under forced redevelopment, gentrification, and occupation, and characterized by razed structures and forgotten lives. The films of the Palestinian filmmaker Kamal Aljafari show a region stranded in history by filming in locations pitted with wrecked buildings, restricted geographical movement, surveilled roadways, and aggressive constructions, where traces of Palestinian lives are violently erased under an expanding Israeli occupation.[17] Patricio Guzmán's *Nostalgia for the Light* (Chile, 2010) uses visual techniques to exhume pasts and bodies lost to the unequal recording of a history that is relentlessly focused on discovering new territories (including outer space) while suppressing Chile's genocidal history.[18] Diasporic and "accented" films, to use Hamid Naficy's term, frequently use the visual trope of ruins and fragments to convey a sense of displacement, as in Atom Egoyan's *Calendar* (1993).[19] As a recorded architectural structure, visual motif, and theoretical optic, the fragmented ruin has represented the lives of people and the histories of places that do not so much exhibit the cultural logic of capitalism and nationalism as the logic of what capitalism and nationalism suppresses, destroys, or finds indigestible in order to manifest itself. In a Derridean sense, ruins may be considered a "hauntology" of history.[20] They provide a spectral account of alternative—residual, affective, resistant, or melancholic—histories of places and communities outside the embrace of a state or a nation; places and people that are nevertheless essential as outsiders and alter-entities to a nation's declarative, visible, and commodified identity.[21]

Photography's coincidental emergence with the expansion of European colonialism and industrialization points to the sordid irony that a cosmopolitan visual familiarity with the world emerged alongside a deeply splintered subjective sense of time and place. This is particularly true in the case of lands violently appropriated from its inhabitants through occupation or displacement, as in the case of slavery and settler colonialisms. In 1857, Indian cities like Lucknow, Meerut, and Kanpur became familiar to the world as strange-sounding names of photographed places involved in an anti-British insurgency. At the same time, inhabitants of these cities were decimated or displaced by counterinsurgent attacks on them and their homes. In this chapter, I focus on commercial Hindi-Urdu–language cinema's visualizations of ruinous places and structures to make the case that they offer an alternative and affective periodization of India's official historical narrative, which was marked by the celebration of commemorative monuments of national and industrial growth (exemplified by N. S. Thapa's Films Division films discussed in chapter 2).

At the center of this chapter's discussion are the topographies of precolonial Lucknow and the architectural forms of the haveli as they appear in Bombay cinema. Lucknow and the haveli have had a checkered history in the social biography of modern India. Havelis began to lose their ability to function as efficient domiciles for the subcontinent's local elite in 1857, when the Indian Revolt or "mutiny" against the British East India Company tore through Lucknow, Meerut, Delhi, Kanpur, Allahabad, Aligarh, Gwalior, and numerous other North Indian cities.[22] As a counterinsurgent measure, Britain established a new form of governance under the Government of India Act of 1858, placing India under the direct rule of the British Crown. The hierarchical and patriarchal system of aristocratic patronage and indirect land ownership that sustained havelis as elite properties under the Mughal Empire was replaced by a new political system under the British. As an architectural form, bungalows came to be better suited to the subcontinent's new bureaucratic elite that constituted the British Empire's governing machinery of anglicized Indian civil servants, administrators, and accountants. Havelis largely receded to the margins of social and political life. In Delhi, for instance, the city literally migrated to a different center by making the havelis inside the walled city of old Delhi peripheral to new hierarchies of power and social capital.[23] In the political and geographical shifts of power from Mughal to British administrative rule, Lucknow similarly ceased to carry political centrality in India's governance.

Despite its diminishing political significance, as a visual image and icon of the East India Company's retributive violence, cities such as Lucknow grew in topical interest with England's mass audiences after 1857. Salacious tales about rebelling native soldiers, black-on-white violence, and climactic British victories appealed to a readership in England that was being constituted as a mass public through pulp fiction and news stories.[24] The popularization of such narratives coincided with transatlantic political alliances between the United States and the United Kingdom. The United States, during this period, was caught between the racial and national aftermath of the Mexican-American War (1846–1848) and the growing momentum of political confrontations that would build up to the American Civil War (1861–1865). Images of dark angry hoards raping white women and slaughtering white children carried an electrifying resonance for antiabolitionists in the United States, and the nascent transnational traffic in photography and film between the two continents gave the wreckage of the 1857 revolt a transatlantic afterlife.

The newsworthiness of 1857 faded from European consciousness when it was superseded by a century of increasingly gruesome wars. But the subcontinent held on to a different memory. Hindi-Urdu cinema continued to imbue Lucknow's cityscape and the structure of the haveli with complex gendered, communalized, and classed meanings long after these sites became irrelevant to the West. The visual images of Lucknow and havelis in Hindi-Urdu films, while still in dialogue with the changing politico-economic and material fates of those environments in modern India, cast India's modernization itself in the alternative light of a *longue durée*. We find few explicit representations of 1857 as a historical event in Bombay's commercial cinema (Shyam Benegal's *Junoon* [1978] and Ketan Mehta's *The Rising: Ballad of Mangal Pandey* [2005] are exceptions). But, as I will be arguing in this chapter, its memory is etched into the mise-en-scène of iconic locations and set designs of commercial Hindi films well into the twentieth century.[25]

Grappling with misalignments between the material destruction of a place against its cultural persistence as a memory, I want to consider how and why iconic forms that belonged to India's precolonial era became resilient signifiers of nostalgia and trauma in post-Independence Hindi-Urdu cinema. An arc of symbolic significance links the revolts of 1857 to India's post-Independence era, pointing to intriguing divergences between the official history of the region (which tended toward triumphant narrations of secular modernity in Films Division shorts, for instance) and the affective histories expressed by the region's popular cinema. Tracking this divergence, I unfix shots of a cityscape and a monument from their function as locational backdrops in British, US, and Indian photographs and films to treat them instead as provocations for an alternative historiography of post-Independence India. A spatial film and media historiography attuned to cinema's affective and expressive negotiations with political memory conveys a different historical timeline than what may be read off the nation's official historical and cinematic trajectory. Bombay cinema's romanticization of Lucknow and the haveli allowed India's feudal past to disconcert the nation's democratic and secular present. In contrast, a contained narration of 1857 confronts us in Western films and photographs, which is where I begin this spatial analysis of India's asynchronous visual modernity.[26]

THE RELIEF OF LUCKNOW, US EDISON COMPANY

Colonial social and spatial relations were violently reordered in Lucknow, a North Indian city that was in the province of Awadh (now Uttar Pradesh) when Indian sepoys (from the Hindi word *sipaahi*, or soldiers) massacred British and loyalist members of the British East India Company in June 1857. Partially as a response to the British usurpation of Awadh from Nawab Wajid Ali Shah, over eight thousand rebelling Indian sepoys besieged women, children, officers, and allies of Sir Henry Lawrence's administration in Lucknow. The ranks of insurgents swelled, as did the number of deaths in the British camp, which rose to two thousand. The "mutiny" was part of a historic rebellion that radically altered the nature of British presence in India and the form of its empire worldwide, ending the British East India Company's economic monopoly and initiating the administrative rationalities of the British Empire in India.

The literary historian Gautam Chakravarty finds that the revolt of 1857 was by far the most popular theme for British novels, producing a greater "literary yield" than any other conflict of the nineteenth century.[27] The popularity of this literature parallels the political and cultural ascendancy of the British middle class, which was the chief consumer of novels. Two icons of rebellion novels validated middle-class values: the treacherous native spy, and the British officer in disguise who penetrates native masses. Chakravarty suggests that both figures offer "a fantasy of mastery that sutured actual intelligence failures during the rebellion" and the "underlying anxieties of a colonial regime . . . exiled . . . from . . . the indigenous world."[28] These figures are prominent in *The Relief of Lucknow* (J. Searle Dawley, 1912), in which they help unfold a narrative about surveillance and conspiracy.

In this single-reel film,[29] Englishmen save their women and children from a colonial city besieged by hostile Indian natives. The spatial tropes of the silent film will be recognizable to anyone familiar with American westerns. Thematically and formally, the text is transportable across time and context through its abstractions of space, achieved by what Ella Shohat and Robert Stam refer to as an "imagery of encirclement" menacing both the camera and the audience.[30] The authors are discussing images from Hollywood westerns that invert history to make Native Americans intruders in their own land by visualizing them as threatening the domestic spaces of white settlers, within which the camera remains nested. Similarly in *The Relief*, the film opens with a cut from the exterior of a fort, with assembled British troops and Indian sepoys, to the interior of a living room, with a piano, two Englishmen, and a woman. A spying native and a letter warning of a mutiny disrupt their peace ("Meerot, May 12, 1857. 'Dear Helen, The native troops here have revolted . . .'"). The film's ensuing drama is articulated around dynamic outdoor shots and interiors that rapidly transform under the siege. Outdoor action is typically shot at an acute angle to the horizontal planes of the camera frame to give it a sense of urgency, while interiors are framed frontally. In the sequence titled "The Death of Sir Henry Lawrence" for instance, Lawrence sits at a table facing the camera when a cannonball slams through a painting on the wall and kills him. The effect of these shots and frames is to create an ideological narrative about the sanctity of English inner space, its threat from an outer space, the violent ingress of that threat, and the final deflection of that threat by the liminal body of an Englishman in disguise.

An Englishman escapes from the garrison in brownface and guides back relieving British forces. With this act, he forges associative links between the radically antagonistic spaces of outside and inside, victoriously ending the spatial drama of encirclement. This volunteer is also romancing a woman in the garrison, which lends the film's historical ambition a personal dimension appreciated by reviewers at the time: "We may say at once that this is quite one of the finest pictures the Edison Company have yet produced. They have taken a great historical theme ... inspired it with the glow and the tumult of real life and action, and at the same time closely adhered to recorded fact. ... Into the web of famous historical happenings, which, of course, forms the subject matter of the film, there has been woven a pleasant little love story, just sufficient to give the requisite touch of more personal human interest."[31] The film adapted a factual episode involving volunteer Thomas Kavanagh, who assisted in an attempt to relieve the Lucknow garrison, though the romance angle was manufactured. Released in Britain on the fifty-fifth anniversary of the Indian Revolt of 1857, *The Relief* traded on discourses of mimesis, authenticity, and sensationalism to be marketed as a "historical picture."[32] The film's exhibition exploited the narrative's and the audience's sense of a communion with past events. In his notes on the production of this film, director J. Searle Dawley writes that nonagenarians who had survived the "Lucknow Mutiny" were driven down for a screening of the film in 1912; one of them was so impressed by the film's realism that he stood up and shouted at the screen, "That's him, that 'Arry' my old buddy."[33]

On a different register, advertisements aimed at potential film exhibitors traded on the film's authenticity as well as the safety of distance. In an announcement in the *Bioscope*, British exhibitors are exhorted to book the film with a playful pun: "If you want your Show *besieged* do not fail to show THE RELIEF OF LUCKNOW .... Because it is an *actual* page from the *actual* history of the past and is historically correct as regards soldiers' uniforms, the fighting, the various wild rushes and mad repulses."[34] The distance of place and time sanctions puns around sieges aimed at film exhibitors, making it grist for humor rather than cause for the righteous outrage exploited by the film's text. Critical praise for the film's accurate replication of a historical place and time showed that the marketing worked well with audiences and reviewers. A review noted, "The suggestion of Indian scenery is quite perfect, tropical foliage, glittering buildings and burning sunshine all complete."[35]

FIGURE 4.1 Publicity for *Relief of Lucknow*. US Dept. of the Interior, National Park Service, Thomas Edison National Historical Park.

FIGURE 4.2 *Relief of Lucknow* advertisement. US Dept. of the Interior, National Park Service, Thomas Edison National Historical Park.

In fact, *The Relief* was shot on location in Bermuda and not in Lucknow. As a British colony that was a satellite island of the United States, Bermuda had played an active part in domestic American politics. During the American Civil War, it served as a Confederate headquarters and post for shipping cotton to England.[36] In 1912, it housed the British Queen's Own Regiment, a regiment that had been involved in suppressing the 1857 revolt in India. For Edison, Bermuda was the perfect answer to the problem of location shooting in faraway India, given its sunshine, good relations with the United States, relative proximity to Edison studios in New Jersey, and the presence of British troops. It was, in other words, authentic in terms of the realpolitik of empire that had brought anti-insurgent British troops to a satellite state of the United States, although this was not the kind of authenticity that interested the film's marketing unit.

As an industrial practice, location shooting—which includes techniques of cheating on locations to visually align different places with each other—cannot be understood exclusively through an analysis of place as a textual or perspectival trope in cinema. The formalization of location shooting is embedded in a range of social and material histories of spectatorship, travel, and commerce.[37] For instance, Edison began to expand his film market by producing films on historically British themes for British audiences onward from 1911. Shooting in foreign locales increased with this trend, with Edison's Dawley shooting films in Cuba and Canada and Ashley Miller taking crews to London.[38] Bermuda had emerged as a popular British and North American tourist destination after Princess Louise, Queen Victoria's daughter, visited the islands in 1883. Wife of the governor-general of Canada, Princess Louise connected the old and new empires of England and North America with her marriage. Edison's paths of access were opened up by an increasing number of steamers filled with the neo-bourgeoisie crossing North America to Bermuda, pursuing leisure and warm weather in imitation of the aristocracy. The film's reality claims depended on a myth enabled by the convenient availability of commensurate subject places and races that could support an ideology of territorial dominance in Britain and the United States, especially as the latter wrestled domestically with debates on imperialism in relation to the Philippine-American War that ended in 1913. In a growing sphere of publics implicated in each other's political events and economic markets, the Edison film about Lucknow exhibited structures of sympathy linking Britain and the United States.

The difference between thinking about visual representations of India in a cinematic text against considering visuality as part of broader historical and geopolitical contexts bears further elaboration. Whereas my initial textual analysis of *The Relief* clarified the film's manipulation of spatial tropes to portray the English as heroes of a historical event and Indian mutineers as historical antagonists, it did little to situate the film in the historical context of visual media's role in the cataclysmic social and spatial reorganization of Lucknow. In fact, visual technologies played a central part in articulating the sociospatial crisis of 1857. Distinct from the print medium, which covered details about the deaths, mutiny-related photographic images of dead bodies remained rare.[39] More often, photographs of ruins and devastated land predominated over images of corpses, providing a visual record of the British policy to level to the ground all Indian cities that supported the insurgency or that neighbored insurgent cities. Administrators, writers, and the public alike wanted to take visual measure of insurgent places, with their shifting boundaries of control and photogenic architectures of ruin, whether to comprehend the events or to officiate and spectate with thrill and horror.[40] Visuality was central to the transformation of a local site of violence into a globally circulated spectacle, and it is in this context—of the circulating images of locational devastation—that we can begin to link the sociospatiality of Lucknow the city with Edison's short film *The Relief of Lucknow*.

In 1858, the *Calcutta Review* reported that England's apathy toward India was radically jolted after "the *electric shock* of the mutiny."[41] Electricity was an appropriate metaphor to convey the speed of the news, which traveled with the recently invented telegraph and resulted in more current reportage of distant events than previously possible. The transmission of accurate reports was still a precarious task, as telegraphed news was unreliable and could be validated or reversed in clarifications arriving by the slower, more detailed and dependable mail by land or sea. Says Karl Marx in the *New-York Tribune* of August 1857, "On the arrival at London of the voluminous reports conveyed by the last Indian mail, the meager outlines of which had been anticipated by the electric telegraph, the rumor of the capture of Delhi [from the insurgents] was rapidly spreading and winning so much consistency as to influence the transactions of the Stock Exchange."[42] Rumors of events, their implications, and the thrust and parry of insurgents and counterinsurgents across unknown terrain were imagined and reacted to in a relatively condensed period of time, courtesy of the telegraph.[43] Constellated channels of information provided by telegraph and mail unfolded stories set in the unfamiliar geography of remote sounding places like Lucknow, Agra, Rohulcund, and Jumna to the British public, even as the spatial boundaries of these cities were erased and rewritten by a spreading insurgency and its suppression.

Representations of the Indian Revolt of 1857 should be treated as an early indication of the centrality of technologies of mass communication and visual reproduction in the surfacing of local sites of violence in a local and imperial/global imaginary. Photographs and early films that depicted sites of a revolt massive in scale and newsworthiness consciously produced unfamiliar regions for cosmopolitan subjects of consumption through a conclave of texts, images, and narratives about the place. Lucknow emerged on the world stage, indeed it *called into existence* a global performative arena, through its part in a hitherto unimagined kind of violence. Like comparable locations today—Fallujah, Ramadi, or Mosul in Iraq; Kabul in Afghanistan; Aleppo in Syria; and Gaza in Palestine—Lucknow was as much a construct of multiplying imaginations as it was a referent. The place became globally familiar at the same time that a spectacular and violent suppression of its sovereignty implanted a local sense of alienation and unhousing. Photography played a crucial part in the incursions of world history into Lucknow's intimate spaces, creating a visceral proximity for the geographically distant and visceral distances for the geographically proximate. Events that caused the "recesses of the domestic space" to "become sites for history's most intricate invasions" were recorded and circulated widely, rendering the place twice estranged from itself, first through acts of violence, and then again through the domicile's photographic reproduction for the edification of foreign audiences.[44] For those who had to continue their lives in places destroyed by counterinsurgency, their home environment would be charged with a traumatic estrangement from the present, nostalgia for the past, and a need to rediscover ways to reconnect with immediate surroundings.

In other words, images of a city laid waste by the revolt cannot be understood exclusively by the ways in which their meanings were controlled by Anglo-American representations that suited the colonial state. They must be thought of simultaneously as part of an event that had multiple implications for several constituencies with varying investments in a place like Lucknow. Let us recall Walter Benjamin, who says that "only a redeemed mankind receives the fullness of its past—which is to say, only for a redeemed mankind has its past become citable in all its moments."[45] The city of Lucknow presented in *The Relief* must be considered in relation to the layered and varied productions of Lucknow's "rival geographies," not only as presented for British and American audiences but also in Indian photographs and films for local viewers.[46] Pursuing this line of argument, a limited-edition photographic album can be seen as providing a cinematic geography of the Lucknow that rivaled the one created by *The Relief*'s spatial design.

The spatial crisis produced by visual technologies becomes clearer when we consider photographs and films not as static images or frames in isolation but as visual records of an event that dynamically circulate among a consuming and meaning-making public, thereby destabilizing an image's formal hierarchies through its spectatorial address, mixed exhibitions sites, and the commercially driven logic of circulation, each of which had to be negotiated anew by the state. One of the most popular modes for circulating photographs of the 1857 insurgency was the photographic album. Photographic "mutiny memorial" albums served as a visual precedent for films about Indian "mutiny" sites as well as mutiny novels, because they revealed the viability of a popular audience for images and accounts of the violent events that would preoccupy the British literary imagination until the first decade of the twentieth century.[47] As the photographer and curator Ben Lifson notes, practical decisions about where to place a camera in a city that was deprived of strategic vantage points because of its systematic leveling by British forces made ruins an unavoidable reality of the city's photographic rendition. Each visual iteration of the city revealed something of the sympathies and desires of its creator, because the recording of photographic images was predicated on literally (if also figuratively) seeking out a perspective by placing the camera somewhere in the rubble.[48]

In the 1800s, "albums" referred to personal collages by Victorian women who pasted together paintings, poems, and mechanically reproduced images to peruse in their living rooms as a sign of their gentility. Additionally, they were the domain of British amateur and professional male photographers who used albums to sample their work and record their travels or experiences.[49] Photographic albums were a transitional artifact of the mid- to late nineteenth century that increasingly grew confined to domestic spaces as art moved into public and museulogical arenas regulated by the prohibition of tactility.[50] As a crafted commodity of one's professional expertise and world travels, displays of photography in the public arena would overshadow the album as a decoupage of visual ephemera, with public exhibitions of photography and art becoming a masculinized domain as opposed to the feminization and deprofessionaliza-tion of the domestic realm.

One instance of a personal mutiny memorial album is Reverend Thomas Moore's album titled "Cawnpore and Lucknow During Mutiny of 1857."[51] The album shares with its feminine counterparts the format of a personal journal, composed of heterogeneous found materials such as sketches, newspaper cuttings, transcribed letters, quoted poetry, and commercial photographs relating directly or indirectly to the revolt. The album offers solemn witness to the revolt through evidentiary texts, but interleaves these with personal thoughts and facts on famous monuments such as the Taj Mahal, alongside copied verses from Alfred Lord Tennyson's poem "The Defence of Lucknow." In other words, the album combines the "somber discourse" of witnessing history with the intimate discourse of personal epistolary and commercial rhetoric of popular tourism.[52] The heteroglossia of this album is our first clue to what exceeds a monocular statist management of perceptions of violence and to the larger context of the circulation of Lucknow's images. Insurgency albums reveal what may be referred to as a form of *colonial disaster tourism* that informed early consumptions of visual violence and complicated visual modes of state and disciplinary power.

A particularly nuanced mode of such a heteroglossic spectatorial address of colonial disaster tourism appears in *The Lucknow Album*, a photographic album of Lucknow's buildings published by the Baptist Mission Press in Calcutta in 1874 and authored by the Indian engineer and photographer Darogha Abbas Ali. This album offers a protocinematic text by binding together fifty albumen prints of Lucknow's architectural landmarks, accompanied by a text presumably authored by Ali.[53] *The Lucknow Album* prefigures the structure of an early travelogue slideshow or film, addressing its viewer by using a kinetic sense of movement across pitted buildings with deep historical residue. It begins with these words: "Ruins, ancient and modern, bearing marks of oriental splendour and extravagance . . . shattered and shot-battered walls, scathed monuments, telling of the horrors of war, rebellion and siege . . . dismantled palaces, fast falling into decay, are all objects of interest and curiosity to the tourist, the antiquary, the historian, the archeologist and the lover of art. The City of Lucknow . . . abounds with objects of this description in all the intense sublimity of ruin . . . that, but for the present volume, would have ruthlessly consigned them to everlasting oblivion."[54] Aligned with Victorian women's albums in its questionable legitimacy because of its Indian authorship, this album's self-conscious deployment of the trope of a "ruin" can be read as a labored self-legitimation to increase its purchase. The book addresses "survivors of the Garrison." Equally, it describes itself as an "illustrated guide" that will "succeed in fostering the spirit of enquiry, to which the histories of objects afore mentioned [railways and ruins] have so manifestly given birth, and to which *the educated Native of India and the traveling public of all nations throughout the civilized world* are so much attached."[55] Shifts between reverential commemoration and sociable gossip are present throughout the album's text, saving its images from the fixity of a frieze. The equivalent of an early limited-edition book, and more seamless than a personal pastiche, Abbas Ali's *The Lucknow Album* carries a multitonality that I wish to convey by the phrase colonial disaster tourism. The album provides salacious details about the lives of those who inhabited places before they were ruined, in addition to making those sites worthy of visitation, contemplation, and mourning, exploiting remnants of colonial violence for its potential touristic attraction in multiple ways.

The album proves to be less a commemoration of counterinsurgency than an incorporation of the city's buildings into narrative accounts of an ongoing life. Each monument comes with a surplus of information that exceeds the text's mournful attitude and counters the stunning evacuation of life from the visuals, by placing the deaths on a continuum with other points of significance and making the "mutiny" as much about the consumption of disaster as it is about grief.[56] The text frequently lists exact names and titles of the British dead, as at the infamous Baillie Guard, but it is quick to suggest that the "consecrated ground" is "prettily laid out" with "floral walks," and "without these pleasant additions to such a mournful spot, the ruins themselves are more than sufficient to repay the visit of the most indifferent tourist."[57] Moti Mahal is described as the site of many British deaths during the revolt, and the text lists names of the British officials killed. The same building is also described as a seraglio or harem, a *zenana khana* from which the Nawabs (the rulers of Lucknow) witnessed wild sport such as tiger combats or fights between an elephant and a rhinoceros.[58] It is at the indifferent tourist, perhaps at the potential distractibility of *every* tourist, that this combination of mournful, incidental, and salacious detail is aimed: details about how much money was plundered by trustees of the Husainabad Imambara, and how the Gomti River provided drinkable water despite the English poet William Wordsworth's condemnation that it was poisoned by "the number of dead bodies thrown in it."[59] Here we catch fleeting subversions of the imperial regime and a refusal to strike a singular emotional tone regarding Lucknow's recent past.

The album is instructively different from the Edison film in its visualization of monumental ruin. In *The Relief*, Saint George and Tom Moore's Tavern in Bermuda play the roles of Lucknow's destroyed streets and forts, with staged sets registering destruction to their surface and interiors. The film attempts to make its location cinematic through edits and explosions, showing visible alterations to buildings in a steady progression to the film's climax. *The Lucknow Album*, on the other hand, allows an instrinsic cinematicity of Lucknow's monuments and city space to emerge through its interplay of visual perspective and text.

34—The inside of Bailie Guard.

16—Mottee Mahal.

FIGURE 4.3 *The Lucknow Album* advertising ruins amid "prettily laid out" parks in Baillie Guard. Getty Research Institute, Los Angeles (92-B22782). (ABOVE) FIGURE 4.4 The Moti Mahal witnessed British deaths but was also a harem, according to *The Lucknow Album*. Getty Research Institute, Los Angeles (92-B22782). (BELOW)

30—Chutter Munzil on brink of the Goomtee.

FIGURE 4.5 *The Lucknow Album* comments on the hybrid architectural style of Chattar Manzil. Getty Research Institute, Los Angeles (92-B22782).

If, as Soviet filmmaker and theorist Sergei Eisenstein argued, sequentiality and montage are two essential conditions of cinema, and all arts tend toward the cinematic,[60] then montage computation was already present in Lucknow's architectural ensemble in a manner that was deeply colonial. Lucknow's architecture combined hybrid influences, incorporating the neo-Classical and Greco-Roman revival popular in England with more environmentally friendly local styles. Rosie Llewellyn-Jones offers rich details on how Lucknow's Nawabs, aspiring to British models of structure and notions of the modern, employed British architects to build their palaces and monuments.[61] In the city's architecture was a sedimented sense of time and significance, and in the construction of its cityspace a diachrony that is activated (not repressed) in *The Lucknow Album*. By describing Chattar Manzil as a "mixture of the Oriental geometrical, the Italian, and the French Chateaus," for instance, the album constructs Lucknow as a city of multiple, coexistent pasts. With its subtle celebration of the syncretism of Lucknow's city spaces, the album lets in an ensemble of perspectives on Lucknow, which is no longer defined purely in terms of its role in the insurgency.

Sophie Gordon points out that a multilayered nature of mourning is also conveyed by Abbas Ali's album's organization of the photographs. While the album follows the east-to-westerly path taken by British troops in 1857, Gordon notes that the final three images of the book are geographically incongruous.

The album shifts directionality to conclude with images of three of Lucknow's mosques that were not destinations for British tourists commemorating sites of British deaths, but rather culminations of Shi'ite processions through the city during Muharram. Lucknow's Islamic architecture established its role as a leading Shi'ite city in India, attracting Muslim mourners from all over the region to move through its streets and religious sites when they observed the martyrdom of Ali, Husain, and Hasan on the holy Muharram day.[62] The directionality of this photographic sequencing is thus a subtle perversion of the secular touristic routes through the city. At the same time, by its own proclamation, the album avows to enter the city "by rail from Cawnpore, commencing from a southerly direction."[63] If photography's "talismanic power" in this collection of images draws on photography's link to traditions of sacred mourning, then it also acknowledges new habits of curious looking.[64] A secular perspective attuned to the trivia of architectural and industrial history that is only tangentially related to the history of the rebellion inflects this layered portrayal of mourning that is claimed for both the British tourist *and* the Shi'ite viewer. The album negotiates between diverse modes of perceiving place because of its own historical location at the cusp of a technological transition, where distant and sacred places could become consumable sites through photography, endowing the image (rather than the monument) with talismanic abilities. The photograph destroys the aura of the place by making it available to every reader. The text describing the places invests the photograph itself with auratic attributes when it notes that "this Album will bear a sacred interest, and many a tear will fall at the contemplation of some well-remembered spot, over which a sort of holy radiance will appear to linger."[65] It is the album that bears sacred interest now, not only the place, which makes a viewing of the album *equivalent* to traveling to those places.

As Jennifer Peterson, Charles Musser, Tom Gunning, Lynne Kirby, and Vanessa Schwartz, among others, have argued, modern travel was about the construction of a mode of perception evident in travel films and in technologies of travel.[66] The visual address of colonial tourism, which was a distinct and difficult category of tourism, confronted the challenge of creating compatible sympathies between the "educated" and "civilized" publics among colonizing *and* the colonized elite who would be susceptible to travel, to cut across fundamental antagonisms between those two subject positions. Efforts to incorporate expanding notions of new publics and competing perceptions of sites of destruction account for the emotional variegations of Abbas Ali's precinematic travel album. We are shown places like Chattar Manzil, an extravagant nawabi seraglio that became a United Service Club in Lucknow to rival "the clubs of Pall Mall"

35—Bulrampore Hospital.

FIGURE 4.6 A converted hospital as a sign of Lucknow's alterations post–1857. Getty Research Institute, Los Angeles (92-B22782).

in England.[67] In Awadh, of which Faizabad and Lucknow were capital cities, nawabs had functioned as autonomous rulers under Mughal rule. With an acknowledgment of the resilience of Lucknow's precolonial nawabi architecture as worthy of tourism, alongside an affirmation of British alterations that were rendering Lucknow into a modern cityscape replete with schools, clubs, and hospitals reminiscent of English cities, the album fabricates a perspective that may be shared by the British and the Indian traveler ("the educated Native of India and the traveling public of all nations") *despite* the dividing chasm of an insurgency. This was a bold stance in the post-1857 environment in which Britain officially reviled Lucknow's architectural hybridity as excessive, wasteful, and worthy of imperial destruction, a sign of the degenerate luxury of the nawabs. The British condemned Lucknow's cultural syncretism that had been promoted by its ruling nawabs (such as the art-loving Wajid Ali Shah) as a sign of the powerless effeminacy of Indian rulers. The album counters the effeminization of the colonial male by including him as an equal consumer of the city's visuality.

The broader inclusion of British and colonial perspectives within this album has a repressed gendered dimension. Its manufactured appeal to an interracial Anglo-Indian perspective depends on the active submergence of the colonial female. The female subject position is excluded from the mixed racial address of colonial spectatorship in this album as a precondition to its articulation of a mass appeal based on soldierly grief, salacious violence, feats of architectural antiquity, and engineering modernity. At the figural level, Muslim women are at best a shadowy presence in *The Lucknow Album*. They appear as a passing reference in the texts that accompany images of empty seraglios once built for nawabi wives and female consorts. Absence, nevertheless, has a profound role in an album that is the impress of a city notable for its ruins. All the city's structures captured by the album are represented as empty shells of buildings that are absent of the life evoked by the album's text. Some of these structures, we are told, survived a passage to the present when they were refunctioned into touristic sites and utilitarian hospitals or state banks. We do not, however, see signs of present life and bustle in the images. The remaindered city, as displayed in the album, lacks access to temporal progression and belongs to a lost past.

The feminine is relegated to that lost past, in a move that effeminizes the space of history as time progresses forward through technologies of civil engineering, industrial architecture, and photography, all of which are coded as masculine and signify a triumph over the ephemerality of time. *The Lucknow Album*'s perspective, aimed at the English and Indian male as the neutral touristic position, rests on a masculinization of progress and a consignment of women to monuments of the past. Similar to *The Relief,* which contains its Englishwomen within domestic interiors, *The Lucknow Album* spectrally relegates Indian women to the unseen recesses of Lucknow's architectural landmarks.

CHAUDHVIN KA CHAND, M. SADIQ

Is it possible to write the history of a city as it is imagined in popular films and photographs when time itself is troped and split in a visual archive that feminizes monuments as static accretions of an emptied-out past while masculinizing spectatorial perspectives as mobile and presentist? Dismantling gendered tropes premised on a teleological temporality involves a critical historiography written not only to the beat of historical materialism but also attuned to the affective charge of material objects and the gendering of time itself. This kind of writing becomes particularly relevant to places where time is not merely experienced in relation to a historical present but also as the "deep *fullness* of time, being present to many times at once," to use Anand Vivek Taneja's evocative description of (Old, New, and expanding) Delhi's multiple coexisting archeological pasts and presents.[68] Walter Benjamin has suggested a path for such historical writing that refuses to think of the past as complete, and of movement as singular or advancing, with reference to the Paul Klee painting *Angelus Novus*. Benjamin's alternative historical account is swept up in a vertiginous temporality like the forward-moving angel in Klee's image, whose eyes are prized open by a past of recursive visions and memories. Following the angel, I consider it not incongruous, or just incongruous enough, to use a Hindi-Urdu sound film shot on location in Lucknow in 1960 to demonstrate the complicity between an early Indian photographic album and a silent US film about Lucknow, both of which erase the subaltern female from their images to depict a city destroyed and remade as a touristic and cinematic attraction through predominantly masculinist tropes.

Chaudhvin ka Chand (also called *Moon of the Fourteenth Day* or *Full Moon*, 1960) unravels the feminization of the ruin and masculinization of progress in its brief introductory credit sequence, which spins a complex referential web with the use of mobile bodies, stationary cinematic images, moving lyrics, and static monuments. The film was a commercially successful tragicomic love story produced by India's critically acclaimed filmmaker Guru Dutt (who was also rumored to be its uncredited editor and, more controversially, its director). Set in Lucknow, *Chaudhvin* depicts characters of the feudal Muslim aristocracy preoccupied with the pursuit of love, poetry, music, artful conversation, and courtship. The film's credit sequence, or prologue, is shot on location in Lucknow and takes us past some of the city's landmark buildings, such as the Husainabad Bazaar Gateway and the Asafi Mosque in the Bara Imambara complex. Other than what I am calling the film's prologue, the film's narrative action occurs mostly on set in modern studios in Andheri, Bombay. The spatiality and temporality of the prologue sequence that is shot on location is, in this sense, exceptional in comparison to the remainder of the film.

Chaudhvin opens with a brief tour of the city as the camera shadows the ghostly figure of a woman in a *burqa*. She walks past the city's landmark architecture, her ghostly tour accompanied by Shakeel Badayuni's nostalgic lyrics about Lucknow, sung by the popular male playback singer Mohammad Rafi:

> This soil of Lucknow.
> This orchard of color or country of heady love and beautiful forms,
> where Awadh's setting sun seeks a destination.
> This place of bewitchment. This place of youth.
> This land of Lucknow.[69]

> *Yeh Lucknow ki sarzameen, yeh Lucknow ki sarzameen.*
> *Yeh rang-roop ka chaman, Yeh husnon-ishq ka watan,*
> *Yehi to woh muqaam hai, Jahaan Awadh ki shaam hai.*
> *Jawaan-Jawaan Haseen-Haseen, Yeh Lucknow ki sarzami.*

FIGURE 4.7 *Chaudhvin ka Chand* poster combining the (un)veiled woman with skylines of Lucknow and havelis. Courtesy of the National Film Archive of India.

The song is a paean to a fallen city that was once the epitome of exquisite beauty. The buildings are filmed to reproduce the city's grandeur. A burqa-clad woman—a restricted participant of Lucknow's public spaces during the city's nawabi past, the British Indian past, *and* India's nationalist present—guides us. The combination of her attire, her solitude, and her touristic visitations make her difficult to read. To which temporal and spatial axis does she belong? Is she of Mughal India, partitioned India, or unified India? How does she see the architecture? This figure becomes more inscrutable as the film's narrative unfolds. The film's story opens with Pyare Mohan (Rehman), a man at a fair, who falls in love with a woman when she briefly raises her burqa. The veil adorned by Jameela (Waheeda Rehman) becomes the start of several erroneous attempts at identifying, misidentifying, and wooing the woman. In the confusing and frequently comic events that follow, Jameela is caught in a love triangle between the two male friends Aslam (Guru Dutt) and Mohan, who must weigh their loyalty to each other against their desire for her. The matter is decided fatally when Mohan swallows his diamond ring to clear the path for his friend.

In contrast to Jameela's imprisonment in a mesh of male priorities in the film's narrative, the unidentified woman in the prologue is a lone traveler free of a consort or companion as she wanders in public places of mourning (at the Imambaras) and pleasure (as promised by the lyrics about Lucknow's *rang-roop* and *husnon-ishq*). Historically, a solitary veiled female wanderer could not have laid claim to Lucknow's public spaces and promised pleasures in the same way as male connoisseurs of its art, music, monuments, and culture. Yet this burqa-clad woman is our guide through the city's monuments and romanticized past. The traveling veiled figure disturbs iterations of Lucknow's city space as presented in the other visual documents discussed here, such as the Edison company's *Relief*, Abbas Ali's photographic mutiny memorial album, and *Chaudhvin's* own narrative segments, because the credit sequence's mixed registers of lyrics, cityscape, and body suggest impossible yearnings. They express desire for a kind of inhabitation of place and time that was never in this figure's possession in the first place. By her impermissible wanderlust, the atypical female flaneuse who is confined to gender-segregated domestic spaces and socially restricted public appearances within the film's narrative allows us entry into something *perverse* in Lucknow's architecture.

As a figural presence out of her usual habitat, the moving veiled body evokes a place that is displaced from its past. The spectral and veiled female wanderer is compelling because she offers spectators a way to experience the "unhomely" in Lucknow.[70] To recall Anthony Vidler's argument, "Film not only depicted movement in space and space in movement, it also unpacked the modern subject's spatial unconscious and its layers of (repressed) memories."[71] In *Chaudhvin's* credit sequence, the past exists mainly as a form of longing. This veiled solitary flaneuse is historically an impossible form, much as returning to Lucknow's feudal glory as promised by the lyrics is an impossible feat. Caught in the rupture of a cataclysmic destruction, this sequence's combination of images and lyrics suggests that Lucknow's cityscapes are left with no easy passage to the present within the realm of visual representation. In 1960, the Lucknow of Hindi-Urdu cinema was still living with unresolved sentiments of loss and desire that had no place in the triumphant and militant space of Lucknow in Edison's 1912 *Relief*.

Discussing links between cinema and travel, theorists of visuality note that modernity was foundationally defined by new technologies of automated motion that changed relationships between the human body, place, and perceptions of space. As Giuliana Bruno argues, understanding cinematics as a new form of mechanized mobility allows us to see how its modes were embedded in evolving urban architectures that became conducive and adaptable to habits of flânerie in public spaces. Cinematic spectatorship opened avenues for the female flaneuse traditionally restricted from perambulatory forms of freedom in city spaces available to men.[72] What is gripping about Lucknow, or indeed any site of insurgency and counterinsurgency, is that the place emerges as a visual commodity and as a subject of popular literature and imagery *after* acts of violence explicitly rewrite its gendered and racial rules of mobility. It is in the context of violence (which produces restrictions on who can or cannot travel) that visual media introduces new spatial rules of mobility and immobility into such spaces, defining who can participate in the virtual and visceral pleasures or horrors of viewing destruction, who can access the cosmopolitanism of consuming places visually, and who must be consumed as part of the topography.

In the two colonial texts discussed previously, the subaltern female remained topographic. She was either part of the landscape or she was erased from the image to produce a masculine, patriarchal, and bourgeois mode of spectatorship. *Chaudhvin*'s fleeting retrieval of the topographic feminine as the spectator's tour guide through this prologue sequence produces the shock of a new perspective, briefly unsettling the gendered troping of time, monumental landscape, and spectatorship. As a traveler within the modern cityspace, the shadowy figure at the opening of *Chaudhvin* is not *of* the ruins. But given the lyric's nostalgic register, the figure is also not entirely of the modern world. The sequence animates strange intimacies and distances in relation to a lost place and time by making the uncanny figure into a tourist in her own land and of her own past. It conveys her sense of being at home and exiled from home at the same time. Consequently Lucknow as a place is conveyed to us through uncanny affective registers.

Nostalgia of this kind does specific cultural work in post-Independence India, evident not only in depictions of Lucknow as mise-en-scène but also in the genre of "Muslim socials" in which such visualizations of Lucknow most often appeared. *Chaudhvin* is a classic Muslim social, which is described by Ira Bhaskar and Richard Allen as a film set in "a Muslim milieu and with Muslim characters as protagonists" with a focus on "the conflict between inherited, feudal values and forces of social change."[73] Referring to Muslim socials, Moinak Biswas rightly notes that they have "always been marked with nostalgia."[74] A popular site for Muslim socials, Lucknow provides an appropriate backdrop for *Chaudhvin*'s romanticization of an elite nawabi culture. Its narrative is nostalgic in the sense that it transports viewers to a timeless Islamic milieu by erasing traces of colonial and contemporary (post-Partition) India, and valuing codes of an imagined past of ritual and honor. The film's prologue stages a slightly different kind of nostalgia when the camera follows the veiled, unaccompanied female figure across Lucknow's iconic public monuments and ruins, evoking the city's repressed history of violence. With a greater acknowledgment of the real environments of Lucknow, the initial sequence uses location shots, lyrics, edits, and a moving veiled figure to stage complex affective connectivities between a figural subject and the violent fate of its built environments. In the remainder of the film, the havelis on-screen are staged sets standing in for the actual architectural and habitational form, but they provoke an equally complex range of emotions about India's feudal past as their inhabited equivalents.

FROM LUCKNOW TO HAVELIS

Scholars Rachel Dwyer, Ira Bhaskar, Richard Allen, and Meheli Sen have insightfully discussed the haveli as a motif in Muslim socials and as part of Bombay cinema's gothic narratives.[75] Shifting away from their focus on cinematic genres and aesthetics, I want to attend to the social meanings attached to havelis as a vernacular architectural form of domicile. Edward Said remarked regarding historical methodology that points of departure are important because they *"enable* what follows from them."[76] Taking a circuitous route to the cinematic haveli of Hindi cinema through the social life of havelis as buildings changes our critical sightlines in a couple of ways. First, it enables us to see architecture in film as an expressive sociocultural form, doing as much cultural work as the film's narrative, theme, or generic structure. Emotions about how class, religion, and gender have been managed in the biography of a modern nation coalesce around the imagination and tropic use of its built environments. Second, the obdurate persistence of the cinematic haveli against the declining or changing social and material fate of actual havelis throws into relief the confounding place of the feudal in India's history.

Mirza Ghalib, the renowned nineteenth-century Urdu and Persian poet, lived through the degradation of his haveli and his life after the British deposed Ghalib's patron, the last Mughal emperor, Bahadur Shah Zafar, in 1857. In the years following Ghalib's death in 1869, his haveli became a coal storage unit and a tin factory. In 2011, this haveli in a narrow lane of Galli Qasim Jaan in Old Delhi's Walled City was renovated.[77] Reports of the renovation reveal the haveli's difficult status in India today. As a residential building that became financially unsustainable in the late nineteenth century with the emergence of new architectures and urban centers of trade and power under the British, havelis struggled

FIGURE 4.8 Ghalib's renovated haveli, now open for tourism. Photograph courtesy of Kalpana Ram.

to survive, especially in locations beset by modern civic neglect. The residents of Galli Qasim Jaan in Ballimaran complained of open drains and poor sanitation when superficial repairs were completed in time to inaugurate Ghalib's haveli as a heritage monument in 2011. To celebrate the event, Ghalib's poems played in continuous loop over a loudspeaker as an act of aural memory or urban noise pollution (or more likely both).

Today, with the exception of a few properties sustained by India's tourism industry, havelis largely populate North India's landscape as decaying, uninhabited, or partially inhabited buildings parceled out among multiple owners, or inhabited seasonally by out-of-town owners. It comes as no surprise, then, that anthropologists and architectural historians have largely studied the haveli as a sign and relic of another era.[78] The picture is very different for literature and media scholars because havelis have thrived in India's post-Independence novels, television shows, and commercially successful Hindi films.[79] Films such as *Chaudhvin*, *Mahal* (Kamal Amrohi, 1949),[80] *Madhumati* (Bimal Roy, 1958), *Sahib Bibi aur Ghulam* (Abrar Alvi, 1962), *Bees Saal Baad* (Biren Nag, 1962), *Mere Mehboob* (1963), *Kohra* (1964), *Bahu Begum* (M. Sadiq, 1967), *Lal Patthar* (Sushil Majumdar, 1971), *Kudrat* (Chetan Anand, 1981), and *Purani Haveli* (Shyam and Tulsi Ramsay, 1989) have endowed havelis with an affective life that creatively processed and reflected on the structure's material decline

FIGURE 4.9 Meena Kumari and Ashok Kumar in a poster for *Bahu Begum*. Courtesy of the National Film Archive of India.

in India's post-Independence (and preglobalization) era.[81] Whereas Ghalib's haveli was salvaged from ruin only recently, his poetry has been remembered continuously and intimately in India and Pakistan in recordings on popular albums or sung live by performers such as Ghulam Ali, Muhammad Rafi, Mehdi Hassan, Jagjit Singh, and Farida Khanum. Film lyricist and dialogue writer Gulzar, key to the commemoration of the dead poet's haveli, authored the successful TV series *Ghalib* (1988) that brought a simulation of Ghalib's haveli and his verses into contemporary living rooms.

In telling the story of Ghalib's haveli, the difficulty in reconciling its quotidian decay with Ghalib's timeless inscription in India's popular culture and his haveli's sudden reclamation as a heritage monument reverts us to those points in time when alignments between the everyday, the popular, and the statist realms have been broken in India, pushing us to tell affective histories of the

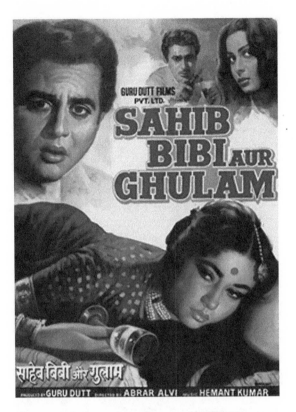

FIGURE 4.10 The principal actors in a poster for *Sahib Bibi aur Ghulam*. Courtesy of the National Film Archive of India.

haveli and consider asynchronous temporalities embedded within a modern nation's architectural form.[82] These misalignments show us that the state and the popular have registered India's modernization of property, gender roles, and religion in divergent ways, revealing postcolonial India as inhabiting a kind of asynchronous time that escapes the conventions of chronological political accounts. Perhaps this is why a snapshot of the haveli's commemoration in the neglected Galli Qasim Jaan—where Chief Minister Sheila Dixit and lyricist/director Gulzar arrived amid puzzled crowds and disgruntled shop owners—has the quality of a Benjaminian dialectical image. In this event, a ruin came to life with the clamor of its designation as a memorial when a lyricist invoked its Mughal-era inhabitant, and people rubbernecked to see why an ordinary building on their street was obstructing traffic, drawing ministerial acclaim and rare municipal attention. Institutional memorialization, poetic empathy, and public disruption

FIGURE 4.11 Haveli facades now subdivided on a narrow street in Jodhpur. (ABOVE) FIGURE 4.12 Havelis blending in with new structures in Bikaner. (BELOW)

produced the kind of constellation that Benjamin describes in his theory of historical knowledge. Arguing against Heidegger's evacuation of history from phenomenology, Benjamin writes about the past as not merely the context of things but as the temporal point at which they flash into comprehensibility or, more poetically, when the "movement at their interior" achieves legibility.[83] These are moments when the meanings that lie at the heart of things are pulled out of their sedimentation in archaic time and into the vagaries of dynamic, historical time.

What of the past leapt into the present with the commemoration of Ghalib's haveli? The building achieved recognition as part of the Indian state's post-liberalization support of commercial tourism, which in this century confronts the government with its uneven funding of heritage projects, the "ennui and indifference" of India's population toward museum culture, and the "combustible domain" of politicized religion easily inflamed around public structures.[84] Claimed today by all Indians, Ghalib was a Muslim who lived in what would later become a ghettoized walled city, which aligns him with a minoritized community under secular nationalist *and* Hindu fundamentalist definitions of modern India. So the commemoration of his house came as a surprise to people living in the haveli's environs in 2011 to whom the salvage of an anonymous house in their street's squalor opened a portal of recognition to their dramatically altered status in the present, in comparison with the neighborhood's more glorious precolonial feudal past.

A CRISIS OF PROPERTY AND PROPRIETY

Historically, precolonial havelis created segregated spaces for women of North Indian Hindu and Muslim families ranging across a wide spectrum of wealth. Indian films of the post-Independence era transformed havelis from nondenominational precolonial structures of segregated living into predominantly Islamic feudal structures inhabited by a wealthy, fading nobility. Hindi cinema's havelis frequently depict the Islamic *milieu* of Lucknow's nawabs or northern India's Muslim elite, even though families of different religious persuasions, including members of the Jain merchant class and Hindu social elite of the Rajputana kingdoms, have owned and continue to own havelis. By collapsing the meanings of a precolonial domicile with a feudal and Islamic era visualized for a postcolonial audience, the films scramble history and erase India's colonial period that was historically central to the haveli's decline as an architectural hub of cities. Faced with such a hermeneutic, a film historian's attention is drawn away from the logic of causality to the logic of signification, to understand what misalignments of time and misremembered identity meant in the popular imagination of an architectural form. The omitted middle of British colonialism has to be analytically recuperated to reveal that a rupture from a sense of continuous history produced this cinematic imagination of a domicile.

Across a range of popular Hindi films, havelis evoke an age of opulence lost through decay, greed, cruelty, madness, murder, and transgression—acts that are confronted with retribution, reincarnation, and haunting within the space of the structure. The Ramsay Brothers' low-budget horror film *Purani Haveli* (1989) is a good place to begin a discussion of what the haveli telegraphs as an architectural landmark in Hindi cinema. The film was made with limited financial resources to exploit the market for sensationalist horror.[85] Of necessity, such a film had to be epigrammatic in its mise-en-scène, to convey a wealth of referential associations with a single prop, sound, lighting setup, or gesture.[86] The opening shots of *Purani Haveli* give us a condensed accumulation of tropes that accompany the appearance of havelis in post-Independence (and preliberalization) Hindi-Urdu cinema. Pillars surround a sunken inner courtyard, or *chowk*, on a misty night.[87] A shrieking bird cry gives way to bestial moans from behind a carved door. A long shot of an imposing, neglected, multistoried haveli is followed by a high-angle geometrically composed shot of ornate steps descending away from the camera. A door creaks, the clock strikes three, and something female shrieks. After the beat of a static high-angle shot of the chowk, we get an external image of the haveli with the (anticipated?) shock of a body falling from the highest *jharokha* (enclosed balcony). The film's titles lunge at us in gruesome red from the location shot of a grand haveli.

Articulated around the haveli are gendered stories of property and propriety.[88] The mansion in *Purani Haveli* is willed to a young female ward whose guardian, her aunt, wants to acquire the property by coercing her niece into marrying her son. But the young woman is in love with someone else, and a murderous monster possessed by the haveli's evil spirit plagues the mansion. In the film *Madhumati*, a raja (king) displaces tribal Santhals from their forest, and his malevolent son attempts to rape the Santhal king's daughter. She hurtles down to her death from the haveli's balcony to escape him, and her ghost returns to avenge the crime so that she may be reborn to a happier life. In *Bahu Begum*, an evil uncle foils his nephew's plans to marry his beloved from a neighboring haveli because the uncle wants possession of his nephew's property. At the climax, an innocent nobleman caught in the middle of these machinations makes the ultimate sacrifice of setting himself and his haveli on fire. In

FIGURE 4.13 Poster for *Purani Haveli*. Courtesy of the National Film Archive of India.

Lal Patthar (as also in *Kudrat* and *Sahib, Bibi aur Ghulam*), havelis pass into ruination haunted by the curse of raped women or hiding the skeletal remains of women killed by a male aristocrat's sexual abuse, violence, and neglect. My plot descriptions flatten great stylistic differences between these films, but they emphasize the extent to which popular films with varying directorial styles and generic predispositions create a dark past to render scandalous a vernacular type of residential property, making it home to murder, sexual assault, female victimization, false inheritance claims, and improper possession.

How do we interpret these visualizations of havelis in Hindi films? What do we make of the overpowering emphasis on sexual violence and retribution in the recuperated memory of the haveli? There is rarely a feminist politics to these depictions of sexual violence against women, but the films do permit a "dizzy satisfaction in witnessing the way that sexual difference under patriarchy is fraught, explosive, and erupts dramatically into violence within its own private stamping ground, the family," or, more precisely in the case of haveli films, in the family's residence.[89] The cinematic haveli of Hindi cinema is metaphoric of a range of social inequities related to the possession of land and property in India's patriarchal and paternalistic society. Representations of the architectural space replay the haveli's decline, but the aesthetics of ruin invite reflection on a history of violence and perversion within domestic spaces. In this sense, the haveli's architectural form offers a critical and melodramatic optic on India's so-called heritage and allows us to think of haveli films as a distinct collection or genre of films in Hindi-Urdu cinema.

In *Mourning the Nation*, Bhaskar Sarkar offers a compelling account of post-Independence Hindi and Bengali cinema as modes of representation pre-occupied with depicting Indian modernity as a traumatic event.[90] Sarkar focuses on popular films as a figuration of the deep trauma of India and Pakistan's Partition in 1947, which carved the lives and land of British India into separate sovereign nations. Sarkar's analysis of the haveli in *Garam Hawa* (M. S. Sathyu, 1975) is a useful point of departure to grasp the structure's function in a wider range of commercially popular Hindi films. *Garam Hawa* depicts the fates of Salim Mirza's family members when their lives are devastated by Partition. As Muslims, Mirza and his family become outsiders in their own land and haveli.[91] If *Garam Hawa* depicts the traumatic uprooting of Muslims from India with the overt symbolism of a family's dispossession of their haveli, the haveli's function in commercial films is more tropic and ambient. In contrast to the socially conscious, realist modes of new Indian cinema (illustrated by *Garam Hawa*), commercial cinema transforms havelis into an abstracted aspect of feudal India's past. This past appears as aristocratic, ornamental, obsessive, immoral, misogynistic, and homicidal across a range of stylistic registers, including, most powerfully, the spatial register of the haveli. In this, the haveli of Hindi cinema grapples with another historical event: not (or not exclusively) the partition of the subcontinent, but the new regime of landownership and property possession and dispossession initiated by India's integration as a modern nation-state from dispersed colonized territories that were parceled out between the princely states and British India provinces.

THE AFFECT OF PARAMOUNTCY

In 1947, the British Crown gave the princely states of India the option of legal independence from India and Pakistan, or the choice of a union with either dominion. A detailed history of this period of India's constitutional birth as a consolidated union formed through the assimilation of British Indian provinces and princely states is outside my purview, but some analysis is essential to highlight the North Indian aristocracy's changing role and relationship to property and political authority under the new regime of secular national modernity. Here I want to lay the foundations for an argument that the architectural form of Hindi cinema's haveli temporally and affectively evokes what is referred to in political history as the "Accession of Princely States" in the integration of modern India. Shyam Benegal's *Zubeida* (2001) makes this period a self-conscious part of the cinematic narrative. But my argument will be that the historical affect of paramountcy and accession were subliminal aspects of most of commercial cinema's depictions of havelis until the era of deregulation, when the nation's spatial relation to its imagined and architectural pasts altered fundamentally (as discussed in the next chapter).

Starting in the late 1700s, a new system of relational power was proposed under the "doctrine of paramountcy."[92] It provided an unusual prescription of state power in over a third of the subcontinent's territory where sovereignty would be shared between India's princes and the British East India Company (and later the British Crown). It was the bargain that England would extend protection against internal rebellion and external attacks to India's aristocrats in return for the British resident's (and later the British government's) paramount power in those regions. In other words, by guaranteeing indirect British rule, the Indian princes were in turn to be "insured against the consequences of misrule."[93] The *Butler Committee Report* of 1929 defined paramountcy as a contract based on "a living, growing relationship shaped by circumstance and policy" combining "history, theory and modern fact."[94] This deliberately vague status shored up the combined powers of the British government and the Indian princes against the people. Officially, the practice ended in 1947 when the dynastic right to govern and own land was ostensibly terminated with the nation's independence.

Paramountcy effectively suspended princely states between feudal and modern state processes by simultaneously investing the governing body with what philosopher Michel Foucault describes as sovereign power (which is visible, external, transcendent, and primarily land-based), retained to all appearances by the princes, *as well as* disciplinary power (which is invisible, bureaucratic, and contract-based) assumed by the British resident.[95] Thus the colonial government's modern dispensation did not rupture a feudal order but guaranteed a social habituation to the links between dynastic power, land control, and governance that has persisted well after the redistribution of private property following 1947. A recent manifestation of feudal power over land is illustrated in the example of Satara, the first state annexed by Governor General Lord Dalhousie in 1848.[96] Udayanraje Bhonsle, thirteenth descendant of Satara's Maratha king Shivaji, represented Satara as minister of parliament in 2012. Contravening the Indian government's Kul-Kayda Act, under which the state reassigned land from landlords to tillers in 1957, the descendants of Satara's royalty had claimed twenty-two villages allegedly awarded to a family temple in an application accepted by local revenue officials, leaving little recourse to public appeal for the local populace because the Bhonsle family also represented the region in parliament.[97]

One of the scandals of Indian democracy has been that the strategically vague legal invention of paramountcy under colonialism—namely, an ostensibly contract-based definition of governance that was in fact an opaque combination of social prerogative, class privilege, and state protection—provides a good description of how several citizens experienced the rule of the democratic state after India's independence, despite the highest principles of India's first lawmakers and statesmen. The legal documentation for land ownership and redistribution of rights to land acquisition entered the country with colonialism, bringing with it tools of democracy *and* corruption. Effectively this not only produced a distrust of democracy in modern India but also gave traction to noncontractual forms of kinship such as caste and tribe. Situated in this context as the central architectural icon of India's feudal era, Hindi cinema's haveli emerges as a highly ambivalent cultural symbol of an unresolved past in the post-Independence era. Although the haveli occasionally represents the tyranny of the feudal (as in *Madhumati*, where a cruel prince vitiates the memory of his benevolent father), more frequently the structure is imbued with affective contradictions. It conveys the renewable hold of social hierarchies in postcolonial India while also expressing anxieties about feudalism's worst sins that are reinvented under the new Indian state. The horrors of paramountcy and the pathos of Indian royalty's accession to a secular order, which bring with them a fear of arbitrary regimes of power alongside a nostalgia for aristocratic grandeur, permeate the filming of this monument.

THE HAVELI AND ITS CHOWK

As affective topos, the cinematic haveli invokes the social sphere through one of the structure's key architectural features made iconic in film, namely, the haveli's inner courtyard, or chowk. A chowk is typically enclosed within the tiered space of multilevel rooms and passageways. In post-Independence Hindi films, the haveli's chowk and the segmented rooms around the chowk become multiphonic symbols of India's hierarchically segregated but ritualistically integrated social spaces. There is a danger in claiming architectural specificity for building types in films, because cinema participates in turning built environments into promiscuous icons that are disloyal to social history and absorptive of all forms for cultural meaning. Thus, as Rachel Dwyer and Divia Patel note, grand cascading stairwells become a generalizable visual mark of grandeur incorporated into the filmic iconography of any set design connoting wealth in commercial Hindi cinema.[98] Nevertheless, architectural forms lend to their imagined and derived versions on-screen a set of *assumptions* about the conduct and aesthetics of life in private and public spaces, which is my focus here.

Dynamic relations between interiors and exteriors were foundational to the structure of precolonial havelis that were designed around a central courtyard both enclosed within the house and open to the elements. Inga Bryden points out that the term "haveli" borrows from the Arabic *haola*, meaning partition, and the Hindi word *hava*, or wind.[99] In havelis, segregated structures with separate accommodations for the haveli's men, women, and servants as well as appointed places for entertaining guests, transacting business, and celebrating religious or family occasions were articulated around one or two chowks. These chowks were separated into the external male courtyard (*mardana*) and the interior female courtyard (*zanana*) in North Indian households, predominantly in Lucknow, in the Rajputana states, and in Delhi. Havelis were nodal points of social life in their neighborhoods, and therefore a haveli's spatial segregations did not *preclude* public transactions; rather, they defined the terms of public interaction. In the larger havelis of Delhi, which had been given by Mughal emperors to grantees such as the "magistrate, army chief, landlord," the *amir*, or head, of the haveli officiated over his own home, over his "accountants, clerks, and personal servants," and over "artists, poets, calligraphers, physicians and astrologers," all of whom may have lived near or on the premises of the haveli, giving havelis and their streets the feel of "miniature cities within the city."[100] The haveli's women, presided over by the patriarch, ran its everyday business with the assistance of a network of servants and retainers.

In commercial Hindi films, life comes together for the companionate commingling of extended families in these open interior spaces governed by strict rules of patriarchal conduct. As a liminal space enclosed within a structure and yet exposed to external (public and environmental) influences, the chowk also becomes the site most vulnerable to change. In Hindi films, the mardana and zenana are frequently sites where the strength of communal bonds sustained by expectations of female behavior before and after matrimony are tested, to manage anxieties about the dissolution of the haveli's respectability. The chowk's surrounding rooms, connecting passageways, and enclosed chambers hide secrets that cast long and unsettling shadows on its carefully regulated sociality; a sociality that is also under threat from the outsiders who are allowed ingress. Herein lies the haveli's gothic darkness.

FIGURE 4.14 A lobby card for *Bahu Begum* in a studio-constructed chowk. Courtesy of the National Film Archive of India.

In *Bahu Begum*, misunderstandings and coincidences bring together the families of three havelis in Lucknow—one in decline, with its nawab on a meager monthly pay from the government; another in debt, as an uncle squanders his ward's wealth; and a third still resplendent. In the film, the chowk of these three havelis spatially concretizes the public stakes of private decisions, particularly regarding romance and marriage, which effect questions of property and inheritance. The tropes of eavesdropping, misunderstanding, and confessions are central to Hindi cinema's imagination of the haveli's chowk because it is a partially closed and regulated private space as well as a partially open and covert public space, making it ripe for intrigue.[101] In *Bahu Begum*, Zeenat (Meena Kumari) is in love with Yousuf (Pradeep Kumar), but she is to be married to Nawab Sikandar Mirza (Ashok Kumar). The wedding commences in the outer male courtyard, the mardana. Only the bride's father, the male *vakil* (lawyer), and *gavah* (eyewitness) are permitted into the zanana to get the bride's acquiescence to the wedding, although they must remain outside the bridal chamber. They are unaware that the bride has fled. Sound replaces vision in this case, and social expectation trumps reality. The wedding is legalized in the absence of the

FIGURE 4.15 Circumscribed space and vision elicits the plot twists of *Chaudhvin ka Chand*. Courtesy of the National Film Archive of India.

bride-to-be when her faithful girlfriend cries out in alarm, and her cry is taken by unseeing male witnesses to be the sound of a bride's acquiescence. An empty palanquin leaves the bridal home. After the shock of finding his bride's palanquin empty, Sikander Mirza enters into an elaborate charade with his sister and Zeenat's father to pretend that the absent Zeenat is in fact living with him as his wife. The façade of a marriage can be maintained to preserve the honor of the bride and groom's haveli only because of each family's sanction to spatially block public entry into the segregated interiors of its structure.

Acts of eavesdropping lead to tragic misunderstandings (such as Zeenat and Yousuf's misconception that they are the intended bride and groom, until it is too late) and dishonorable deeds (such as an uninhabited palanquin leaving Zeenat's father's haveli), precisely because the chowk constitutes a liminal boundary between the outside and inside. It defines the limits to which anyone other than familial elders can enter the inner chambers. In distinction to the bazaar's (marketplace's) open spaces,[102] the chowk is where the family interacts with the community in circumscribed ways by exteriorizing and displaying the family's honorable standing, while also interiorizing the community's judgment. It is thus a vulnerable space within the lexicon of haveli films.

The historical haveli and chowk were features of a vernacular and syncretic architectural form used by Hindu and Muslim families alike. Havelis in the Rajputana states were built to correspond to Vedic principles of *vaastu*, or ancient Hindu principles of spatial arrangement.[103] So why was it stylized and memorialized with Islamic overtones in popular cinema? What had to be misremembered or forgotten for such visual recuperations to occur? The answers lie in the constitutive elements of the Indian gothic in Hindi cinema, which derive from the nation's particular historical emergence into political modernity based on secular-democratic principles of universal franchise that were abruptly extended to an overwhelmingly patriarchal and feudal society. The difficult place of gender relations, social equality, and religious identity in modern India (discussed in turn) are central to popular culture's gothic reconfiguration of the haveli and its chowk.

The globally recognizable aesthetic of the gothic identifies the "sustained (though largely doomed) attempt to articulate a form of opposition to the culture of modernization."[104] Hilary Thompson defines the gothic as "the genre in which the unresolved demands of one time come to call on another," making it particularly well suited for tales of reincarnation and haunting.[105] As a relic of the past lingering in the present, havelis in Hindi cinema become a favored site for reincarnation narratives. Using David Punter's definition of the gothic as history written with the logic of the revenant, Meheli Sen builds on Rachel Dwyer's argument that the gothic aesthetic in Hindi cinema is a commentary on the nation's hybrid modernity, constituted as a simultaneously oppositional *and* "derivative discourse" (cf. Partha Chatterjee) of European Enlightenment.[106] Sen focuses on the male protagonists of such films, who represent the "masculine subject-citizen" antonymous to the hero of dominant Nehruvian socials from the same period. As she shows, in opposition to the nationalist and modernizing arc of the Nehruvian hero, the male protagonist of Hindi cinema's gothic tales moves from cities to provincial locations to collapse dramatically in havelis haunted by (real or staged) female spirits.

Shifting attention from the masculine protagonist to the spectral female figure in this disillusion with/dissolution of the national uncovers how the past is etched onto architectural forms. In discussing the dominance of nostalgia in the twentieth century, Svetlana Boym expands on the notion of "heritage" as a past without guilt.[107] Heritage is the past commodified and made consumable. The haveli film in this sense is an antiheritage film.[108] It is a past recollected with guilt, as conveyed by the mansion in decay (*Sahib Bibi aur Ghulam, Bahu Begum, Kudrat, Mahal*), the haunted mansion, or the mansion under a curse (*Kohra, Lal Patthar, Bees Saal Baad, Purani Haveli*). The haveli's walls mutely witness the rape or attempted rape of women (*Lal Patthar, Bees Saal Baad, Madhumati*) and their neglect, suicide, or murder (*Purani Haveli, Madhumati, Sahib, Bibi aur Ghulam, Kudrat*).

In the haveli of Hindi films, subaltern forces—primarily the Muslim and the female as dispossessed subjects of the nation—demand the price of their suppression in a manner that resonates with modern India's schizophrenia. Social hierarchies sustaining the architecture of the haveli become an object of fascination and vilification because they are the antithesis of the architectures of a new democratic state. Amit Chaudhuri describes this in terms of India's crisis of adopting a universal adult suffrage in the absence of an educated or middle-class populace. In his words, the state "has had, thus, to negotiate two languages, two (I am borrowing from Ruskin) architectures, from its inception." In addition to the architecture of a democratic nation-state, the "other language or architecture of the Indian state might be called a Gothic experiment, a space in which the 'rude' or 'savage' are indispensable to the life of the structure."[109] Subordinated in the state's experiment within its own architectures of democracy, the "rude," "savage," or what has been more deeply theorized as the subaltern, erupts in the cinematic imagination of India's aristocratic past. In this internal conversation, the British are erased from historical memory, and the myth making and account taking occurs most deeply in terms of oneself.[110] At the same time, the colonial lingers as a memory of definitive rupture: it is what makes the past unbridgeable with the present.

In the haveli as artistic *chronotope*, to borrow Bakhtin's conceptual apparatus, "spatial and temporal indicators are fused into one . . . concrete whole. Time, as it were, thickens, takes on flesh, becomes artistically visible; likewise, space becomes charged and responsive to the movements of time, plot and history."[111] As a concretization of time, the cinematic haveli is not a metonymy of India's feudal past. It is a reminder of its experience of falling out of joint with its own past, ruptured by colonialism and modernized through an incomplete democratization and irrevocable communalization of self and state identity. Scholars discuss the emergence of "Muslimness" as a stylistic effect in twentieth-century Indian literature and cinema in terms similar to the antinomies of modernity characterizing the style of the European gothic.[112] Their argument is relevant to discussions of the gothic as a sort of antimodern force or "antihistory,"[113] in that the gothic style attends to the darkness lurking within brightly teleological narratives of the nation.[114] The Islamicate of haveli films can be read along the grain of this argument, as an antihistory to nationalist narratives of India.[115] The Islamification of the haveli in cinema safely contains India's Islam within the nation's noble past, but the ambivalent charge haunting havelis is an acknowledgment that horrors accompany the nation's polyglot modern form.

GENDER AND THE CINEMATIC HAVELI

The haveli's ambivalent affect in Hindi cinema is evident in *Lal Patthar*, starring Raaj Kumar, Hema Malini, and Raakhee. *Lal Patthar* was a commercially successful film produced by F. C. Mehra and directed by Sushil Majumdar in 1971. Similar to several Bombay filmmakers of their generation, the lives of the film's director and producer were defined by the political turbulence of 1947. F. C. Mehra was a Lahori who migrated to India after Partition. Sushil Majumdar was born in a part of Bengal that became East Pakistan and subsequently Bangladesh. The commercial film effaces these privations at the level of explicit theme, though the film's mise-en-scène is saturated with an affective displacement of trauma.[116] The film's story is set in the abstracted town of "Raj Nagar," and its lead characters are Hindu. Nevertheless, locational and atmospheric elements usher in memories of another time, place, and religious allegiance. The film largely plays out in Fatehpur Sikri, an iconic site of Hindi cinema.[117] A walled city built by the great Mughal emperor Akbar in the sixteenth century to serve as his capital but abandoned soon after, Fatehpur Sikri lies in ruins as a well-preserved marker of the glory and eventual desolation of India's Islamic architectural and political past. Laid out with an important shrine to the Sufi saint Salim Chishti, with monuments that housed Akbar's advisors and wives from varying regions and sects in India, Fatehpur Sikri symbolizes India's polyglot history.

The film's opening sequence presents Fatehpur Sikri from the perspective of modern tourists while also undercutting the visual modalities of tourism. Following a group of sightseers, camera movements animate the monument with pans and zooms from the vantage point of framing arches, terraces, and gardens. Aurally, this tour is disturbed by a disembodied voice-over. A man tells the audience that Fatehpur Sikri beckons to a deep emptiness, or *virani*, in his soul. *Lal Patthar* is a story told by Raja Kumar Bahadur Gyan Shankar Rai (Raaj Kumar) to a group of tourists visiting Fatehpur Sikri. It is the story of a madman obsessed with a monument: he is seen perusing its catalogue; it is the site of his crime; and he returns to it repeatedly after his slide into insanity.

FIGURE 4.16 Privilege, trauma, and feudal violence in *Lal Patthar*. Courtesy of the National Film Archive of India.

Studio shots of Rai's mansion as well as location shots and studio mock-ups of Fatehpur Sikri reference architectural elements of havelis. Most of the dramatic action in Fatehpur Sikri is set in its pillared and open chowks, while the set design of Rai's mansion contains a range of narrow, confining, and claustrophobic spaces, including women's bedrooms and passageways connecting multiple rooms that are shot with a clutter of taxidermy and European furniture. Rai keeps his mistress and wife at different levels of his mansion, and their rooms open out to an interior foyer of mutual rivalry as Rai ascends and descends from one room to another. The visual design of the film reflects Rai's schizophrenia. The trouble in Rai's haveli has originated from its past: Rani Swarnamayi cast a curse of insanity on his family after she was raped by Rai's grandfather in the bedchamber that he inherits. The young scion's father proves equally loathsome. Rai is sent away from the mansion after he witnesses his father attempting to rape a woman. Rai grows up vowing never to marry, and dedicates himself to acquiring a double master's degree in history and psychology (which is appropriate, given the subliminal canvas of this film).

Despite efforts to escape his ancestral blight, Rai falls in love with two women. He is dogged by alcoholism and jealousy, and devolves into an uxorious drunk who kills his wife and best friend in a ghostly tableau staged at Fatehpur Sikri. The shots of the film's opening and climax edit together actual and staged locations of a chowk, infecting the historical site of Emperor Akbar's religious and marital syncretism with the darkness of Rai's bedrooms and passageways. After the double homicide, the Masjid chowk echoes with Rani Swarnamayi's vindictive cackle and Rai's insane laugh as the haveli's curse comes true and a camera zooms dizzyingly around Fatehpur Sikri's courtyard. A woman's curse reverberates between a haveli and Fatehpur Sikri, but is mellowed by the sudden appearance of Rai's mistress, who has devoted her life to his care. As the film concludes, she appears from behind the pillars to gently guide the old madman away, now exhausted from reliving his criminal past.

The dual affects of horror and reverence that the film creates around Kumar Bahadur Rai through the figures of his wife and mistress (and Raaj Kumar's star status) reinscribes the principle of social paramountcy. In contrast to Rai, who is a man obsessed with an architectural structure that endlessly triggers his past, the inattentive consumerist tourists in Fatehpur Sikri appear superficial and callow even after the past is exposed for its monstrous violence. The present is let into the secrets of the past, but it is diminished by an encounter with older primal structures of allegiance. Compared to the devaluation of personal relations in the present, old bonds command respect for their grandeur and, in equal measure, are excoriated for their epic demands. The monument belongs to past generations that can only partially reveal their monstrously consuming passions to the new, because these emotions cannot be fully translated into the present ethic.

This is the hermeneutic of the cinematic havelis. They conjure lives that hide terrible secrets and make us mourn their decline. Similar to the tourists, the film's viewers are but secular moderns getting glimpses into an epic past. They are consumed by the haveli's melodramas for the duration of their spectation, but they are inadequate to its raging furies. Figures like Rai inhabit an expectation of social paramountcy with their arbitrary demands of unquestioning loyalty and authority defining the terms of their social relationships, particularly with women. Increasingly unviable, this modality of power is nevertheless given its emotional due and its erosion mimicked and mourned in the ruin of a domicile, so that both the relationships and the architectures sustaining them are fraught with contradictory significance. In *Lal Patthar* (as also

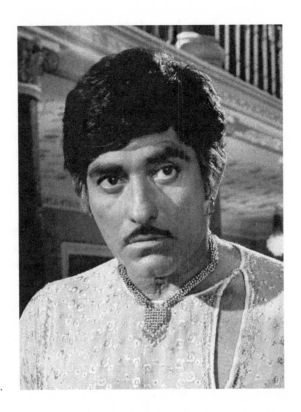

FIGURE 4.17 Raaj Kumar is a haunted feudal aristocrat in *Lal Patthar*. Courtesy of the National Film Archive of India.

in *Kudrat, Sahib, Bibi aur Ghulam, Bees Saal Baad*, and others) violent acts against women committed in the rooms and passageways hidden from sight lurk underground in dungeons or in dark attics and stairwells and erupt to the surface to exact their price. These gothic spaces represent a kind of antihistory by revealing the criminal basis of patriarchal and dynastic power, but their allegiances to the architectural and relational structures of paramountcy lead to ambivalent critiques of sexual violence and asymmetrical power at best. Democratic futures appear feeble.

The film *Kudrat* produces a similar affect. It contrasts two archetypal spaces of Hindi cinema—the court and the haveli—in the cold case trial of a feudal Choudhury (played again by Raaj Kumar), who raped and killed Chandramukhi (Hema Malini), his servant's daughter, which led to the accidental death of her lover, Madho (Rajesh Khanna). In the film's present, Choudhury's accuser, Paro (Hema Malini), and legal prosecutor, Mohan (Rajesh Khanna), are the dead lovers reincarnated. The crimes of the haveli are not, however, resolved through the arbitrations of a modern court but by a return to the haveli when Chandramukhi's skeleton is found walled into the attic. An older retributive justice swallows the haveli's stairwell, attic, and its hidden skeleton in flames when a fire consumes not only the incriminating evidence but also the Choudhury's daughter (Priya Rajvansh), who is his defense attorney. In court, a grieving Choudhury offers a grandstanding acceptance of his culpability as a rapist and killer. He anoints Mohan his new legatee, and Mohan touches the Choudhury's feet reverentially. The film presents the criminal nobleman sympathetically as a benign aristocrat guilty of but one past aberration. It recuperates a sense of honor for the haveli's patronage as the camera pans slowly across the weeping faces of the public at court—more *praja* (subjects) than *bahumat* (democratic majority). Although human agents drive the recuperation of this social order, it is finally restored by the inexorable forces of *kudrat*, or "nature." The past in *Kudrat* (as also in *Madhumati*) demands that crimes condoned by patriarchical and class-ridden societies be settled outside secular forums of justice. The end of an era plays out in the perspectival melodramas of socially segregated protagonists who are brought together by acts of violence, rape, madness, and death, leaving the film's characters and its spectators too emotionally depleted for any hope that a democratic future might portend.[118]

In Hindi cinema, the haveli exhibits the ritualized traditions and terrors of hierarchical social relations. As an open-air space (*hava*) that is also enclosed and partitioned (*haola*), the chowk in a cinematic haveli represents the socialities that are subject to the structure's segregated spaces and hoary traditions while also being exposed to the winds of change. In Hindi-Urdu–language films, these enclosures shelter acts of criminality against women, but Bombay cinema's obsessive return to such sites gives melodramatic voice and form to the suffering and dead women hidden away in a haveli's enclosures, making the structures an expressive rather than a silencing location in film. In using the haveli to produce such meanings, Hindi cinema far exceeds the social history of its architectural form. It offers an affective meditation on Indian history by working against the colonizer's material devaluation of the Indian haveli and remythifying the structure with Islamic overtones. Hindi cinema also contaminates its nostalgia for havelis by making them into architectures abhorrent to modernity with their assumptions of dynastic loyalty and patriarchal authority, although these allegiances seem to come from a place that is neither unimaginable nor obsolete in postcolonial India.

Statist regulations of India's territorial space do not help us grasp the numerous ways in which its people have experienced, negotiated, or remembered the land's history. Discrepancies between regulations that sought to produce a territorially unified democratic nation and the more inchoate, ambivalently processed, variably enforced, sluggish, and traumatic social readjustments from feudal to democratic structures in India create asynchronicities that disable direct correlations between the nation's politico-economic history and its culture's or cinema's affective content. Affective histories are important because they tell us how popular accounts diverge from political chronologies as registers of change. Affective histories carry different assumptions about the continuing imbalance between (purportedly equitable and legal) secular rights and (birth- and caste-based) dynastic rights, or between social contract and natural law, when a territory is hailed as a nation. This is evident when we compare the official histories presented by Films Division documentaries against the affective histories presented by commercial Hindi-Urdu films. In this chapter, I have written about Hindi cinema's use of the city of Lucknow and the architectural form of the haveli as an image and icon to link those representations back to formative historical periods when the significance of the city and the built structure was violently split for an expanding mass audience, which included colonizers and the colonized, Muslims and Hindus, men and women. The photographic and cinematic imagination of Lucknow and havelis far outlasted the sociopolitical ascendance of the city and the structure. A spatial film historiography allows us to thread Hindi cinema's representations of a city space and an architectural form back to their translation from locations and structures into affective sensibilities and visual forms.

PART III

COMMODIFIED SPACES

5

GLOBAL:
FROM BOLLYWOOD LOCATIONS
TO FILM STOCK RATIONS

A nation-state's fiscal boundaries and its population's spatial imaginaries change with the adoption of neoliberal rationalities. In film, visual traces of privatization and globalization present themselves in an altering mise-en-scène: how and where films are shot and what they look like begin to alter. Concomitant changes in the film industry's technological and professional practices and in the material conditions of its workers additionally force us to think of the filmic mise-en-scène as an aspect of labor's social space. This is connected to, but distinct from, globalization's textual trace. My fifth and final argument for a spatial film historiography is founded on the complex roles played by a film industry's social composition, pre-production practices, and industry cultures in transforming actual locations into visual images when a state privatizes its national economy.

Marx lays bare the causal connection between economy and culture. For us, what matters is the thread of expression. It is not the economic origins of culture that will be presented, but the expression of economy in its culture.

WALTER BENJAMIN, THE ARCADES PROJECT

When Gulshan Kumar of T-Series was around, we used to shoot together, we enjoyed ourselves in a group, there was a sense of belonging, there was no tension. Now it's all a new-new environment. People stay to themselves.

T-Series ke Gulshan Kumar thé jab, saath shooting karte thé, ek group main enjoy karte thé, ek apnapan lagta tha, koi tension nahin tha. Ab sab naya-naya mahoal ho gaya hai. Sab apney-apney main rahtey hain.

RUKHSANA, JUNIOR ARTIST (SUPERCLASS)

Sonu Srivastava, who describes himself as a "coordinator, choreographer, and business manager" of Bollywood dancers, notes that Boney Kapoor's *Bewafaa* (2005) was the first film to bring twenty white Russian women and twenty black British women ("white girls" and "black girls" in his parlance) to India, rather than going abroad for its shoot. In his words, "Nowadays foreigners are essential for every movie . . . even if it's Holi, there's foreigners" (*Ab har movie main foreigners zaroori hai . . . Holi bhi ho, to bhi foreigners*), referring to the "Balam Pichkari" song from the film *Yeh Jawaani Hai Diwani* (Ayan Mukherjee, 2013).[1] The sequence depicts rambunctious celebrations of the Indian spring festival of Holi, with lead actors Deepika Padukone, Ranbir Kapoor, and Kalki Koechlin dancing at the center of a young crowd in which white Caucasians mingle unremarkably with Indians. The song is set on a street in Himachal Pradesh but shot in Kashmir. To those in the know, this is a Hindu festival being staged along the lanes of a predominantly Muslim territory that has been historically fractured by Indian state violence and local civil and militant rebellion. In order to shoot in this location, Dharma Productions would have had to control local crowds, recruit Indian and foreign dancers, and get shooting permits from the Jammu and Kashmir Regional Transport Office (J&K RTO), the Srinagar Municipal Corporation, and the Local Police Commissioner in Kashmir.

Whereas crowd management for location shooting is as old as filmmaking in India, and Hindi films have sought domestic and foreign locations for fantasy and song sequences at least since the 1960s,[2] extensive location-based filmmaking and generous budgets for location shoots are recent to mainstream films. *Bhopal Express* (1999), *Lagaan* (2001), and *Dil Chahta Hai* (2001), which use location shoots with synchronized sound (or sync sound, not widely used in the Indian film industry until the late 1990s, as discussed below) supervised by sound engineer and mixer Nakul Kamte, are repeatedly invoked as trendsetters.[3] Industry insiders benchmark the rising dominance of sync sound, location shoots, and cosmopolitan backgrounds in Bollywood to the entry of corporations such as Reliance BIG Entertainment, Walt Disney India, UTV, Eros, and Studio 18 into the commercial film industry. Efforts to make India an alluring place for the capital generated by domestic and international film shoots have been of a piece with the expanding privatization of India's economy following decades of state protectionism, with the country's central and state governments now devising ways to market India as an ideal filmmaking location. As Ben Goldsmith and Tom O'Regan note, a mix of factors contribute to making countries attractive to international and domestic audiovisual productions, such as their "locations (including their built and natural environments), their film services infrastructure (including studio complexes and related facilities and personnel), and an international-production-friendly context often underwritten by an explicit policy framework."[4] The India Film Commission of the Indian Ministry of Information and Broadcasting (I&B Ministry) hopes to create single-window clearance for Indian location filming in order to attract lucrative foreign productions to India, to facilitate domestic shoots, and to eliminate or reduce the myriad inconsistent laws pertaining to filming across the country's different states.

At the time of writing, a system of single-window clearance is not yet entirely operational in India, and conditions for shooting on location remain far from seamless. Local productions receive limited tax exemptions—for instance, Marathi-language shows receive tax credit for shooting in Maharashtra, while Hindi-language Bollywood films produced by the Maharashtra-based film industry do not—and in general filming in India's major cities remains challenging given the country's bureaucratic and political obstructionism, cinephilic public,[5] heavy traffic, and noise congestion. Most states in India still lack tax incentives and require several levels of clearance for location shoots. But 1998 initiated structural changes for filmmaking in India when it was granted official status as an "industry" by the Indian government, ushering in the entry of banks, insurance companies, corporate finance, and international investments into the industry on a rapidly expanding scale. A growing body of work from film scholars such as Adrian Athique and Douglas Hill, Anustup Basu, Anupama Chopra, Rachel Dwyer, Rajinder Dudrah, Tejaswini Ganti, Ajay Gehlawat, Sangita Gopal, Nitin Govil, Anandam P. Kavoori, Aswin Punathambekar, Amit Rai, Shanti Kumar, and others shows that India's economic liberalization and its socioeconomic impetus are influencing Hindi cinema's form, content, production, distribution, and exhibition practices, while also lending the industry a self-reflexive brand awareness.[6] International familiarity with the term "Bollywood" over the past two decades is itself a sign of the industry's rapid commodification and globalization, as discussed by Ashish Rajadhyaksha and Madhava Prasad.[7]

The move to privatize the industry has thrust Indian cinema into a dynamic period of change with regard to location filming, as a zealous adoption of film aesthetics favoring real locations and sync sound emerges despite the challenges of dealing with India's teeming crowds, loud cities, cultures of risk and informality, and labyrinthine bureaucracy. As India's film industries move away from an informal economy to a more organized (but still semiformal) economic sector, Hindi cinema's backgrounds are changing both in terms of their "aesthetics of frame" and their "cultures of production." John Caldwell introduces these terms to analyze film and television space in Los Angeles, defining the aesthetics of frame as the "perceptual and cognitive frame of the viewer created via the mise-en-scène" through elements such as the placement of cameras and actors, the blocking of action, and the creation of perspective.[8] In variance, production cultures cluster around work sites, filming locations, sound stages, and production studios. Trade talks, off-the-lot deals, social rituals, and iconography through which film workers organize their "turf" are included in the latter category.

Caldwell's conceptual armature is useful in threading through the ways in which location shooting has an impact on cinema's aesthetics as well as its cultures of production during a film industry's corporatization. Traditionally, popular Hindi cinema's aesthetics of space have been considered unique because of a Hindi film's epic length, musical interludes, interrupted format of narrative and spectacle, melodramatic content, and nonrealist style. Its traditional infrastructure of "unevenly developed market capitalism" and "haphazard and individualized mode of production" funded not by banks but by several "fragmented and decentralized . . . independent financiers, producers, distributors and exhibitors," at odds with Hollywood's practice of vertical integration, have been considered determining factors of Hindi cinema's discontinuous aesthetics.[9] Coeval reconfigurations of Bollywood's textual and economic spheres with the entry of corporates into the industry provide a compelling opportunity to assess the relationship between Hindi cinema's textual spaces on the one hand, and its industrial and professional spaces on the other.[10]

Stylistically, contemporary Bollywood films are beginning to espouse a strong preference for location-based realism, whether we consider debut films such as *Masaan* (Neeraj Ghaywan, 2015), shot extensively in Benaras, or productions fronted by Bollywood stalwarts such as Shah Rukh Khan in *Raees* (Rahul Dholakia, 2017), shot in Ahmedabad in Gujarat and Navi Mumbai in Maharashtra, among other places. Following the "thread of expression" that connects a nation's economy to its culture (using Walter Benjamin's phrase), in this chapter I focus on the culture of location shooting in Indian cinema to study India's paradigmatic shift from economic protectionism to privatization. I interpret "culture" broadly, just as Benjamin does—that is, not to refer exclusively to a visual text, but rather to its cultures of production and underlying assumptions of lifestyle, consumption, professional, and leisure practices. As cultures of filmmaking reorganize with the corporatization of the Bombay film industry, they inevitably entangle as well with the ground realities of Indian cities. In filming *Raees*, for instance, Maharashtra's far-right pro-Marathi political party, Maharashtra Navnirman Sena, shut down the film's shooting because *Raees*'s female lead, Mahira Khan, is from Pakistan. Maharashtra Navnirman Sena condemned all production companies using Pakistani talent and crew as antinationalist during a time of escalating Indo-Pakistan tensions and pro-Hindutva sentiments.[11] Stalled productions, political and street-level negotiations, and covert filming locations are part of the story of how the privatization and corporatization of the Hindi film industry is unfolding in India today, to reorganize its production practices.

Conceiving of filmed space once again as the tensile relationship between on-screen spaces and social spaces, which together constitute cinema's visual appearance and its institutional materiality, I propose that location shooting registers politico-economic transitions with great acuity because it hinges on multiple factors. These include the relative politico-economic stability of places that invite onsite filming, regulatory incentives that attract production crews to the place, aesthetic commitments of filmmakers and industrial predilections for shooting on location, industrial access to necessary technology, and street-level interactions conducive to shooting in public spaces. As I will show, cinema's heterogeneous artifactual status—as a regulated and profit-making commodity, technological apparatus, representational medium, and employment opportunity—links the changing look of Hindi cinema's mise-en-scène to the current commodification of land and leisure, and a shifting social range of Bollywood's professional workers in globalizing India.

In this sense, a film's location and the appearance of its background actors are more than textual elements of a film, although they are also that. The circulation of infrastructural material (such as film stock, cameras, sound-recording technologies) and resources (such as institutional finance) play a significant part in shaping the industry's structural conditions for filming on location. The composition and appearance of a film's background encodes, in this case, larger socioeconomic histories of India's transition from an era of economic protectionism and high taxation under a quasisocialist secular state to the current phase of aggressive privatization, rising neo-fascism, and the commodification of everyday life. I explore the practice of location filming and the appearance of cinematic backgrounds as an expression of these clusters of factors, paying particular attention to film's taxation as a commodity, statist assumptions regarding consumerism and leisure underlying those regimes of taxation, social attitudes toward wealth and travel sustaining a film's background cues, and the social classes involved in producing and consuming a film's geographical canvas.

To construct a story of this vast socius behind the particular appearance of locations and backgrounds in film, I draw on historical research, policy analysis, textual analysis, and interviews with below-the-line Bollywood workers conducted during my research visits to Mumbai in 2009 and 2013. I prefer the term "socius" to "habitus" to capture a habitus-in-formation, although French sociologist Pierre Bourdieu's concept of habitus as the realm of a person's disposition, tastes, and behaviors reflecting socialized norms remains a primary reference point.[12] As we will see, the socius or dispersed social body implicated in Bollywood's location work, with its diffuse class base and its attendant cultural norms, is as yet too amorphous and undefined to express a unified habitus. In Tejaswini Ganti's phrase, the "gentrification" of Bollywood's production culture and visual image is part of tectonic socioeconomic changes under India's globalization, which leads every film image and production practice to unspool into a display of the complex transformations under way in the country's social spaces.[13] Analyzing individual films for their representations of a place does not give us an accurate sense of how the practice of location shooting is part of this broader restructuring of India's social matrix as the nation turns to neoliberalism and a free market economy. An account of location filming today is necessarily part of a networked story of the forces of consumerism transforming the appearance, habitation, and governance of public places in India. A dilating cultural sphere of Brand India, discussed further, is commodifying the very notion of place in a manner that redefines the work of Bollywood's below-the-line professionals who are involved in location filming.

Designations such as "above-the-line" and "below-the-line" work point to the film industry's intrinsically spatial framework. The term "below-the-line" refers literally to the line drawn in a film's budget, separating above-the-line salaries of talent and management (typically of a film's director, producers, writers, and lead actors) from below-the-line production expenses of technical crews, camera equipment, film stock, film printing, travel, location costs, and background actors. Typically, above-the-line contracts are negotiated, while below-the-line wages are fixed. A line producer or line manager—common in Hollywood but nonexistent in the Hindi film industry until its formalization in 1998—is the person who straddles the line by planning budgets.[14] In an informal industry known for its disregard for scripts, paperwork, budgets, and written contracts, Hindi cinema's production lines have always been more malleable, provisional, and opaque than those in Hollywood. The industry's corporatization has led to attempts at formalizing and rationalizing the industry into discrete areas of professional competence. But such attempts at streamlining location shoots emerge alongside habituated social arrangements within the nation's film industries and cities, in a manner that complicates both the new forces of economic and professional change and the preconditionings of social habit. Current redistributions of work between above- and below-the-line professionals involved in location shoots are therefore an important locus where the forces of corporatization and commodification confront all sorts of local pushbacks and vernacular adaptations. Line producers—who supervise everyday details of location shoots—are at the liminal, mundane, and negotiated spaces of this encounter. As the industry and the nation turn to free market economics, the line producer's centrality to defining Bollywood's new professional practices on the ground is belied by their largely taken-for-granted work. To foreground their centrality, I let the line producers, location managers, and background coordinators working in India's mainstream Bollywood industry take center stage as the lead protagonists of this chapter.

In 2002, when India's share of the global traffic in tourism was at a stagnant 0.38 percent, Indian Ministry of Tourism's Joint Secretary Amitabh Kant was tasked with selling India to the world. As a combined effort that brought together talents from the private and public sectors of India's film, tourism, and hospitality industries, Kant oversaw a highly promoted "Incredible !ndia" campaign—the exclamation point of the "I" in India eye-catchingly dotted with a large red bindi. The campaign had the following vision statement: "Put India on the world tourism map and develop it as a premier holiday destination for high-yielding tourists; India should be a global brand, with worldwide brand recognition and strong brand equity, especially in the trade and among the target audience."[15] The campaign's targeted audience of "high-yielding tourists" refers to extravagant "high net worth" visitors, using a global managerial phrase designed to normalize extreme class and wealth differentials promoted by free market economics.

Of a piece with various industrial shifts under way in the 2000s, the Incredible India campaign expanded and streamlined India's international tourism, updated its image, and upgraded its technological outreach through websites and advertising campaigns. In the advertising business, it is held up as an early and highly successful example of public-private collaboration in India, between the Indian Ministry of Tourism, the advertising agency Ogilvy & Mather, Indian filmmakers, and the Experience India Society, which is a private-sector partnership of luxury hoteliers such as the Taj, Oberoi, Hyatt, and others. Bharat Bala, director of the first of many campaign films for the Incredible India project (available online),[16] characterizes the Incredible India shorts by noting that "India cannot be thought of without acknowledging the irony of it being an ancient country with a modern outlook."[17]

India as a land of contradictions plays into an old trope, as we have seen in discussions of colonial-era nontheatrical films, Films Division shorts, and transnational feature productions. Yet the Incredible India campaign films—depicting the tactile movements of Indian dancers in desert landscapes, and sculpted bodies in yoga poses on mountains, all cut to the pounding beats of Indian drums and classical ragas—are experienced as ecstatic and novel. This is in part because the tourism campaign shorts offer a self-exoticizing image that is made by the cosmopolitan Indian consumer for their global counterparts, using what Anustup Basu calls a "geo-televisual aesthetic."[18] Discussing India's contemporary media sensorium, film scholars Anustup Basu and Amit

FIGURE 5.1 Incredible India poster in Salar Jung Museum, Ahmedabad. Courtesy of the Baishyas. (ABOVE)
FIGURE 5.2 Incredible India poster on a bus in Alappuzha, Kerala. Courtesy of Vivek Shreedhar M. (BELOW)

Rai find it useful to shift away from discussions of Bollywood within a "representational frame" tied to the content of discrete films, and instead evaluate the industry in terms of its "assemblages" of global media.[19] Unlike Basu and Rai, I am not concerned here with theorizing the networked and synesthetic affects of global media, nor with the somatic nature of media consumption under globalization. I also retain a sense that individual films matter in their specificities in addition to the significance of their role within multiple assemblages. But I am persuaded that we must think of Bollywood as a media event dispersed across a range of products, platforms, and experiences, particularly because Bollywood is not working as an industry in isolation in the transformation of India into Brand India.[20]

Bharat Bala Productions

The professional itineraries of the people who are currently setting the standards for filming Indian locations demonstrate that Bollywood is part of a larger media assemblage by the simple fact that the same people work across different media platforms and industries. Bharat Bala's production company can serve as a nodal institution in tracing some of these intersections in the contemporary transformations of Bollywood's aesthetic image and production practices. Bala directed the Incredible India campaign films, in addition to codirecting and producing music videos for the songs "Maa Tujhe Salaam" ("Mother, I Salute You," about India as motherland) and "Jana Gana Mana" (India's national anthem) with Kanika Myer. "Maa Tujhe Salaam" was the lead single in A. R. Rahman's first nonfilm music album *Vande Mataram* (translated as "I bow to thee, Mother" by Sri Aurobindo Ghosh), which was released in 1997 to mark the fiftieth anniversary of India's Independence. Bala's "Jana Gana Mana" video was released in 2000 to commemorate fifty years of India as a republic. Both music videos were composed as riffs on India's unofficial and official national anthems and proved tremendously popular when televised across India. They continue to garner enthusiastic digital audiences on YouTube.[21]

Rahman, who is Tamil and Hindi cinema's innovative and celebrated music composer, came to international prominence with his Oscar-winning musical score for *Slumdog Millionaire* (Danny Boyle, 2008) in 2009. Strikingly, in his music video for *Vande Mataram*, there are no images of urban India. Tibetan monks, Kathakali dancers, Rajasthani women, costumed tribals, and turbaned villagers appear against auburn sunsets, ochre sand dunes, and yellow skies in a romanticized display of indigenous exotica. The short film intersperses close-ups of people looking directly into the camera with strong diagonal and geometrical long shots of figures cutting across the visual frame in static and mobile patterns, while holding aloft the fluttering tricolor Indian flag. Rahman strides across the frame in an open white button-up shirt that picks up the stark whites of several frames. He sings a Hindi-language song about his homeland, saluting the nation as his Maa, Amma, and Mother while "Vande Mataram" is repeated in the chorus, or *sthayi*. "Vande Mataram" is the Sanskrit phrase that anchors Bankim Chandra Chatterjee's rousing poetic composition in praise of the wealth, beauty, and geographical variety of the land that would be India.[22] The song was adopted by Indian nationalists during the nation's freedom struggle and became independent India's national song alongside the anthem "Jana Gana Mana." With its images of India's borders, provinces, and marginalized populations, Bala's music video infuses the mobile aesthetics of a television commercial with the weight of nationalist sentiment.

Vande Mataram's release in 1997 as part of India's top-selling nonfilm music album hints at the admixture of nationalism and commercialism that has characterized globalizing India. As Christiane Brosius points out, "While capitalism was previously identified with a lack of patriotism, members of the new middle classes now consider themselves as motors of a new national revitalization, both in terms of economy and moral values."[23] At the same time, nationalism and patriotism have been genies in a bottle that, once released, are not entirely domesticated by the forces of commercialism. The commodification of nationalism under right-wing populism has encountered its twists and turns in the extended story of the Incredible India campaign. Accompanying the branding of India for high-net-worth foreign tourists was a second campaign aimed at domestic audiences titled the *Athithi Devo Bhava* project. Explaining the phrase, Amitabh Kant says, "Parallel to 'Incredible India,' a complementary campaign, entitled *'Atithi Devo Bhava'* or 'Guest is God,' was launched domestically to create a sense of pride in India as a tourism destination and qualitatively improve the services provided by taxi drivers, guides, immigration and customs officials. The campaign, using India's leading film actors—the popular Shah Rukh Khan and now, the versatile Aamir Khan—has been broadened, focusing on aspects such as garbage collection and stopping defacement of monuments."[24] Indeed, this campaign revives an older Emergency-era promotion to teach Indians proper etiquette around foreign tourists launched by Films Division in 1977, as I discuss elsewhere.[25]

As the campaign has expanded under Prime Minister Narendra Modi's government, messages of nationalist pride are also harnessed in promotions of the "Swachha Bharat," or Clean India, campaign and in the National Movement for Clean Ganga, or *Namami Gange* campaign.[26] Worthy as these goals are, the promotional and inspirational images and music used with the campaigns gloss over several realities. As Aileen Blaney and Chinar Shah observe in their analysis of contemporary photographic protest art critical of government-sponsored campaigns, in order to promote a cleaner India, the Modi government imposed a 0.5 percent service tax on the population.[27] Additionally, presenting public cleanliness as a civic issue with strong India-as-Hindu overtones (conveyed by the campaign's Sanskritized anthems) hides India's caste-based infrastructure of sanitation, which rests overwhelmingly on a Dalit workforce with no protection of labor rights, a theme explored in Chaitanya Tamhane's *Court* (2014).[28] Concern with public cleanliness—reminiscent of the coerced urban beautification projects under the Indian Emergency (1975–1977), which involved forced evictions and slum clearance—extends under the Modi administration to politically motivated panic around cultural "pollution" (*sanskritik pradushan*). Demands for cultural and linguistic "cleansing" involve draconian revisions of school curricula and national history as well as attacks on the democratic governance of India's leading educational and cultural institutions. They sanction discourses of ethnic cleansing and increasingly violent assaults on India's free press, creative artists, social activists, and minorities, particularly Muslims and Dalits, on the grounds of maintaining the purity of India's Hindu past and Aryan lineage.

In other words, while the goal of cleanliness and environmental consciousness is laudable, under the current administration the mission is announced on the backs of the government's antidemocratic and pro-Hindutva agenda. In this charged environment, Aamir Khan, Bollywood star and celebrity spokesman of the *Atithi Devo Bhava* campaign, became a target of cyberbullying when he expressed his (Muslim and Hindu) family's anxieties about the atmosphere of rising religious intolerance in India condoned by the Modi government.[29] The abrupt termination of his contract as India's brand ambassador for the campaign and his replacement with the iconic Amitabh Bachhan and Priyanka Chopra clarified that for the Modi regime at least, the commodification of India's image could not harbor any criticisms of right-wing ideologies.

Sunitha Ram and Kaushik Guha

Despite such collusions with the nation's "saffronization" (right-wing indoctrination), the private industry's collaboration with state organizations in producing India's new image is led not by nationalist ideologues but by career professionals. Codes of corporate management and professionalization, while not unaffected by national or local politics, hew to different priorities that produce disavowals of dominant political trends among those in charge of filming locations (and filming on locations) in India and abroad. Sunitha Ram, who was a producer with Nirvana Films when I interviewed her in 2013, had worked with Bharat Bala Productions on A. R. Rahman's *Vande Mataram* in 1997. She went on to work as line producer for the commercial feature films *Taare Zameen Par* (2007), shot on location in Bombay and Panchgani, India,[30] and *Dhobi Ghat / Mumbai Diaries* (2010), shot in Bombay. She was also executive producer of *Zindagi Na Milegi Dobara* (ZNMD, 2011), shot in San Fermin, Spain. Kaushik Guha, who was on Bala's team for the Incredible India film campaigns, subsequently worked as production manager for the Indian segments of *Eat,*

Pray, Love (2010), *Zero Dark Thirty* (2012), and *The Reluctant Fundamentalist* (2012). He was also line producer for *Delhi Belly* (2011) and unit production manager for *Life of Pi* (2012). Bharat Bala Productions served as Ram's and Guha's platform to launch into subsequent high-profile projects that required filming locations as well as handling local and international film crews in India and Indian crews abroad.[31] Professionals such as Ram and Guha act as cultural translators and creators of a new aesthetic of territorial visuality within a globalizing Indian media industry. They have little to no personal investment in politics, although the governing political regimes shape their working environment in ways described below.

These professionals mediate between transnational multimedia corporations and local operatives by using their familiarity with both worlds to develop globally competitive national standards for location shooting in India. Guha notes that (through his companies Moon Rise Productions and Kaushik Guha Productions) he has been able to handle requests considered unorthodox in India fifteen years ago. He was able to provide "intangibles" to Ang Lee's production team for *The Life of Pi*, he argues, by contributing to design decisions and finding places to park the crew's eighty-seven tractor-trailers near the shoot location, which was an unusual demand by Indian standards at the time. Prior to the recent compartmentalization of professional competencies, art directors of Hindi films rarely delegated design decisions to anyone. And Bollywood stars still do not park vanities next to filming locations for fear of being mobbed. An increasing influx of international crews shooting in India began to stretch the resources and capacities of local operatives with their demands in the early 2000s. Guha thrived in this environment because of his ability to bridge international standards in production practices with local contacts and a familiarity with India's ground realities. He has evolved modes of visually presenting India to his clients by combining techniques used in the United States (of digital images and Google Earth coordinates displaying film locations) and Britain (of traditional paper briefs and descriptions) with a fluency in the working parameters of Indian hotels, local art and transportation departments, model coordinators, and junior artists.

Similarly, New York–based Anadil Hossain (a Bangladeshi-British expatriate), president of the production company Dillywood, line producer for *Kal Ho Naa Ho* (2003) and *The Namesake* (2006), coproducer of *Darjeeling Limited* (2007), and executive producer of *Kabhi Alvida Na Kahna* (2006), speaks of her role in assisting Indian crews in the United States as a "training of the minds."[32] *Kal Ho Naa Ho* was one of the first in a wave of Bollywood films to shoot entirely in the United States and Canada. According to Hossain and location manager Joseph White, *Kal Ho Naa Ho* was mostly shot in Toronto, which doubled for New York, because of its generous tax breaks.[33] Ten days of exteriors were shot in New York (particularly in Brooklyn and Queens) until traffic gridlocks created by New York City's South Asian cabdrivers and a stern cautionary letter from the governor's office persuaded the crew to use New York primarily for its skylines and exteriors, while decamping to shoot in Toronto. Hossain ran *Kal Ho Naa Ho* like an American indie film by creating a template for its production crew. She helped them anticipate factors that were not a typical part of Hindi cinema's regimen, such as conducting a technical reconnaissance of locations, prelighting tests, camera tests, viewing dailies, and so on, all of which are now routine practice in Hindi films but were not so twenty years ago.

The sheer volume of Indian films shot abroad today forces Indian location managers to adapt to different cultures of production. Bollywood's sizable international location shoots, too numerous to list here, may be conveyed by the fact that VisitBritain, the United Kingdom's national tourism agency, published a "Bollywood map of Britain" to coincide with the International Indian Film Academy Awards hosted in Sheffield, South Yorkshire, in 2007. The map displayed prominent Bollywood films shot on location across the United Kingdom (with several featuring the star Shah Rukh Khan). To publicize the map, Tom Wright, chief executive of VisitBritain, cited the growth in tourism among India's new middle classes in hyperbolic terms by observing, "Although the average Indian earns only about £300 each year, the fast-growing middle classes—numbering 50 million—have an average disposable income of £12,000. By 2025, it is predicted that 41 per cent of the population—about 83 million people—will be from the middle classes."[34] The claim that fifty million people in India have an expendable income of £12,000 is absurd for various reasons, including its unverifiability given how many Indians remain outside the tax net.[35] But it confirms the giddy enthusiasm surrounding the Indian market's consumerist potential and anticipatory grabs to exploit it.

For Indian filmmakers and film production units, a steep learning curve in dealing with production practices from other countries occurs in lockstep with a working knowledge of the ground realities of the Bombay film industry. In other words, whereas economic and political vectors had to shift to make India an attractive proposition for domestic and international location shoots, such cosmopolitanism exists alongside a familiarity with local work habits. In an analysis of Hollywood's use of India as a location to represent Indian and other "location-proximate" places, Nitin Govil discusses Take One Productions as a prominent line producer for foreign shoots in India, credited with films such as *Alexander* (2004), *Mission: Impossible—Ghost Protocol* (2011), and *Life of Pi* (2012).[36] The company itself, however, is not a self-contained unit but dependent on contracting out work to a large number of individuals. Take One's apparent streamlining fronts a more chaotic range of negotiations between professionals who operate at different levels of the local location-management chain, interfacing with both international production companies and ground-level operatives. Line production companies like Take One tend to be place-holders for subcontracted individuals navigating between international crews and networks of local workers, who have location-specific knowledge and are adept at India's informal modes of sociality. Line production companies front complex interactions on the ground as Bombay-based productions use func-tionaries operative in regions neighboring the city, such as Pune, Madh Island, and Wai, that are more viable for outdoor location shoots. Making an often-heard comment in India, Ankit Mehta, CEO of Inega Models (which repre-sents Indian and international models in India's media industries) remarks that "doing business in India is about building relationships."[37]

Even as the process of getting permissions and the management of locations gets streamlined in a corporatizing industry, film director Tarsem Singh points out that permissions "mean nothing on the grassroots level" in India, referring to his experience of shooting *The Fall* (2006) partially in Rajasthan.[38] His point is that any union member, police officer, or government employee in India can potentially appear on location to demand more money or more paperwork to get more money. Director Govind Menon euphemistically refers to this as India's "additional location fee."[39] In the 1960s, these "additional" location fees, or bribes, were another layer of corruption exacerbated by the nonavailability of institutional financing for the film industry, which encouraged the entry of a range of off-the-record monetary transactions. Recent efforts to create a single window for permissions streamlines the process and reduces the num-ber of people who can legitimately claim to be representatives of municipal authorities, law enforcement agencies, and political and workers unions. For Tarsem Singh, however, even in the new millennium, "there's only two ways you can shoot on location in India . . . absolute control or no control. In the middle, you are screwed. And one can turn very quickly into another."[40] The *Bourne Identity* franchise, according to Singh, went with the "absolute con-trol" method. Referring specifically to *The Bourne Supremacy* (Paul Greengrass, 2004), shot partially in Goa, Singh observes that they acquired their filming permissions from local authorities but sent a decoy team to a separate location while a smaller crew did the actual filming at a second permitted location.[41] Singh himself claims to prefer the no control model.

Such strategies of coping with the unexpected in India make vernacular ground-level adaptations a significant part of location filming in the country despite the industry's top-down corporate makeover. This is also why subcontractors and middlemen remain key. To get to the complex socius involved in the film industry's management of filming locations and background actors as the industry gets corporatized, I interviewed over thirty-five professionals in the field between 2009 and 2013. My interviews and field notes revealed a significant socioeconomic shift in the composition of those involved in below-the-line work related to location filming. As I suggest, these changes reflect the amorphous nature of India's new middle class, in which people with varying degrees of job security and disposable income lay claim to the imagined life-style of consumerism and social mobility. The negotiation of social and class difference among Bollywood's new professionals in location shooting belies the Bollywood blockbuster's on-screen depiction of seamlessly cosmopolitan places, where "transnational . . . *gopinis*" gyrate in the background when Bolly-wood stars take center stage.[42] Despite the fact that today, a few years since my field trips, there is more variation in commercial Bombay cinema's content, the blockbuster films continue to favor images of extreme wealth, financial mobil-ity, and a global cosmopolitanism that is connoted by international locations and white or multiracially international background actors. The class of Indi-ans that is excluded from these backdrops nevertheless remain active producers of the images, in that they constitute a critical part of the industry's below-the-line labor. As we will see, accounting for them makes evident that the visual commodification of place involves workers who are coopted into collaborating in their own visual erasure, even as they remain vocal and active defenders of their social rights and professional contributions.

THE SOCIUS OF LOCATION FILMING

Unlike a film's above-the-line personnel, such as the film's director, producer, or lead actors, who can get away with interacting primarily with industry pro-fessionals during the filming process, the location management crew has to negotiate with a broader section of the Indian public as they acquire permits, arrange transportation, cast background actors, and coordinate crowds. The significance of this larger and more inaccessible socius that defines the terms of filming in the city asserted itself during my research visits to Bombay in 2009 and 2013, when, depending on the time of day, it was not unusual to be stuck in traffic for two hours to get to a thirty-minute interview. This was particularly true when traveling from Worli in the wealthy southwestern part of the city to northern suburbs such as Kandivali and Borivali, or Oshiwara in Jogeshwari West, where many below-the-line workers have their offices and homes. The experience recalled advice from Ted Skillman (executive producer, *Bollywood Hero*, 2009) to US-based filmmakers interested in shooting in Bombay that they should "never change location during the day."[43]

Gathering information about Bollywood's new professionals in location management was an introduction to the city's transportation system and the sociality of its public spaces. In 2013, during the months leading up to India's national elections, in which Narendra Modi of the Bharatiya Janata Party (BJP) swept into political office as the nation's prime minister, I found myself repeatedly in the midst of volatile conversations that revealed a groundswell of rage against India's past. In this imagined past, Hindus were India's persecuted victims, secularism and liberalism were emasculating political compromises, and the tolerance of difference a derisible weakness. The Modi campaign's nationalistic and antiminority Hindutva rhetoric, combined with Congress leader Rahul Gandhi's ineffectual opposition, was bringing about the death of nuance in ways that have become familiar in the United States under Donald Trump's presidency. In contrast to the political polarizations, I encountered a shared public mode of navigating the city's sprawl by using networks of local knowledge and social relations, which exerted a countervailing force on the pervasive nationalism of intolerance. This sociality, a surviving locus of civil and civic life in the polemics of a politically polarized nation, emerged whenever I looked for my appointment venues. Visits to the frequently provisional workspaces of Bombay's below-the-line workers were not guided by addresses, GPS maps, or street names but by conversations with strangers, references to mundane landmarks, older and idiomatic street names, people's memories of streets, and shared mobile phones.

The contact addresses I received were short on street numbers and names but long on a list of adjacent landmarks. Paras Mehta, whose visiting card describes him as a "Pre-Production Controller, Line Producer, Model Co-ordination, Models for Background, Junior Artist Coordinator, Suppliers [*sic*] of Foreigners, Suppliers of Nigerians, Suppliers of Chinese" (more on this job description further), located his office as being near the Royal Hardware Store, above the Maruti courier shop, beside Jagannath Bank, and next to Hotel Bhavna. When finding his office proved elusive, my taxi driver requested Mehta to meet us at Hotel Bhavna. After speaking with three passersby and twice to Mehta himself on my cell phone, I found that the hotel was more of a bar in a back alley. There, a man gestured at me to follow him, and through narrow lanes we reached a room with no apparent access to the main road. This, I surmised, was the reception to Mehta's office. I would not have chanced upon it without intermediaries who translated the address through social networks rather than numerical coordinates. My silent guide watched a television exposé on the forced imprisonment of women while I sat with mounting apprehension about my position. Shortly after, however, Mehta appeared, dispelling my anxieties and displaying more generosity than I had accommodated in the narrow confines of his office or of my circumspection.

Possessing the knowledge to navigate public spaces in India, which is essential to location shoots, brings us to the highly gendered, classed, and ethnically coded nature of public spaces in cities. Accelerated demographic mobility and gentrification of India's urban spaces have produced combustible gendered and classed encounters. Social spaces are charged with the micropolitics of individual desires at a time when a privatizing economy brings new job opportunities and puts the dream of belonging to India's middle class within the reach of many, despite chronic income differentials and class and caste hierarchies. In location filming, for instance, the industry's corporatization has dispersed location work, which in India was supervised by the film's executive producer and art director until the 1990s. Bollywood's location shoots now involve line producers, location managers, unit production managers, production controllers, sync-sound engineers, sound-lock security personnel, and coordinators of foreign and Indian models, all of which are new professions in the industry. The fragmentation and specialization of work around location shooting reflects higher film production budgets, a more systematic capitalization of domestic and global tariff rebates, and rising expectations of technical finesse in film production. Such jobs also require varying levels of skilled and unskilled work, drawing people from a wide social strata into the industry. The redistribution and rationalization of location-related jobs mirror the altering professional landscape of the nation's "new middle class," a contested category in India. As sociologist Leela Fernandes notes, actual figures for the Indian middle class vary vastly ("from tens of millions to 250 million")[44] depending on whether class calibrations are structural and income-based or founded on consumption patterns and the nation's new credit economy. Disparities between statistical definitions of an emerging socioeconomic group with aspirational affiliations to the middle class are redoubled by idealized media images of the "English-

FIGURE 5.3 White background dancers with Shah Rukh Khan in *Ra.One*'s "Chammak Challo" number.

speaking urban white-collar segments of the middle class" that is abstracted to represent all of India's middle classes.[45] The result is the kind of vision conjured up by background dancers in the "Balam Pichkari" song that Sonu Srivastav referred to in this chapter's opening or by the "Chammak Challo" number in *Ra.One* (2011).

Such screen images have been the bad objects of sociological studies that contrast celebratory media representations of cosmopolitanism and consumerism with India's real social inequities. Fernandes refers to the selective visual construction of India's urban middle classes that excludes or marginalizes other social groups as a "politics of forgetting."[46] However, this politics of forgetting takes on a different inflection when we consider the professional conditions, social status, and everyday lives of those creating Bollywood's locational backdrops. Cinematic images that erase certain bodies and faces in the portrayal of globalization on-screen remain the products of a workspace that includes varied social classes of professionals. The trick to not forgetting, it turns out, is to expand our understanding of film beyond its function as an abstracting image to its function as a production practice.

THE REORGANIZATION OF WORK

An expansion in location-based film work has meant that a wider social spectrum of people are drawn into industry work at the unskilled and skilled ends of the profession. A significant number of below-the-line film workers involved in location shoots tend to be Hindi- and Marathi-speaking and drawn from the working and lower-middle classes typically excluded from the cultural capital of India's anglicized, transnational elite. Although rarely visually represented as part of Bollywood's cosmopolitan locales, they are essential to the global make-over of the industry not only because they do the grunt work involved in shooting films on location, but also because the industry's adoption of new production practices depends on their assistance. Their experiences and responses to the industry's corporatization inflect the social and spatial manifestations of Bollywood's globalization.

Mahendra Kumar Singh is not a native English speaker and has not had any formal education in media and communication, but he cut his professional teeth on various jobs as a location manager and has worked on several big-budget international film shoots. He was given the chance to make what he considers intangible creative decisions on projects such as *Slumdog Millionaire* (2008) and *Mission: Impossible* (2011), when they filmed in India. For these films, he assisted with finding locations suitable to the script. He compiled photographic images of places and decided where vanity vans should be parked. Such decision-making opportunities have led him to desire a broader scope for his job in Bollywood productions, which usually assign him the work of acquiring permits. Reorganizations of work in Bollywood's location shooting practices are reflective of larger changes in the professional makeup of the industry, where new opportunities for employment bring different social classes into closer proximity in the workspace. Where there was previously no social conflict, because the division of work in the mainstream Hindi film industry hewed to preexistent class (and often caste) hierarchies, today the simultaneous entry of an anglicized and educated professional elite alongside a wider range of social and professional classes agitates the industry's demographic profile. These proximities create misunderstandings—or conflicting interpretations—about what the job of a Bollywood location manager constitutes.

For instance, Sunitha Ram, who has organized innovative location shoots (for *Dhobi Ghat* and ZNMD, for instance), agrees that the terminological designation of a location manager is new to the Hindi film industry. However, she maintains that the work accomplished by Indian location managers remains much the same, although there have been changes to the *kinds* of background used in Hindi films today. In her words, location managers in India are "people who'll deal with the *babus*." *Babu* is Hindi slang for "bureaucrat." Babus are known to be afflicted with "babu mentality," which means that they have the kind of job security that makes them obstructionist, corrupt, and lacking in any incentive to work (akin to the British jobsworth). Dealing with babus in India can be a laborious task. In the Hindi film industry, this job was traditionally delegated to unskilled workers willing to run from one controlling authority

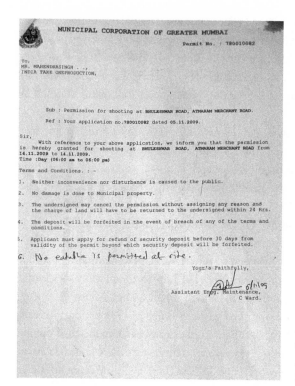

MUNICIPAL CORPORATION OF GREATER MUMBAI

Permit No. : 780010082

To,
MR. MAHENDRASINGH . .,
INDIA TAKE ONEPRODUCTION,

Sub : Permission for shooting at BHULESHWAR ROAD, ATMARAM MERCHANT ROAD.

Ref : Your application no.780010082 dated 05.11.2009.

Sir,
    With reference to your above application, we inform you that the permission
is hereby granted for shooting at BHULESHWAR ROAD, ATMARAM MERCHANT ROAD from
14.11.2009 to 14.11.2009.
Time :Day (06:00 am to 06:00 pm)

Terms and Conditions. : -

1. Neither inconvenience nor disturbance is caused to the public.

2. No damage is done to Municipal property.

3. The undersigned may cancel the permission without assigning any reason and
    the charge of land will have to be returned to the undersigned within 24 Hrs.

4. The deposit will be forfeited in the event of breach of any of the terms and
    conditions.

5. Applicant must apply for refund of security deposit before 30 days from
    validity of the permit beyond which security deposit will be forfeited.

6. No eatable is permitted at ride.

Your's Faithfully,

6/11/09

Assistant Engg. Maintenance,
C Ward.

FIGURE 5.4 No Objection
Certification (NOC) permit for
location filming. Courtesy of
Mahendra Kumar Singh.

to another, such as the local police commissioner, Brihanmumbai Municipal
Corporation (BMC), and the state's Regional Transport Office (RTO) to get
permission to shoot. These unskilled workers do not have the class currency of
the creatives. The pervasiveness of bribes and the opaque process of getting permissions makes their work necessary and important, but finally a thankless and
invisible job requiring no prior training other than the doggedness to pursue
bureaucratic paperwork in India and a familiarity with the cast of petty officials
who can grant permissions. Ram feels that this remains the main responsibility
of Indian location managers.

New entrants to the expanding below-the-line work in location management such as Singh chafe at the suggestion that their job is merely dealing with
babus. Singh got his break working on the comedy *Hadh kar di Aapne* (Manoj
Agrawal, 2000) but subsequently worked as location manager for *Slumdog
Millionaire, Mission: Impossible—Ghost Protocol,* and *Bombay Velvet* (Anurag
Kashyap, 2013). Singh, who freelanced for Take One Productions, among other
companies (demonstrating again that it is not so much a centralized organi-

zation as a set of independently contracted people managed by a company), argues that it is the Indian film producers who misunderstand a location manager's job. According to him, producers and production designers in India typically retain jurisdiction over all creative decisions, including those pertaining to locations. Unlike Bollywood producers, international production companies provide him with a script and a brief and allow him latitude for creative input regarding a film's ideal location venue and look. This is possibly because they are unfamiliar with the Bombay film industry's internal hierarchies or are less less observant of India's internal social divisions of labor, but collaborating with Hollywood-facing companies has occasionally granted more flexibility in the work responsibilities of an independent contractor like Singh. Consequently, Singh's definition of his work as a location manager in India varies from Ram's. For Ram, a location manager "is not a person who's going to put your film together after reading a script. It's literally the person who gets permission . . . from bureaucrats, BMC, police, and RTO, whatever else. That is what the definition of a location manager is and was. I mean, even now, I have yet to find the person in India who is actually going to read a script . . . break it down . . . imagine a color palette . . . presenting ideas like that. I don't think that still exists," she argues. Singh disagrees.

Ram may be both right and wrong. The work of coordinating permissions has typically gone to those who lacked the credentials to receive social and professional acceptance into skilled below-the-line work. Professional distinctions that bleed into class divides (and vice versa) hold true of other below-the-line professions in India as well, as with the costume designers discussed by Clare Wilkinson-Weber. She notes that the "splitting of mental labor from manual labor is fundamental to the creative elevation of designers over tailors, and its persuasiveness depends upon a parallel separation of their social lives and professional discourses."[47] A professional dependence is accompanied by mutual skepticism and condescension between the designers and the tailors. Similar developments may be observed in location management with some difference. Unlike costume design, where tailors and craftspeople in subordinate ranks find their "areas of autonomy" shrinking with the appearance of professional costume designers, workers like Mahendra Kumar Singh find more autonomy and opportunities for input while working on Hollywood productions rather than Bollywood shoots.[48]

As someone who studied with Jeroo Mulla in the Social Communications Media (SCM) department at Sophia's College in Bombay, Sunitha Ram is socially progressive and well aware of media's impact on social ideology. She would never dismiss the contributions of someone like Singh. Ram is one of the women in Bollywood who is changing the hoary ways in which the patriarchal industry functions, and she possesses an acute sense of the representational politics of images in Bollywood. At the same time, to the extent that she finds location management stuck in the realm of unskilled labor in Bollywood, she reinvests in traditional class hierarchies of the organization of work. Social class, fluency with English, access to accredited international and domestic film schools, and cultural capital collectively distinguish those who are an acknowledged part of Bollywood's corporate makeover and those who are not.

MATERIAL BACKGROUNDS AND IMMATERIAL LABOR

Italian sociologist Maurizio Lazzarato talks about the organization of work in the context of defining "immaterial labor" as the characteristic part of postindustrial modes of production that dismantle old binaries between mental versus manual labor posited by Georg Simmel.[49] According to Lazzarato, the reorganization of work in postindustrial society transforms all workers into living labor through a "participative management" of their work and social spaces.[50] Simple examples of participative management might include a large corporation that conducts self-motivation and mindfulness seminars for its workers while disallowing overtime pay, or a state that cuts public school funds while sponsoring incentives for private individuals to start charters and select vouchers to schools to create the illusion of individual choice while structurally reinforcing social inequality. Both measures disproportionately benefit those already wealthy and participate in erasing institutional responsibilities toward an equitable distribution of rights and the possibility of a commons. These are fundamental aspects of how the state and the market get reorganized with privatization, wherein every worker and citizen is repositioned as a potential consumer and consequently a presumed manager/entrepreneur of their own time, lifestyle, and choices, despite having no ability to initiate structural changes.

In an idea extended by Michael Hardt and Antonio Negri's writings on affective labor, Lazzarato argues that postindustrial societies restructure work as an extension of "management thinking" where control appears to reside in subjects and in the communicative processes of consumerism (or, more correctly, in the processes of production *and* consumption that become indistinguishable under the postindustrial system).[51] The worker is restructured as a perennial consumer and traditional boundaries between work and life break down as commodification spreads well beyond localizable factory processes. Aware that this idea of inescapably prescriptive subjectivities veers too close to a totalizing theory of ideology, Lazzarato argues that the commodification of life does not erase the potential for conflict but disperses its terrain. According to him, immaterial labor becomes the "very real terrain and condition of the conflict between social classes" because of its dependence on a new kind of subjectivity and collective form. This difference in subjectivity "has immediately expressed itself as a clash between social classes within the organization of work."[52] "Clash" is too aggressive a word for current renegotiations in the distribution of work within Bollywood, but it points to forces that could either turn toward a greater rationalization of professional responsibilities, a deeper eruption of social conflict within the workspace, or both. As the career trajectories and experiences of individuals involved in a range of professions dealing with Bollywood and Hollywood film locations and backgrounds in India demonstrate, the socioeconomic forces of accelerated liberalization in India are disturbing traditional social and professional hierarchies.

Without reducing Bollywood professionals to mere representatives of their class, I can confirm based on my conversations in the field that the assorted workers involved in locating shoots in India today come from a range of social classes. Their range reveals the disparity between a Bollywood blockbuster's on-screen transnational backgrounds and the social diversity of those involved in producing them. On-the-ground compositions of pre-production and production crews are more hybrid than a Bollywood blockbuster's flat images of urbane cosmopolitanism convey. For instance, recording sync sound on location in a noise-congested country is drawing unskilled crews to work as security personnel on film sites, in addition to the highly trained sound engineers who handle the technological and creative end of recording on-site.[53] Until the late 1990s, Hindi cinema followed the norm of looping all dialogue ("dubbing") at the post-production stage, commonly referred to as post-sync sound. In a change that occurred over a relatively accelerated period of time, a majority of India's commercial films moved from MOS (motor only sound, or no sync) to recording sound coupled with the image during a film's shoot. Today, an amalgam of on-location camerawork, sync sound, and Automated Dialogue Replacement or ADR characterizes Bollywood cinema's visuals and soundscape. Bollywood's increasing deployment of method acting, sync sound recording, and seamless continuity in editing and lighting brings its production quality and technological practices closer to its Hollywood counterpart than in previous decades. The technical effect of audio-visual realism announces Hindi cinema's self-conscious entry into popular global aesthetics.

This change in film sound has not only created a demand for trained creative technicians and sound engineers; it has equally drawn the semiskilled and unskilled labor of security personnel and bouncers. Many of those working in this pool of unskilled labor come from Bombay's economically depressed migrants, who have traveled to the city in search of employment. According to line producer Raj Hate (with television commercials and the location-heavy *Miss Lovely* [2012] to his credit), the practice of "sound lock ups" started with television commercials in India during the late 1990s before it was adopted on film shoots. "Sound lock" is a phrase used by a few professionals to describe the practice of securing an area to ensure silence in order to get the best location sound. Security provider Narendra Baruah, who started with security work for *Lagaan*, the first big-budget film shot with sync sound, employs a few regulars and hires additional men, several on a temporary basis from a pool of local Mumbaikars and immigrants seeking employment in the big city. He retains a small group of men on a monthly salary with additional per diem top-ups during assignments, which may range between INR 5,000 and 10,000 to over INR 20,000 a day, depending on the nature of the shoot.

Baruah's company is in competition with actor Ronit Roy's security company, ACE, and movie star Salman Khan's Tiger Security. He lacks their star profile but has made a name for himself through his entrepreneurial practice and his expertise in shooting at *jhopad pattis* (slums) for films such as *Barah Aana* (Raja Krishna Menon, 2009) and *Slumdog Millionaire*. Baruah's practice of hiring temporary workers for security is partially what Lazzarato means when he discusses the "anthropological realities of work" that are reconfigured in a global workspace, where "polymorphous self-employed autonomous work has emerged as the dominant form" inserting itself into the market.[54] Mahendra Kumar Singh and Narendra Baruah represent these self-employed autonomous workers who can be contracted by various domestic and international production companies. They constitute a different demographic of the global middle class than the one represented by Ram, Guha, or myself. As Hagen Koo argues in relation to the shrinking middle class in America and Western Europe against the expanding middle classes of India and China, representations of the global middle class that narrowly refer to "the upper segments . . . in developing countries, whose members are affluent and globally oriented in their lifestyle and mobility pattern," are woefully inadequate.[55] The socially diverse range of background actors and their handlers provides a counterpoint.

MODELS VERSUS JUNIOR ARTISTS

Dil Chahta Hai (Ritesh Sidhwani, 2001), a film that portrays the close friend-ship between three young men who have differing attitudes to love and rela-tionships, used sync sound, a nontraditional plot structure, extensive location shooting in Sydney, Australia, and a lifestyle-oriented display of global urban "cool." The film displayed the urbanity of its characters by their clothes and gelled hairstyles, their minimalist and well-appointed home interiors (discussed by Ranjani Mazumdar),[56] their air travel in first-class cabins, and by the venues they visited. *Dil Chahta Hai* is also among the films that popularized white and Westernized Indian youths as background actors, which is a trend that has cre-ated an opening for a new kind of handler and agent for film extras. Tradition-ally, Hindi cinema's background actors were drawn from the unionized Junior Artists Association (JAA) for men, and the Mahila Kalakar Sangh (MKS) for women. Junior artists are internally differentiated into B-grade, A-grade (referred to sometimes as A-class, B-class), and "Superclass," based on their caliber of looks as adjudicated by junior artist coordinators. Wages are calibrated accord-ingly. The recent influx of models in the Hindi film industry has effectively led to the disappearance of A-grade junior artists in all but nominal terms, as the extremes of presentability and class appearance have diverged more radically in India's postglobalization era.

"Models"—a term applied broadly in Bollywood to any nonunionized background actor usually contracted for a day—designates anyone who looks like they could be a model or a seamless part of a cosmopolitan urban setting. This covers a wide range but primarily the designation distinguishes a higher social class of background actors from the unionized "junior artists" or film extras who have traditionally acted in nonspeaking background roles in Hindi cinema. Whereas junior artists have historically belonged to India's working and economic underclasses, Bollywood's models may be Indian college stu-dents looking for pocket money, foreign tourists visiting India and interested in a walk-on part for a lark, or someone recruited via street casting by local location managers and casting agents. The term "model" is also applied in conventional ways to the professional Indian or foreign models who are repre-sented by model management companies. Changes in the management, cast-ing, and coordination of junior artists and models illustrate some of the ways in which Bollywood's globalization is leading to renegotiated relationships in society and in the professional spaces of the industry.

FIGURE 5.5 *Dil Chahta Hai* poster conveying urban "cool" in 2001. Courtesy of the National Film Archive of India.

"Pappu" Lekhraj Nanda and Paras Mehta

Paras Mehta's career as a "pre production controller, line producer, model co-ordination . . . junior artist controller" and so forth has been made possible by postliberalization changes in the Bombay film industry. He supplies junior artists for films and television, and he has represented models for films such as *Saarawaria* (2007), *Ghajini* (2008), *Black* (2005), *Guzaarish* (2010), and *Dhoom 2* (2006) and for commercials made by foreign production companies in India. Mehta divides his international collaborations into two categories. In his first category are foreign producers who contact him because they want their films to have an "Indian look." In this category he also places foreigners looking for some sort of Bollywood tourism. These are tourists who want to experience a Bollywood shoot and are indifferent to the film's quality or their own wages. About the international companies looking to shoot in India, he says, "They prefer the girls real Indian-looking. They don't want the actors.

They want the real-looking, street-looking people. *Jiska* camera face *nahin kiya hota hai*" (Meaning: "Those don't have a camera-face," although it could also mean "Those who have never faced a camera"). For these shoots, traditional junior artists can sometimes be a good fit. Salaries for unionized junior artists, according to Mehta and others, range from INR 1,000 a day for Superclass and A-grade male junior artists, and INR 1,200 a day for the Superclass women (female junior artists are higher paid because they are more scarce than men).[57] B-grade men and women make INR 800 a day. Junior artists of all categories make 25 percent less if they are hired for television. Mehta quotes higher rates for models (or what he terms "featured background actors"), ranging from INR 2,500 to 7,500 per day, defining models as background actors who are more "presentable" and "superior to Superclass" junior artists.[58] They are also invariably fairer. Models do not have the same work protections (such as regulated hours of work) as junior artists, as they are not unionized.

Lekhraj Nanda, whose family has been in the business of providing junior artists to film productions since 1945 (compared to Paras Mehta's fourteen years), and whose company has coordinated background actors for international films including *Man with the Golden Arm* (1955), *Slumdog Millionaire*, *Salaam Bombay!* (1988), and *City of Joy* (1992), observes that "foreigners are very organized and they mostly want to show poverty. Their requirements are very easy, because they don't want good-looking people. For slums we use B class junior artists" (*Baahar ke log bahut* organized *hote hain aur unko garibi chahiye. Unka* requirement *karne ke liye bahut* easy *hota hai, kyunki unko achhe log nahin chahiye hote hain. Slum mein* B class use *karte hain*). In contrast, as Anadil Hossain says bluntly, "Indian filmmakers want white people."

The social legitimation of Bollywood over the last decade (elaborated by Tejaswini Ganti[59]) has led to what junior artist and model coordinator Lekhraj Nanda identifies as the phenomenon of *acche ghar ki ladkyian* (girls from respectable homes) in India clamoring for nonspeaking background parts in films. Lekhraj Nanda specifically pegs the increasing popularity of nonspeaking Bollywood roles among affluent youths to Shah Rukh Khan's entry into films and to the film *Kuch Kuch Hota Hai* (1998). The precision of this claim feels spurious, but as observers of Bollywood have argued, Khan's media persona has developed in tandem with the industry's globalization and commodification.[60] The star's successful self-branding as "SRK" across a range of media platforms and corporations is a good example of this trend. Perhaps what Lekhraj Nanda intuits is not so much SRK's causality to the entry of so-called models into background work but a sense that his stardom is symptomatic of this larger trend. Shifts in Bollywood's backgrounds are closely related to the expansion of consumerism, the commodification of leisure, the monetization of Bollywood's international market, and the changing architectural landscape of urban India (all of which have also contributed to SRK's success as a brand). This is clear when we attend to the places where Nanda's employees scout to recruit upper-middle-class youths to background film work. As he informed me, in addition to maintaining a regular photographic portfolio of hopefuls and "strugglers," his employees hand out fliers and visiting cards at Bombay's upscale malls (such as the Highstreet Phoenix mall in Lower Parel and Infiniti Mall in Malad), automobile showrooms, wedding parties, and property fairs.

Nanda, who claims to handle 80 percent of all junior artist needs for the Hindi film industry (notably mentioning that, despite these statistics, it is television rather than films that keep him in business) offered a lower number for the daily pay scales of models in 2013. According to him, models' earnings ranged between INR 1,500 and 2,500 a day, always remembering that these payments count as wages for junior artists but expendable income for models, given their class differential. The influx of models, "white people" (tourists or those on an "E" or employment visas), young upper-middle-class, and affluent Indians into Bollywood's backgrounds has had a deep impact on the employment of Hindi cinema's junior artists. Confrontations between production companies that want to hire models and junior artists unions that want to protect their members open up avenues of conflict and mediation that are managed by the likes of Mehta and Nanda.

Wage Loss Agreement

Faced with a large-scale loss of jobs to models, the JAA (the union representing male junior artists) and MKS (JAA's female counterpart) intervened to negotiate a wage loss agreement in 2008. According to the wage loss agreement, film producers agreed to pay a compensatory amount to the main background artist unions for wages lost whenever they hired a model instead of a junior artist. In return, the JAA, MKS, and the Cine Dancers Association agreed that if producers could demonstrate that the union was not in a position to fill their particular requirements by using one of the union members, they would not disrupt film shoots that employed models for background work.[61] Unlike Hollywood, where SAG-AFTRA (Screen Actors Guild-American Federation of Television and Radio Artists) membership rules apply equally to unionized principal actors and background actors, both of whom can get membership in the organization, the JAA for junior artists and CINTAA (Cine and Television Artist's

Association) for principal talent are distinct organizations in Bombay's industry. Social and class divisions are pronounced between them. Moreover, not all top Bollywood stars are members of CINTAA. Twenty-two craft unions under the parent Federation of Western Cine Employees represent film and media workers in Bombay, and JAA has been important in arbitrating for improved work conditions for junior artists. The wage loss agreement's negotiation is one way in which the transformation of Bollywood's visual space has had a concrete ramification on contractual and informal arrangements constituting the professional space of below-the-line workers.

Junior artists and junior artist coordinators have largely welcomed the wage loss agreement as a victory. Arguably, however, the proposal effectively forces junior artists to participate in their own erasure from on-screen backgrounds. Their lack of work is now legitimated as an option to *not* work for less pay, so that they become willing partners in their own dismissal when they accept payment in lieu of losing their jobs to nonunion labor. Their visual replacement is compensated by a partial remuneration, which transforms the actual labor of junior artists into immaterial labor in that it allows them to become tacit accomplices in their own redundancy. Not being hired for work acquires an equivalency with being hired when workers can be bartered into accepting remuneration for their replacement. Being made redundant can be framed as a choice rather than a function of the market's compulsion or exigency.

Moreover, the specifics (amount and distribution) of wage loss compensations are undefined and left to active negotiations on set, so the terms are opaque to the workers. One of the job descriptions of Paras Mehta is to serve as an intermediary between film producers, junior artists, and models to conduct wage loss negotiations on set. Discussing the challenges in getting this compensation, Mehta notes, "*Producers to kahenge jo cheez maine* use *nahin kara uska main* payment *kyun karoon?*" [Producers will say, why should I pay for something that I did not use?] It is usually very difficult to make them understand, because the producer is correct on his part. Association is right on his part. So what do you do? That's the big challenge." Mehta sees his role as keeping both parties satisfied, and he suggests that his job would be redundant if there was agreement between film producers who used models in lieu of junior artists, and junior artists who wanted wage loss compensation. "If those people ask and these people give, then what job is left for me to do?" (*Agar unhone maanga aur inhone dey diya, to hamara kaam hya hai?*) When asked how he brokers this delicate negotiation between the two parties, he responds in English, "That's business, professional, that can't be disclosed."

Professionalization and transparency, which are ostensibly the promise of the Indian film industry's corporatization following decades of the industry's operation as an informal sector, would make intermediaries like Mehta and his social negotiations redundant. It would constitute their ouster. Such a dramatic change does not seem anywhere near the horizon. Stalwarts of coordinating background actors such as Lekhraj Nanda and relative newcomers to location work, model coordination, and sound security work, such as Paras Mehta and Mahendra Kumar Singh, remain indispensable for grappling with the ground realities of shooting on location in Bombay, because by definition location shoots must exit studios to enter the hurly-burly of the everyday. These below-the-line professionals decipher the rules of sociality that govern personal interactions, lived experiences, and everyday politics in Bombay and its film industry. Accessing them becomes important because such information cannot be gleaned off the pages of any brief, read off a statistic, or seen on-screen as a cinematic image.

Shiv Sena and Maharashtra Navnirman Sena

Bombay's day-to-day politics are also the turf of the Shiv Sena (or Sena). As the far right pro-Maharashtra political party whose alliances with the national Bharatiya Janta Party (BJP) have recently fallen afoul, the Sena is one of the many pieces of the puzzle that confront professionals responsible for organizing location shoots within Bombay's territory. The Sena's history as a political party is outside the scope of my analysis, but a few aspects of the party's impact on Bollywood's location choices and background actors are significant to note. It was under the fiscal policies of the BJP-led Hindutva government, as Nandana Bose points out, that filmmaking received its industry status in 1998.[62] Local BJP and Sena activists in Bombay who had a long-running role in the industry's financing, casting, and shooting through illicit dealings with the city's underworld did not disappear with media corporatization but took on a different guise.[63] In addition to the Sena, which has had a history of sponsoring film workers unions in Bombay to protect regional interests, its splinter group, Maharashtra Navnirman Sena (MNS), led by Raj Thackaray, and MNS's prominent cine-wing, Maharashtra Navnirman Chitrapat Karmachari Sena (MNCKS), remain extremely active in monitoring, aiding, and obstructing film shoots based on their political agendas.

Efforts to streamline the multiple unions championing regionalist Marathi *manoos* (Maratha people) and Hindutva ideologies led to the formation of an umbrella wing under the Bharatiya Chitrapat Sena, which was also an effort on the Shiv Sena's part to wrest control from Raj Thackaray's breakaway MNS.[64]

A Bollywood production's ability to shoot on location in Bombay depends on maintaining good relationships with this welter of right-wing political units and agents that are entangled in internecine rivalries among themselves. In recent years, film unions sponsored by the MNS have shut down location shoots by protesting, rioting, or vandalizing film sets, vans, and star vehicles for any number of reasons. These have included allegations that productions are employing foreign nationals as models or background actors without appropriate visas, underrepresenting Maharashtrian actors and crew, misrepresenting India, demeaning Indian women, demeaning Indian culture, or blocking access to public spaces.[65] Such confrontations put Bollywood crewmembers in a variably obsequious, adversarial, or rebellious stance in relation to local politics and politicians. Ramesh Sippy (director of yesteryear's classic *Sholay*, 1975) was among the filmmakers who represented the Film and Television Producers Guild of India in a petition to Chief Minister Prithviraj Chavan and Home Minister R. R. Patil, threatening that the film industry would geographically "shift base if the Maharashtra government does not ensure to protect the industry from political vandalism."[66] Indian cinema's location shoots become battle-grounds for the new millennium's pitched battles between those who benefit financially from globalization and those who benefit politically from whipping up rage against globalization's real and imagined beneficiaries.

While union activism sponsored by right-wing political parties is a significant problem for Bollywood's local film shoots, the appeal of labor unions sponsored by regionalist political parties lies in their outreach to underserved Marathi and other non-English-speaking working-class and low-income entrants who are seeking access to background work in Bollywood. MNS and Sena unions provide them with some representation as well as a familiar and familial set up. They offer modes of belonging that are not open to them when the decision makers are composed of India's anglicized socioeconomic elite. Sitaram Kadam, one of Pappu Lekhraj Nanda's long-term employees, entered the industry by becoming a member with the MNS in 1974 because of its accessibility. For Kadam, who has had little formal education and who transitioned from being a junior artist to working full-time as a coordinator for Pappu Lekhraj's company in 1986, MNS provided an important stepping-stone.[67] From a film producer's point of view, however, having to negotiate with multiple organizations and unions potentially stalls film shoots and increases what New York–based Anadil Hossain identifies as India's "middle management syndrome" of too many intermediaries and no centralized responsibility.[68] The problem of middle management is another factor that makes one-point intermediaries such as freelance location managers or unit production managers valuable to line production companies in India, because they handle all ground-level negotiations and have a roster of autonomous contacts to manage location-based filming in Bombay, or in India more generally. For this reason, a majority of such essential but also tedious negotiations are left to intermediaries such as Nanda and Mehta.

The realm of corporate transactions and the realm of ground-level negotiations entail two entirely different kinds of social cultures. Tejaswini Ganti has discussed the ways in which traditional networks of "kinship" have been central to Bollywood.[69] To some extent, at the pre-production and production levels, the kinship networks that dominated the Hindi film industry in the preglobalization era are relaxing to allow the entry of a wider range and class of professionals. Young middle-class professionals who found the film industry socially undesirable and opaque in its working two decades ago now see legitimacy in media-related work and welcome the shift. At the same time, the industry's professionalization brings higher levels of anxiety for workers to whom corporate Bollywood connotes inaccessible social capital and the distancing formality of professionalism. It feels corrosive to below-the-line workers who have depended on a sense of adoptive communities as a primary way to survive in their jobs, where they have otherwise had little real negotiating power beyond relying on trust and word-of-mouth deals.

Superclass junior artist Rukhsana, quoted in this chapter's epigraph, has worked in the industry for twenty-three years in the backgrounds of films such as *Chauraha* (1994), *Roop ki Rani Choron ka Raja* (1993), *Dil Hai ki Manta Nahin* (1991), and *Saajan* (1991). She has also served as a body double for Monisha Koirala and Karishma Kapoor. She experiences the industry's corporatization in terms of a loss of a sense of belonging, or *apnapan*. A member of the (nonreligious) Mahila Kalakar Sangh union, she thinks of her employer, Pappu Lekhraj Nanda, as her brother, and her professional community as her family. Out of a sense of loyalty, she will work only on assignments that Lekhraj Nanda sends her way, and he returns the favor by having his employees call her at home for work so that she doesn't have to sit for hours in the MKS office in Adarsh Nagar, Oshiwara, waiting to see if she will get an assignment for the day. Aligning herself with intermediaries such as her junior artist coordinator is Rukhsana's primary means for finding continued background work in an industry that is changing its look and locations.

Ground-level MNS agitations that resist the hiring of Indian models and foreign crews represent local reactionary antiminoritarian forces, but they also

FIGURE 5.6 Superclass junior artists Rukhsana and Kanchan.

have to be assessed as part of the complex ways in which Bollywood's corporatization impacts Bombay's local population and politics. Parallel to the development of a corporate workspace of professionals exists an alternative sphere of social communities, from the sisterhood of the MKS to the brotherhood of the Sena and the MNS. Intermediaries such as Lekhraj Nanda and Mehta, who are businessmen first and care little for political alliances, have to negotiate with these forces while also satisfying their clients, who range from Indian or international film producers and models to junior artists. Junior artists are in the most precarious position in this environment, as they are edited out of film backgrounds for not fitting into contemporary visual conceptions of global spaces. Despite this, Superclass junior artists Rukhsana and Kanchan are satisfied with their career choices. It has enabled them to provide for their extended families and educate and support their siblings and children with and without the assistance of male partners. As they affirm, "We are masters of our own choice. We face no restrictions" (*Hum apni marzi ke malik hain. Koi bandish nahin hain*). While it is undeniable that their position is more precarious with the nation's zealous adoption of consumerism and the erasure of such figures as stand-ins to represent affluent locations and lifestyles on-screen, their work as junior artists in Hindi cinema has allowed them to overcome the gendered and economic denial of basic opportunities to women of their class in India. As they perceive it, they have retained the opportunity to exercise a choice.

Kanchan and I disagreed on the extent to which her profession is becoming more precarious under the new corporate order. She perceived more freedom in her situation than I did. If she is not entirely trustworthy because confessing to her professional precarity in front of a stranger may have been unnerving to her, my own account is equally unreliable. I have assessed the film industry to the exclusion of television, which is also a source of employment for background actors such as Kanchan, and the picture may look different if I took television into account. The common ground between our positions lies in our mutual agreement that the Bombay film industry is newly invested in spectacles of urban cosmopolitanism and consumerism in ways that exclude people such as Rukhsana and Kanchan. This shift has come with a concomitant professionalization of work environments in which, they observe, they feel alienated.

CONSUMERISM AND LEISURE IN THE ERA OF REGULATIONS

Contemporary efforts to corporatize the Indian film industry and move it away from informal, familial, and trust-based systems are uneven and far from systematic, but these shifts relate to larger transformations in the social attitudes toward individualism and the legitimacy of capitalist enterprise in India. Movie theaters and movie production have historically borne the brunt of a slew of taxations and regulations when the state categorized them as inessential and potentially immoral. Several things shifted as a deregulating state actively legitimated consumerism and the monetization of entertainment and leisure. To see the material and social links between India's embrace of neoliberalism and the changing look of Bollywood's backgrounds, we need a brief detour through the regulation of commodities categorized as leisure, particularly as it influenced film (as a regulated product, a social activity of leisure, and a medium that could represent leisure). Spatial thinking turns our attention to cinema's on-screen spaces, to the status of film as a material object,[70] and additionally to film's function in the creation of public and private spaces. Cinema's object status, aesthetic appearance, and social roles are not homologous, but changes across each of these registers can be used to calibrate shifts in a nation's historical and political priorities. If we are to assess film's definition in relation to a dispersed range of (social, regulatory, aesthetic, political) spaces, as I am attempting to do in this book, then we must consider the co-implicated aspects of its spatialization as a commodity, a social activity, and a representational medium.

As we will see, prior to the era of deregulation, the Indian state's restrictions on foreign exchange, film stock, and film technology materially shaped the Bombay film industry's options for location filming. I am not proposing a purely technomaterialist optic here. The film industry was neither unified nor passive in its response to state regulations. However, I am suggesting that the state's shifting categorization of film as a taxable commodity of leisure that could serve as a monetizable source of income, versus film's treatment as an instrument of social uplift worthy of state sponsorship, shaped the film industry's regulatory and financial environment and the material terms of the industry's creative production. Competing social outlooks on the question of austerity versus expenditure played their parts in the debates that raged between the Indian government and Bombay film industry over the taxability of film as leisure. At the same time, conflicting social attitudes about the need to cultivate a sense of public obligation against prioritizing the acquisition of private wealth and expenditure influenced the content of Hindi cinema's narratives and locational mise-en-scène. In other words, *attitudes* regarding the illegitimacy or legitimacy of consumption and leisure have made their appearance in debates over the appropriate regulation of popular entertainment as much as they have manifested in images on-screen. These shifting attitudes also influenced the kinds of places that were filmed, the styles for filming them, and the possibilities for filming on location, as discussed below.

A Regime of Taxation and Regulation

The grounds for thinking about theatrical venues as a nuisance were laid in a debate about film's potential taxability in 1923, and at issue in that debate was the voluntary and inessential nature of film viewing, categorized with leisure activities such as horse racing and golfing that were considered taxable to support essential nation-building activities such as education.[71] As Manishita Dass argues in relation to colonial India, cinema's potential to reach audiences beyond the print-literate elite produced a sense of film spectatorship linked to evolving and expanding notions of national citizenship.[72] This imagination of an untutored audience skewed the colonial and national state into a paternalistic treatment of cinema. The idea of levying high taxes on entertainment in Bombay was mooted in 1923 as part of the Bombay Presidency Bill (in imitation of a similar tax in England), the provisions of which had been recently inserted into an act of the Bengal Legislative Council. The bill proposed a tax "on admission to theaters, cinemas and places of public entertainment."[73] Debates over the bill show that cinema was associated with activities of public entertainment and leisure that were taxed heavily because they were perceived to carry a counterweight in social obligation. They were defined as part of the colony's inessential industries, as opposed to core public interest and utilitarian industries that needed state support.

The argument that film production and exhibition should receive some tax breaks did not gain traction in postcolonial India until 1998.[74] Close to six decades after the Bombay Presidency Bill, the Indian film industry would still be arguing for a fundamental revision in the "philosophy" behind national policies on film taxation and theater licensing by pitching theaters as "community centers" and places of "public utility and a place of cultural activity" rather than "a cause of public nuisance" that could be slapped with the equivalent of a sin tax.[75] Some of the taxes on film traditionally levied by the central (akin to the federal) government in India included import duties, censorship fees, storage fees, newsreel rental fees, income tax, and super tax. Taxes by the state governments included entertainment tax, sales tax, theater license fees, and electricity duty. Various local bodies levied additional show tax, taxes on posters, license fees, octroi taxes, and so on.[76] A tax proposal that attracted a fair amount of controversy in 1960 was the excise tax, introduced by the central government as an inland duty to be levied in proportion to the footage of exposed film. Excise tax was not related to the income or profit generated by a film but to the metric length of its prints. Members of the Bombay film industry found that the state excise tax affected them more severely than it did India's other regional filmmakers because, they argued, Hindi cinema had wider distribution and needed a larger number of prints. The state's changing tax structure made their condition precarious.[77]

When infrastructural supplies such as raw stock, cameras, lighting equipment, and electrical supply are subject to the vagaries of state taxation and regulation, the regimes of control have an immediate impact on the look of films. As already discussed (in chapter 2), film stock was a highly rationed commodity and this rationing affected commercial film producers more severely than it did state-supported documentarians such as N. S. Thapa. Recall that in response to the rationing of film stock in the 1960s, the Hindi film industry created regional committees referred to as "steering committees" to scrutinize producers' applications for film stock. The idea was that such committees would "safeguard the legitimate interests of *bona fide* producers, keep out the speculative and wasteful entrepreneur," and also allow the industry some measure of representation while "leaving the final control with the Government."[78] One unspoken consequence of such committees was that established producers who had industry clout, a strong social network in the industry, and access to bankable stars, were more likely to receive film stock. Another was that directors became prone to combining color stocks to make their films, irrespective of what they claimed on a film's final credits.

For instance, the color stocks most commonly used in the 1960s and 1970s were Fujicolor, Gevacolor, ORWO color, and Eastman color. Surveying films from 1975, Feroze Rangoonwalla observes that the availability of Fujicolor (used in *Rafoochakkar* and *Rani aur Laal Pari*) and Eastman color declined that year. With the exception of *Sholay* (made with Technicolor) and *Jai Santoshi Ma* (made with ORWO color), there was "*no certainty that all of the prints were from the same stock*" for the other films released.[79] State control over color film stock and state restrictions on foreign currency exchange for color stock purchases as well as foreign location shoots had a profound influence on industry practices and on the films produced. Director and Producer G. P. Sippy, then president of the Indian Motion Picture Producer's Association, noted, "Colour pictures are produced with raw film imported against export guarantee and bonds. . . . A producer plans his movie on the basis of current costs of materials. When the costs go up in the middle of production due to increase in taxation, the entire scheme is upset."[80]

Few producers could afford to plan and execute location shoots outside India given the paucity of stock and the precarious supply of foreign exchange. The government released money for foreign location shoots on the guarantee of returned earnings. According to *Picturpost*, Finance Minister Sachin Chaudhuri reported on the Lok Sabha floor that the Government of India released INR 4.09 lakhs in foreign exchange in 1965 and INR 1.75 lakhs in 1966 for shooting Indian films on foreign locations "on the condition that the producer gave a guarantee to earn at least four times exchange of the amount released to each producer. In 1964 film exports from the country earned Rs. 2.13 crores as foreign exchange. The earnings up to September 1965 were INR 1.67 crores."[81] Over the next ten years, demand for a return on the released foreign exchange rose steadily, with rumors that in 1976 film producers had to return up to eight times the foreign exchange released to them by the government. Whatever the exact figure, restricted foreign exchange stalled the completion of several big-budget productions that were filming in foreign locations, including *Aashiq hoon Baharon ka* (1977), *Dream Girl* (1977), and *The Great Gambler* (1979). "Will Government adopt the pragmatic view and allow the producers of incomplete movies made on foreign locations to go yet again, finish their work and come back?" demanded Bunny Reuben, in his coverage of this episode.[82]

Thwarted international location shoots and rising interest in domestic tourism contributed to popularizing Indian locations for film shoots in places such

FIGURE 5.7 *Dream Girl* lobby card showing international location. Courtesy of the National Film Archive of India.

as Darjeeling, Kodaikanal, Himachal Pradesh, and Kashmir. Kashmir appears to have had the added advantage of not charging a location fee for film shoots, unlike all other Indian states. Shakti Samanta points out that "this might be one additional reason for producers to have their extensive outdoors there, rather than pay location rent elsewhere."[83]

In sum, high box office returns were all-important to commercial filmmakers working within a speculative market that depended on government authorization for the release of color stock and foreign exchange for location shoots abroad. Economy-of-scale productions could withstand the state's restrictive terms by aggressively targeting domestic and export markets through star-studded (and, in popular Indian parlance, "multistarrer") color extravaganzas, guaranteeing quadruple and octuple returns on investment as a condition of their production. Two of the largest films of the 1960s, *Love in Tokyo* (Pramod Chakravarty, 1966) and *Evening in Paris* (Shakti Samanta, 1967), were, using these strategies, planned as too big to fail. *Love* was promoted as "the first Indian movie to have a commercial run in Japan," with Pramod Chakravarty reediting the film "to suit Japanese tastes." By September 1966, Chakravarty was reported to have "put back more hard currency in the Union coffers than had been given to him for his location shooting in Japan."[84] Foreign location shoots had the additional advantage of placing the lead star cast in one place for the entirety of a shoot, which was important before the industry's corporatization introduced call sheets to the notoriously tardy and high-maintenance top stars of Hindi cinema. *Love* and *Evening* are also exemplary in displaying spectacles of travel, conspicuous consumption, and cosmopolitanism in an era of high protectionism, and must be understood for their content as much as for their contexts of production.

AMBIVALENT CONSUMERISM

The 1960s and 1970s marked India's first foray into free market ideology. The memorable song "Evening in Paris" from Shakti Samanta's eponymous film released in 1967 is a paradigmatic image of this decade. Ranjani Mazumdar has argued that the box office successes of what she terms "global travel films" such as *Sangam* (Raj Kapoor, 1964), *Love in Tokyo*, and *Evening in Paris* "brought jet age aviation, tourism, consumerism, color film stock, fashion and music into a distinct cultural configuration" in India.[85] In the introductory song that opens the film, star Shammi Kapoor lip-syncs directly to the camera as he promises his audiences the unrepeatable experience of a glorious "Evening in Paris." He is in the city of romance and flanked by a row of white Caucasian (presumably Parisian) women who are part of a spectacle that he insists we should see, repeating the word "see" (*dekho*) five times. Whereas there is much about post-1998 Bollywood cinema that celebrates its own novelty, the use of foreign nationals and foreign locations to connote Western standards of consumerism and excess is not new to Bollywood. To retrace mainstream Bombay cinema's move to outdoor locations in the sound era, and to the promotion of consumerism and tourism in the culture at large, we need to look to its precursors in the 1960s and 1970s, as Mazumdar reminds us.

After the nation's foreign exchange reserves plunged to a perilous low in 1966, the Indian government devalued the Indian rupee. Following droughts, food shortages, depleted foreign currency reserves, and wars with China and Pakistan in 1962 and 1965, respectively, the government under its new prime minister, Indira Gandhi, was forced to accept terms set by the United States

FIGURE 5.8 Surf's Lalitaji.

and the International Monetary Fund (IMF), as the artificially inflated rupee was no longer viable. The rupee was devalued by 40 percent, and tariffs import and export subsidizations, which had been severe since 1957, were temporarily reduced. In other words, the 1960s in India witnessed a new spatialization of film as a commodity because older boundaries of taxation and revenue were redrawn in accordance with a nation making its borders more porous to international capital. The acceptance of trade terms from the IMF to liberalize India's economy in exchange for hard currency was withdrawn equally rapidly, however, when the Indian state reverted to import substitutions by 1969.[86] Any significant shift toward privatization would have to wait until the 1990s.

Rhetorical modifiers such as "despite" and "notwithstanding" frequently accompany descriptions of the 1960s as an era when the visual attractions of consumer culture thrived in Hindi cinema "regardless of" the state's restrictive economy.[87] In fact, crisis over the nation's insolvency in relation to the rest of the world was *central* to the emergence of a complex affectivity of desire in commercial Hindi films of the period, which combined a sense of revulsion with envy, and covetousness with condescension, toward capitalism and conspicuous consumption.[88] This complex affectivity is evident in commercial Hindi cinema's backdrops of the 1960s and 1970s, a period that Mukul Kesavan describes as "materialism in the age of high tariffs" when the "history of middle-class India . . . [could] be written in soap and detergent."[89] Indian television and movie viewers of the 1970s will remember the iconic "Lalitaji" of Surf detergent advertisements created by ad-filmmaker Alique Padamsee. A housewife who doesn't waste money on buying new clothes but instead prefers to wash her family's clothes with the most expensive detergent in the market, Lalitaji was a fictional character who appeared in a range of Surf advertisements to emphasize the importance of balancing consumerism with thrift. Tapping her head with her index finger to indicate her street smarts, she recommends the pricier detergent, Surf, because it is the sensible choice (*Surf ki khariddari mein hi samajhdari hai*).[90] A Lalitaji-like ambivalence toward consumerism is notable in the spatial aesthetic of Hindi films of the 1960s and 1970s.

Teen Bahuraniyan, S. S. Vasan/S. S. Balan

The successful domestic living-room drama *Teen Bahuraniyan* (Three Daughters-in-Law, 1968) is a film that can be placed at the opposite end of the spectrum from the era's global travel films discussed by Mazumdar. Produced by Gemini Studio, the Hindi film was part of the studio's stable of bilingual productions.[91] A successful remake of the Tamil *Bama Vijayam* (K. Balachandar, 1967), this family comedy contains practically no location shots (other than a disorienting shot of a car arriving outside a house) and is staged entirely inside studio sets depicting living rooms and bedrooms. All the action is composed frontally with static camera set-ups. There is a preponderance of medium shots, which are held while characters enter from screen left or right in a pattern that predominates over the lexicon of shot and reverse shot. If, as Mazumdar notes, *Evening* and *Love* are films in which "the plot is thin and quite marginal to the drama of space,"[92] then *Teen Bahuraniyan* is all plot with little action. It denies us picturesque locations, tourist sites, mobile cameras, or aerial photography. Nevertheless, unkempt consumerist desires threaten to unnerve the film's visual display of a middle-class family that appears to be perennially tempted to line up by height and smile for the camera.

Teen Bahuraniyan is the story of a joint family of three brothers and their wives (Shankar and Parvati, Ram and Sita, Kanhaiya and Radha, covering three iconic Hindu deities and their consorts) who live in a modest house but become obsessed with a movie star who takes up residence in a neighboring mansion. Whereas the movie star, Sheela Devi (Shashikala), befriends the couples because of their apparent simplicity (*saadgi*), the women and their husbands are titillated by the star's wealth, fame, and lifestyle. Viewers first glimpse Sheela Devi descending a curved staircase (which was Hindi cinema's visual

FIGURE 5.9 Film still of "Aamdani atthanni" song in *Teen Bahuraniyan*. Courtesy of the National Film Archive of India.

code for luxurious interiors, as Rachel Dwyer and Divia Patel note).[93] She is in conversation with her private dressmaker (Jagdeep), who is showing her a style magazine to design clothes in the latest figure-hugging trend. Soon the wives start pawning off items from their bridal dowries (*dehéj*) to replace generic household goods with named brands in order to invite Sheela Devi into their home. The wives savor the name of each desired product in English. They want to replace a *lakdi ki purani almari* (an old wooden cupboard) with a Godrej (an Indian brand eponymous with steel cupboards because of its monopoly), a *bijli ka pankha* (electrical fan) with an air conditioner, a *gandi khatiya* (dirty cot) with a "double bed" and "Dunlop pillow." Hapless husbands transform the shared family space littered with stainless steel utensils, clothes, lawn chairs, and paper calendars into a model middle-class living room. The family room is now remodeled as an aspirational middle-class living room with upholstered sofas, throw pillows, vases, curtains, painted walls, statuary, a coffee table, and eventually a telephone to call Sheela Devi. It is father-in-law Dinanath (played by veteran actor Prithviraj Kapoor), a retired schoolteacher, who manipulates events to teach his daughters-in-law and sons the valuable lesson that such showiness (*dikhava*) gives them only false respectability (*jhooti izzat*).

The film is a two-hour-and-forty-minute lesson against credit economy. The family's three sons present three ways of living beyond their means, using Hindi

FIGURE 5.10 Sheela Devi (Shashikala) and her designer (Jagdeep) in *Teen Bahuraniyan*. Courtesy of the National Film Archive of India.

as well as English words to describe their methods of purchase. They get their desired consumer nondurables "*bhade par,* on hire," "*mahiney ke hisaab se,* on [monthly] installments," and with "*udhaar,* on credit." The sons ask Dinanath condescendingly, "Do you know the meaning of 'installment,' father?" (Installment *kisko kehten hain, malum hai pitaji?*) To which he replies, "Do you know the meaning of 'insolvent,' sons?" (Insolvent *kise kehte hain, jaante ho bete?*) These opposing ideologies of wealth are summarized in a mathematical song sung by the children of the household under Dinanath's tutelage:

> One rupee spent for every half rupee earned,
> Oh Brother, what a joke.
> The result is: Mr. Broke!
>
> *Aamdanni atthanni, kharcha rupaiya,*
> *Oh Bhaiya, Na poocho na poocho haal.*
> *Natija Than-Than Gopal!*[94]

On learning the error of their ways, the daughters-in-law dutifully accept their father-in-law's pronouncement that women are the root cause of all good and evil.[95] What leads the housewives astray and what must be corrected is female desire for products and lifestyles far in excess of their husband's lower-middle-class incomes. As it happens, the first wife's husband teaches music at a school, the second's is an office clerk, and the third's is a sales representative for a medical company. The wives have been lying about their husband's jobs in their conversations with Sheela Devi and transforming them into desirable white-collar professionals.

Like the middle-class films of Basu Chatterjee and Hrishikesh Mukherjee that it preceded by a decade, *Teen* depicts male leads that are employed in a range of nondescript service sector jobs somewhere in the amorphous social middle. Cinematic representations of the Indian middle class have often been a bellwether for the nation's attitudes toward consumerism.[96] Despite a national job market overwhelmingly dominated by a flexible or informal sector with a dearth of written contracts, social security, pensions, and eligible paid leave in India (in 2014, 73 percent of the employed urban population was reportedly working without contracts),[97] the visual image of a modest income and secure job anchoring the middle class has been a staple of Indian films, television, and commercials at least since the 1970s. The Indian economy's liberalization following 1991 cemented the rhetorical position of middle classes as the primary beneficiaries of the nation's economic growth.[98] Sociologists argue that screen images of a globalizing middle-class consumer (portrayed in films such as *Yeh Jawaani Hai Diwani* [2013], *Break ke Baad* [2010], and *Karthik Calling Karthik* [2010]) are contrary to "the actual labor market of the 'new' upwardly mobile urban middle classes" that face "processes of retrenchment, increased job insecurity and a structural shift to subcontracting work."[99] With the liberalization of India's economy, more people identify as middle class and aspire to its cultural capital despite lacking the real income, access, social opportunities, or mobility to belong to it.

Contemporary Bollywood's celebrations of consumerism indicate that this ambivalence toward capitalism, neoliberalism, and individualism is largely anachronistic in India today. The expectation that materialism was opposed to moral integrity seeped away in the 1990s when it no longer served the state's financial model or the national narrative.[100] India's middle class was no longer made to feel subservient to a sense of collective national responsibility. The new middle class is more likely to lay its claim to economic individualism and the pursuit of profit without guilt, and in this sense it becomes more akin to the

American middle class. In contrast, the expectation that India's middle classes would sustain the nation's commercial growth while being prudent and seeing through the superficiality of material possessions was founded on a socially ambivalent embrace of consumerism in the 1960s and 1970s. Even in the films that explicitly celebrate consumerism and travel, such as *Love* and *Evening*, we see some traces of this ambivalence writ small.

Love in Tokyo *and* Evening in Paris
Despite their use of spectacular camera movements and foreign locations, *Love* and *Evening* share some unexpected affinities with *Teen*. Both films trade on the visual and sensorial lure of consumption within a measured hermeneutics of suspicion toward it. *Love* and *Evening* show us a consumerist paradise embedded in plots that seem thin until they reveal a moral and ideological weight in their gendered messages of sacrifice. In *Evening*, Sharmeela Tagore's character disavows her wealth and swaps identities with her maid to find true love, although this elaborate set-up quickly becomes irrelevant to the film's plot twists and capers. In *Love*, Asha Parekh's character volunteers to sacrifice her eyes for her boyfriend, thus winning over his mother. This alarming proposal marks no particular emotional high point for a film that moves swiftly to its next dramatic episode. What the volunteering of sight achieves, however, is proffering the idea that female sacrifice is a necessary precondition for parental consent (even among Parisian Indians). Sketchily formulated plot points seem like fleeting set pieces and make little sense within the films' regimes of visual pleasure until we realize that they are part of a larger cultural narrative about wealth. Protagonists—particularly women—must situate their consumerist display within a show of selflessness to be redeemed within the narrative. A later film such as *Bunty aur Babli* (2005) would give audiences the vicarious and picaresque experience of travel, high living, and easy money absent of any sense of self-abnegation or guilt. Bollywood films today lack, as others have noted, qualms about getting rich and staying rich.[101]

It is useful to reprise Ranjani Mazumdar's and Madhava Prasad's contesting positions on these films in this context. As Mazumdar notes, against Prime Minister Nehru's anticapitalist and Third Worldist internationalism that "bracketed and filtered" the idea of the global within nonaligned pacts with Asian and African nations, a parallel "consumerist imaginations of excess held sway and sought to break free" of post-Independence politics during the 1960s.[102] She finds evidence of this in global travel films such as *Sangam*, *Love*, and *Evening*, in which "foreign locations were incorporated into the narratives of the films as tourist site, as the place of romantic possibility, and as the space of encounter with new forms of urbanism."[103] Citing the same films (and on occasion the same sequences) as Madhava Prasad, Mazumdar suggests that what "Prasad reads as an ideological need to establish the uniqueness of the national culture, emerges as a deeply ambivalent space, working creatively to generate alternative maps of desire."[104] Whereas Prasad emphasizes the state's ideological hold as moral guardian and authorizer of national identity, Mazumdar focuses on the desire for change represented in commercial cinema's embrace of urban modernity and consumerist fantasies, echoed in the extra-cinematic worlds of advertisement, fashion, and style magazines of the 1960s. Prasad's Marxist historiography omits the realm (and fantasy) of consumerism during the so-called period of formal subsumption that Mazumdar effectively recuperates.

Reading across both Prasad's and Mazumdar's interpretations of commercially successful films in the 1960s helps us see the extent to which this decade was defined by debates over the status of film as a pedagogical medium versus commercial entertainment for the masses. A sentiment of ambivalence toward free market economics was of a piece with debates over the regulation of entertainment and consumer goods in the 1960s and 1970s. When held in comparison to images from the 2000s, spectacles of leisure and consumer nondurables appear to enter national consciousness via visual images that were charged not only with desire but also with some guilt. A historical affect of ambivalence, noted by Mazumdar but marginal to her argument about the decade's regimes of desire, acquires greater significance when we think through the differences between the policies and the affective economies of globalization in the late 1990s in opposition to the 1960s and 1970s. The look of the background actors and the approach to location filming vary correspondingly between these two eras.

ANTIREALISM AND REALISM AS PRODUCTION PRACTICES

In the early sequences of *Love* set in India and shot in a studio, we witness an archetypal Hindi movie party sequence of the era. These parties were typically composed of adults in a large mansion or bungalow, with background elements including elaborate chandeliers, bejeweled women, suited men, and the occasional piano or cake (as in Vijay Anand's *Jewel Thief*, 1967). Other than featured leads, junior artists typically played background parts in such scenes. Ambient actors who filled out well-heeled party scenes in commercial films from the 1960s through the 1990s were drawn largely from the daily wage category of Superclass junior artists discussed previously. Postglobalization, background actors in such sequences are predominantly not junior artists but models. Shifts in the visual look and patterns of employment of background actors are linked to transformations in Bombay cinema's aesthetic from a largely *antirealist* to a *realist* style.[105] While neither the ambient junior artists of the preglobalization era nor the post-2000s models can be described as accurate representations of any empirical or statistical composition of Indian society (if such a representation were at all possible), the appearance of background actors in Indian films prior to the 1990s was in keeping with the overall *in*significance of set and lighting continuity in commercial Hindi films that prioritized the emotional logic of sequences over their visual coherence or credibility.[106]

Comparing background actors who portray college students in the Aamir Khan starrer *Dil* (1990) with Farah Khan *Main Hoon Na* (2004) over a decade later, with Shah Rukh Khan in the lead, shows the extent to which ambient actors conjure up a different visual universe pre- and postglobalization. Prior to the 1990s, background actors in Hindi films did not vary greatly in age or appearance irrespective of whether they were playing teenagers in a college classroom, middle-aged office workers, or angry mobs on the street. They were uniformly drawn from the unionized JAA or MKS. Sitaram Kadam, a junior artist coordinator who has worked in the business since the 1990s, points out that demands on his business have changed greatly in recent years:

> So, this is the era of models. . . . In a disco scene, producers want half-clothed girls. The thing with union people is, it's the same people in all the movies, you see them everywhere. So we tell the producers, mate, union people are union people. We can't change them. So they say, pal, then give me a model.

> *Toh abhi hai* model *logon ka zamaana . . . toh disco ke scene mein* half *kapde pehanne waali ladkiyan chahiyen hai . . . ye union ke logon ke saath aisa hota hai ki, har picture mein wohi hain, har jagah wo hi dikhte hain. Toh hum log un* [producer] *ko bolte hain, yaar, jo union mein hain woh hain. Unko hum* change *nahin kar sakte. Toh phir bolte hain, yaar, phir* model *daalo.*

Prior to the new millennium, a commercial Hindi film was not judged as qualitatively inferior if it used lighting, sound, or background actors in discontinuous and antirealist ways. In the first twelve minutes of *Love*, for instance, the film provides its two key male protagonists with MacGuffinesque rationales for traveling to Tokyo. We witness Ashok (Joy Mukherjee) and Mahesh (Mehmood) in brief episodes of drama and high slapstick. Story- and plotwise,

FIGURES 5.11 AND 5.12 Junior artists portraying a college scene in *Dil*.

these early episodes represent a continuous segment of time. Yet we follow Mahesh through romantic hijinks in outdoor shots that are darkened to indicate nighttime, while in indoor shots within the same block of time we see Ashok's mother Gayatridevi (Lalitha Pawar) in her mansion with windows lit for daytime. Such discrepancies were commonplace in commercial Hindi films when lighting and visual continuity were not priorities in the way that they are for Bollywood films today. The global travel films and domestic melodramas of the 1960s were formally antirealist in this sense, which translated into an equivalent latitude in expectations of realism from the kinds of people hired to

FIGURES 5.13 AND 5.14 Models as background actors portraying a college scene in *Main Hoon Na*.

play ambient parts in films. Background actors did not have to reflect changes in spatial locations as dramatically and could remain the same from one scene to the next without disrupting the codes of a fictional universe.

Filmmakers from India's parallel cinema movement in the 1970s who wanted to make films that maintained a sense of realism in environments as well as a shot-to-shot consistency in appearance, background, lighting, and sound struggled against this regime. The rationing of film stock added material obstacles to their efforts to gain a unified artistic vision. To quote filmmaker Shyam Benegal, "Film you can't measure like that. In feature films, performances matter. So many hits and misses, so many improbables, you are taking a chance on performances, on camera movement, on focus pulling, on recording, on lighting, in each one of these things something can happen, something can go wrong and you have to re-shoot. . . . But the government decided how much stock you got, how much work you could do."[107] Although there were certainly exceptions in the world of commercial cinema, it was the art, experimental, and middle cinemas of India that aesthetically invested in a sense of actual location and nonactors, nonstars, or deglamorized stars to recover a sense of real locations in India, or to experiment with the real as an artifice. Examples range from Ray's *Apu* trilogy (1955, 1956, 1959) and Ghatak's *Nagarik* (1952, released in 1977) to later productions such as Benegal's *Ankur* (1974), Basu Chatterjee's *Rajnigandha* (1974) and *Chitchor* (1976), Govind Nihlani's *Ardha Satya* (1983), and Adoor Gopalakrishnan's *Elippathayam* (1981). The aesthetic commitment to location filming was frequently made despite limited technological infrastructure.

In his documentaries, for instance, Benegal improvised a sort of sync sound effect. He tied pillows to the noisy Arriflex 35 IIC camera, muffling the motor noise of the camera in order to film images while recording the sound simultaneously. To shoot his first feature *Ankur* on location in Yellareddiguda, outside Hyderabad, Benegal used a heavy studio Seiki camera ("a kind of Japanese copy of a Mitchell") with a soundtrack to record sound directly on location on 35 mm sound tape because, according to him, "I value the ambience of the location, the sense of the place, which you must feel tangibly." Benegal and Ray both decided to use studio cameras rather than more portable cameras to shoot on location for *Ankur* and *Pather Panchali*, respectively, because the studio cameras were more silent. This meant that they had to improvise by taking studio paraphernalia to actual locations. For the Apu trilogy, Ray had actors recording their dialogue immediately following the film shoot on a pilot track (an audio track with controlled speed to assist synchronization). Effectively, because of their commitment to an aesthetic of audio-visual realism, these filmmakers ventured to record sound on location and simulate a sort of sync sound effect prior to the arrival and adoption of potable silent cameras in India. They worked in what Benegal describes as an "amateurish" territory, confronting India's "technological irregularities" with "the ingenious search of solutions, or *jugaad*" to use Ravi Sundaram's words from another context.[108] The bifurcated industry model framed—in the sense that it enabled—how Indian filmmakers would define their options for shooting and representing locations visually and aurally.

India's parallel cinema's aesthetics of realism was a response, in part, to the audio-visual discontinuities and irrelevance of visual and narrative continuity in blockbuster films such as *Evening* and *Love*. If the commercial films' spectacular exploration of romance in foreign lands made them typical of the blockbusters of their era, their antirealism was equally characteristic of a bulk of mainstream films from the preglobalization period. And while unreliable supplies and variable qualities of rationed film stock in the 1960s and 1970s did not *create* Hindi cinema's discontinuous aesthetics (or what Lalitha Gopalan calls the "cinema of interruptions"),[109] they certainly encouraged and materially contributed to them. The potential patchwork of raw stock and unpredictability of film finance gave Hindi cinema's aesthetic more to work *against* in order to achieve visual continuity and formal realism. Bollywood's contemporary move toward an aesthetic of audio-visual realism (combined with a postmodern self-reflexivity) stands in contrast to mainstream popular cinema's antirealist production practices of previous periods. The contemporary impetus of big-budget Bollywood productions to demand models rather than junior artists to populate the upscale location favored by its blockbusters is, in this sense, not only an erasure of all but the most affluent classes on-screen. It is also Bollywood's attempt to cater to an audience that possesses, or prides itself in possessing, a discriminatory taste for visual continuity that marks (via nostalgic affect, technological finesse, or winking references) the distance between itself and pre-1990s Hindi cinema.

The push toward using actual locations and a formal commitment to audio-visual realism can be seen across a range of films with vastly different scales of production in the post-2000 period, ranging from the ventures of Yash Raj and Dharma Productions to the smaller-scale genre films of Mukesh Bhatt.[110] Boosted by a growth in middle-class consumerism, Bollywood's visual artifices of global travel and cosmopolitanism appear alongside localized representations in alternative, *hatke* (different, off-the-beaten path), and multiplex films that abound in heterogeneous and detail-rich images of India's cities, shantytowns, urban slums, and rural locations.[111] Despite their opposing themes, styles, and locations of representation, the Bombay film industry's blockbusters and alternative films reveal commonalities in their stylistic and production choices, namely, that both adhere to a formal audio-visual realism that prioritizes actual locations and sync sound recording. As demonstrated, these aesthetic shifts occur alongside, and motivate, changes in the professional spaces of Hindi cinema that are yoking together a combustible range of social classes as the film industry negotiates its informal past with a corporatizing present, to attract new social groups to expanding below-the-line professions. It also leads to a greater bifurcation in the appearance of places and people that count as cosmopolitan and a transfer of background work from unionized labor to nonunion models.

Corporatization and globalization depend on transforming spaces of production into markets for the consumption of space itself. The production of Brand India is a prime example of this. Henri Lefebvre notes that the more people become consumers of space, whether as tourists or as viewers of glossy images, the more they forget what is involved in the production of those spaces.[112] In this chapter, I have argued that taking the appearance of Brand India at face value, as it presents itself in Bollywood's cosmopolitan backdrops and in India's touristic marketing of itself, ignores the everyday and lived messiness of its production. Locational backdrops of Bollywood blockbusters that depict the consumerist nonplaces of globalization and iconic locations of international tourism are abstracted surfaces.[113] These abstracted spectacles of consumption belie the checkered history of consumerism in post-Independence India, and the heterogeneous labor of workers from a widening range of socioeconomic classes that produce the images.

An ethnographic profile of those involved in the pre-production work of putting together the look of Hindi cinema's locational backgrounds reveal technical, business, and film school graduates carving out jobs from a disorganized working-class sector, resulting in assorted filmmaking practices and significant social readjustments within the film industry. As the nation redefines itself within a changing ecology of privatization, globalization, and Hindutva, those producing the look of its commercial cinema's backgrounds represent a range of social classes colliding and cohabiting in India today. At one end, corporate-speak, professionalization, and streamlined filmmaking technologies are increasingly significant in Indian location filming. At the other end, people working on organizing locations for films in India have to be conversant with modes of spatiality and sociality defined by municipal practices and local, regional, or urban environments. Large-scale structural changes introduced by media corporatization do not obliterate the need to grapple with paperwork, crowds, noise, and (professional as well as Sena-supported) workers, unions in Bombay. Negotiations on the ground mark India's filming locations as the site of a new kind of interface between skilled and unskilled below-the-line film workers who identify as India's emerging amorphous middle class.

CONCLUSION:
CINEMA AND HISTORIOGRAPHIES
OF SPACE

The critical hermeneutic is still enveloped in a temporal master-narrative, in a historical but not yet comparatively geographical imagination.... Space still tends to be treated as fixed, dead, undialectical; time as richness, life, dialectic, the revealing context for critical social theorization.

EDWARD SOJA, *POSTMODERN GEOGRAPHIES*

It would seem that Soja's objection, which closely echoes Foucault's complaint ("Did it start with Bergson, or before? Space was treated as dead, the fixed, the undialectic, the immobile. Time, on the contrary, was richness, fecundity, life, dialectic"[1]), is now passé. In the December 2007 issue of *Rethinking History*, Edward Dimendberg noted that challenges from theories of space to "the hegemony of temporality" were so well entrenched in the humanities that it was the historian who was beginning to feel "discredited in the wake of the postmodern rejection of metanarratives about the meaning and direction of history."[2] Certainly, the critical appeal to comprehend the twentieth century's continuing legacy as the "epoch of space . . . the epoch of simultaneity . . . the epoch of juxtaposition, the epoch of the near and far, of the side-by-side, of the dispersed" has been issued by a number of philosophers, social theorists, and geographers since the 1970s.[3] In the new millennium, offshore accounts of the global 1 percent, cross-border networks of terrorism, geographies of antiimmigrant and antiminority rage,[4] legions of destitute and refugee populations, and feeble national responses to a planetary climate crises make it clear that something dramatic is shifting once again in how humanity organizes its economic, political, ecological, and social space.

As a field, film studies is ideally positioned to examine the double helix of sociality and spatiality because of the form and distributive logic of its object of analysis. Cinema's use and simulation of places, settings, and landscapes mimics, extends, subverts, or presages natural and social environments, of which films are also a part. Its dependence on circuitries of technological hardware, networks of trade practices, regulations of commodity, conventions of practitioners, places of communal exhibition, and habits of private screening make it part of a range of spatial scales and sites. These include political and fiscal territories, geographies of taste, and, in Giuilana Bruno's evocative phrase, the human "atlas of emotion."[5] If the spatial turn in film studies is nothing new, however, navigations of cinema's hybrid status as a representative medium, technomaterial commodity, phenomenological experience, and affective matrix—all of which are an integral part of (and traffic with) our social worlds—remain challenging to operationalize. Ontological and methodological segregations are commonplace. I started writing this book with the assumption that while the verticality of periodized and geographically defined research may be the traditional remit of film history, the scope of a spatial critique in film studies could be fully announced only if it cut across methodological differences to consider the role of space in cinema's representational, cultural, commodity, and technomaterial forms. I called this project a spatial film historiography because, through a study of films about places in India, I aimed to (a) show the scales of cinema's spatiality as a screen image, a social and economic commodity, and an affective medium; (b) consider how cinema was constituted in relation to a range of socioeconomic, disciplinary, experiential, and geopolitical spaces; and (c) maintain an autocritical approach toward my own analytic categories and words, because they actively participate in demarcating and normalizing epistemic boundaries in our discipline.

My intent has been to dislodge the centrality, though not the significance, of cinema's representational space. Representational space—the filmic space of the image on the screen—has historically dominated conversations about cinematic space because it is the most visually spectacular of its spaces. The sheer visual force of the cinematic image has been such that Henri Lefebvre, the philosopher central to the spatial turn in social theory, condemned the entire medium for it.[6] Partially as a function of his Marxist critique of ideational forms, Lefebvre conceived of cinema as an abstracting form of art at the expense of attending to its productive infrastructures. "Take images, for example, photographs, advertisements, films. Can images of this kind really expose errors concerning space? Hardly. Where there is error or illusion, the image is more likely to secrete it and reinforce it than to reveal it. No matter how 'beautiful' they may be, such images belong to an incriminated 'medium' . . . images fragment; they are themselves fragments of space. Cutting things up and rearranging them, *découpage* and *montage*—these are the alpha and omega of the art of image-making."[7] Lefebvre's argument about film (defined here primarily in terms of its images and frames) is of a piece with his objection against two forms of illusions—the "illusion of reality" and the "illusion of transparency"[8]—that, according to him, conceal the nature of space as a social product. The illusion of reality stems from the belief that things have a reality independent of subjects, discourses, and thought. The illusion of transparency makes the opposite error of fetishizing representation, the word, and design. The "material idealism" of the former (objects determine reality) and the "philosophical idealism" of the latter (language and discourse determine reality) are related, in that both hide the manner in which each society creates its space and the rules governing it.[9] Cinema stands indicted here because it promotes the illusion of transparency, and its visuality overwhelms its object-status. "People *look*, and take sight, take seeing, for life itself."[10] So when Lefebvre asks, "how many errors, or worse, how many lies, have their roots in the modernist trio, triad or trinity of readability-visibility-intelligibility," film stands in a lineup of suspects. For the leading philosopher of space, film is preemptively culpable because it trades on its excessive visuality to present abstracted fantasies of (and to) the real world.[11]

Where Histories Reside has been a response to Lefebvre's specter haunting film studies with two unanswered questions. First, if the cinematic form abstracts space, can its privileged position at the seam of mental space (that is its canvas) and socioeconomic space (where lie its technologies and institutions) reveal anything *beyond* the abstraction of space? This question is about ontology because it rests on how we define cinema. Second, as states, markets, corporations, and industries produce their cinemas, is it possible to see these structures as themselves reified forms of institutional space? How are the boundaries of their territorial, economic, and ideological power exercised and negotiated through the management of film, which has the power to visually represent such institutions? This question is about historiography because it makes assumptions about how institutional structures and creative forms interrelate, and how we should study and write about them. My short answer to both questions is, yes. The preceding chapters have been the longer response.

One of the challenges in writing this response has been that space is defined in widely divergent ways in film studies, and perhaps appropriately so. In enumerating social, material, and immaterial spaces, Soja adds to Michael Dear's roster and enumerates so many that they have to be alphabetized, from "absolute, abstract, appropriated, architectonic space" to "urban, utopian, and women's space."[12] There are ways in which cinema can be considered as a part of all such spaces. I conclude this book by returning to the question of how space has been parsed as a cinematic and social concept in film studies, a question I first pursued in the introduction, in order to reflect back on my own approach to the question. In writing about space, cinema, and historiography, I found myself turning to the wealth of relevant scholarship in film and media studies, in addition to a bibliographic cluster that combined Lefebvre and Bazin with Marxist, feminist, and anticolonial theorists such as Massey, Spivak, Mohanty, Kaplan, and others. A (reductive) categorization may consider Lefebvre a materialist, Bazin an idealist, and neither as avowedly anticolonial or feminist, which makes my adoption of their perspectives seem incoherent. My concluding reflections on this book's spatial film historiography will refer to the expanding scholarship on film, space, and place and to the spirit (if not strictly to the letter) of Lefebvre's and Bazin's arguments to defend their cohabitations in my book.[13]

HISTORICIZATIONS OF FILM AND SPACE

Scholarship in film studies has long been involved in a careful historicization of cinema's formal, narrative, and aesthetic spaces. David Bordwell, Janet Staiger, and Kristen Thompson's analysis of classical Hollywood cinema and Madhava Prasad's study of the realist and melodramatic conventions of Indian cinema show film aesthetics and style to be both a reflection and product of dominant modes of production.[14] Writing from neoformalist and Marxist traditions, respectively, the historians analyze commercial film style to expose links between material and aesthetic spaces, attesting to film's status as a product of its economic and industrial context even when the films themselves obscure such relationships of homology.[15] These histories of cinema expose the mechanisms through which state, capital, and industrial practices are naturalized at the level of film style, to present the materialist basis of filmic space. Further, film and media scholars studying cinema's emergence as an aspect of nineteenth- and twentieth-century industrial and technological modernities foundationally frame cinema in the context of social spaces.[16]

Historians of early cinema and visual cultures such as Tom Gunning, Miriam Hansen, Anne Friedberg, Vanessa Schwartz, and Jeannene Przyblyski discuss film as a form embedded within the spatiality and sensorium of new architectures, optics, and technologies that emerged with European modernity.[17] Zhang Zhen and Ranjani Mazumdar turn the lens toward non-Western modernities.[18] Offering a scrutiny of films that use maps in *Cartographic Cinema*, Tom Conley sees similarities between the topographical representations of maps and the projections of a film, because both re-create a multidimensional world through flat surfaces while carrying their legends within them, to help viewers graphically rearticulate real spaces. Conley finds (by way of de Certeau, Deleuze, and Foucault) that in particular cinematic remappings of the world "what goes in the name of the archive becomes a tactics because it resists any and all complacency that inheres in pregiven truths."[19] If cinema promises revelations of the social rules undergirding the management of real places in this instance, the "spatiovisual" art of cinema transform Giuliana Bruno's theoretical prose into a poetics when she elaborates on film's function as part of "the haptic map designed by the modern age."[20]

The historical work of film and visual studies scholars overcomes the potential impasse of presuming cinema to be ontologically split between its mimetic and symbolic impulses.[21] Jonathan Crary argues that the photographic apparatus, functioning independently of the spectator's body, reorganizes the heterogeneous human senses of vision and sound under a singular optical perspective.[22] Crary considers cinematic technology and vision on a continuum with the historical disaggregation and reassembly of the subject, who is rendered into abstractable units that can be manipulated by modernity's techniques of power and knowledge. The danger of universalizing Crary's particular technological narrative of sensory abstraction is averted if we understand cinema's emergence to be a spatially dispersed phenomenon, mired in a range of political and institutional uses the world over. As Gunning argues, "Considering historically the definitions of film as a medium helps us avoid the dilemma of either proscriptively (and timelessly) defining film's essence or the alternative of avoiding any investigation into the diverse nature of media for fear of being accused of promoting an idealist project."[23]

Although a concern with the digital is his immediate provocation, Gunning's point is that as a medium, cinema has always been defined within a "welter of new inventions" and "models and uses."[24] He calls for an account of cinema's dispersed contexts to enable a nonproscriptive and historicist return to the question, once again, of what is cinema?[25] "Rather than myths of essential origins, historical research uncovers a genealogy of cinema, a process of emergence and competition yielding the complex formation of an identity."[26] Gunning's invitation, and that of media archeologists, to begin with "thick descriptions of how media work, that is, phenomenological approaches that avoid defining media logically before examining the experience of their power," brings us unexpectedly back to a realm valued by Lefebvre: namely, the *processes* through which objects, institutions, lives, and realities take shape in (material and immaterial) spaces, rather than a passive acceptance of our world through the categories presented to us. Despite the difficulty of speaking outside given taxonomies, in *The Production of Space* Lefebvre uses a form of argumentation and structure that Soja compares to a "fugue, a polyphonic composition," filled "with Aleph-like references to the incapacity of language, texts, discourses, geographies and historiographies to capture fully the meanings of human spatiality"[27] at the intersection of lived, perceived, and represented spaces. Lefebvre tries to infuse his book-length argument with the cadences of music in order to give up inert terminologies and grasp the active emergence of social space within the "dialectics of the lived and the conceived, the "real" and the "imagined" worlds."[28]

Cinema, with its simultaneously referential and representational technology,[29] turns out to be an exemplary form through which to grasp the dialect between our lived, conceived, and perceived worlds. Constituted between the material, social, and imagined spheres, the moment when a place or event is captured as a moving image can serve as a node from which to explore each of those constitutive planes. Such a project is allied with the work of film historians and theorists Noa Steimatsky, Paula Amad, and Anand Pandian.[30] The authors start from the camera's relationship to place to write broader histories. Attending to the moment of encounter with an interest in writing an ethnography of the present, Pandian provides an account of location shoots in the contemporary Tamil film industry. Steimatsky's study of Italian neorealist films draws out their contradictory modernisms in depicting postwar Italian landscapes, and Amad's work articulates the fascist as well as the avant-garde drives behind aerial photography during World War I. Both Steimatsky and Amad bring out ambivalences and conflicting affiliations within a period, technology, and style. An inquiry that begins with how places were actively experienced and visually constituted in the process of filming also denaturalizes presumed unities (such as those of genres, nations, periods, and institutions). Such agnosticism can provide the basis for both a self-reflexive historiography and a historicist framework for cinema's ontology.

BETWEEN CHAOTIC PLACES AND INSTRUMENTAL SPACES

Grappling with history not through the presumptively determinative or homologous relationships between political economy and culture but rather through the more chaotic relationships between a place, the context of filming, and the cinematic apparatus offered me substantial promise. I found that it could help me trace (a) the *dependence* of cinematic commodities on (regulatory, capitalist, and aesthetic) institutions; (b) the *difference* between screens and their profilmic and environmental elements, as well as the unpredictable afterlives of moving images; and (c) the *consolidation* of politico-economic regimes through their strategies of managing the visuality and meaning of territories and bodies through film. Let me begin by addressing the first two aspects of this study. Differences between screen images and profilmic elements have included, in this book, the lived experiences of production personnel involved in a shoot, and the social histories (and memories) of recorded places that exist in excess of their images on film. This kind of information remains difficult to recover, particularly from the past and particularly from archive-impoverished India, but staying alive to their possibility changes the ambition and scope of historical narratives.

For instance, we know from the notes of Eugene Lourié, production designer on *The River*, that a two-year-old deaf and mute destitute Indian girl helped lift bricks to build huts for Renoir's film. We also learn from these notes that this child "cried uncontrollably," "ran after the departing vehicles," and "threw herself on the ground despondently" when the foreign crew concluded their filming schedule.[31] On a few rare occasions, such incidental stories and occurrences are incorporated into a film's text, but more often than not they linger as uneasy or additional memories. In the self-reflexive *Akaler Sandhaney*, for instance, the film's opening sequence shows a farmer laughing at the urban film crew that arrives in his village to shoot a film about the colonial Indian famine. This scene was based on Mrinal Sen's crew's real encounter with "an aged farmer, his body nothing more than a bundle of bones." According to Sen, the farmer shouted "almost in jest, 'Hey, look, they, the cinema *babus*, have come from the city looking for a famine. But here we are, the famine itself,' before laughing out loud."[32]

What is a historian supposed to do with this information? The easiest thing would be to ignore it. Information related to the profilmic and preproduction processes of a film are mostly incidental to the final product and difficult to grasp as part of a film's history. This is particularly true in the case of institutional analysis (as mine partially is), in which the argument leaves little room to track incidental or contingent occurrences and events. But what if we were to take seriously Walter Benjamin's injunction to the chronicler to recite "events without distinguishing between major and minor ones in accordance with the following truth: nothing that has ever happened should be regarded as lost for history"?[33] The purpose is not to lose sight of the causal determinants of events but to bring into sight its multiple, dispersed, and predictable as well as unpredictable impact across time. This is, in a way, reminiscent of film theorist André Bazin's idea that cinema can make us realize that "everything... is of like importance."[34] Bazin is talking about the lack of visual hierarchy created between events occurring in Florence during Liberation, as shown in one of the episodes in Rossellini's *Paisan* (1946). A woman learns in passing that the man she seeks is dead. If the camera makes her discovery narratively incidental and visually fleeting, it is not because her loss is unimportant. Rather, it is because grief such as hers is all pervasive. In a world crowded with people and events, this camera has allowed us to see "in the eyes of those who stand aside the reflections of other concerns, other passions, other dangers."[35] There is a similarity between the neorealist camera making the ordinary consequential by equalizing the weight of all events, and a historian allowing the caustic laughter of a farmer or the despair of a child, provoked by a film crew's arrival to and departure from a filming location, to linger beyond a filmmaker's memory or a production designer's log. These sounds were powerful enough to make their way into a newspaper interview with, Sen or an archived box of material on Renoir. Including them in a historical narrative about the films does not compound our scholarly knowledge of the films. It expands to *unsettle* it.[36]

A similar turn occurs when we consider how place-images consolidate particular regimes of looking. Let me revert to the example of Darjeeling in West Bengal, India, first offered in this book's introduction. *Darjeeling* (1954), a post-Independence short by Films Division (FD) documentarian K. L. Khandpur, celebrates the hill station as a picturesque tourist site. A few decades earlier, a Gaumont-British Instructional (GBI) short, *A Foothill Town: Darjeeling* (1937), purports to present a factual account of the hill station town but omits incendiary events that occurred there such as the 1930–1933 Chittagong youth rebellion; the assassination attempt on Bengal's governor, Sir John Anderson; and

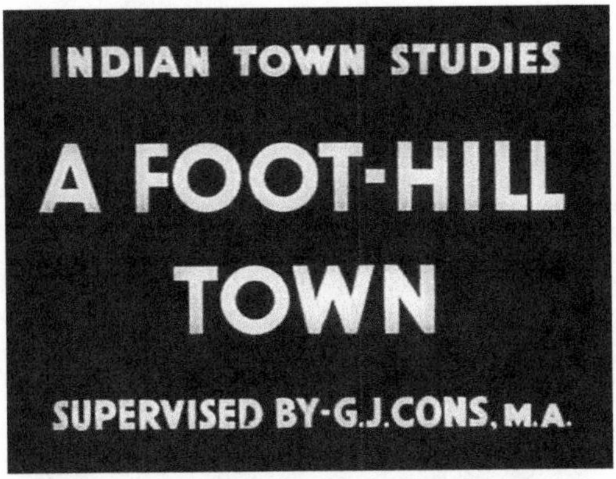

INDIAN TOWN STUDIES

A FOOT-HILL TOWN

SUPERVISED BY·G.J.CONS, M.A.

FIGURE C.1 Title frame of GBI's
instructional short *Darjeeling*.

the repressive state backlash.[37] The same Darjeeling plays a key role in Satyajit Ray's *Kanchanjungha* (1962), in which the winding and looping paths of the town become overdetermined sites for a family melodrama involving Bengal's elite *bhadralok*. And in the same decade as Ray's film, the commercial Hindi films *Hariyali Aur Rasta* (Vijay Bhatt, 1962) and *Aradhana* (Shakti Samanta, 1969) transform Darjeeling into a scenic location for illicit young romance. Although there is no equivalence between these perspectives on place in terms of their contexts of circulation, ideological power, or commercial popularity, bringing them into one analytic space denaturalizes the meanings they each attach to Darjeeling.

Each perspective posits a different relationship between film and location. Historicizing these relationships with a deliberate unruliness toward their genre segregations disperses "India" to reveal the perspectival and political regimes through which a territory has been produced as a visual environment over the years: in this instance, Darjeeling through a colonial-educational perspective (of the GBI short), national-regulatory perspective (of the FD short), regional-critical perspective (in Ray's film), and national-commercial perspective (in Bhatt's and Samanta's films). In relation to such abstractions, the organization and chaos of actually filming a location are a finally unverifiable substratum of the cinematic image. We can never go back to *that* location or *that* instance of filming. We can never know of the passersby who scoffed, inhabitants who watched, farmers who laughed, or children who cried. Their time is past and their reimagination is only available through various mediated cinematic visions, inconsequential to the gravitas of film history. In the face of this historical muteness and textual abstraction, one of the things a film historian *can* do

FIGURE C.2 Darjeeling as it appears in an *Aradhana* poster. Courtesy of the National Film Archive of India.

while scanning images for their ephemeral index is diversify archives, memories, and historical accounts of the image to undermine the image's exclusive claim to the real.

Acknowledging the multiplicity of referential records and their mutual interrogation turns on its head the notion that cinema's photographic image has a privileged (referential) connection to reality; a position associated most often with Bazin. However, it arguably maintains Bazin's interest in seeking a frame of historical analysis that can convey that *some*thing always escapes the film's screen and its historicization, because of the fecundity and ambiguity of reality in relation to the delimitation of interpretive frames. Despite drawing attention to perspectival constructions, I emphatically do not assume relativism (I am not ending with "everyone has a perspective"). As this book shows, I am calling for a reckoning with the *processes* through which places are framed by particular dispensations as the first and essential step to denaturalizing the politics of their vision and a reckoning with their power. Scanning everything from "the great strategies of geopolitics to the little tactics of the habitat" in the construction of these perspectives does not produce, in my view, a total history or "*histoire* *total*" as proposed by Fernand Braudel, and elaborated by Barbara Klinger in the context of film.[38] Rather, it creates a Foucauldian "space of a dispersion."[39] Klinger's assumption is that the pursuit of synchronically rich historical data and diachronic historical flux will provide, finally, a more comprehensive material history. However, when we see films and records from *competing* political regimes and opposing styles or transcriptional practices that describe and visualize the same place (mapping the Saidian "rival geographies"), the quest for a more complete history finally destabilizes the objects of inquiry and fields of knowledge themselves. The heterotopia of such a historiography[40]—created by holding within one analytic space a range of regimes to assess their mutual politics—breaks down the seamlessness of social spaces extended visually by their films.[41]

Holding within one analytic space a range of visual regimes: this historiographic device allows historiography to mimic cinema's spatial techniques while also revealing the camera's/screen's unreliability and partiality. I am asking that we expand our frame of analysis to consider the multiple underlying determinants of a moment, not only in time but also in space. A case in point is the previous chapter's assessment of Bollywood films. Bombay's blockbusters conjure up a sense of cosmopolitan place by using Indian and non-Indian youth as background actors. As noted, in several cases India's unionized junior artists (extras) are paid wage loss compensation for disappearing from the shots. Expanding the historical lens to accommodate lives that are valued differently, valued less, or broadening it to include labor that is visually erased despite being a central part of the production of that image makes historical analysis aspire to a kind of cinematic vision described by Bazin. The French film theorist argued for a realism that may be achieved when all things are kept in a camera's line of vision to maintain "photographic respect for the unity of space."[42] Bazin's point was that the photographic lens, despite its dependence on artifice, has the ontological ability to access the continuous space of real places, whereas other plastic arts must necessarily fabricate that sense of continuity. Underlying Bazin's argument I discern the sentiment that all things (places, beings, histories) should be maintained in line of sight because they are of like importance. Hierarchized filmic narratives or socioeconomic arrangements rarely structure things with equivalence, but outside of these constructions objects may be presumed to possess their own singularity in the world. This notion expresses a radical egalitarianism that I have wanted to take seriously.[43]

Other schools of continental philosophy—flat ontology, for instance, which proposes to apprehend the world outside the idea of scales and hierarchies—consider the implications of treating every object and being as if they were on the same plane.[44] My interest is not in the metaphysics of this question, which threatens to lose sight of systems, structures, and relations by abstracting material objects.[45] I have merely asked how presuming the fundamental equivalence of things and beings that are made unequal by a deeply hierarchical world shaped under modernity by the histories of colonialism and capital can transform the act of film historiography. Recall, once again, Walter Benjamin's words that "only a redeemed mankind receives the fullness of its past—which is to say, only for a redeemed mankind has its past become citable in all its moments."[46] In other words, history happens everywhere, all the time, and to all people. Accounting for the scattered yet co-implicated nature of our lives, and of our different encounters with the world based on our embodied subjectivities, alters the ambition and sightlines of any historical project. It also taunts language, description, and analysis with the "all-inclusive simultaneity"[47] of seeing everything and everyone at once, akin to what is experienced by the narrator in Jorge Luis Borges's short story "The Aleph." It becomes what the protagonist in Penelope Lively's novel *Moon Tiger* wishes to narrate from her deathbed: "The works, this time. The whole triumphant murderous unstoppable chute—from the mud to the stars, universal and particular, your story and mine."[48] Faced with the "murderous unstoppable chute" of reality, film and media historiographies attuned to a spatial politics therefore need to ask themselves: What are the (geographical and epistemological) locations from which we write our particular film and media histories and theories? And what if, despite this world's entrenched and seemingly intractable sociopolitical hierarchies, we write histories with the assumption that every being and event has a radical spatial equivalence in terms of their right to be acknowledged in history?

The notion of everything accreted into a complex reality returns us to the two enabling paradoxes that have framed my discussions of cinema and of history. One, that cinema reproduces the images of things and places that, while ordered by the "despotism of the director" for the screen, exist in the "chaos" of the material world.[49] And two, that history is similarly both structured and dynamic, because while it is framed by and assimilated within the context of official, national, politico-economic, and disciplinary frames, it happens to us as part of our inchoately subjective, discrete, and embodied experiences in an evanescent present. Put differently, films (particularly photographic films) are born perpetually astride the flux of the real/referential and the form of the constructed/plastic. Cinema's abilities to simultaneously reproduce and abstract reality have created fault lines in apprehending its spatiality. I turn to these fault lines next, before returning to their implications for film and to the writing of its histories.

A divergence of views over the value of cinema's ability to represent but also manipulate reality produces the first fracture on the issue of cinema's spatiality. According to Lefebvre, as already noted, cinema's technological ability to abstract reality in the process of representing it makes the medium ontologically irredeemable. For him, cinema's paradox ("images fragment; they are themselves fragments of space") becomes the grounds to repudiate the medium. Film theorists from the realist and avant-garde traditions considered some of these same properties of cinema, that is, its ability to register but also reorganize and reinvent space, as endowed with an almost talismanic power to clarify our perception, not just of reality but also of its unseen truths.[50] For instance, Siegfried Kracauer finds that objects hidden in plain sight by humanity's prejudice and habituated blindness are "cinematic" because of the medium's way of "disintegrating familiar objects and bringing them to the fore."[51] Equally interested in the cinematic medium's unique properties in relation to spectatorial effect, but focused instead on editing and arrangement (the *montage* and *decoupage* lamented by Lefebvre) are Lev Kuleshov's experiments in manipulating human anatomy and landscape by constructing a "creative geography" to push the revolutionary potential of cinematic form.[52] Writing about cinematography, experimental filmmaker Maya Deren is centrally concerned with the creative tension of transforming "spatial images" into a "time form."[53] And cinema's abilities to record spatial detail and accrete environmental minutiae into a deeper apperception of reality produce this startling assessment from Bazin, writing about Renoir: "There is no point in rendering something realistically unless it is to make it more meaningful in the abstract sense."[54] In Bazin's vision, cinema not only showed us the world in front of a lens. It could also do something more elusive and profound. It could "drive home into the mind the sharp end of an unforgettable moral truth."[55]

For these film theorists and filmmakers, the cinematic capacity to extract and reshape meaning from profilmic visual particulars meant that film was not so much an eternally "incriminated medium," as in Lefebvre's indictment, but a perceptual apparatus with the potential to be utopian as well as critical. For them, cinema functioned much like Lefebvre's theoretical apparatus. It could break our habit of seeing *through* space in order to look *into* the mechanics of its meaning production. Cinema, depending on how it was used, had the capacity to offer radically new ways of perceiving how space was socially fetishized and ossified. Such faith in the capacity of film's formal spatiality is not always part of Lefebvre's neo-Marxist critique of cinema's spatial abstractions.[56]

A second fault line in disciplinary thinking around cinematic space emerges from the tendency to separate ontological discussions of cinema from historical and geopolitical ones. Although a focus on cinematic space was central to 1970s film theory, its foundation in psychoanalysis, linguistics, and semiotics (with Lacan, Saussure, and Althusser as inspirational figureheads) meant that social and power hierarchies, primarily of patriarchy, secondarily of race, though rarely of colonialism, were addressed in relation to the cinematic apparatus, which was exemplified in most cases by European and American mainstream and art films.[57] Perhaps as a consequence of this exemplarity,[58] interrogations into space and geography today are largely particularized within the study of regional, national, postcolonial, and transnational cinemas, which are designated (or self-designate) to the analytic rubric of cultural studies and political economy but rarely of film theory. There are important exceptions,[59] but as all disciplines are hierarchical configurations and systematizations of knowledge,[60] it is important to question why the analysis of film aesthetics and theory rarely intersects with geopolitical analysis in our field, and why theoretical exemplarity still remains the burden of case studies drawn from American and European cinemas against the particularity of others. This returns us to Foucault and Lefebvre's concern with spatial distributions of knowledge as an aspect of a discipline's internal segmentation of ideas.

To briefly interrogate one of Thomas Elsaesser's statements while giving due deference to the inherently spatial metaphor and method of his generative proposal to rethink film history as media archeology,[61] Elsaesser situates Bazin "at the center of a renewal of film theory in the spirit of discovery and disclosure, terms Deleuze would endorse in opposition to aesthetic programs serving social constructivism or cultural studies."[62] One might ask why the spirit of discovery and disclosure should presumptively oppose the aesthetic program of social constructivism and cultural studies, even if it habitually does so in current field formations? This book shows, I hope, that something is gained in bringing a consciousness of the social battles fought in cultural arenas to debates in film theory and aesthetics, just as more formal precision and historicization of aesthetic form adds to cultural studies approaches that otherwise tend to concern themselves primarily with discursive politics.

Spatial thinking foundationally (as in, at the level of restructuring foundations) must engage in the practice of critical border thinking. Proposing a form of literary analysis that approaches textual and cultural comparitivism by dissolving geographical and disciplinary boundaries in *Death of a Discipline*, Gayatri Chakravorty Spivak invokes Jacques Derrida, whose work on the concepts of friendship and death push against the limits of thought and being.[63] Derrida writes, "Up to this point, we have rightly privileged at least *three* types of *border limits*: *first*, those that separate territories, countries, nations, States, languages, cultures . . . ; *second*, the separations and sharings between domains of discourse . . . ; *third*, to these kinds of border limits we have just added the lines of separation, demarcation or opposition between conceptual determinations, the forms of the border that separates what are called concepts or *terms*—these are the lines that necessarily intersect and overdetermine the first two kinds of terminality."[64] Similar to Edward S. Casey, who extends "liminological" thinking by writing about landscapes from an intermediate zone between the salient and subtle rims of a vista, and akin to Gloria Anzaldúa's and Walter Mignolo's border thinking or Mezzadra and Neilson's proposal to consider the "border as method,"[65] writing about cinema and space invites thinking across habituated separations between the ontological, the politico-economic, and the sociohistorical programs for cinema.

In pursuit of such a practice, we may consider Jacques Rancière's critique of Gilles Deleuze's movement-image (which galvanizes cinema's spatial dimension) and time-image (mobilizing its temporality). Although the complexities of Deleuze's philosophical arguments are outside my expertise and purview, Rancière's and Tom Conley's elaboration of the role of historical rupture in *Cinema 1* and *Cinema 2* are of interest for my analysis. As Conley argues, "Inasmuch as the author disclaims history . . . history sustains what he calls a taxonomical project."[66] Deleuze describes a subordination of movement, matter, and space in the postwar world as a crisis of the "action image" unleashed by the traumas of modernity. Rancière focuses on the Deleuzian assumption that it was the ruins of World War II, the horrors of concentration camps, and mass human dislocations that rendered the cinematic image (borrowing Conley's words) "in deficit in respect to what it was showing."[67] Rancière wonders if this rendering of world history, which is understood as initiating the emergence of time-image, has any option *other* than to "sanction a crisis."[68] If the postwar period inaugurates a pure optical and sound situation because the image attempts to grasp at "something intolerable and unbearable," then the sensory-motor exhaustion imputed to images is less endemic to the images than to a particular narrativization of European history, in Rancière's view.[69]

Rancière's question about the historical basis of such a divide does not refute Deleuze's philosophical meditation on cinema inasmuch as it reaffirms cinema as a modern technology of vision congenitally defined by a dialectic between material (spatial) and ideational (temporal) registers. As he notes, "The rupture that structures the opposition between the movement-image and the time-image is a fictive rupture, so that we may do better to describe their relationship not as an opposition, but as an infinite spiral."[70] Holding on to a sense of a definitive historical rupture between movement-image and time-image may in any case be problematic because the notion that movement is transcended in the actualization of optical and sound situations potentially consigns the former to an anachronistic mode of expression, thought, and being. Rancière's interrogation of the spatial and geographical basis of Deleuze's philosophical narrative here exposes how a particular trajectory of European history can become universalized into a philosophy of cinema itself. Acknowledging multiple and non-Eurocentric histories does not demand that we arbitrate over competing trajectories of cinematic form or competing degrees of human trauma and suffering.[71] Nor does it negate theories and philosophies drawn primarily from Euro-American histories and films. But it does delink the *ontology* of cinema from a particular *spatial universalization* of world history to turn the critical lens back upon historiography itself.

So while Rancière's critique of Deleuze may be debatable, at minimum he draws attention to the submergence of the geographical underpinning of history in Deleuze's philosophical taxonomy of cinema. In ways unintended by the original authors of the concepts, I suspect that conceptualizations of cinema as a *time-image*, as a *clock for seeing*, and as *change mummified* have resulted in the disciplinary habit of prioritizing theories of cinematic temporality over spatiality in ontological discussions.[72] Consequently, theories of cinema's temporality have borne a lighter burden of proof in demonstrating their relevance to the medium's ontology than theories of cinema's spatiality. An important area of innovation in the latter field is work on cinema and motion, if we understand movement as a key spatial component of the cinematic form.[73] Another is work that elaborates on a theory of film historiography with global exemplars. Phil Rosen's work, for instance, brings a spatial dimension into film history and theory by considering parallels between historiographic method and cinema's ontological form while accounting for geographical variation, as discussed next.

BETWEEN THE CREDULOUS AND SKEPTICAL VIEWER

In *Change Mummified*, Rosen influentially argues that we need to "conceptualize the interpenetration of cinema and history" in a manner that will "enrich film theory."[74] He proposes that the "attempt to conceptualize historicity in theory or practice must implicitly or explicitly acknowledge the referential ambitions of any historiography."[75] For Rosen, Bazin's film theory illuminates what lies at the core of any historical thinking: specifically, historiography's referential ambition. To count as historical, a narrative must refer to something that actually happened in the past, however effaced the past or the event. In this aspect, historiography reveals its affinity to cinematic form as theorized by Bazin. Like historiography, which "purports to be real" and is tested against a standard of reality, cinema's realism trades on spectatorial faith in the reality of the photographic image.[76] Following Bazin's writings on the ontology of the photographic image, Rosen notes that what persuades the spectator about the cinematic image's realism is therefore not its spatial likeness to the real (unlike realistic painting) but faith in a preceding moment of temporal simultaneity between reality and its mechanical capture. By "disentangling spatial likeness from the evidentiary in photographic and cinematic images, Bazin makes a crucial move," argues Rosen, when he "displace[s] considerations of the special appeal of cinematic 'realism' from the spatial similarity and dissimilarity between image and world, to issues of temporality."[77]

Admittedly, as Rosen notes, "spatial likeness and deviance are finally not the crux of Bazinian realism."[78] But I think interpreting space primarily in terms of the spatial contiguity between the world and its image permits an ascendency to issues of temporality in Bazin only because that is what obsesses the Bazinian subject with regard to the *credibility* of a photographic image.[79] The "special credibility of the automatically produced image" comes from its ability to garner spectatorial belief in the fact that, at some point in time, a real object in front of the camera created its trace on the screen's image.[80] I want to pursue Rosen's point that spectatorial affect is key to any reading of Bazin in another direction, because I think it teaches us a different lesson: that in addition to the credibility of the photographic image, Bazin is interested in the cinematic lens's ability to endow all objects with a spatial *equivalence*, stripped of discrimination that derives from a narrative's structure or humanity's habituated forms of seeing. Bazin's phenomenology asks whether a cinematic image subordinates profilmic realities to the camera's framing, movement, narrative, character development, and so forth, or whether cinema's entire artifice and arsenal of representative and symbolic techniques are at the disposal of freeing profilmic objects from such trappings.[81]

I am guided by Rosen's impulse to insert a sense of historicity into film theory, but have wanted to take a different route to get there. Rosen introduces history into theory by thinking through the significance of the temporal, indexical, and referential in Bazin's theory of film. For Rosen, the referential—as a locus of our temporally bound and changeable world—serves as the portal through which historical and geopolitical questions can be ushered into film theory.[82] My interest in excavating the role of space in the cinematic form reveals an alternative emphasis in Bazin's writings, evident in his use of spatial metaphors to realize temporal concepts. As Rosen agrees, space is "also a basic Bazanian category."[83] Although there is little room to develop it here (and Conley and Ludovic Cortade have already written on this more extensively[84]), I briefly point to a range of spatial metaphors that convey the importance that Bazin places on the weight or "centrifugal properties" of images outside the logic of their narrative.[85] In tracing the "aesthetic geology"[86] of neorealism, for example, Bazin posits that the smallest unit of cinema is the "fragment of concrete reality"; he imagines that these fragments allow the "surface of the scene" to manifest a "concrete density"; particularly when the "special density" of scenes allow them to relate to their "material context."[87] The phrases convey the mass, texture, and accretion of objects that leave their impress, in spatial terms, on images.

If cameras unmoor places and things from their temporal reality by mummifying them, then the neorealist camera does not ascribe them with meaning solely based on stories "invented by the mind."[88] Rather, it frees them from the logic of a (temporal) reality and a (symbolic) narrative to allow them their own concrete density. Consequently, even the progression of time in a neorealist film becomes not a series of abstracted moments but so many "concrete instants of life" filled with the clutter of every thing, place, and object that carries its own weight.[89] Cinematic time freed of superimposed dramatic interests is transformed into "the concrete duration of the character,"[90] because the story and plot are not much more than the minutiae of things with which a character interacts, as with Maria the maid's morning routine in *Umberto D* (De Sica, 1952).

In other words, in exploring neorealist actualizations of the cinematic camera, Bazin is not asking for a spatial likeness between image and reality, as Rosen rightly notes. Bazin is seeking camera framings and movements with the power to delink objects, places, and people from a preordained hierarchical significance within a dramatic totality in such a manner that each person, object, and place is liberated from a symbolic frame to carry their own centrifugal weight. In my view, under the Bazinian vision the camera consequently acquires a new sense of *scale*, which is always a physical measure, but here also an ethical and juridical one. Within such a cinematic world, as Bazin notes, "Man himself is just one fact among others, to whom no pride of place should be given a priori."[91] Surprisingly, this is not far from what Lefebvre asks for, when he suggests that we release objects, ideas, and relationships from their spatialization by markets, ideologies, and politics. He asks that we free them from their place in the production of totalities that subsume or consume their meanings by exposing the processes of their production to critical scrutiny. Identifying and airing in the open the mechanics through which objects, ideas, and institutions acquire an abstracted self-evidence and homogeneity becomes a critical, ethical, and political gesture.

The notion that neorealist cameras can enable new ways of spatializing objects and people permits an interpretation of cinema less invested in the form's referentiality. To return this discussion to the question of history, we could say that placing primary emphasis on the temporality of cinema (and, by equivalence, on the referential dimensions of historiography) too readily overlooks the relevance of spatial questions to the medium (of cinema) and the discipline (of history), by insufficiently accounting for the spatiotemporal dislocations against which the reconstituted continuum of both film and history are founded. While Rosen's reading of Bazin may adhere more closely to Bazin's arguments,[92] I am convinced that the spatial metaphors undergirding Bazin's film theory can be recovered to understand film and historiography outside exclusively referential urges in order to legitimate an alternative reading. Faith or belief in the temporal simultaneity of a recorded event characterize the credulous spectator in Bazin, but such a credulity is wrested from a skepticism that stems from the subject's knowledge of the differences between cinema and reality. This spectator is someone who "can say at one and the same time that the basic material of the film is authentic while the film is also truly cinema."[93]

A skeptical rather than a credulous spectator comes to the fore when we measure film's spatial reconstructions of reality in relation to the world's materiality, reminding us again (from this book's introduction) of David James's evocation of a "double hermeneutic."[94] The same may be said of history.[95] If film and history are to maintain their power over audiences, then consumers of film and of history must believe in the referentiality of cinematic or of historical narratives despite knowing about their reconstructed natures. In Bazin's words, "If the film is to fulfill itself aesthetically, we are to believe in the reality of what is happening while knowing it to be tricked."[96] So whereas space is not the provocative agent of Bazin's realism, it serves the important function of providing the material *friction* against which film's referential realism must assert itself. Following Rosen, we may use Bazin to think of film in relation to history and historiography once again, but this time to consider the spatial densities of both forms rather than their referential and temporal impulses.

Writing histories of film from the spatial perspective requires us to leverage our way into the gaps between our knowledge of cinema's plastic abilities to manipulate reality while also retaining our wonder at its powers to overwhelm that knowledge, much like Bazin's spectator. The writer of cinema's spatial histories is someone who possesses the contrary natures of a skeptical subject and the passionate cinephile within her,[97] allowing her to grasp both aspects of the cinematic simultaneously. Lefebvre did not anticipate such a viewer or writer when he cast film aside for its overwhelming powers of visual abstraction and propaganda. Cinema's foundational ability to be / to appear referential while also being manipulative is worth recuperating as inspiration for a spatially informed writing practice in film history.

In this book, I have worked to recover the function of space in (location-based) films in a number of ways: by considering the relationship between real, social, and screen spaces in documentary and commercial films; by studying cinema as an instrument of a state's territorial and ideological boundary-constructions; by examining cinema as a force for the visual reorganization of architectures and landscapes within varying political and regulatory regimes; by considering cinema's iteration as object, commodity, social profession, and visual trace within various (industrial, regulatory, economic, social, and memorial) spaces; by considering the experiences of cinema's practitioners and below-the-line workers; by assessing cinema as subject to disciplinary and archival categorizations; and by assessing my own categorical assumptions. I have also frequently shifted my geographical orientation to consider the filming of places in India by British colonial, Euro-American, and Indian production companies. What remains, then, is an assessment of these geographical shifts by way of a conclusion.

A POLITICS OF LOCATION IN HETEROTOPIC HISTORIOGRAPHIES

The following three excerpts are notes from my research for this book, and they convey the book's geographical ambit.

Mrinal Sen's *Akaler Sandhaney* (the film that opened this book) is a fictional account of a film crew traveling to an impoverished village in modern Bengal to shoot a film set during a colonial famine. *Akaler Sandhaney* interrogates the presumptions of well-fed urban actors who think they can know and represent a place of endless famine. The film questions its own presumptions of proximity and empathy.

Similar to Sen's film, Renoir's *The River* sets its fiction in a West Bengal village. Renoir constructed a village for this purpose, not far from the Indian Planning Commission's Multipurpose River Valley Project at the Damodar Basin. Neither the location's recent history of famine nor the influx of monumental technology and human displacement find a place in the film's story, but *The River* is a meditation on the experience of estrangement and exile.

In the same decade as *The River*, G. J. Cons, senior lecturer in geography at Goldsmiths, University of London, revised a textbook for British school geography instructors called *Handbook for Geography Teachers*. He added a section on teaching with visual media. Writing in 1955, Cons was an expert on visual geography because he had supervised short films on India produced by Bruce Woolfe's GBI in 1937. Even as the project to impart visual education in colonial geography was gaining traction in England, a certain Colonel D. J. Campbell, director of Map Publications, and Brigadier C. G. Lewis, surveyor general of India, were facing obstructions in standardizing Indian maps. In 1937, Lewis wanted to institute a new series of maps for Indians. Campbell's prior investigation had shown them that maps were not much in use by locals, either because "there is no general demand for maps at all, i.e., absence of map-mindedness" or "the particular map or series does not meet a demand."[98] Their efforts to create a new map series that could simultaneously standardize cartographic representation and satisfy the needs of India's inhabitants met with failure, because the topographical uses of land in India were deemed too irregular and untranslatable to the standardized grids and legends required by the Carte Internationale du Monde.

In transcribing my notes, I was taken with Brigadier Lewis and Colonel Campbell's assessment of Indians as potentially a people with an *absence of map-mindedness*. I decided to more or less embrace this assessment in structuring my narrative. Presented in the analytic space of this book are accumulated notions of India as a cinematic location that do not, collectively, yield any recognizable map. I have desired, like the English patient in this book's epigraph, an alternative cartography. This book has created its cartography by pursuing the motivations underlying various political and epistemic dispensations or *dispositifs* that cinematically organized a territory and designated it "India." Across this book's geographical and historical leaps there have been overlaps in infrastructure, personnel, and institutional precedents. This historiography may be thought of as heterotopic in defining its archives in relation to different orders of knowledge production about a region. A heterodoxy guides the material sourced in this book as well, to provide different shards of knowledge on the place-images of India. An expanded and multisited archive allows ingress to material excluded from any one version, and, more important, it invalidates the prerogative of any one interpretation of India to complete historic truth.

It may be useful, then, to think of this book's historiography as a heterotopic account of India's natural and human geography as represented in educational, documentary, and commercial films produced in Britain, India, and the United States. I am borrowing Michel Foucault's well-worn concept that describes a kind of space that exists relationally to other social spaces (hetero=other; topos=space) but contradicts them because it contains within itself a juxtaposition of different, mutually incompatible sites. According to Foucault, such sites "have the curious property of being in relation with all the other sites, but in such a way as to suspect, neutralize, or invert the set of relations they happen to designate, mirror, or reflect."[99] As a concept, heterotopia is (over)used in the humanities to analyze physical, social, and imagined sites,[100] but outside a few exceptions it is not often deployed as a mode of critical analysis.[101] In fact, Foucault's deceptively schematic essay slides between defining heterotopias as real places and proposing them as "a set of relations" or a "systematic description," inviting us to think of heterotopic *methods*.[102] Stretching Foucault's definition of "heterotopia" to imply a form of analysis and description allows us to define as heterotopic the kinds of research and writing that work "to suspect, neutralize or invert" the objects of study that they presume to "designate."[103] Applied to historiography here, it suggests a method that works with materialist tools and poststructuralist doubts as it commits to fact-based research while remaining alert to each archive's, and its own, political complicities, privileges, and alliances. At its best, a heterotopic historiography may permit an epistemology of humility, self-critique, and self-awareness of its own location to coexist with a commitment to historical facticity.

In the 1980s, Adrienne Rich made an appeal for feminism to avow a "politics of location."[104] For Rich, devising a politics of location was the means to dismantle the "position, identity and privilege of whiteness" in her feminism. In subsequent debates, a few scholars hailed Rich's concept as a feminist landmark but found it fell short of its promise and premise.[105] To Rich's argument that US feminism should acknowledge its geopolitical privilege and mobilize against the violence of US foreign policy, Kaplan responded with concern about Rich's tropic recourse to foreign policy and the geographical other in order to correct white feminism's shortcomings. For Kaplan, this made domestic gender and racial inequalities secondary; it made white feminism the norm; and it instrumentalized one inequality to get conscientized about another. Kaplan aligned herself with Michele Wallace, who asked for an "unlocated" and "schizophrenic" place of critique that neither settled into one identity nor romanticized fragmentation in organizing its politics.[106]

I take this debate in transnational feminism as a lesson on the need for a coalitional politics (even between Rich and Kaplan) that nevertheless acknowledges the inability of any one platform to serve all. This is a position that accepts the risks of a precarious (because autocritical and perpetually renewed) solidarity. Other intellectual and social movements have sought to redress sociospatial hierarchies while defining a contingent politics of location and identity, some cited by Rich and Kaplan (such as Haraway, Probyn, Lugones, and Anzaldúa), and some that we may enlist today (such as Soja's thirdspace and the politics of intersectionality[107]). Writing that calls for a politics of location while simultaneously questioning its position of privilege, normativity, and access to political representation both designates and offsets the authority of its location,[108] and is heterotopic in this sense.

A heterotopic historiography that combines a commitment to evidentiary records with a skepticism toward the politics of knowledge production is well suited to film. Despite cinema's (and history's) technological proximity to the real and the referential, the expectation that cinema (or history) will deliver the totality of the real has ever been more of a faith than a fulfillment. If nothing else, Bazin and Lefebvre would agree on this. As Bazin wrote using a spatial metaphor, "The film maker [and, we may add, the historian] does not ordinarily show us everything. . . . The mind has to leap from one event to the other as one leaps from stone to stone in crossing a river. It may happen that one's foot hesitates between two rocks, or that one misses one's footing and slips. The mind does likewise."[109] Histories reside everywhere, but institutional and visual regimes ensure that we look at only that which we are conditioned to see, or see in particular ways. It follows that film histories must divulge the spatial epistemologies guiding their definition of cinema and of history. This book has been about films shot on location in India. Equally, it has been about the institutions and relations that have produced India *and* cinema as a spatially bound image and commodity. The promise of this book has been that both can be potentially unbound by a critical spatial film historiography.

APPENDIX:

AUTHOR INTERVIEWS

BENEGAL, SHYAM. November 5, 2009. New Delhi.

DAWRA, SANJAY. October 5, 2009. Pune.

FONSECA, BAYLON. October 28, 2013. Bombay.

HATE, RAJ. September 19, 2009, and October 28, 2013. Bombay.

HOSSAIN, ANADIL. March 30, 2009, and April 15, 2009. Phone interviews LA–NY.

IRANI, SOHRAB. November 1, 2013. Bombay.

KADAM, SITARAM. October 26, 2009. Bombay.

KANCHAN. October 29, 2013. Bombay.

KUMAR, ANIL. September 7, 2009. Bombay.

MAPUSKAR, RAJESH. September 17, 2009. Bombay.

MEHTA, ANKIT. November 5, 2013. Bombay.

MEHTA, PARAS. November 5, 2013. Bombay.

NANDA, PAPPU LEKHRAJ. October 29, 2013. Bombay.

RAM, SUNITHA. October 31, 2013. Bombay.

RUKHSANA. October 29, 2013. Bombay.

SINGH, MAHENDRA KUMAR. November 1, 2013. Bombay.

SINGH, TARSEM. May 12, 2009. Los Angeles.

WHITE, JOSEPH. April 15, 2009. Phone interview LA.

Note: The list does not include film industry personnel interviewed for this project but not quoted in the book.

NOTES

INTRODUCTION

1　Traditions of thought that consider the arguments, tropes, and claims through which history acquires its historical status have made this point. See Boym, *Future of Nostalgia*; Chakrabarty, *Postcolonial Thought and Historical Difference*; Cook, *Screening the Past*; Gaines, *Pink Slipped*; Gaines, "What Happened to the Philosophy of Film History?"; Lipsitz, *Time Passages*; Nora, "Between Memory and History"; Rancière, *Names of History*; Rosenstone, *Visions of the Past* and *History on Film*; Scott, *Gender and the Politics of History*; Sturken, *Tourists of History*; Spivak, *Death of a Discipline* and *Aesthetic Education*; White, *Metahistory* and *Tropics of Discourse*.

2　Gunning defines the profilmic as "everything placed in front of the camera to be filmed" in *D. W. Griffith*, 19. In Kuhn and Westhall's *A Dictionary of Film Studies*, profilmic event and profilmic space are defined as (333) "The slice of the world in front of the film camera; including protagonists and their actions, lighting, sets, props and costumes, as well as the setting itself, as opposed to what eventually appears on the cinema screen." My book primarily deals with location-based (fiction and nonfiction) films, though there are also references to studio-based films that incorporate locations or a sense of real location (particularly in chapter 4).

3　Nichols makes this distinction in *Representing Reality* (120; emphasis added). Also referenced in Bowles and Mukherjee, "Documentary and Space," 1–13.

4　Several essays characterizing this approach were published or excerpted in Rosen's landmark anthology *Narrative, Apparatus, Ideology*, particularly Mulvey's "Visual Pleasure and Narrative Cinema"; Silverman's "Suture"; Metz's "The Imaginary Signifier"; and Heath's "Narrative Space." See also Kuhn, "*Screen* and Screen Theorizing Today." Burch and Lane offer a detailed reading of cinematic space in *The Theory of Film Practice*. Central to 1970s *Screen* theory was the Althusserian critique of ideology and psychoanalytic concepts of absence and suture in the construction of cinematic forms, influenced by Lacanian thought. *Screen* theory is historically significant, but as should be clear, I find that their approach to ideology from within the formal and discursive particularities of filmic space constrained the political ambitions of their critique.

5　See note 37 for representative examples.

6　I find alliances with and inspiration from other material culture and media archeology studies, such as Couldry and McCarthy, eds., *MediaSpace*; Huhtamo and Parikka, *Media Archeology*; Lyon and Plunkett, *Multimedia Histories*; Zielinski, *Deep Time of the Media*.

7   It is a question revived thought provokingly by several scholars in face of the apparent dissolution of cinema's specificity in the digital era, preeminent among them Rodowick in *Elegy for a Theory* and *The Virtual Life of Film*. My response, formulated through a Lefebvrian take on cinema and space, follows a different track.

8   Soja uses the term "sociospatial" in *Postmodern Geographies* to indicate the ways in which society is both space forming and space contingent. My interest is in the interrelationships between the spatial qualities of film (as object, image, affect) and the spatiality of society (as a collective of institutions, people, ideologies, policies, capital, and so forth).

9   Tuan, *Space and Place*. Regarding my use of "Bombay" for Mumbai despite the city's name change in 1995 after the electoral victory of Shiv Sena, the far-right regional (pro-Maratha and Hindu) party, I will be referring to the city as Bombay for the sake of consistency. I also don't use "Mumbai" because my discussion moves too frequently to the past (when the city was Bombay); Bollywood is still referred to as the Bombay film industry; and I oppose Shiv Sena's politics of name change.

10 de Certeau, *Practice of Everyday Life*, 112.

11 Massey, "Global Sense of Place," 24–29; Harvey, *Condition of Postmodernity*; Jameson, *Postmodernism*.

12 Harvey, *Condition of Postmodernity*, 257.

13 Harvey, *Condition of Postmodernity*, 303.

14 Massey, "Global Sense of Place," 29.

15 Massey, "Global Sense of Place," 25. She is thinking in particular of those structurally outside enclaves of power such as the poor, racial, ethnic, and sexual minorities, and women.

16 Rhodes and Gorfinkel, *Taking Place*, xii, xiii.

17 Rhodes and Gorfinkel, *Taking Place*, xii, xi.

18 Rhodes and Gorfinkel, *Taking Place*, xvii.

19 Rhodes and Gorfinkel, *Taking Place*, vii; Kracauer, *Theory of Film*.

20 Sandberg, "Location," 23–46.

21 Jacobson, *Studio before the System*, chapter 5, 168–200.

22 For more on this, see Elmer and Gasher, *Contracting Out Hollywood*. For online discussions on movie mistakes, accessed November 20, 2018, http://www.moviemistakes.com (contributor-based site); and Brian D. Johnson, "Toronto and Vancouver: Hollywood Can't Quite Disguise Them." February 17, 2012, accessed April 28, 2015. http://www.macleans.ca /culture/movies/toronto-and-vancouver-barely-incognito/.

23 Rhodes and Gorfinkel, *Taking Place*, vii.

24 Tuan, *Space and Place*, 6.

25 Massumi, *Parables for the Virtual*; S. Ahmed, *Cultural Politics of Emotion*; Puar, *Terrorist Assemblages*. See also this book's epigraph and part II, "Affective Spaces."

26 Rhodes and Gorfinkel, *Taking Place*, xii.

27 Other spatial history projects offer models for a spatial film and media history, such as the Holocaust Geographies Collaborative, https://holocaustgeographies.geo.txstate.edu, and the Stanford Spatial History project, http://web.stanford.edu/group/spatialhistory/cgi -bin/site/index.php, accessed January 2017.

28 H. Lefebvre, *Production of Space*, 21.

29　See this book's epigraph. The effort is to move away from thinking through taxonomic segmentations and toward perceiving social and conceptual relations, as elaborated in this introduction and in the conclusion's appeal for a methodological heterodoxy.

30　Taxonomically, filmed spaces would cover real and artificial environments. This book's study relates primarily to filming "actual locations" (to use an industry term) rather than sound stages, back lots, animation, special effects, or digital simulations, not to diminish such backgrounds but to delimit the scope to manageable proportions, while maintaining the theoretical ambition to critically analyze filmed space.

31　Ramaswamy, *Goddess and Nation, Lost Land of Lemuria*, and *Terrestrial Lessons*; Goswami, *Producing India*; Pinney, *Camera Indica* and *Photos of the Gods*.

32　Kuhn and Westwell, *Dictionary of Film Studies*, 165.

33　Wolfe, "From Venice to the Valley," 28.

34　Dimendberg, *Film Noir*; Bruno, *Streetwalking on a Ruined Map*; Shiel, *Hollywood Cinema*. For more examples, consult the book's conclusion.

35　James, *Most Typical Avant-Garde*, 18.

36　James, *Most Typical Avant-Garde*, 18. This similarity was pointed out by Wolfe in "Response to 'Wrong Living.'"

37　A representative selection includes Allen, "Relocating American Film History"; Amad, *Counter-Archive*; Bean, Kapse, and Horak, *Space and the Politics of Silent Cinema*; Conley, *Cartographic Cinema*; Couldry and McCarthy, *MediaSpace*; Dimendberg, *Film Noir*; Elmer and Gasher, *Contracting Out Hollywood*; Elison, *The Neighborhood of Gods*; Fay, *Inhospitable World*; Fortmueller, "Encounters at the Margins of Hollywood"; Fowler and Helfield, *Representing the Rural*; Gleich, *Hollywood in San Francisco*; Gleich and Webb, *Location Shooting*; Halberstam, *In a Queer Time and Place*; Hoyt, *Hollywood Vault*; Jacobson, *Studios before the System*; Kirby, *Parallel Tracks*; Lamster, *Architecture and Film*; Mazumdar, *Bombay Cinema*; McCarthy, *Ambient Television*; Mukherjee, *Cine-Ecology*; Parks, *Cultures in Orbit*; Peterson, *Education*; Penz and Koek, *Cinematic Urban Geographies*; Penz and Thomas, *Cinema and Architecture*; Wojcik, *Apartment Plot*; Rhodes, *Stupendous, Miserable City* and *Spectacle of Property*; Rhodes and Gorfinkel, *Taking Place*; Ruoff, *Virtual Voyages*; Schwartz, *It's So French!*; Shiel and Fitzmaurice, *Cinema and the City*; Starosielski, *Undersea Network*; Steimatsky, *Italian Locations*; Tongson, *Relocations*; Tierney, *Public Space*. Also notable are the dissertations by Fortmueller, "Part Time Work, Full Time Dreams"; Paul, "Unraveling Countryside"; and Latsis, "Nature's Nation on the Move."

38　The concept of fetishized space is in several sections of H. Lefebvre, *Production of Space*, 5, 28, 81.

39　Maier, *Location Scouting*, 7.

40　Soja, *Thirdspace*, 53. "Perceived, conceived, and lived" are Soja's terms.

41　This is reminiscent of the statement "If space is produced, if there is a productive process, we are dealing with *history*," H. Lefebvre, *Production of Space*, 46.

42　Soja, *Thirdspace*, 66. Also H. Lefebvre, *Production of Space*, 38–39.

43　Bourdieu, *Distinction*, 170. Against the backdrop of this provisional taxonomy, it could also be argued that Michel de Certeau's notion of "space" as "a practiced place" encourages a conflation of *perceived* and *lived* spaces, wherein places as static points on maps created by city planners and cartographers are transformed into itinerant spaces by walkers and travelers. de Certeau, *Practice of Everyday Life*.

44 Caldwell, *Production Culture*.

45 Pandian, "Reel Time," 203.

46 Pandian, "Reel Time," 197, expanded in Pandian, *Reel World*.

47 Examples of existing work include Dwyer and Patel, *Cinema India*; Dwyer, *Yash Chopra*; Mazumdar, *Bombay Cinema*; and San Miguel, *World Film Locations*.

48 Foucault, "The Eye of Power," 149.

49 On "minor instrumentalities," see Foucault's *Discipline and Punish* quoted in de Certeau, *Practice of Everyday Life*, 96.

50 Reorienting the history of colonial cinema as one of exchange (in addition to repression and censorship) was central to my first book, *Cinema at the End of Empire*.

51 See Peterson, *Education*, for a historical study of scenics in early cinema.

52 Consult Colonial Film: Moving Images of the British Empire, http://www.colonialfilm.org.uk/home, codirected by MacCabe and Grieveson.

53 Borges, "Funes, His Memory," 131–39.

54 Rhodes and Gorfinkel, *Taking Place*, vii.

55 Wolfe, "Response to 'Wrong Living,'" 2.

56 The sublime, typically treated as an aesthetic category, is used here to refer to an affective mode wherein apprehension and sensation are defeated in encountering something overwhelming and inexpressible. In that sense, the sublime belongs to the same order of things as the disciplinary, regulatory, and so forth, because they all describe a form of encounter and comprehension (or, in the case of the sublime, *in*comprehension).

57 This is akin to Steimatsky's study of Italian postwar directors in *Italian Locations*. She argues that the directors mobilize Italy's past through cinematically reinhabiting local sites and structures by using certain "tropes" for the "figuring of space," which also serve as the organizing structure of her book.

58 See Blackburn, *Oxford Dictionary of Philosophy* (119, 318–19) for the differences between empiricist versus rationalist thought. As Blackburn notes (318), "The Continental rationalists, notably Descartes, Leibniz, and Spinoza, are frequently contrasted with the British empiricists (Locke, Berkeley, and Hume)."

59 Consult the early cinema catalogue *The "Elge" List*, which includes such sensational fare as "Nauch Girls Dancing" (75B), "A Hindoo Sacrifice" (84B), and "Bathing Ghat" (86B).

60 A similar argument is made in another context by A. Ahmed, "Jameson's Rhetoric," 3–25.

61 Anthony Vidler argues that the sublime is created by transcending the uncanny, by pushing the uncanny, mythic, and occult to the margins. Vidler, *Architectural Uncanny*, 26–27.

62 Forster, *Howards End*, 195.

63 Tiedemann, "Dialectics at a Standstill," 942.

64 Barthes, *Camera Lucida*, 13–14.

65 Soja, *Postmodern Geographies*, 35.

66 See Martin Lefebvre's argument in *Landscape and Film*.

67 H. Lefebvre, *Production of Space*, 281.

68 Adarsh, *Film Industry of India*, 547; *Report of the Film Inquiry Committee*, 199.

69 These terms ("boundaries," "emplacements," "relationalities") mimic Michel Foucault's tracing of the western history of space in his essay "Of Other Spaces."

70 *Report of the Film Inquiry Committee*, 17, 199; Adarsh, *Film Industry of India*, 547. For additional scholarship on censorship and the Central Board of Film Censors, now Central Board of Film Certification (CBFC), see M. Mehta, *Censorship and Sexuality in Bombay Cinema*; Baskaran, *Message Bearers*; Mazzarella, *Censorium*; and Jaikumar, *Cinema at the End of Empire*.

71 For references to other inquiries on this point, and its own assessment, see *Report of the Working Group on National Film Policy*, 4–5.

72 The *Report of the Film Inquiry Committee*, also called the *Patil Committee Report* after its chairman, S. K. Patil, quotes the following passage from the poem, in English translation, to convey the film industry's long endeavor against the "stranglehold" of regulations (17): "In the net of every wave, exist / A hundred gaping mouths of crocodiles: / See what the rain drop goes through, / Before it becomes a pearl" (*"Daam-e har mauj mein hai halqah-e sad kaam-e nihang / dekhein kyaa guzre hai qatre pe guhar hone tak"*). The title's translation is mine.

73 Mazumdar elaborates on this in depth in a forthcoming monograph, some of which appears in "Aviation, Tourism and Dreaming."

74 For a detailed analysis of this form of cinema, see Peterson, *Education*.

75 Many others have exhaustively studied this (e.g., Pinney, *Camera Indica*), but I briefly discuss one aspect with regard to photographic albums in chapter 4.

76 Differentiating between a film's "setting" and "landscape," Martin Lefebvre argues that settings are the subordinated background of narrative action while the idea of landscape emerges when space is *"freed from eventhood,"* to invert the superiority of narrative and endow the land with perspectival autonomy. Lefebvre, *Landscape and Film*, 22.

77 This dynamic is described in Lefebvre, *Production of Space* (chapter 5 in particular).

78 Said, *Culture and Imperialism*, xx.

79 Sontag, *Regarding the Pain of Others*, 111.

80 Hill stations were retreats created by British colonial administrators in various parts of India as a cooler alternative to the plains during the subcontinent's hot summer months. They thrived as vacation spots after Independence.

81 Bois, "Introduction," 111.

82 Bois, "Introduction," 111.

83 "The adverb 'off' confuses our sense of direction. It makes us explore side shadows and back alleys, rather than the straight road of progress; it allows us to take a detour from the deterministic narratives of history." Boym, "Nostalgia and Its Discontents," 9.

84 Spivak, *Aesthetic Education*, 11.

85 For instance, McClintock, *Imperial Leather*; Lim, *Translating Time*.

86 Chakrabarty, *Provincializing Europe*, 40.

87 Similar questions are taken up by all the essays in Salazkina, "Dossier."

88 For an enduring paradox explored in film theory, particularly in *Screen*, see Wollen, "Ontology"; and McCabe, "Theory and Film."

89 Presner, "Hegel's Philosophy," 205. Bringing multiple histories into simultaneous view has a political intent, as demonstrated by Tara McPherson's concept of a "lenticular" lens in

Reconstructing Dixie, which sees the racialized subtext in popular images and narratives of the American South; or by the different scales and national contexts of Holocaust history, in Knowles et al., *Geographies of the Holocaust*. With the benefit of a nonlinearity derived from their operational matrix, scholars working with the digital medium have used this optic to illustrate parallel and rival geographies. They remain an inspiration for my entirely linear book format.

90 For an elaboration on the idea of perspectival equivalence see the book's conclusion. Several scholars make an argument for locating knowledge, including Alcoff, "Problem of Speaking for Others"; Gould, "Geography of Comparative Literature"; Kaplan, *Questions of Travel*; and Alexander and Talpade Mohanty, "Cartographies of Knowledge and Power."

CHAPTER 1. DISCIPLINARY

Epigraphs: Walt Whitman, *Handbook for Geography Teachers*, 1; J. B. Holmes, "G.P.O. Films," 159; G. J. Cons, *Handbook*, 115.

1 Bruce Woolfe's British Instructional Films merged with British International Pictures in 1931, but, unhappy with his marginalization within the new company and the loss of his distribution arm Pro Patria Films, Woolfe left the organization to start British Independent Productions, which became Gaumont-British Instructional (GBI). Woolfe took some of his regular staff (such as Percy Smith and Mary Fields) and rights over his educational footage and shorts to GBI. See the entry by Simon McCallum, "British Instructional Films (1919–1933)," Screenonline.org, accessed August 2009, http://www.screenonline.org.uk/film/id/5439966.

2 Consult www.colonialfilm.org.uk/home. Specifically http://www.colonialfilm.org.uk/node /1774 for *Bikaner*; http://www.colonialfilm.org.uk/node/451 for *Udaipur*; http://www .colonialfilm.org.uk/node/1645 for *Darjeeling*. *Bikaner* (1937) is available for viewing but inaccurately filed under the 1934 *Secrets of India* series. (All four films from the *Indian Town Studies* series were produced by Mary Field, supervised by G. J. Cons with diagrams by R. Jeffreys.) See "'Appraisal' of 'Foothill Town: Darjeeling,'" *Monthly Film Bulletin* 4, no. 8 (December 31, 1937): 261–62.

3 *To-day's Cinema* 49, no. 3708 (September 9, 1937): 1; "'Appraisal' of 'Foothill Town: Darjeeling,'" 261–62.

4 McCallum, "British Instructional Films"; Low, *History of the British Film*, 107; 129.

5 See their *Catalogue of Films* (1928) available at the British Film Institute. The films are organized by geographical territories (e.g., India, Malay Peninsula, Palestine, Mesopotamia, and so on). Film titles are accompanied by descriptive summaries and rare guidance on how the films may be used.

6 This is Hansen describing Kracauer's theory of film experience in Hansen, "Introduction," xxi.

7 For more on this, see Pinney, "Introduction," 6.

8 Harvey's discussion is more philosophically far-reaching than my deployment of his categories. See Harvey, "Space as a Keyword," 270–93; and Harvey, *Spaces of Global Capitalism*.

9 Foucault, "Of Other Spaces," 22–27.

10 Amad, "Visual Reposte," 52.

11 Said, *Culture and Imperialism*, 81.

12 For a larger discussion of film's role in "the elaboration of a capitalist and imperialist governmentality," see Grieveson, "Cinema and the (Common)Wealth," 73; and Grieveson, *Cinema and the Wealth of Nations*, especially chapter 8. Also see the forthcoming study of the Colonial Film Unit's productions for colonies, Rice, *Films for the Colonies*.

13 Kearns, *Geopolitics and Empire*, 5.

14 See note 2 for viewing options on the http://www.colonialfilm.org.uk/home site.

15 Malitsky, "Science and Documentary," 250.

16 This is based on distinguishing between the index and icon following C. S. Peirce, who was also an expert on map projections.

17 Cons, *Handbook for Geography Teachers*, 23. In 1932, Miss D. M. Forsaith, a lecturer in geography at Goldsmith's College, edited the *Goldsmith's College Handbook for Teachers of Geography*. The Standing Sub-Committee in Geography of the University of London undertook revisions of this version in 1955, under the editorship of G. J. Cons. I use the revised version, which adds a section on visual aids.

18 Cons, *Handbook*, 12–13.

19 Consult Jaikumar, *Cinema at the End of Empire* for an analysis of Korda's empire films.

20 "'Appraisal' of 'Foothill Town: Darjeeling,'" 261. Also http://www.colonialfilm.org.uk/node/1645.

21 A. R. H., "Photographs."

22 George Kerevan, "Remembering the Scots Who Flew over Everest Some 80 Years Ago," *Scotsman* (March 25, 2013), accessed January 10, 2014, and November 21, 2018, https://www.scotsman.com/news/remembering-the-scots-who-flew-over-everest-some-80-years-ago-1-2855400.

23 Buchan, "Foreword," 13; A. R. H., "Photographs."

24 "'Appraisal' of 'Foothill Town: Darjeeling,'" 261. Also http://www.colonialfilm.org.uk/node/1645.

25 Compare *Fair City of Udaipur* (1934) at http://www.colonialfilm.org.uk/node/857 with my descriptions of the 1937 series.

26 The "Elge" List.

27 "'Appraisal' of 'Foothill Town: Darjeeling,'" 262; and *Monthly Film Bulletin* 2, no. 23 (September 1935): 182.

28 The BFI organized regional conferences, Films for Schools, the first of which was held in Manchester in the autumn of 1937, and the second in Leeds in the spring of 1938. In conjunction with these, reports were published on the use of film in schools, including *History Teaching Films, Science Teaching Films, Foreign Language Teaching Films*, and *Geography Teaching Films*. Fletcher, "Science Teaching Films."

29 "'Appraisal' of 'Foothill Town: Darjeeling,'" 262.

30 Said, *Orientalism*, 72.

31 Appadurai, "Number in the Colonial Imagination," 323.

32 Cons, *Handbook*, 6.

33 Cons, *Handbook*, 6.

34 Cons, *Handbook*, 6.

35 Field and Smith, *Secrets of Nature*, 4.

36 Easen, "Mary Field," 247.

37 Field and Smith, *Secrets of Nature*, 190.

38 McCallum, "British Instructional Films."

39 Easen, "Mary Field," 248.

40 Field and Smith, *Secrets of Nature*, 189.

41 On *Mystery of Marriage*, see McCallum, "British Instructional Films." Easen, "Mary Field," 248.

42 Gaycken, *Devices of Curiosity*. See in particular "Juggling Flies and Gravid Plants."

43 Field and Smith, *Secrets of Nature*, 72.

44 See Amad's reading of Ousmane Sembene's comment to Jean Rouche that the French ethnographers "look at us as though we were insects"; Amad, "Visual Reposte," 49.

45 Mbembe, "Necropolitics," 23.

46 Comparing the Indian geographicals to the animated GBI short *The Expansion of Germany 1817–1914* (1936), produced by Mary Fields and photographed by R. Jeffreyes (both of whom would later be part of the *Indian Town Studies* production team), clarifies this point. The film, made at the brink of World War II, offers a fascinating economic analysis of Germany's expansion as a prelude to World War I, revealing there was some vigorous experimentation with economic analysis via short format films.

47 For more details, see Vasudevan, "Geographies of the Cinematic Public," 101; and Bhaumik, "Emergence of the Bombay Film Industry," 94.

48 Koch, *Franz Osten's Indian Silent Films*, 1; Jaikumar, "DVD Review."

49 "Shiraz," *Bioscope*, September 16, 1928, 41.

50 "A Throw of Dice," *Bioscope*, October 23, 1929, 36. See also chapter 4.

51 "'Appraisal' of 'Foothill Town: Darjeeling,'" 261–62.

52 Fairgrieve quoted in Kent, "Geography," 4.

53 For more on the significance of visualization to education in general, and its relation to instructional media, see Gaycken, *Devices of Curiosity*; Peterson, *Education*, especially chapter 3; Orgeron, Orgeron, and Streible, *Learning with the Lights Off*; Acland and Wasson, *Useful Cinema*; and Naficy, "Lured by the East."

54 Cons, *Handbook*, 2, 1.

55 Male suffrage was expanded with the Representation of the People Act (1884), and the state mandate to educate the working classes was inaugurated by making education compulsory in 1880 and free after 1892. For the "institutionalisation and professionalization of geography" from 1830 to 1918, see Maddrell, "Discourses."

56 Mackinder, "Teaching of Geography," 80. For more on Mackinder's use of visual media in geographical education and geopolitics, see Ryan, *Picturing Empire*; and Kearns, *Geopolitics and Empire*.

57 Cons, *Handbook*, 10.

58 Mackinder, "Teaching of Geography," 80.

59 Ryan, *Picturing Empire*, 208–9; Kearns, *Geopolitics and Empire*, 165.

60 Mackinder, "Teaching of Geography," 79.

61 Mackinder quoted in Cons, *Handbook*, 10.

62 Mackinder, "Teaching of Geography," 80.

63 Cons, *Handbook*, 2.

64 Mackinder, "Teaching of Geography," 82.

65 Heidegger, "Age of the World Picture."

66 Mackinder, "Teaching of Geography," 83; emphasis added.

67 For an application of Heidegger's essay in discussions of photography, maps and early cinema, consult Gunning, "Whole World within Reach," 25–41; and Pinney, "Future Travel," 409–28.

68 Heidegger, "Age of the World Picture," 57.

69 Heidegger's theses on the boundaries between the calculable and the incalculable aspects of modern life are beyond the scope of my argument, but the underlying sense of the aesthetic realm rearticulating every conceivable aspect of cultural and human life in the modern industrial era is of significance and applicable to a range of modern European thinkers, from Walter Benjamin to Lacanian and Marxist philosophers such as Louis Althusser, Chantal Mouffe, and Fredric Jameson. Given the disciplinary foundations of film and media studies in psychoanalytic and Marxist cultural and literary theory, arguably the entry of the ordinary into the realm of aesthetics upon which the emergence of a modern sensibility (and, for Heidegger, modern science) was predicated is also the very grounds to presume that a media scholar's object of analyses extends to politics, economics, society, and everyday beliefs and experiences, insofar as they control and are framed by mediated representation and communication.

70 Lloyd and Thomas, *Culture and the State*, 7.

71 Grieveson, "On Governmentality and Screens."

72 Spivak traces the expanded role of the aesthetic in contemporary life as a legacy of European Enlightenment (via Immanuel Kant), but proposes a subversion of European liberal thought that begat concepts of freedom and liberal democracy on the backs of imperialism. Literature, she argues, provides a conscious and conscientious way of being, "but as long as we take the literary as substantive source of good thinking alone, we will fail in the task of the aesthetic education we are proposing: *at all costs to enter another's text*." Spivak, *Aesthetic Education*, 6.

73 This is a phrase used by Mackinder in his slideshow "Site of the Black Hole" about Calcutta. Kearns, *Geopolitics and Empire*, 167.

74 See also U. Mehta, *Liberalism and Empire*.

75 Cons, *Handbook*, 58.

76 Cons, *Handbook*, 58–59.

77 Emphasis mine. Explaining the significance of his title, "The Teaching of Geography from an Imperial Point of View," Mackinder points out that he is specifically using the term "imperial" and not "imperia*list*" because he stands in opposition to the narrowly political or purely scientific view. Imperial for him was inclusive of a global and aesthetic outlook.

78 Reading Hodgson Burnett's *The Secret Garden* to my daughter as I edit this book, I am struck by how closely the novel replays this ideology.

79 Mackinder, "Teaching of Geography," 84.

80 Mackinder, "Teaching of Geography," 84–85.

81 Cons, *Handbook*, 118.

82 Cons, *Handbook*, 120.

83 Grieveson's "Cinema and the (Common)Wealth of Nations" is particularly enlightening on the historical roots of state and market collaboration during the 1920s, in helping us grasp how the contradictions between capitalist and territorial power operated in the British state's attitude toward cinema. My reading of the Quota Act (1927) as a policy aimed at mobilizing the empire as a unit of trade rather than territory was along the same lines of inquiry (Jaikumar, *Cinema at the End of Empire*).

84 Cons, *Handbook,* 115–49.

85 The event is noted (without transcript) in *To-day's Cinema* 48, no. 3620 (May 27, 1937): 7.

86 Letter from Major Keating to the Colonial Office, August 9, 1927, National Archives UK, CO 323/985/83 (1927).

87 Letter from Keating to Colonial Office, August 9, 1927. See also Rice, "Exhibiting Africa."

88 Letter from the Comptroller-General, Development and Intelligence, to the Undersecretary of State, Colonial Office, August 5, 1927, National Archives UK, CO 323/985/23.

89 "Imperial Institute," National Archives UK, CO 323/985/83 (1923).

90 Letter from H. A. F. Lindsay, Director, Imperial Institute, to the Secretary of the Department of Overseas Trade, March 31, 1937, National Archives UK, T 161/844 (1938); Holmes, "G.P.O. Films," 159.

91 Letter from Lindsay to the Secretary of the Department of Overseas Trade, March 31, 1937.

92 Letter from Lindsay to the Secretary of the Department of Overseas Trade, March 31, 1937.

93 For more on the BFI's role, see Nowell-Smith and Dupin, *British Film Institute*; see also "The BFI Turns 80," accessed June 2015, http://www.bfi.org.uk/news-opinion/news-bfi/features/bfi-turns-80.

94 Letter from H. A. F. Lindsay of the Imperial Institute to J. H. Jones of the Department of Overseas Trade, May 20, 1937, National Archive (T161/844).

95 H. Lefebvre, *Production of Space*, 96.

96 H. Lefebvre, *Production of Space*, 75.

97 C. S. A. G. Savidge, Undersecretary to the Government of India, External Affairs (EA), memorandum dated December 13, 1937, National Archives of India, Home (Political), "Afghan Travel documents: Request to the Afghan Govt That All Passports Issued to Afghan Subjects Should Contain a Specimen Signature or Thumb Impression of the Holders," National Archives of India, Home (Political), F 17/437/38. According to this docket, Afghans and Rahdaris came to British India from the northwest frontier as well as Assam, Shillong, and Burma with travel documents that did not conform to Indian passport rules.

98 Letter from Savidge to R. B. Elwin, Undersecretary to the Government of India, Home Department, May 18, 1938, National Archives of India, Home (Political), "Afghan Travel documents." F 17/437/38.

99 Letter from Elwin to Savidge, July 15, 1938, "Afghan Travel documents," National Archives of India, Home (Political), F 17/437/38.

100 The only indication of a rupture between Afghan reality and the hermetically sealed world of the film's ideology erupts in an absurd misinterpretation of facts. Showing an image of a *pan-wallah* (a man who sells fragrant beetle-leaves consumed widely in the subcontinent),

the voice-over in the Afghanistan short describes him as "a merchant who collects beetles and sells their multicolored wing cases for decorating embroideries and jewelry."

101 For more on this, see Pinney, *Coming of Photography in India*; and Mahadevan, *Very Old Machine*.

102 For an extended discussion, see Conley, *Cartographic Cinema*.

103 "Carte Internationale."

104 Crone, "Future of the International Million Map," provides conference details.

105 See Edward J. Wheeler, ed., *Current Literature*, 53 (July–December 1912): 55 for the Edinburgh Review's report that reproduces "The International Map of the World" in the "Science and Discovery" section.

106 National Archive of India, Education, Forests, 32–14/37, 1937, "Survey of India-Map policy conference," see Appendix II to notes on conference on Map Policy in relation to the 1/M maps of India. Also consult prior discussion in National Archive of India, Home (Public) 516/1928. "Herewith a sample volume of a proposed new series of map for India."

107 This was the system followed by the preexisting map series referred to as the India and Adjacent Countries (I and AC) series, which was to be replaced by the Carte Internationale or 1/M series. National Archive of India, Education, Forests, 32–14/37, "Survey."

108 National Archive of India, Education, Forests, 32–14/37, "Survey."

109 The conferences occurred in London in 1909 and in Paris in 1913. National Archive of India, Education, Forests, 32–14/37, "Survey." In this file, see "Response: Carte Du Monde Au Millionieme, Bureau Central, Ordnance Survey office," Southampton, October 25, 1937, Captain R. E., to the Surveyor General of India, Calcutta.

110 Examples include the Colonial Film project (http://www.colonialfilm.org.uk/) and the British Pathe newsreel archive (http://www.youtube.com/user/britishpathe).

111 Similar questions are raised in Amad, *Counter-Archive*; Bloom, *French Colonial Documentary*; Grieveson and McCabe, *Empire and Film*; Grieveson and McCabe, *Film and the End of Empire*; Larkin, *Signal and Noise*; Larkin, "Imperial Circulation"; Limbrick, *Making Settler Cinemas*; Maingard, "African Cinema and *Bamako*"; and Sanogo, "History of Documentary."

112 H. Lefebvre, *Production of Space*, 352–400.

CHAPTER 2. REGULATORY

1 Thapa, *Boy from Lambata*, 35.

2 Thapa, *Boy from Lambata*, 39, 43, 56. B. D. Garga also discusses the Army Film Center in Ballard Estate, Bombay, which served the purpose of training army personnel in movie making (Garga, *From Raj to Swaraj*, 76). More details on Bryan Langley's career and films can be found at http://www.colonialfilm.org.uk/node/6357 and at Ann Ogidi, "Langley, Bryan (1909–2008)," *BFI Screen Online*, accessed January 2014, http://www.screenonline.org.uk/people/id/778563/index.html; "Bryan Langley: BECTU Interview Part 3 (1987)," *BFI Screen Online*, accessed December 2018, http://www.screenonline.org.uk/audio/id/946226/index.html.

3 These organizations are discussed at greater length in Garga, *From Raj to Swaraj*; Woods, "From Shaw to Shantaram," 293–308; Narwekar, *Films Division*, especially 18–22; Cowan, Judith. "'Women at Work for War . . . Women at Work for the Things of Peace': Representations of Women in the British Propaganda Newsreel in India in the Second World War, Indian News Parade," accessed January 16, 2014, http://bufvc.ac.uk/wpcontent/media/2009/06/cowanessay.pdf; Jain, "Curious Case of the Films Division," 15–26; S. Roy, *Beyond Belief*, especially 35–39; Rice, "Indian News Parade"; Deprez, "Films Division of India," 149–73; Vasudevan, "British Documentary"; Sutoris, *Visions of Development*. Recent works on Indian documentary include Battaglia, *Documentary Film in India*; Kishore, *Indian Documentary Film and Filmmakers*; Vasudevan, ed., "Documentary Now."

4 Thapa, *Boy from Lambata*, 53, 59.

5 Narwekar, "Rewind to 1948," 6.

6 Narwekar, "Rewind to 1948," 5.

7 Sutoris, *Visions of Development*.

8 Narwekar, "Rewind to 1948," 12.

9 Thapa served as regional officer of the Film Censor Board in Bombay during the suppression of the political satire *Kissa Kursi Ka*. This is not an aspect of his career examined here but part of a rich history about media and media personnel during the Emergency waiting to be written.

10 Aretxaga, "Maddening States," 393–410; Butler, *Psychic Life of Power*.

11 Hull, *Government of Paper*, 1.

12 Appadurai, *Social Life of Things*.

13 Appadurai, *Social Life of Things*, 4. Appadurai's later work on globalization is enabled by this mode of conceptualizing regimes of socioeconomic value, as in "Disjuncture and Difference," 295–310.

14 S. Roy, *Beyond Belief*, 7.

15 Crampton and Elden, *Space, Knowledge, and Power*; Brenner and Elden, *Henri Lefebvre*; Poulantzas, *State, Power, Socialism*; Brenner and Elden, "Henri Lefebvre," 358.

16 See the Indian Mountaineering Foundation website, accessed November 21, 2018, https://www.indmount.org/IMF/welcome; Barry C. Bishop, John Hunt, Wilfrid Noyce, Norgay Tenzing, and Stephen Venables, "Mount Everest," *Britannica Academic Edition*, accessed January 22, 2014, http://www.britannica.com/EBchecked/topic/197160/Mount-Everest; Barry C. Bishop and Shiba P. Chatterjee, "Himalayas," *Britannica Academic Edition*, accessed January 22, 2014, http://www.britannica.com/EBchecked/topic/266037/Himalayas.

17 Murthy, "Foreword," 12; Thapa, *Boy from Lambata*, 77.

18 Thapa, *Boy from Lambata*, 121.

19 The antidam movement can be traced to the Mulshi Satyagraha in the 1920s but has attracted national and global awareness since the 1990s. Vora, *World's First Anti-Dam Movement*; A. Roy, "Greater Common Good."

20 S. Roy, *Beyond Belief*, 44.

21 Bourne, "Ten Weeks," 17. The essay was originally published in the *British Journal of Photography*, February 1 and 15, 1864, 15–23.

22 Talukdar, "Picturing Mountains"; Kabir, *Territory of Desire*, 60–70; Bourne, *Photographic Journeys in the Himalayas.*

23 Talukdar, "Picturing Mountains."

24 Dimendberg, *Film Noir*, 6. In the Indian Himalayan films, the assertion of a centripetal pull of the camera titling up (the verticality of) mountain ranges sets up the (horizontal) border as a unifying fortress against the potential dispersal of a nation's regions and populations.

25 Oettermann, *Panorama History*. I assume that the functions of the panorama as theorized within a European historical context in Oettermann's work are "both indispensable and inadequate" to the Indian context, echoing Dipesh Chakrabarty in *Provincializing Europe*, 6.

26 In this sense, Thapa's films also shared an affinity with Nehru's treatment of the Himalayas in *The Discovery of India*, as discussed by Kabir, *Territory of Desire*, 99.

27 S. Roy, *Beyond Belief*, 24, 3.

28 The Planning Commission's Five-Year Plan guided India's economic development after its independence, setting the agenda for resource allocation and industrial prioritization. See "Twelfth Five Year Plan 2012–17," Planning Commission Government of India, accessed January 2014, http://planningcommission.nic.in/plans/planrel/fiveyr/welcome.html.

29 Oettermann, *Panorama History*, 22.

30 Steimatsky, *Italian Locations*, xi.

31 Williams, *Notes on the Underground.*

32 Prakash, *Another Reason.*

33 Mani, *Sacred Secular*. Also see Gandhi, *Sita's Kitchen.*

34 Following this line of argument would take me too far from my current discussion, but one could start on this path from Spivak, "'Draupadi' by Mahasveta Devi," and Grim, *Indigenous Traditions.*

35 The following special issues of the *Weekly* from 1966 convey the erasure of the region's Islamic history: Syed Mir Qasim, "Kashmir's Ties with India," *Illustrated Weekly of India*, 87 (March 1966), 26–27; D. R. Raghavan, "Kashmir in Ancient Times," *Illustrated Weekly of India* 87 (March 1966): 38–39; and, in the same issue, S. M. Das, "Kashmir's Contribution to Science," *Illustrated Weekly of India* 87 (March 1966): 44–45. For more on the requisition of Kashmir for Shaivite Hinduism, see Kabir, *Territory of Desire.*

36 Ramaswamy, "Visualizing India's Geo-Body," 154; and Ramaswamy, *Goddess and Nation.*

37 Thapa describes his research for the film in *Boy from Lambata*, 118–19.

38 The term is usually reserved for Christian theological traditions (dating to Saint Thomas Aquinas) that sought to reconcile revelation with rationality in defending the existence of God. Honderich, *Oxford Companion to Philosophy*, 45; Edwards, *Encyclopedia of Philosophy*, 133–35.

39 Manu Goswami, in *Producing India*, provides an account of the influence of precolonial temporal and spatial concepts from the Puranic Itihas (vernacular nineteenth-century histories based on ancient Hindu texts) on the formation of modern Indian geography. As she notes, despite precolonial spherical maplike representations of the world in India since the sixteenth century that differed from "Puranic inspired cosmographies" that were flat, the topography of both "were inscribed with religious deities and human figures," and used scale (if at all) "as an index of the relative social and religious importance of particular places" (157–58).

40 Oregeron, Oregeron, and Streible, *Learning with the Lights Off*, 9.

41 In post-Independence India, state-controlled media channels included India's radio (All India Radio), theatrically screened film shorts and documentaries (FD), and television (Doordarshan).

42 Kaplan, *Aerial Aftermaths*; Weems, *Barnstorming the Prairies*; Parks and Kaplan, *Life in the Age*; Dorrian and Pousin, *Seeing from Above*; Amad, "From God's-Eye to Camera-Eye."

43 Kaplan, *Aerial Aftermaths*.

44 Scott, *Seeing Like a State*.

45 Thapa, *Boy from Lambata*, 131–32.

46 Thapa, *Boy from Lambata*, 141.

47 Thapa remembers cameraman Prem Vaidya atop a Sherman tank in the Indo-Pakistani war of 1965. Thapa, *Boy from Lambata*, 141.

48 Scott, *Seeing Like a State*.

49 One aspect of the film that shows its distance from the subject is its frequently punning humor: "Things are looking up when they are dropping down," says the voice-over as supplies airdrop to soldiers in remote outposts. This film's address is radically different from another series of military films that Thapa shot in his early career for Britain's Directorate of Army Welfare titled *Calling Blighty* (1944–1946), in which the camera allows the voices and vulnerabilities of each soldier to come through. For example see "Calling Blighty India (c. 1944), The Norfolk Regiment calls home from India," East Anglian Film Archive, University of East Anglia, http://www.eafa.org.uk/catalogue/431.

50 The Doon School, an elite private boy's school at the Himalayan foothills of Dehradun, played a pioneering part in mountaineering as its first headmaster, Arthur Foot, was an avid climber and member of the Alpine Club. Nalni D. Jayal, "Early Years of Indian Mountaineering," *Himalayan Journal*, accessed January 29, 2014, https://www.himalayanclub.org/hj/62/16/early-years-of-indian-mountaineering/.

51 Nehru quoted by SVV, "The Western Himalayan Mountaineering Institute," *Illustrated Weekly*, April 1, 1962, 46.

52 Bharat Mathur, "Climbing Mt. Everest," *Illustrated Weekly of India* (June 1965): 8–15; Lt.-Cmdr. M. S. Kohli, "Nine Atop Everest," *Illustrated Weekly of India* 87, no. 22 (May 1966): 28–31; Swami Sundarananda, "Twenty Days at the Himalayan Mountaineering Institute," *Illustrated Weekly of India* 87, no. 20 (May 1966): 36–37; defense minister Y. B. Chavan, "Foreword," Special Army Day Number: Accent on the Armed Forces, *Illustrated Weekly of India* 87, no. 3 (January 1966): 9; Brigadier Gyan Singh, "Indians on Everest," *Illustrated Weekly of India* 87, no. 4 (January 1966): 44–47; Mariner, "Defending India's Coastline," *Illustrated Weekly of India* 87, no. 4 (January 1966): 37.

53 Amardeep Singh, "Khushwant Singh's Journalism: The Illustrated Weekly of India," quoting Khushwant Singh's preface to collection of columns in 1981 (Friday, August 4, 2006), accessed November 21, 2018, http://www.lehigh.edu/~amsp/2006/08/khushwant-singhs-journalism.html; and Vikas Kamat, "Kamat Research Database: The Illustrated Weekly of India," accessed November 21, 2018, http://www.kamat.com/database/sources/weekly.htm. Roychoudhuri, "Documentary Photography," includes a discussion of *The Weekly*.

54 Kirby, "Male Hysteria and Early Cinema," 68.

55 The exact height is a matter of some controversy, but in 2010, China and Nepal agreed that the official overall height was 8,848 meters. "Nepal and China Agree on Mount Everest's Height," BBC News, last updated April 8, 2010, accessed January 10, 2014, http://news.bbc .co.uk/2/hi/south_asia/8608913.stm.

56 A. R. H., "Photographs," 54–60; George Kerevan, "Remembering the Scots Who Flew over Everest Some 80 Years Ago," *Scotsman* (March 25, 2013), accessed January 10, 2014 and November 21, 2018, https://www.scotsman.com/news/remembering-the-scots-who-flew-over -everest-some-80-years-ago-1-2855400.

57 Ahluwalia, *Everest Within*; Thapa, *Boy from Lambata*, 139. The nine members to reach the summit were Sonam Gyatso, Nawang Gombu, Captain A. S. Cheema, C. P. Vohra, Ang Kami, Sonam Wangyal, Captain H. S. Ahluwalia, H. C. S. Rawat, and Phu Dorji.

58 Thapa, *Boy from Lambata*, 142.

59 Thapa, *Boy from Lambata*, 124–25.

60 Thapa, *Boy from Lambata*, 151. The basis of the truth-claims of documentary has been a subject of fertile inquiry by Winston, *Claiming the Real*; Renov, *Theorizing Documentary*.

61 The attributed quote is repeated in several places. Rotha, *Documentary Film*, 70; and Ellis, *John Grierson*, which analyzes all three terms in Grierson's definition. Thapa remembers Grierson's definition of documentary as "a creative interpretation of reality"; Thapa, *Boy from Lambata*, 151. The documentarian Sukhdev deliberately rephrases it as "the creative interpretation of RECREATED reality" in "Documentary in Theory and Practice," 13. For an assessment the British documentary movement's influence on FD, see Deprez, "Films Division of India"; Vasudevan, "Geographies"; and Sutoris, *Visions of Development*.

62 Winston, *Claiming the Real*; Ellis, *John Grierson*.

63 Thapa, *Boy from Lambata*, 151.

64 Credit for this observation goes to the audience at Jawaharlal University, New Delhi, following one of my talks.

65 For a discussion of how the industrialization of everyday life creates its corresponding catastrophe and pathology, see Schivelbusch, *Railway Journey*.

66 Thapa, *Boy from Lambata*, 124.

67 Bourne, *Photographic Journeys*, 24–61.

68 Reassessing Ray's films and their changing critical response, Moinak Biswas is sympathetic to the historical relevance of charges that Ray's films frequently embed social critique in marginal characters, but also notes that "the moral degeneracy of our heroes is brought out through their alienation from the people of the region they have chosen to visit. . . . The chowkidar (watchman), the errand boy, the tribal girl, instead of forming a backdrop to the protagonists, come to signify their hollow insides"; Biswas, *Apu and After*, 6–7.

69 Thapa, *Boy from Lambata*, 62.

70 Garga, *From Raj to Swaraj*, 101. Garga writes that the American War Production Board had no such stipulation, though it did cut down supplies to countries dependent of US film stock because the material for film base was needed by the munitions industry.

71 The *Report of the Working Group on National Film Policy* observes, "The main drawbacks in the performance of HPF are defective collaboration (with ORWO color), insufficient

collaboration, lack of developmental consciousness, inadequate quality control and quality consciousness, and insufficient expansion of product range" (34).

72 See editorials in *Filmfare* 6, no. 14 (July 5, 1957): 3; and *Filmfare* 6, no. 19 (September 13, 1957): 3.

73 IMPEC was merged with NFDC in 1980. For details of the laws, see *India Business Law Handbook*, 125.

74 *Report of the Working Group on National Film Policy*, 54; "Vague Laws," *Filmfare* 21, no. 26 (December 15, 1972): n.p.

75 Editorial by B. K. Karanjia, "A Commendable Scheme," *Filmfare* 6, no. 6 (August 2, 1957): 3. The Film Federation of India is a representative body of the film producers, distributers, and exhibitors.

76 "On Film Length Control," editorial, *Filmfare* 6, no. 19 (September 13, 1957): n.p.; Irani, interview with author (see appendix).

77 See chapter 5 for the Steering Committee's impact on commercial filmmakers.

78 Irani interview with author.

79 "Due to crisis of Eastmancolor Negative, producers are being forced to use either Geva or Fuji and the sale of these less popular stocks was highest during the last two weeks. Also black marketers made a tidy sum by selling Eastmancolor Negative at Rs. 6000 per 1000 feet!" "Believe It or Not," *Trade Guide*, August 7, 1976, 7. For silver trading, see *Report of the Working Group on National Film Policy*, 32.

80 Sutoris, *Visions of Development*, 70.

81 Acland and Wasson, *Useful Cinema*.

82 See Sutoris, *Visions of Development*, for an analysis of FD's atypical directors such as S. Sukhdev, Shyam Benegal, S. N. S. Satry, Fali Billimoria, and Prem Vaidya. Also see Kaushik, "Sun in the Belly," for experimentation in FD between 1965 and 1975. Independent and alternative documentary also covered by Battaglia, *Documentary Film*; Kishore, *Indian Documentary*; Sharma, *Documentary Films*.

83 Sutoris, *Visions of Development*, 67.

84 My synopsis is based on *Films Division Manual*, 183–87, which breaks down the procedures for producing newsreels rather than documentaries, although later annexures outlined similar requirements for documentary. According to Sutoris, *Visions of Development*, 251–53, footnotes 24, 35, 37, and 44, the following annexures (which I have not seen) related to documentary specifically. These were "Report on Study of FD" (Administrative Staff College of India, Consulting and Applied Research Division, Hyderabad for the Ministry of Information and Broadcasting, October 1971, FD); Annexure A: Line of Approach, updated in 77, internal FD publication; Annexure 3B, "Various Stages in the Production of a Documentary Film"; Annexure XVI, "Statement Showing the Ration of Consumption of Raw Stock for Various Broad Categories of Films Produced by FD."

85 *Films Division Manual*, 184.

86 *Films Division Manual*, 185. The overall procedures synopsized here are outlined in chapter 12, "Newsreel Section."

87 According to Sutoris (*Visions of Development*, 70), every director was expected to complete at least four films a year.

88 Thapa, *Boy from Lambata*, 143.

89 See chapter 5.

90 Accounts of this are available in most essays on FD's creation, such as Garga, *From Raj to Swaraj*; S. Roy, *Beyond Belief*; and Jain, "Curious Case of the Films Division."

91 Thapa, "Life behind the Camera," 21–22.

92 "Cinematograph Act No. XXXVIII of 1952 (as modified up to the 12th March 1959), Part III, 12 (4)," reproduced in Adarsh, *Film Industry of India*, 552.

93 Known as the *Patil Committee Report* after its chairman, S. K. Patil, Member, Constituent Assembly, this is from *Report of the Film Inquiry Committee*, 23, 222. The Central Government of India is equivalent to the US federal government as opposed to regional state governments.

94 Adarsh, *Film Industry of India*, 551.

95 *Gazette of India*, May 15, 1943, no. 20, part I, section 1, page 503. I am grateful to Ravinder Singh for making this document available to me.

96 Alternative modalities of documentary making have, of course, always existed and came into their own with the breakdown of FD monopoly in the 1990s. Work on independent, amateur, and nonstate documentary filmmaking in India include Sarkar and Wolf, "Indian Documentary Studies"; Jain, "Suffering and Spectatorship"; and Hariharan, "Private Modernities."

97 *Report of the Film Inquiry Committee*, 23. The committee also felt that the industry needed to be encouraged to produce nonfiction and documentary (179).

98 The Films Division prioritized quantity to feed "a network of all-India theaters . . . with new films 52 times a year." Narwekar, "Rewind to 1948," 8.

99 The Films Division levied a charge of 1 percent of the net collections (i.e., collections after deducting entertainment tax from gross earnings) of theater exhibitors every month.

100 Anil Kumar, then a senior branch manager at FD, interview with author (see appendix); G. Seetharaman, "Short Films and Documentaries Aired before Movies in Cinema Become a Laughing Stock," *Economic Times*, June 2, 2013, accessed October 15, 2012, http://articles.economictimes.indiatimes.com/2013–06–02/news/39675389_1_films-division-short-films-such-films.

101 "Union of India and Others vs. the Motion Picture Association," July 15, 1999, accessed November 10, 2013, http://indiankanoon.org/doc/921638/; E. Padmanabhan, "Tamil Nadu Film Exhibitors . . . vs The Branch Manager, Films," accessed January 5, 2014, https://indiankanoon.org/doc/1188748/.

102 Anil Kumar, interview with author (see appendix).

103 "Indovision Media" and "Indian Infotainment Media Corporation," accessed October 15, 2013, http://www.indovisionmedia.com/Approved%20Films.html and http://www.iimcindia.com/aboutus.php (Indovision link no longer operative).

104 See, for instance, "FD ZONE," accessed November 21, 2018, http://filmsdivision.org/category/the-fd-zone and its collaboration with University of Westminster's India Media Center since March 16, 2015, https://www.westminster.ac.uk/events/fd-zone-london-launch.

105 As geographers Jeremy W. Crampton and Stuart Eldon have shown, while Foucault "did not write primary texts that foreground spatial concerns . . . spatiality was more than just a passing interest," in the sense that it undergirds his body of work on state power. Crampton and Elden, *Space, Knowledge, and Power*, 8.

106　W. Brown, *States of Injury*, ix.

107　See Burchell, Gordon, and Miller, eds., *Foucault Effect*; and Grieveson, "On Governmentality and Screens." Thinking in terms of state space falls within a longer intellectual tradition starting with Hegel's spatial ontology of the state as the territorial spirit of perfected reason. Western Marxist theories of state countered Hegelian idealism by rethinking the state in relation to capitalism and the class struggle; Foucault extended this thesis with his study of the procedural institutionalization of power in discourse and knowledge.

108　See Brenner and Elden's *Henri Lefebvre* and H. Lefebvre, *Production of Space*, specifically the following passage: "The relationship between institutions other than the state itself (for instance, university, tax authority, judiciary) and the effectiveness of those institutions has no need of the mediation of the concept of space to achieve self-representation, for the space in which they function is governed by statutes . . . which fall within the political space of the state. By contrast the state framework, and the state as framework, cannot be conceived of without reference to the instrumental space that they make use of. Indeed each new form of state, each new form of political power, introduces its own particular administrative classification of discourses about space and about things and people in space." (H. Lefebvre, *Production of Space*, 281).

CHAPTER 3. SUBLIME

Epigraphs: Renoir, *Renoir on Renoir*, 241; Bazin, *Jean Renoir*, 113; Shahani, "Film as Contemporary Art," 34.

1　The shooting started in India in 1949 and, according to some accounts, the final scene was filmed on May 15, 1951. Isobel Silden, "'The River': A One-Shot Deal that Became a Classic," *Los Angeles Times*, Sunday, March 9, 1980, 28; LoBianco and Thompson, *Jean Renoir*. DVDs of the restored film print with superior special features and extras are available from the BFI and Criterion Collection.

2　For more on the significant "initiations," see Renoir, *Renoir on Renoir*, 242; Renoir, "Introduction"; Jhaveri, *Outsider Films*, 26. My published conversation with Jhaveri initiated my own thoughts on *The River*, and I am grateful for the opportunity.

3　Bergan, *Jean Renoir*, 281; and Bergan, *Eyewitness Companions*, 244.

4　Mitra, who later worked with Ray and James Ivory, was still a science student in college, but his impromptu sitar-playing sessions on *The River*'s set were used in the film and incorporated at the film's opening. See Arnaud Mandagaran's documentary *Around the River* (2006), included as a bonus feature in the US Criterion Collection DVD of *The River*, which includes a wealth of archival visual material and interviews. I am grateful to Professor Janet Bergstrom for sharing the documentary with me in 2012.

5　Rich troves of material continue to be added to our knowledge of Renoir and *The River* and this is an enviable bounty to any scholar of Indian cinema, which lacks deep archives and restored prints.

6　Renoir, "Introduction."

7　Seton, *Portrait of a Director*, 323.

8　Renoir, *Renoir on Renoir*, 31. He repeats this in various interviews.

9 On orientalism, see Bhatia, "Whither the Colonial Question," 51–64.

10 Renoir, *My Life and My Films*, 253; Bazin, "Pure Masterpiece," 114.

11 Renoir, *Renoir on Renoir*, 242. Octave's character in *Rules of the Game*, played by Renoir himself, repeats this (noted as well by Bazin, *Jean Renoir*, 9). *The River* is also discussed in Merigeau's exhaustive biography *Jean Renoir*, although the book was published in English translation after completing the bulk of my writing, so I am unable to engage it here. I am grateful to Jonathan Buchsbaum for drawing it to my attention.

12 Letter from Melvina McEldowney to Hedda Hopper, December 17, 1949, Hedda Hopper Collection, #3962, Margaret Herrick Library (hereafter MHL).

13 Coco Fusco and Guillermo Gomez-Peña's *Undiscovered Amerindians* (1992) brought the concept of "reverse ethnography" into prominence with the performance of "The Couple in the Cage." Also relevant is Fusco, "Other History," 148.

14 For notes on shooting by the Hooghly River, consult "E. Lourié Notes on Location Shooting," Box 9, Folder 4, Renoir Paper Notes, UCLA, Archives, Los Angeles.

15 Shaw, *Sublime*, 4.

16 Burke, *Philosophical Enquiry*.

17 For this discussion, see Almond, *History of Islam*; Battersby, *Sublime*; Crowther, *Kantian Sublime*; Kant, *Critique of Judgment*; Longinus, *On the Sublime*; Lyotard, *Lessons*; Ram, *Imperial Sublime*; Shaw, *Sublime*; Žižek, *Sublime Object of Ideology*.

18 Mishra, *Devotional Poetics*, 9.

19 Texts that influenced my thinking in the debates over what film enables and what it constitutes include Andrew, *André Bazin*; Andrew with Joubert-Laurencin, *Opening Bazin*; Arnheim, *Film as Art*; Bazin, *What Is Cinema?*, vols. 1 and 2; Benjamin, *Arcades Project* and *Work of Art*; Buck-Morss, *Dialectics of Seeing*; Eisenstein, *Film Form*; Gunning, "Moving Away," 29–52; Hansen, "Benjamin, Cinema and Experience," 179–224; Kracauer, *Theory of Film*; Rosen, *Change Mummified*, among others.

20 Bazin, "Myth of Total Cinema," 17.

21 Renov, *Subject of Documentary*, particularly "Technology and Ethnographic Dialogue," 148–58.

22 I am, of course, deliberately misquoting Robert Browning's poem "Andrea del Sarto": "Ah, but a man's reach should exceed his grasp, / Or what's a heaven for?" See Poetry Foundation, https://www.poetryfoundation.org/poems/43745/andrea-del-sarto.

23 Butler, *Frames of War*, 46.

24 Butler, *Frames of War*, 52–53.

25 And, to a lesser extent, Wes Anderson's *Darjeeling Limited* (2007). I edited out my discussion of this film because of a lack of space, but it may be productively discussed in this context. See Chabon, "Introduction," and Seitz, "*The Darjeeling Limited*."

26 Said, *Orientalism*, 5.

27 On "encounters" between film industries, see Govil, *Orienting Hollywood*.

28 Said, *Culture and Imperialism*, 48.

29 Said, "Always on Top," 3; also noted in Said, *Culture and Imperialism*.

30 In making this argument, I am disagreeing mildly with Amit Chaudhuri, who compares Said unfavorably to Dipesh Chakrabarty. Chaudhuri, "In the Waiting Room."

31 Said, *Culture and Imperialism*, 134.

32 Examples include Ngai, *Ugly Feelings*; Ngai, *Our Aesthetic Categories*; Goodstein, *Experience without Quality*; and Galt, *Pretty*.

33 Kumar Shahani talks of his changing response to *The River* in his introduction to BFI's DVD release.

34 The term is borrowed from Donna Haraway, "Situated Knowledges." For a parallel discussion, see Said, "Always on Top," 5.

35 From Kristin Thompson and David Bordwell, "David Bordwell's website on cinema: Observations on Film Art. Class of 1960," accessed February 16, 2015, http://www.davidbordwell.net/blog/2009/08/02/class-of-1960/.

36 Bazin, "Pure Masterpiece," 109.

37 Mignolo, *Local Histories*.

38 B. Brown, "Thing Theory," 1–22; republished in B. Brown, *Thing Theory*.

39 B. Brown, "Thing Theory," 9.

40 Letter from McEldowney to Hopper.

41 Renoir, *Renoir on Renoir*, 33–34.

42 Faulkner, *Social Cinema*, 173; Renoir, "Quelque chose m'est arrivé," 32, as quoted by Faulkner, *Social Cinema*, 173.

43 Renoir, *Renoir on Renoir*, 39. Approximately eighteen of the film's ninety-eight minutes are documentary sequences.

44 Nichols, *Introduction to Documentary*.

45 This is underscored by the extra features in the film's BFI DVD, which includes early travelogues of Indian riverbanks.

46 Bazin, "Ontology," 15.

47 Derrida develops these ideas in a few places, such as Derrida, "Hostipitality," and Derrida, *Of Hospitality*.

48 Renoir, *Renoir on Renoir*, 37.

49 Godden reported that she was nearly murdered by her domestic Indian staff, who mixed crushed glass with her food, according to Matthew Dennison, "Rumer Godden's life is a story in itself," *The Telegraph*, January 5, 2008, https://www.telegraph.co.uk/culture/books/3670310/Rumer-Goddens-life-is-a-story-in-itself.html. Gayatri Chatterjee is working on *The River*'s adaption from Godden's novella and I am grateful to her for sharing her unpublished essay "Jean Renoir and Rumer Godden Make a Film in India."

50 Bazin, *Jean Renoir*, 107.

51 Lefebvre, *Production of Space*, 306–8, and 402 especially.

52 Younger offers an illuminating reading of Bazin through *The River* in "*The River*," 166–75 (the above quote is from 167, emphasis in original); Younger, "Re-thinking Bazin through Renoir's *The River* Part 1," and Younger, "'Re-thinking Bazin through Renoir's *The River* Part 2."

53 Bazin, "Evolution," 24.

54 Bazin, "Evolution," 34.

55 Conley, *Cartographic Cinema*, 40–64.

56 According to Mandagaran, *Around the River*, the film contains seven hundred shots, usually sufficient for three films by Renoir.

57 Seton, *Portrait of a Director*, 324.

58 Renoir, *My Life and My Films*, 250–51.

59 Renoir, *My Life and My Films*, 251.

60 James Blue, "Interview: Satyajit Ray," Film Comment 1968 issue, accessed October 2016, http://www.filmcomment.com/article/interview-satyajit-ray/.

61 Renoir, *Renoir on Renoir*, 39.

62 Renoir, *My Life and My Films*, 256.

63 Bazin, *Jean Renoir*, 117, 118.

64 Bazin, *Jean Renoir*, 117.

65 Bazin, *Jean Renoir*, 118.

66 Braudy, *Jean Renoir*.

67 Morgan, "Rethinking Bazin," 449. Rosen offers a different analysis of Bazin in his prior publication, *Change Mummified*.

68 Morgan, "Rethinking Bazin," 452.

69 Gunning, "Moving Away," 33.

70 Gunning, "Moving Away," 39.

71 Morgan, "Afterlife of Superimposition," 130.

72 Bazin, "Pure Masterpiece," 107–8.

73 Bazin, "Pure Masterpiece," 107–8.

74 Bazin, "Pure Masterpiece," 107–8.

75 Bazin, "Aesthetic of Reality," 27.

76 It is for this reason, I think, that Gunning finds "the challenge of cinema as an art form lies neither in expressing individual subjectivity nor in simply reproducing the traits of movement, color, sound and relief as components of illusion, but rather in presenting the world in its own image, a task that must be more elusive than it might first appear." Gunning, "World in Its Own Image," 123.

77 Bazin, "Pure Masterpiece," 109.

78 Bazin, "Pure Masterpiece," 113, 114.

79 Bazin, *What Is Cinema?*, Vol. 2, 68. During his Hollywood years, Renoir reached for something similar in his film *The Southerner* (1945). See "The Southerner," New York State Writer's Institute, accessed October 2016, http://www.albany.edu/writers-inst/webpages4/filmnotes/fns03n10.html.

80 Bazin, "Pure Masterpiece," 107.

81 Rosen, "Belief in Bazin."

82 Bazin, *Jean Renoir*, 107. Recall again how this is strangely reminiscent of Lefebvre's concrete abstraction from *The Production of Space*.

83 In talking about *Rules of the Game*, Renoir identifies his style as something "between a certain realism—not exterior, but realism all the same—and a certain poetry," influenced by the literary works of the eighteenth-century French novelist Pierre de Marivaux and nineteenth-century dramatist-poet Alfred de Musset. Renoir, *Renoir on Renoir*, 4.

84 Watts, "Eloquent Image," 223.

85 Watts, "Eloquent Image," 223.

86 Details of this episode recorded in Mandagaran, *Around the River*.

87 Bazin, "Pure Masterpiece," 111.

88 Rowland, "Films from Abroad," 137.

89 Godden interviewed by David Thompson in *The River* BFIVD619 booklet, n.p.

90 Bernier's memories in Mandagaran's *Around the River*. Of this period, Renoir says he lived without any "meat, tobacco or alcohol." Renoir, *My Life and My Films*, 258.

91 Renoir, *My Life and My Films*, 252, 40.

92 In this context, see Bergstrom, "Jean Renoir's Return to France"; Bergstrom, "Oneiric Cinema"; and Bergstrom, "Jean Renoir and the Allied War Effort."

93 Waldman, *Hollywood and the Foreign Touch*, 243; Renoir in Mandagaran, *Around the River*.

94 Renoir, *My Life and My Films*, 248–49; "J. K. McEldowney, 97; Florist Made Movie after Wife Dared Him," *Los Angeles Times*, obituary, last modified January 16, 2004, accessed May 22, 2015, http://articles.latimes.com/2004/jan/16/local/me-passings16.2, McEldowney in Mandagaran, *Around the River* (2006).

95 Pumphrey, "Cameras Finally Roll," *New York Times*, February 26, 1950, clipping, Folder: "The River" [Oriental-Inter. 1949], Hedda Hopper Collection, MHL.

96 Mandagaran, *Around the River*.

97 Godden interview by David Thompson.

98 For details on what is involved in below-the-line work, see chapter 5.

99 Mandagaran, *Around the River*.

100 Pumphrey, "Cameras Finally Roll."

101 Letter from Melvina McEldowney to Hopper, December 17, 1949, Folder: "The River" (United Artists, 1951) #3962, Hedda Hopper Collection, MHL; Pumphrey, "Cameras Finally Roll" reproduces material from Melvina's letter.

102 Reports of obstacles to the shoot in Bergan, *Jean Renoir*, 278; Hedda Hopper, "Hollywood Story, Stranger Than Movies," *Chicago Sunday Tribune*, April 8, 1951, Hedda Hopper Collection: Folder "The River" [Oriental Inter. 1949]. MHL; Mandagaran, *Around the River*.

103 Golsan, "Desperately Seeking Radha," 119.

104 There is much more that could be said here about the film's use of Technicolor that I omit for a lack of space.

105 Bergan, *Jean Renoir*, 278; LoBianco and Thompson, *Jean Renoir: Letters*, 246.

106 Godden interview; Bergan, *Jean Renoir*, 278. According to Bergan, the man was manager of the screening facility. I am going with Godden's memory that it was the local customs officer.

107 Pumphrey, "Cameras Finally Roll."

108 "E. Lourié Notes on Location Shooting"; Pumphrey, "Cameras Finally Roll." See this book's last chapter, "Reflections," for the story of a little girl who helped with building huts.

109 Renoir, "Introduction," 242.

110 Renoir, *Renoir on Renoir*, 37.

111 Not to be confused with the Brāhman caste in Hinduism.

112 Audi, *Cambridge Dictionary of Philosophy*; see entries for Advaita (9) and Vedanta (832–33); Blackburn, *Oxford Dictionary of Philosophy*; see entries for Advaita (7), *moksha* (247), and Shankara (350); R. Prasad, *Historical Developmental Study*; and Rajagopalachari, *Upanishads*.

113 Wessinger, "Hinduism Arrives in America."

114 Bergan, *Jean Renoir*, 279; Renoir, *Renoir on Renoir*, 37.

115 Bazin, *Jean Renoir*, 45. For a study of the unanimism of Romains, see Norrish, *Drama of the Group*.

116 Bazin, *Jean Renoir*, 46.

117 Ellwood, "Theosophy."

118 Viswanathan, "Ordinary Business of Occultism," 2.

119 Viswanathan, "Ordinary Business of Occultism," 3.

120 I thank Tom Gunning for this observation.

121 Golsan, "Desperately Seeking Radha," 117. I thank Janet Bergstrom for drawing my attention to this essay.

122 Renoir, *Renoir on Renoir*, 37.

123 Golsan, "Desperately Seeking Radha."

124 Golsan, "Desperately Seeking Radha," 111–12.

125 Coorlawala, "Ruth St. Denis"; P. Srinivas, *Sweating Saris*; Golsan, "Desperately Seeking Radha," 112.

126 Golsan, "Desperately Seeking Radha," 113. Golsan very effectively uses my gradations of imperial narratives to demonstrate that *The River* accepts an attrition of its fictional world in allowing India a stronger sense of place. Jaikumar, *Cinema at the End of Empire*.

127 Renoir, *Renoir on Renoir*, 37.

128 Renoir, *Renoir on Renoir*, 37.

129 Bazin, *Jean Renoir*, 11–12.

130 Renoir, *Renoir, My Father*, 19.

131 Renoir, *Renoir, My Father*, 19.

132 Hansen, "Introduction," xi.

133 Renoir, *Renoir, My Father*, 23.

134 Renoir, *Renoir, My Father*, 23.

135 Hansen, "Introduction," xxvi.

136 Hansen, "Introduction," xxxvi.

137 Renoir, *Renoir, My Father*, 6.

138 Jhaveri, *Outsider Films*, 19.

139 Godden, *The River*, 107.

140 Renoir, *Renoir on Renoir*, 32.

141 Captain John is played by Tom Breen, son of Joseph Breen, who enforced the Hayes Code.

142 "Film Music Article by Ann Rovell," Box 12, Folder 13, UCLA Renoir Papers; "Musician and Instrument List," Box 9, Folder 3, UCLA Renoir Papers.

143 Renoir, *My Life and My Films*, 251.

144 Renoir, *My Life and My Films*, 251.

145 Also noted by Jhavery in Jaikumar, "Dialogue on *The River*," 29.

146 For more see Street, *Black Narcissus*; and Jaikumar, *Cinema at the End of Empire*, 165–91.

147 Durgnat, *Jean Renoir*, 276.

148 Bazin, *Jean Renoir*, 39.

149 I expand on this argument in Jaikumar, "Dialogue on *The River*," 21. See also Thapar, *Past as Present*.

150 Nichols, *Representing Reality*.

151 Bazin, "Aesthetic of Reality," 24. See also Caminati's discussion of documentary aesthetics in the director's body of work in *Roberto Rossellini Documentarista*.

152 Rosenbaum, "Creation of the World," 53.

153 Rosenbaum's version of the translation varies from this one. He follows Ted Gallagher's subtitles, while I am using the subtitles provided in TMC's telecast of the film on March 13, 2013, at 12:30 am. Despite recent digital restoration by the Cinecittà Studios and Cineteca Nazionale (CSC), it remains difficult to access a good copy of the film with English subtitles at the time of writing. I thank my friends Peter Sarram in Italy and Angela Wood in Los Angeles for getting me a copy of the film.

154 Bazin, "Pure Masterpiece," 107; Bazin, "Virtues and Limitations of Montage," 48; Bazin, "Pure Masterpiece," 118.

155 Ghatak, *Cinema and I*, 86.

156 Sarkar, *Mourning the Nation*, 207.

157 This ferocity erupts in Ghatak's *Megha Dhaka Tara* (1960), when the camera spins on the Shillong landscape echoing with a dying and consumptive Neeta's plea: "I want to live." Shahani refers to this as Ghatak's "circular panoramics" in conversation with film scholar Ashish Rajadhyaksha. Rajadhyaksha, "Dossier: Kumar Shahani," 80.

158 Sarkar, *Mourning the Nation*, 225.

159 Rajadhyaksha, *Ritwik Ghatak*.

160 Ghatak, *Cinema and I*, 86–87.

161 Also, as Hansen argues in her reading of *Theory of Film* through Kracauer's Marseille notebooks, the "problematic of the subject" always remains a part of Kracauer's focus on "camera reality." So Ghatak may have had more affinity to Kracauer than his review would allow.

162 Hansen, "Introduction," xi.

163 Rajadhyaksha, *Ritwik Ghatak*; O'Donnell, "'Woman' and 'Homeland.'"

164 Ghatak, *Cinema and I*, 15.

165 See Morgan, "Rethinking Bazin," 461; see also 458–75.

166 Morgan, "Rethinking Bazin," 469–75.

167 Rajadhyaksha, "Dossier: Kumar Shahani," 107.

168 Shahani observes that Ghatak "freed the form [of film] from the classical supernatural and the later romantic individualistic concepts by replacing Hamlet's 'particular fault' by socio-historical forces" (Rajadhyaksha, "Dossier: Kumar Shahani," 79). Similar observations are made in Sarkar, *Mourning the Nation*, 200–229; Rajadhyaksha, *Ritwik Ghatak*; and Rajadhyaksha, "Introduction to Kumar Shahni's Essays," in "Dossier: Kumar Shahani," 68–70.

169 As Biswas notes, "The mythic power of return will fascinate Ghatak; he was not satisfied with a form that enacts the historical flow but sought to turn history itself into an object of investigation." Biswas, "Her Mother's Son."

170 Bazin, "Aesthetic of Reality," 37.

171 Bazin, "De Sica," 68.

172 The "ethic of realism" is a phrase from Watts, "Eloquent Image," 223. For more on my argument about the ethic of equivalence, see the book's conclusion.

Epigraphs: Jawaharlal Nehru, *The Discovery of India*, 51; Borges, *Collected Fictions*, 288.

1   Guha, *India after Gandhi*, 755.
2   P. Chatterjee, *Nationalist Thought*; Chakrabarty, *Postcolonial Thought*; Prakash, "Writing Post-Orientalist Histories," 383–408; Majumdar, *Writing*; and, from the perspective of transnational critique, see Spivak, *Critique of Postcolonial Reason*.
3   See Chakrabarty, *Provincializing Europe*, especially 40, 41, and 235.
4   Kosambi, "Indian Feudalism," 148–49; Shelvankar, "Indian Feudalism," 150–54.
5   Princely states lost their special status with the adoption of the constitution in 1949. Prime Minister Indira Gandhi abolished titles and the Privy Purse in 1971 under the Derecognition of Indian Princes Proclamation.
6   This is not to disregard nuanced historical analysis such as Rudolph and Hoeber's *Essays on Rajputana*, which address micronegotiations between feudal and democratic social registers that cannot be described as a "narrative of success."
7   Rhodes, *Spectacle of Property*; Steimatsky, *Italian Locations*; Dimendberg, *Film Noir*; Robertson-Wojcik, *Apartment Plot*.
8   Rhodes, *Spectacle of Property*, 11.
9   Dimendberg, *Film Noir*, 3.
10 Dimendberg, *Film Noir*, 3.
11 Filmi Duniya Mein Awadh was the theme of the Sanatkada Lucknow Festival in 2015, subsequently published as an encyclopedia by Saman Habib.
12 Hell and Schönle, *Ruins of Modernity*, 5.
13 Hell and Schönle, *Ruins of Modernity*, 5.
14 Under postmodernity, Jameson argues that society can at best manufacture a nostalgia for nostalgia, in imitation of an emotion for the past that it can no longer experience.
15 I am primarily drawing on Benjamin, *Writer of Modern Life* and *Arcades Project*. For Jameson's reading of Benjamin, consult Jameson, "Walter Benjamin, or Nostalgia."
16 The dialectic works against the commodification of a ruin as a heritage monument, which potentially freezes its temporal dialectics.
17 Limbrick, "Contested Spaces."
18 Jonathan Perel's *Toponymy* (Argentina, 2015) does the same in relation to settler townships. Thanks to Jennifer Peterson and Brian Jacobson for introducing me to this film and their film notes at "May: Toponomy," accessed May 2017, https://docalogue.com/may-toponymy/.
19 Naficy, *Accented Cinema*.
20 Derrida, *Spectres of Marx*.
21 In this context, see also Ramaswamy, *Lost Land of Lemuria*.
22 Marx's controversial stance in the debate is discussed by Jani, "Karl Marx." For more on the unstable description of the "mutiny" as "revolt," also consult my essay "Insurgent Place as Visual Space," reworked in this chapter.
23 Hosagrahar, "Mansions to Margins."
24 Chakravarty, *Indian Mutiny*.

25 For a similar argument in the context of what he terms "Islamic" films such as *Pakeezah* (Kamal Amrohi, 1972), *Coolie* (Manmohan Desai, 1983), and *Muqaddar ka Sikandar* (Prakash Mehra, 1978), see Taneja, *Jinnealogy*.

26 "Visual modernity" is defined here as the experiential reorganization of space and time with the industrialization of technologies of vision.

27 Chakravarty, *Indian Mutiny*, 72.

28 Chakravarty, *Indian Mutiny*, 7.

29 For my brief description and analysis of this film on the Colonial Film website, see "The Relief of Lucknow," http://www.colonialfilm.org.uk/node/1836.

30 Shohat and Stam, *Unthinking Eurocentrism*, 119.

31 *Bioscope* 16, no. 307 (August 29, 1912): 664 (no author or title).

32 *Bioscope* 16, no. 307 (August 29, 1912): 664.

33 Notebook #2 (*The Relief of Lucknow*), 204, "Dawley Collection," MHL, Los Angeles.

34 *Bioscope* 16, no. 307 (August 29, 1912): 652–53.

35 *Bioscope* 16, no. 307 (August 29, 1912): 663.

36 Deichmann, *Rogues and Runners*.

37 See Sandberg, "Location, "Location"; Palmer, *Shot on Location*; Roan, *Envisioning Asia*; Gleich and Webb, *Hollywood on Location*; Gleich, *Hollywood in San Francisco*.

38 Musser, *Thomas A. Edison*. Another example of location shooting aimed at British audiences is Dawley's *Charge of the Light Brigade* (1912), accessed June 12, 2009, http://www.bfi.org.uk/films-tv-people/4ce2b6a4e28ee.

39 An exception is Felice Beato's Sekunderbagh image, analyzed in Chaudhary, "Phantasmagoric Aesthetics"; and Jaikumar, "Insurgent Place as Visual Space."

40 Perception and social practices are central to the consumption and narration of place, echoing de Certeau's formulation that "*space is a practiced place.*" de Certeau, *Practice of Everyday Life*, 117.

41 Martineau et al., "India Question," 358.

42 Karl Marx, "State of the Indian Insurrection." Transcribed by Tony Brown. *New-York Tribune*, August 18, 1857, accessed October 10, 2007, http://www.marxist.org/archive/marx/works/1857/08/18.htm.

43 News from India arrived in Britain within a month or two of an event's occurrence through a combination of the telegraph, military dispatches, and mail carried by steamers.

44 On "sites for history's most intricate invasions," see Bhabha, *Location of Culture*, 33. On war and disaster photography, Sontag's *Regarding the Pain of Others* has a similar meditation.

45 Benjamin, "Theses on the Philosophy of History," 254.

46 Said, *Culture and Imperialism*, xx.

47 Examples of mutiny-themed films of the early 1900s include *Historic Mutiny Sites* (c. 1916), *A Visit to Lucknow* (c. 1913), and *A Sepoy's Wife* (Vitagraph Fiction Films, 1910), among others. Pinney, *Coming of Photography*, studies photographic albums related to the mutiny.

48 Lifson, "Beato in Lucknow."

49 There are a few examples of female mutiny albums, though less numerous than their male counterparts. See Lifson, "Beato in Lucknow"; and Klaver, "Domesticity Under Siege."

50 Di Bello, *Women's Albums*.

51 Reverend Thomas Moore, "Cawnpore and Lucknow during Mutiny of 1857: 8 Diary, Sketches, Photographs and Plans by Reverend T. Moore, 1958," Manuscript Department (Add. 37151), British Library, London.

52 I am paraphrasing Bill Nichols's well-known description of the institutional discourses of medicine, science, and educational policies as "discourses of sobriety," in Nichols, *Introduction to Documentary*.

53 These arguments on Ali's album first appeared in my chapter "Insurgent Place and Visual Space."

54 Darogha Abbas Ali, *The Lucknow Album* (Baptist Mission Press, 1874), (Getty Research Institute). Abbas Ali is also spelled as Ubbas Alli, and this album is now in the public domain. Full text available online at https://archive.org/details/gri_00003312500860833.

55 Ali, *Lucknow Album*, 2; emphasis mine.

56 Sturken, *Tourists of History*, offers an argument linking consumer culture, memory, and mourning in the contemporary United States.

57 Ali, *Lucknow Album*, 45.

58 "Nawab" was the title given to a Muslim nobleman or governor under the Mughal Empire.

59 Ali, *Lucknow Album*, 52–54, 47–48.

60 Bois, "Introduction," 111.

61 Llewellyn-Jones, *Fatal Friendship*.

62 Gordon, "City of Mourning," 80–91.

63 Ali, *Lucknow Album*, 6.

64 Ali, *Lucknow Album*, 3.

65 Ali, *Lucknow Album*, 2.

66 Peterson, *Education*; Musser, "Travel Genre," 123–32; Gunning, "Whole World within Reach," 25–41; Kirby, *Parallel Tracks*; Schwartz, "Dimanche à Orly."

67 Ali, *Lucknow Album*, 31. "Nawabi" means "of nawabs."

68 Taneja, *Jinnealogy*. See chapter 2 on "Saintly Visions," 55–88.

69 The translation is mine, but I am indebted to Iftekhar Dadi and Shohini Ghosh for assistance.

70 A rumor from *Chaudhvin*'s location shoot has it that the filmmakers persuaded a local male auto driver (a driver of three-wheelers) to don a burqa for this short sequence (as told to me by my friend, filmmaker and scholar Shohini Ghosh, based on narratives from the convention *Filmi Duniya Mein Awadh*). Made doubly uncanny by this rumor, the cross-dressing male or presumptively female presence inhabits an estranged space in relation to the urban environment. For similarly estranging encounters between space, time, monument, and flesh in literary, poetic, cinematic, and rumored texts, see Taneja's use of the phrase "elsewhen" in "Saintly Visions."

71 Vidler, "Foreword," ix.

72 Bruno, *Atlas of Emotion*; Friedberg, "Mobilized and Virtual Gaze," 15–32. Also see Schivelbusch, *Railway Journey*.

73 Bhaskar and Allen, *Islamicate Cultures*, 65.

74 Biswas, "Mourning and Blood Ties," 78–85.

75 Dwyer, "Bombay Gothic"; Sen, "Haunted Havelis," 116–36; Bhaskar and Allen, *Islamicate Cultures*, 65–90. Sen's argument is expanded in her monograph *Haunting Bollywood*.

76 Said, *Orientalism*, 16; emphasis in original; see also Said, *Beginnings*.

77 "Mirza Ghalib's Renovated Haveli Opened," *Times of India*, Last modified December 28, 2011, accessed June 30, 2013, http://timesofindia.indiatimes.com/city/delhi/Mirza Ghalibs-renovated-haveli-opened/articleshow/11273415.cms?referral=PM.

78 Tillotson, *Indian Mansions*; Hosagrahar, "Mansions to Margins," 26–45; Bryden, "There Is No Outer Space," 26–41; Parmar, *Haveli*.

79 Novels set in *havelis* include Mehta's *Inside the Haveli*, Staples's *Shabanu* and *Haveli*, and pulp haveli romances such as Mahal, *Haveli*.

80 In "Bombay Gothic," 130–55, Dwyer notes that the film *Mahal* was originally titled *Haveli*.

81 The cultural significance of objects and monuments alters with India's economic shift to privatization and globalization in 1991, seen in a self-consciousness toward history in Hindi films in *Hazaron Khwaishen Aisi* (Sudhir Mishra, 2003) and *Om Shanti Om* (Farah Khan, 2007); the latter's burnt ruin and reincarnation site is a winking reference to haveli films.

82 This echoes Lim's analysis of heterogeneous time in *Translating Time*.

83 Benjamin, *Arcades Project*, 462.

84 Guha-Thakurta, *Monuments, Objects, Histories*, xviii, 303.

85 For more on the Ramseys, consult Nair, "Taste, Taboo, Trash"; and Sen, *Haunting Bollywood* (see in particular chapter 2 on "The Ramsey Rampage").

86 McCarthy and Flynn, *King of the Bs*.

87 *Purani Haveli* can be viewed online and is available as a DVD through Mondo Macabro. All other films discussed are available through induna.com. *Laal Patthar* streamed on Netflix in 2017.

88 See Rhodes, *Spectacle of Property*, for a discussion of the house in American cinema as a visual and architectural mediation of private property on-screen.

89 Mulvey, "Notes on Sirk and Melodrama," 75.

90 Sarkar, *Mourning the Nation*, 21.

91 Sarkar, *Mourning the Nation*, 192.

92 According to *The Government of India White Paper on Indian States*, earliest articulations of paramountcy were made during Lord Richard Wellesley's residency as governor-general of India in 1797–1805.

93 *White Paper on Indian States*, 9.

94 Phadnis, *Towards the Integration of Indian States*, 46.

95 Foucault, "Governmentality," 87–104; Foucault, *Discipline and Punish*.

96 The annexation was legally permitted by disenfranchising the direct heir to the Maratha king Shivaji under the new law Doctrine of Lapse, which denied royally adopted heirs the right to inherit land or title.

97 Niranjan Takle, "What in Goddess's Name!" *Week*, July 8, 2012, 22–25.

98 Dwyer and Patel, *Cinema India*, 71–73.

99 Bryden, "There Is No Outer Space," 27.

100 Hosagrahar, "Mansions to Margins," 29, 31.
101 Contradictions between the public nature of artistic forms and private aspects of its content are discussed by Bakhtin, *Dialogic Imagination*, 123; emphasis in original.
102 For an analysis of bazaars, consult Chakrabarty, *Habitations of Modernity*, 65–79.
103 Bryden, "There Is No Outer Space."
104 Makdisi, *Romantic Imperialism*, 9. Gothic, antirationalist, and antirealist impulses in eighteenth-century European poetry and art (by Horace Walpole, William Blake, George Byron, Percy B. Shelley, and others) are understood as articulating resistance and antinomy to the historical rupture of modernity. Ng, *Asian Gothic*; Banerjee, "Political Economy," 260–71, 319.
105 Thomspon, "Encrypted Ancestries," 76.
106 P. Chatterjee, *Nationalist Thought*; Dwyer, "Bombay Gothic"; Sen, "Haunted Havelis."
107 Boym, "Nostalgia and Its Discontents," 9, expanded in Boym, *The Future of Nostalgia*.
108 Despite sharing an emphasis on monumentality and mise-en-scène with the British heritage film genre, Indian *haveli* films combine the modalities of heritage cinema with a gothic aesthetic. For more on British heritage films, see Higson, *English Heritage*.
109 Chaudhuri, *Clearing a Space*, 167.
110 This echoes an argument by A. Ahmed, "Jameson's Rhetoric of Otherness."
111 Bakhtin, *Dialogic Imagination*, 84.
112 Mufti, "Greater Story-Writer," 1–36; Taneja, "Muslimness in Hindi Cinema."
113 "Anti-history" is Makdisi's term (contrasting with William Blake's prophetic poetry to the historical writing of J. S. Mill) "to seek out the heterogeneous and the unexpected in the present, as well as imagine the unimaginable" (Makdisi, *Romantic Imperialism*, 3).
114 Taneja, "Muslimness in Hindi Cinema," n.p.
115 Bhaskar and Allen (following Marshall Hodgson and Mukul Kesavan) elaborate on the Islamicate in *Islamicate Cultures*.
116 See similar arguments in Sarkar, *Mourning the Nation*, chapters 1 and 2.
117 Dwyer talks of Fatehpur Sikri's significance in "I Am Crazy," 123–34.
118 See Elsaesser, "Tales of Sound and Fury" for such an emotional toll being the general province of family melodramas.

CHAPTER 5. GLOBAL

Epigraphs: Benjamin, *Arcades Project*, 460; Rukhsana, Junior Artist (Superclass) interview with author (see appendix).

1 Sonu Srivastava, interview with author.
2 See Dwyer and Patel, *Cinema India*; and Mazumdar, "Aviation, Tourism and Dreaming." Ranjani Mazumdar's unpublished manuscript, currently titled *Travel, Design, and Colour: Bombay Cinema and the Global Sixties*, promises an expansive analysis of this decade.
3 Hate (pronounced Ha-tey) and Dawra, line producers, interviews with author (see appendix).
4 Goldsmith and O'Regan, "The Policy Environment," 41. Similar factors are also discussed in S. Kumar, "Mapping Tollywood."

5 I am using "cinephilia" here to describe the extent to which a devotion to popular Indian cinema infiltrates every aspect of life in India.

6 Athique and Hill, *Multiplex in India*; Basu, *Bollywood*; A. Chopra, *First Day First Show*; Dwyer, *Bollywood's India*; Dudrah, *Bollywood*; Ganti, *Producing Bollywood*; Gehlawat, *Twenty-First Century Bollywood*; Gopal, *Conjugations*; Govil, "Hollywood Effects" and *Orienting Hollywood*, among others; Kavoori and Punathambekar, *Global Bollywood*; Punathambekar, *From Bombay to Bollywood*; Rai, *Untimely Bollywood*; S. Kumar, *Gandhi Meets Primetime*; Kumar and Punathambekar, *Television at Large*.

7 Rajadhyaksha, "Bollywoodization"; M. Prasad, "Surviving Bollywood." I join others in the field in using the descriptor "Bollywood" exclusively in reference to the postliberalization avatar of Bombay's Hindi-language cinema.

8 Caldwell, *Production Culture*, 69.

9 M. Prasad, *Ideology of the Hindi Film*, 48; Ganti, *Producing Bollywood*, 338; M. Prasad, *Ideology of the Hindi Film*.

10 Works that address this include Gopal, *Conjugations*; Rai, *Untimely Bollywood*; Basu, *Bollywood*; S. V. Srinivas, *Megastar*; Dudrah, *Bollywood Travels*.

11 "Mahira Khan to Complete Raees Shooting with Shah Rukh Khan at a Secret Location," Express Web Desk, October 22, 2016, accessed May 22, 2017, https://tinyurl.com/hebzz2b.

12 Bourdieu, *Distinction*.

13 Ganti (*Producing Bollywood*, 4) develops the phrase "gentrification" in the context of the "rising cultural legitimacy of popular Hindi cinema" since the industry's corporatization.

14 The line producer is the person that looks after the physical and logistical rather than the creative decision-making processes of film production. Some line producers I spoke with disagreed with this definition and claimed more creative freedom in India.

15 A. Kant, *Branding India*, 6.

16 See "Bharat Bala Productions" website for the "Incredible India" shorts at http://www.bbp.co.in.

17 A. Kant, *Branding India*, 21. Recent campaign films can be viewed on YouTube (accessed December 1, 2018), http://www.youtube.com/watch?v=CilRScdUibE; on Vimeo (accessed December 1, 2018), http://vimeo.com/28498949; and on "Bharat Bala Productions" website, http://www.bbp.co.in.

18 Basu, *Bollywood*, 6.

19 Rai elaborates on adapting Deleuze and Guattari's concept in *Untimely Bollywood*, 3.

20 For more on the idea Brand India, see also Kapur, *The Politics of Time and Youth*.

21 "Jana Gana Mana: A.R. Rahman," accessed December 1, 2018, https://www.youtube.com/watch?v=redlx8mSTok; "A.R. Rahman: Maa Tujhe Salaam," accessed December 1, 2018, https://www.youtube.com/watch?v=jDn2bn7_YSM.

22 For more on this trope, see Ramaswamy, *Goddess and the Nation*.

23 Brosius, *India's Middle Class*, 11.

24 A. Kant, *Branding India*, 28.

25 Jaikumar, "Hospitality in the Time of Regulation."

26 The music video accompanying the official Namami Gange anthem by Chennai's Trichur Brothers also uses familiar tropes for visualizing India's rivers and mountains.

27 Blaney and Shah, "Aesthetics," 7.

28 Blaney and Shah, "Aesthetics," 8.

29 Deepshikha Ghosh, "Aamir Safe in India, His Comments Insult to Fans, Says Government," NDTV.com, November 24, 2015, accessed June 2016, https://www.ndtv.com/india-news/aamir-khan-says-wife-kiran-suggested-leaving-india-alarmist-says-bjp-1246837.

30 The Panchgani scenes were shot in New Era High School (a Baháʼí school).

31 Ram also credits ten years of work at Prahlad Kakkar's Genesis Films for her professional training.

32 Anadil Hossain, interview with author (see appendix).

33 Hossain interview.

34 Wynne-Jones, "UK Makes Movie Map for Bollywood Buffs," *Telegraph*, May 27, 2007, accessed May 25, 2016, http://www.telegraph.co.uk/news/uknews/1552735/UK-makes-movie-map-for-Bollywood-buffs.html.

35 In 2010–2011, the top 1 percent in India were those with an annual income of over 12.5 lakhs, according to Centre for Macro Consumer Research (CMCR) of the National Council of Applied Economic Research (NCAER). Their disposal income would be approximately 30 percent of this. Susan Viveat et al., "The Case of the Growing One Percent Indians," *Business Standard,* January 24, 2012, http://www.business-standard.com/article/economy-policy/the-case-of-the-growing-one-per-cent-indians-112012400073_1.html.

36 Govil, "Producing 'India' as Location," 237.

37 Ankit Mehta, interview with author (see appendix). The idea that experiences outside textbook knowledge carry more weight in a "greenfield business" such as India (which lacks the competition of a crowded market such as the United States) is the received wisdom of tech and service startups entering developing markets. Anita Raghavan, "For Indian Startups, Tenacity Beats High Tech," *New York Times*, April 11, 2016, B1.

38 Tarsem Singh, interview with author (see appendix).

39 Govind Menon, "International Co-productions," panel discussion, April 23, 2009, Westfield Mall, Century City, Los Angeles.

40 Singh interview.

41 The same method was used in *Munnabhai MMBS* to shoot scenes with Sanjay Dutt and Arshad Warsi. The team kept packing up and moving to different locations to mislead a crowd of over 100,000 people congregated on Marine Drive to watch the shoot. Mapuskar, interview by author (see appendix).

42 Basu notes that "in recent popular Hindi films like *Janasheen* (Feroz Khan, 2003) or *Jab Pyar Kissise Hota Hain* (Deepak Sareen, 1998), transnational women, covering a remarkable racial spectrum, replace the earthly *gopinis*"; Basu, *Bollywood*, 87. *Gopinis* are devotees, and the word is often used in relation to the village girls entranced by Lord Krishna's flute and his roguish ways.

43 Ted Skillman, "International Co-productions," panel discussion, April 23, 2009, Westfield Mall, Century City, Los Angeles.

44 Fernandes, *India's New Middle Class*, 226 (note 13).

45 Fernandes, *India's New Middle Class*, xxxiv.

46 Fernandes, "Politics of Forgetting."

47 Wilkinson-Weber, *Fashioning Bollywood*, 22.

48 Wilkinson-Weber, *Fashioning Bollywood*, 9.

49 Lazzarato, "Immaterial Labor."

50 Lazzarato, "Immaterial Labor," 134.

51 For Lazzarato, "production" includes the sense of a reproduction of social relations based on communication, which is an aspect of consumption. Feminists such as Susanne Schultze would later contend that Lazzarato, Hardt, and Negri's notions of immaterial labor and affective labor nod tokenistically to reproductive and nonwage work, reproducing traditional understandings of gendered labor divisions. Schultze, "Dissolved Boundaries."

52 Lazzarato, "Immaterial Labor," 134.

53 Jaikumar, "Out of Sync."

54 Lazzarato, "Immaterial Labor," 139.

55 Koo, "Global Middle Class," 441.

56 Mazumdar, *Bombay Cinema*, 142–48.

57 This is up from approximately INR 4,000 to 5,000 a month in 1985–1986, according to Pappu Lekhraj Nanda.

58 As negotiated by the JAA and the MKS in 2012, Bombay's junior artists do not work more than twelve-hour days, although models have no work-hour protection, as they are not unionized.

59 Ganti, *Producing Bollywood*.

60 A. Chopra, *King of Bollywood*; Dudrah, Mader, and Fuchs, *SRK and Global Bollywood*; Shankar, "Star Gazing via Documentary," 100–118; Kapse and Sen, "Introduction to Dossier."

61 Mehta interview with author; Lekhraj Nanda interview with author (see appendix); Chanana, *Missing 3*, 128.

62 Bose, "Situating Right-Wing Interventions."

63 Mecklai and Shoesmith, "Religion," 316–33; Rajagopal, *Politics after Television*; Pendakur, *Indian Popular Cinema*.

64 HT (Hindustan Times) correspondent, "Shiv Sena Plans to Have Single Union for Film Industry," *Hindustan Times*, March 30, 2013, https://www.hindustantimes.com/mumbai/shiv-sena-plans-to-have-single-union-for-film-industry/.

65 For a few examples, see PTI (Press Trust of India), "MNS Film Wing Stops Shooting of John Abraham's Force 2," TOI (*Times of India*), April 22, 2016, https://timesofindia.indiatimes.com/city/mumbai/MNS-film-wing-stops-shooting-of-John-Abrahams-Force-2; ANI (Asian News International), "Give Screen Space to 'Deva' or Won't Allow Shooting after This," *Business Standard*, December 20, 2017, http://www.business-standard.com/article/news-ani/give-screen-space-to-deva-or-won-t-allow-shooting-after-this-mns-to-yrf-117122000603_1.html; "MNS Corporation, 6 Party Men Held for Vandalising Film Set," accessed August 2017, http://www.rediff.com/news/report/mns-corporator-6-party-men-held-for-vandalising-film-set/20120730.htm.

66 Aditi Raja, "Film Industry Threatens It Might Have to Move Out of 'Unsafe' Mumbai," *Daily Mail*, July 31, 2012, accessed July 20, 2015, http://www.dailymail.co.uk/indiahome/indianews/article-2181689/Film-industry-threatens-unsafe-Mumbai.html.

67 Sitaram Kadam, interview with author (see appendix).

68 Kadam interview.

69 Ganti, *Producing Bollywood*, 196–202.

70 See chapter 2.

71 National Archive of India, "A Bill to Impose a Duty in Respect of Admission to Entertainments (Bill No. XX of 1922)," October 4, 1922, 2–12 (hereafter "Entertainments Bill"). Mr. R. G. Salgar of Sholapur argued, "In the case of horse racing can we say that the idea of entertainment is primary, seeing that the primary object is the breed of horses and even as entertainment, it is not entertainment pure and simple, but betting and making money? I doubt if race courses are within the scope of this bill," 3.

72 Dass, *Outside the Lettered City*.

73 National Archive of India, *Home Judl. Bombay Entertainment Duty, F1565* (June 1921 to December 1922), "Act No.— of 1923," 1 [blank space in original] and "Entertainments Bill," 2.

74 The Indian state initiated a tax-free policy to support the growth of multiplexes in 1998. For more, see Athique and Hill, *Multiplex in India*.

75 *Report of the Working Group*, 25. Sin tax, a sumptuary tax levied on objects considered socially undesirable (such as alcohol and tobacco) is imposed by many nation-states, but there is no consensus on which commodities should cost more to pay society for the moral burden of their consumption. In the entertainments bill debate, see the positions of Salgar and Dadchandani of Bombay City South ("Entertainments Bill," 3 and 7, respectively). Also see Prasad's discussion "Social Tax" in M. Prasad, *Ideology of the Hindi Film*, 121.

76 Entertainment taxes vary on a state-by-state basis in India, although they are not levied on local film and media products in some states. See also chapter 2 of this book, and Ganti, *Producing Bollywood*, 54–55.

77 The tax was borne by distributors as part of the cost of the print. G. P. Sippy, "Taxation and the Film Industry: A Symposium—2," *FF* January 7, 1966, 33, 35; Mittal, *Cinema Industry in India*, 62.

78 "On Film Length Control."

79 Feroze Rangoonwalla, C6.02, "Comment: Pointers from 1975 Releases," *Star & Style* 25, no. 1 (January 2 1976): n.p.; emphasis added.

80 Sippy was fresh from the success of *Mere Sanam* with Asha Parekh and Biswajeet in 1965. Sippy, "Taxation and the Film Industry," 33. See also Karanjia's untitled editorial in *Filmfare* on April 21, 1972; and B. R. Chopra. "Hindi Cinema Is Still in Tears," *Filmfare*, September 30–October 13, 1977, 17, 19. In 1957, the government appears to have considered restricting the length of films to eight thousand feet (approximately 1 hour and 30 minutes of running time), which would have been impossible for commercial Indian films. "On Film Length Control."

81 "Newsreel," *Picturpost*, October 1966, 93.

82 Bunny Reuben. "Spotlight: Overseas Shootings: Yes or No?" *Trade Guide* 22, no. 28 (May 8, 1976): 12.

83 "Shakti Returns with Mission Accomplished," *Cinema Advance Weekly Entertainment* 39, no. 36 (September 15, 1966): 14. The location rent doesn't seem to have been a hefty fee (Madras state demanded approximately Rs. 1500 or more per day in 1966), but presumably any cost was a disincentive.

84 "'Love in Tokyo' for Japan," *Cine Advance Weekly Entertainment*, September 1, 1966, 11. Comparisons are also made, in this period, between films such as "Round the World," which is criticized for going around the world for location shoots without making money, and

Sangam, which "went abroad only once and earned record foreign exchange with its release in foreign countries." "'Round-the-World' for the Fifth Time," *Cine Advance Weekly Entertainment*, September 15, 1966, 7.

85 Mazumdar, "Aviation, Tourism and Dreaming," 130.

86 Mukherji, "India's Aborted Liberalization," 375–92.

87 For instance, Poduval uses these modifiers in "Affable Young Man," 37. I do not disagree with Poduval's perceptive analysis but want to tease out what lies behind the contradictions frequently assumed to exist between the financial crisis of the 1960s and the exuberant consumerism in films from the same period.

88 This is also evident in state-sponsored films of the period, in Films Divisions tourism shorts such as *Don't Be That Greedy* (*Itne Laalchi Na Baniye*, Prem Vaidya 1975); *Come Again* (Loksen Lalvani, 1975); *Jaan Bachi aur Lakhon Paye* (*Getting Away with Your Life Is Worth a Million*, Upadhyay, 1975); *Preserving Our Heritage* (Samiran Datta, 1975); *Honored Guest* (B. N. Mehta, 1975); *All the Way* (B. G. Devare, 1975); *Kashmir: A Dream in Winter* (Ashok Sagar, A. K. Sagar, 1975); *Tourism: An Economic Boon* (G. C. Bharadwaj, 1977), some of which I analyze in "Hospitality in the Time of Regulation."

89 Mukul Kesavan, "Remembrance of Things Past: Materialism in a Time of High Tarriff Barriers," *Telegraph*, May 6, 2012, http://www.telegraphindia.com/1120506/jsp/opinion/story _15457508.jsp#.UCyBS05C8fP.

90 "Surf Lalitaji Commercial." The commercial is on YouTube, https://www.youtube.com /watch?v=CN_plnOolf8. See Masoom Gupte, "40 Years Ago and Now . . . Unsmiling Lalita ji to Celebrating Stains," *Business Standard*, August 27, 2014, accessed January 2016, http:// www.business-standard.com/article/management/40-years-ago-and-now-unsmiling-lalita -ji-to-celebrating-stains-114082701206_1.html.

91 Rajadhyaksha and Willeman, *Encyclopedia of Indian Cinema*, 231.

92 Mazumdar, "Aviation, Tourism and Dreaming," 139.

93 Dwyer and Patel, *Cinema India*, 72.

94 The translation is mine and not literal. I take poetic license. "Athanni" is 8 annas, or approximately 50 paise. Annas followed the predecimal system, when the Indian rupee was subdivided into 16 annas.

95 As with all Indian melodramas of the preglobalization era (including global travel films and *haveli* films), female bodies are the site for negotiations between tradition and modernity. In *Teen Bahuraniyan*, this is explicit when one of the wives performs a cabaret number for her husband, repeating a trope present in several films, including *An Evening in Paris*.

96 As Satish Poduval argues, the intermediary position of this class is linked not only to socioeconomic status but also to their "access to significant forms of cultural capital which includes . . . the acquisition of crucial 'non-material' attributes such as taste, style, and social networking," which play "a crucial role in the reproduction of class relations and capitalist culture." Poduval, "Affable Young Man," 39. See also Dwyer, *Bollywood's India*; "Mumbai Middlebrow," 51–68; and "Zara Hatke!," 184–208.

97 C. P. Chandrasekhar, "India's Informal Economy," *Hindu*, September 3, 2014, accessed June 20, 2016, http://www.thehindu.com/opinion/columns/Chandrasekhar/indias-informal-economy /article6375902.ece.

98 Fernandes, "Restructuring the Middle Class," 88.

99 Fernandes, "Restructuring the Middle Class," 102.

100 Uberoi's and Chopra's arguments regarding *DDLJ*'s recuperation of the expatriate global Indian can equally apply to the redemption of the wealthy Indian. A. Chopra, *Dilwale Dulhania le Jayenge*; Uboroi, "Diaspora Comes Home."

101 Tejaswini Ganti makes a similar point when she elaborates on her interview with art director Sharmishta Roy about changing representation of the wealthy in Hindi cinema. Ganti, *Producing Bollywood*, 98–99.

102 Mazumdar, "Aviation, Tourism and Dreaming," 130.

103 Mazumdar, "Aviation, Tourism and Dreaming," 131. Specifically, Mazumdar turns to the performance of a kiss, the female protagonist's acts of masquerade, the use of international architectural icons, and the circulation of scandalous images in and around the publicity of these films.

104 Mazumdar, "Aviation, Tourism and Dreaming," 142.

105 "Realism" here refers to an invisibility of form achieved through the creation of seamless visual effects that do not distract a viewer's attention away from a film's fictional world, in the manner of classical Hollywood cinema.

106 The insignificance of continuity in lighting is evident in several commercial blockbusters prior to the 1990s. As a specific example, scenes from the first twenty minutes of *Love in Tokyo* (Pramod Chakravorty, 1966), a film discussed in the context of foreign location shooting and tourism, show shots lit differently although they are supposed to depict the same unified space and time of day.

107 Shyam Benegal, interview with author (see appendix).

108 Sundaram, *Pirate Modernities*, 2–3; Liang and Sundaram, "India," 339–98.

109 Gopalan, *Cinema of Interruptions*.

110 Bhatt (a veteran of film shoots in Malaysia), president of the Film and Television Producers Guild of India, and Farokh T. Balsara, partner and market leader of Media and Entertainment Sector for Ernst & Young LLP, presented a report on international tariff incentives during the years 2013–2014 systematizing production incentives for shooting in several places (specifically, Malaysia, Australia, Italy, Spain, Ireland, Turkey, the United Kingdom, South Africa, Mauritius, Abu Dhabi, and Canada), providing contacts and the costs and benefits of each location to the Indian film community. Mukesh Bhatt and Farokh T. Balsara, *Incentive Guide: Indian Film Productions Abroad*, Edition 1, The Film and Television Production Guild of India, accessed November 2017, http://www.ey.com /Publication/vwLUAssets/ey-incentive-guide-indian-film-production-overseas/$FILE /ey-incentive-guide-indian-film-production-overseas.pdf.

111 Bollywood blockbusters, multiplex films, and *hatke* films cover a large spectrum of film productions (and such binary divisions are increasingly collapsing with films such as *Udta Punjab*, 2016, that use mainstream actors to explore unconventional themes and styles), but select examples of blockbusters with foreign locations include *Dil Chahta Hai*, 2001; *Jhoom Barabar Jhoom*, 2007; *Dostana*, 2008; *New York, New York*, and multiplex or *hatke* films using real locations include *Black Friday*, 2004; *Delhi 6*, 2009; *Dhobi Ghat*, 2010; *No One Killed Jessica*, 2011; *Kahaani*, 2012; *Talvar*, 2015; *Gangs of Wasseypur* (Part 1 and 2), 2012; *Delhi Belly*, 2011;

Court, 2014. *Hatke* films are "offbeat" films that push the artistic and narrative boundaries of conventional Bollywood fare. They were made financially possible by the growth of multiplexes, fragmentation of audiences, availability of international funding and recognition for Indian filmmakers, and the rise of conglomerates with multiple revenue streams, which allow film producers to be less risk-averse. See also Dwyer and Pinto, *Beyond the Boundaries*.

112 H. Lefebvre, *Production of Space*, 356.

113 Auge, *Non-Places*.

CONCLUSION

Epigraph: Soja, *Postmodern Geographies*, 11.

1 Foucault, "Questions on Geography," 70, reprinted in Crampton and Elden, *Space, Knowledge, and Power*.

2 Dimendberg, "Limits to Emplacement," 513.

3 Foucault, "Of Other Spaces," 22. Key works include Foucault, "Of Other Spaces"; several essays in Crampton and Elden, *Space, Knowledge, and Power*; H. Lefebvre, *Production of Space*; de Certeau, *Practice of Everyday Life*; Bachelard, *Poetics of Space*; Tuan, *Space and Place*; Said, *Orientalism* and *Culture and Imperialism*; Kasbarian, "Mapping Edward Said," 529–57; Massey, *Space, Place, and Gender*; G. Rose, *Feminism and Geography*; Soja, *Postmodern Geographies*, among others; Jameson, *Geopolitical Aesthetic*; Harvey, "Space as a Keyword," 270–93, and *Condition of Postmodernity*; Berman, *All That Is Solid*; and Davis, *City of Quartz*, among others.

4 See Appadurai, *Fear of Small Numbers*.

5 Bruno, *Atlas of Emotion*.

6 David Harvey notes that Lefebvre did not constitute the "originary moment from which all thinking about the production of space derives," Harvey, "Space as a Keyword," 279. This may be true, but his ideas are today the most widely disseminated.

7 Lefebvre, *Production of Space*, 96–97.

8 Lefebvre, *Production of Space*, 28–30; Soja, *Thirdspace*, 63–64.

9 Lefebvre, *Production of Space*, 30.

10 Lefebvre, *Production of Space*, 75.

11 Lefebvre, *Production of Space*, 96.

12 Soja adds to Dear's list in *Thirdspace*, 59; Dear, "Postmodern Bloodlines," 49–71.

13 Discussions with Phil Rosen helped me clarify the purpose of this chapter to a great degree, and I am very grateful for his detailed response to an earlier version of the same.

14 Bordwell, Staiger, and Thompson, *Classical Hollywood Cinema*; M. Prasad, *Ideology of the Hindi Film*.

15 See Oever, *Ostrannenie*; Thompson, *Breaking the Glass Armour*. Independent and avant-garde films may "defamiliarize" normative stylistic strategies, but these film historians argue that such works illustrate the norm by their exceptionality.

16 Consult this book's introduction for examples of spatial film and media scholarship. In "Placing the Past," Ethington makes an eloquent argument for spatially mapping the past, as he does in his ongoing online interactive publication *Ghost Metropolis*. See also Rosenberg and Grafton, *Cartographies of Time*.

17 For example, Gunning, *Films of Fritz Lang* and "Modernity and Cinema," 297–315; Hansen, "Mass Production of the Senses," 59–77; Friedberg, *Virtual Window*; Schwartz and Przybyl-ski, *Nineteenth-Century Visual Culture Reader*.

18 Zhen, *Amorous History*; Mazumdar, *Bombay Cinema*.

19 Conley, *Cartographic Cinema*, 14.

20 Bruno, *Atlas of Emotion*, 8, 46, and more. The term "intimate geographies" is used several times in the book, particularly in "An Archive of Emotion Pictures."

21 If we conclude that film is simultaneously referential and abstracting, where do we go from there?

22 Crary, *Techniques of the Observer*.

23 Gunning, "Moving Away from the Index," 35.

24 Gunning, "Moving Away from the Index," 35.

25 Rodowick, in following the genealogy of theory itself, revisits this question in *Elegy for a Theory* and *Virtual Life of Film*.

26 Gunning, *Moving Away from the Index*, 35.

27 Soja, *Thirdspace*, 58, 57.

28 Soja, *Thirdspace*, 61.

29 I am referring simply to cinema's technological ability to record or closely simulate reality, while embedding reality within a symbolic system of narrative or iconic meanings.

30 Steimatsky, *Italian Locations*; Pandian, *Reel World*; Amad, "From God's-Eye to Camera-Eye."

31 "Notes by E. Lourie re Location Shooting," Box 9, Folder 4, Jean Renoir Papers, UCLA Archives, Los Angeles.

32 Ziya Us Salam, "Changing Contours," *Hindu Magazine: Weekly Edition 2* (August 24, 2008): 2.

33 Benjamin, "Theses on the Philosophy of History," 254.

34 Bazin, "Aesthetic of Reality," 36.

35 Bazin, "Aesthetic of Reality," 36.

36 The question of how to write about a subject from records that yield no trace of them, while guarding against the historian's recovery of the subject as co-optable trace, is thoughtfully explored in Arondekar, *For the Record*.

37 In addition to my analysis in chapter 1, see the entry on "Foothill Town" on the Colonial Film website, http://www.colonialfilm.org.uk/node/1645.

38 Foucault, "Eye of Power," 149; Klinger, "Film History."

39 Foucault, *Archeology of Knowledge*, 9–10. Anthropologist Ann Stoler makes this argument in detail in *Along the Archival Grain*.

40 For more on heterotopic film historiographies, see the last section of this chapter.

41 In this sense, I am more poststructuralist than those who trace their historiography to the Annales school, or to recent ideas in *deep mapping* following Moon's work, which is to provide cross-referenced, varied, multivocal but finally exhaustive information about place. Nevertheless, deep mapping practices remain influential for me. Moon, *PrairyErth*.

42 Bazin, "Virtues and Limitations," 46.

43 As I complete this book under Donald Trump's presidency, it is evident that the argument of radical equality is threatening to authoritarian regimes. The "All Lives Matter" slogan,

deployed viciously against "Black Lives Matter," refuses to acknowledge populations denied the presumption of ontological, historical, or social equivalency. It becomes a ploy for racist and fascist regimes to suppress minorities by claiming the status of victimhood for the majority.

44 "Flat ontology" was originally discussed by DeLanda in *Intensive Science*.

45 J. D. Rhodes enabled me to understand why I had a problem with the metaphysics of this project. See also Rosenberg's critique of object oriented ontology and new materialism in "Molecularization of Sexuality."

46 Benjamin, "Theses on the Philosophy of History," 254. I also quote this passage in chapter 4.

47 Soja, *Thirdspace*, 57. Soja cites "The Aleph" at length.

48 Lively, *Moon Tiger*, 1.

49 Rancière, "From One Image to Another?," 117.

50 Lefebvre's rejections of this line of argument may have resulted from his rift with the Situationist International at the time of writing *The Production of Space*, a text that conveys both an acceptance and critique of literary surrealism (in his references to André Breton and Georges Bataille). H. Lefebvre, *Production of Space*, 18.

51 Kracauer, *Theory of Film*, 54.

52 Kuleshov, *Kuleshov on Film*, 52–53; Leyda, *Kino*, 164–65; Vertov, "From Kino-Eye to Radio-Eye," 87–88; Vertov, "Kino-Eye," 67.

53 Deren, "Cinematography," 154.

54 Bazin, *Jean Renoir*, 85.

55 Bazin, "De Sica," 68. Also see the careful reading of Bazin's realism by Morgan, "Rethinking Bazin," 443–81.

56 I say "not always" because of Lefebvre's association and subsequent falling out with the Situationists International. As noted in note 50, some of his refutation of film's decoupage and montage in 1974 must have been aimed at the surrealist faith in spatial fragmentation and re-assembly as an aesthetic technique and political strategy.

57 See Rosen, "Screen and 1970s Film Theory," and *Narrative, Apparatus, Ideology*, for the context and key essays from *Screen* and *Cahier du Cinéma* in the 1970s. Also consult my introduction for a discussion of and references to this material.

58 Derrida's theory of the supplement and the exemplar is relevant here (in *Of Grammatology*).

59 Specifically, scholars reassessing cinematic ontology on the basis of global exemplars, and scholarship and translations of theories of cinema produced outside the Euro-American world. For examples, see Bao, *Fiery Cinema*; Galt and Schoonover, *Global Art Cinema*; Marks, *Skin of the Film* and *Enfoldment and Infinity*; Rosen, "Border Times and Geopolitical Frames"; Salazkina, "Geopolitics in Film." As I argue in "Feminist and Non-Western Interrogations of Film Authorship" (212), "Cinema and media studies awaits the kind of gravity-shifting moment experienced in comparative studies . . . where understanding that history and literature are multi-sited provoked a radical revision of theory itself." This book is an attempt to hasten that.

60 For the disciplinarization of film studies, see Grieveson and Wasson, *Inventing Film Studies*; and Grieveson, "Discipline and Publish."

61 Elsaesser, "New Film History," 75–117.

62 Elsaesser, "Bazinian Half-Century," 3.

63 Spivak, *Death of a Discipline*, 26–32.

64 Derrida, *Aporias*, 23.

65 Casey, "The Edge(s) of Landscape," 91–110; Anzaldúa, *Borderlands/La Frontera*; Mignolo, *Local Histories / Global Designs*; Mezzadra and Neilson, *Border as Method*.

66 Conley, *Cartographic Cinema*, 10.

67 Conley, *Cartographic Cinema*, 10.

68 Rancière, "From One Image to Another?," 114.

69 Deleuze, *Cinema 2*, 18; Rancière, "From One Image to Another?," 108. In Rancière's analysis, the paralysis of protagonists in Hitchcock's films (such as *Rear Window* [1954]; *The Wrong Man* [1956]; *Vertigo* [1958]), held up by Deleuze as part of the postwar psychomotor hindrance to the linear arrangement of images, may just as easily be understood as the paralysis of characters within a plot, 115. For a detailed discussion of time in Deleuze's writings on cinema, see Rodowick, *Gilles Deleuze's Time Machine*.

70 Rancière, "From One Image to Another?," 119. This sentiment is shared by Conley, who notes that "A close reading of *Cinema 2: The Time-Image* reveals that the movement-image inheres indeed in the time-image and vice-versa"; Conley, *Cartographic Cinema*, 10.

71 Decolonial and postcolonial studies offer critical insights here because, steeped in reading images in the context of local politics and geopolitical hermeneutics, they disable the presentation of any singular form or history as universal template. Historical ruptures endured with the apocalyptic displacement and murder of slaves and genocidal killings of indigenous populations cast as long a shadow on cultural memory and cinematic form as the early twentieth-century horrors of the world wars and the European Holocaust. For more, see chapter 4.

72 On *time-image*, see Deleuze, *Cinema 2*. Spatial metaphors and spatial thinking are, of course, central in Deleuzian analysis, as with the idea of the fold, de- and reterritorialization, smooth and striated spaces, the rhizomatic, plateaus, and so on. On a *clock for seeing*, see Barthes, *Camera Lucida*, 15. And on *change mummified*, see Bazin, "Ontology," 15.

73 See, for instance, Gunning's ongoing work on cinematic movement: "Moving Away from the Index"; "Animating the Nineteenth Century"; "Hand and Eye."

74 Rosen, *Change Mummified*, xxiii.

75 Rosen, *Change Mummified*, 7.

76 Rosen, *Change Mummified*, 7.

77 Rosen, *Change Mummified*, 19, 16.

78 Rosen, *Change Mummified*, 19.

79 "For Bazin the photographic or cinematic image always provides the spectator with absolute brute knowledge that the objects visible in the frame *were at one time* in the spatial 'presence' of the camera, that they appear from an irrefutable past existence. Furthermore, this 'presence' of the camera to object lasted *for a certain amount of time*." Rosen, *Change Mummified*, 29; emphasis in original.

80 Morgan disagrees with this in "Rethinking Bazin." On the "special credibility of the automatically produced image," see Rosen, *Change Mummified*, 18, 20.

81 It is this intuition that allows Bazin to say, in describing *Umberto D*, that De Sica and Zavattini's cinema becomes "the perfect mirror" in which life can be "visible poetry" and "be the self into which the film finally changes it." Bazin, *What Is Cinema?*, Vol. 2, 82.

82 These were blind spots for 1970s film theory, as Rosen argues. Rosen, *Change Mummified*, 175.

83 Rosen, *Change Mummified*, 29.

84 Cortade discusses the cartographic origins of Bazin's theory of spatial mobility and immobility in cinema, in "Cinema across Fault Lines," 20. And in *Cartographic Cinema*, Conley argues that Deleuze draws upon Bazin as an inaugural moment in the historical shift from movement-image to time-image because Bazin values the neorealists' use of local image-facts to disperse totalizing meanings in a film (just as the topography of particular details disperse the cosmography of a map). The spatial singularity of each image and its connection to things in their splendid isolation allow the film to be tethered to something other than a cinema's design and narrative coherence, permitting the entry of other logics and other temporalities.

85 Bazin, *What Is Cinema?*, vol. 2, 37.

86 Bazin, *What Is Cinema?*, vol. 2, 30.

87 Bazin, *What Is Cinema?*, vol. 2, 37, 38.

88 Bazin, *What Is Cinema?*, vol. 2, 37.

89 Bazin, *What Is Cinema?*, vol. 2, 81.

90 Bazin, *What Is Cinema?*, vol. 2, 77.

91 Bazin, *What Is Cinema?*, vol. 2, 38.

92 Rosen's complex argument far exceeds my brief summary here.

93 Bazin, *What Is Cinema?*, vol. 1, 48.

94 James, *Most Typical Avant Garde*, 18.

95 As argued by White, *Tropics of Discourse*, among others.

96 Bazin, *What Is Cinema?*, vol. 1, 48.

97 The cinephile or following Amelie Hastie's phrase from her regular column, "The Vulnerable Spectator," *Film Quarterly*, 2013 onward.

98 National Archive of India, Education, Forests, 32–14/37, 1937, "Survey of India-Map policy conference," section on "Map Policy," 28. Also consult the discussion on standardizing maps in National Archive of India, Home (Public) 516/1928, "Herewith a sample volume of a proposed new series of map for India."

99 Foucault, "Of Other Spaces," 24.

100 See Johnson's collation in "Heterotopian Studies: Foucault's ideas on heterotopia," accessed December 2, 2018, http://www.heterotopiastudies.com/. Also P. Johnson, "Geographies of Heterotopia"; Dehaene and De Cauter, *Heterotopia and the City*; Elliott and Purdy, "Walk through Heterotopia"; Chung, *Media Heterotopias*.

101 The most prominent is Soja, *Thirdspace*. In discussing the use of digital technologies in recent films in "Media Heterotopia and Transnational Filmmaking" (88), Chung proposes "heterotopic perception as a critical reading strategy that more adequately reflects the material realities of transnational filmmaking by taking into account globally dispersed sites of production and bodies of labor" creating seamless finished products. She expands this argument in *Media Heterotopias*. Closer to what I am proposing, Topinka reads Foucault's "heterotopia" as a term referring to the fundamental spatialization of knowledge that makes its order legible. Topinka, "Foucault, Borges, Heterotopia," 56. In "Theater Historian in the Mirror," Bank uses the term similarly.

102 Foucault, "Of Other Spaces," 24. As geographers Crampton and Elden note, while Foucault "did not write primary texts that foreground spatial concerns . . . spatiality was more than just a passing interest." Crampton and Elden, *Space, Knowledge, and Power*, 8.

103 Foucault, "Of Other Spaces," 24. In *Third Space*, Edward Soja evokes this in his elaboration of a thirdspace constituted through a "critique of the bicameralized spatial imagination" that segments institutional and material spaces from mental and social spaces by thinking relationally and experientially, 15. There is, however, more of a sense of utopia to Soja's definition than to my evocation here.

104 Rich, *Blood, Bread, and Poetry*.

105 Kaplan, "Politics of Location," 139. See also the extended debates on the politics of location with essays by Coco Fusco, bell hooks, Laleen Jayamanne, Stuart Hall, and others, published in "Third Scenario: Theory and the Politics of Location," in *Framework: The Journal of Cinema and Media*, no. 36 (1989): 4–81.

106 Kaplan, "Politics of Location," 140.

107 Widely adopted in the women's marches in the wake of Trump's election to the presidency, the term was first used in Crenshaw, "Demarginalizing the Intersection."

108 See, for instance, the discussion in Arondekar and Patel, "Area Impossible."

109 Bazin, "Aesthetic of Reality," 35.

BIBLIOGRAPHY

ARCHIVES

British Film Institute, London, UK
British Library, London, UK
Colonial Film: Moving Images of the British Empire, www.colonialfilm.org.uk/home
Getty Research Institute Library, Los Angeles, US
Imperial War Museum Film and Video Archive, London, UK
Maharashtra State Archives, Mumbai, India
Margaret Herrick Library, Los Angeles, US
National Archive of India, New Delhi, India
National Archives of UK, Kew, UK
National Film Archive, Pune, India
Nehru Memorial Museum and Library, New Delhi, India
UCLA Archives, Los Angeles, US

PUBLISHED BOOKS AND ARTICLES

Acland, Charles R., and Haidee Wasson, eds. *Useful Cinema*. Durham, NC: Duke University Press, 2011.

Adarsh, B. K. *Film Industry of India*. Bombay: Perfecta Printing Works, 1963.

Adorno, Theodor W. "Transparencies on Film." In *The Culture Industry: Selected Essays on Mass Culture*, edited by J. M. Bernstein, 178–87. New York: Routledge, 2001.

Agnew, John. "The Territorial Trap: The Geographical Assumptions of International Relations Theory." *Review of International Political Economy* 1, no. 1 (1994): 53–80.

Ahluwalia, H. P. S. *The Everest Within*. New Delhi: Hemkunt, 2001.

Ahmed, Aijaz. "Jameson's Rhetoric of Otherness and the 'National Allegory.'" *Social Text* 17 (fall 1987): 3–25.

Ahmed, Sara. *The Cultural Politics of Emotion*. New York: Routledge, 2004.

Aitchison, Cara, Nicole E. Macleod, and Stephen J. Shaw. *Leisure and Tourism Landscapes: Social and Cultural Geographies*. London: Routledge, 2001.

Alcoff, Linda. "The Problem of Speaking for Others." *Cultural Critique* 20 (1991): 5–32.

Alexander, M. Jacqui, and Chandra Talpade Mohanty. "Cartographies of Knowledge and Power: Transnational Feminism as Radical Practice." In *Critical Transnational Feminist Praxis*, edited by Amanda Lock Swarr and Richa Nagar, 23–45. Albany, NY: SUNY Press, 2010.

Allen, Robert. "Relocating American Film History: The Problem of the Empirical." *Cultural Studies* 2, no. 1 (2006): 48–88.

Almond, Ian. *History of Islam in German Thought: From Leibniz to Nietzsche.* New York: Routledge, 2010.

AlSayyad, Nezar. *Cinematic Urbanism: A History of the Modern from Reel to Real.* New York: Routledge, 2006.

Amad, Paula. *Counter-Archive: Film, the Everyday, and Albert Kahn's Archive de la Planète.* New York: Columbia University Press, 2010.

Amad, Paula. "From God's-Eye to Camera-Eye: Aerial Photography's Post-humanist and Neo-humanist Visions of the World." *History of Photography* 36, no. 1 (2012): 66–86.

Amad, Paula. "Visual Reposte: Looking Back at the Return of the Gaze as Postcolonial Theory's Gift to Film Studies." *Cinema Journal* 22, no. 3 (spring 2013): 49–74.

Andrew, Dudley. *André Bazin.* Foreword by François Truffaut. New York: Columbia University Press, 1978.

Andrew, Dudley, with Hervé Joubert-Laurencin, ed. *Opening Bazin: Postwar Film Theory and Its Afterlife.* New York: Oxford University Press, 2011.

Anzaldúa, Gloria. *Borderlands/La Frontera: The New Mestiza.* San Francisco, CA: Spinsters/Aunt Lute, 1987.

Appadurai, Arjun. "Disjuncture and Difference in the Global Cultural Economy." *Theory, Culture & Society* 7 (1990): 295–310.

Appadurai, Arjun. *Fear of Small Numbers: An Essay on the Geography of Anger.* Durham, NC: Duke University Press, 2006.

Appadurai, Arjun. *Modernity at Large: Cultural Dimensions of Globalization.* Minneapolis: University of Minnesota Press, 1996.

Appadurai, Arjun. "Number in the Colonial Imagination." In *Orientalism and the Postcolonial Predicament: Perspectives on South Asia,* edited by Carol A. Breckenridge and Peter van der Veer, 314–38. Philadelphia: University of Pennsylvania Press, 1993.

Appadurai, Arjun, ed. *The Social Life of Things: Commodities in Cultural Perspective.* Cambridge: Cambridge University Press, 1998.

Aretxaga, Begoña. "Maddening States." *Annual Review of Anthropology* 32 (2003): 393–410.

A. R. H. "Photographs from the Mount Everest Flight." *Geographical Journal* 82, no. 1 (July 1933): 54–60.

Arnheim, Rudolph. *Film as Art.* Berkeley: University of California Press, 2006.

Arondekar, Anjali. *For the Record: On Sexuality and the Colonial Archive in India.* Durham, NC: Duke University Press, 2009.

Arondekar, Anjali, and Geeta Patel. "Area Impossible: Notes toward an Introduction." *GLQ: A Journal of Lesbian and Gay Studies* 22, no. 2 (2016): 151–71.

Athique, Adrian, and Douglas Hill. *The Multiplex in India: A Cultural Economy of Urban Leisure.* London: Routledge, 2009.

Audi, Robert. *Cambridge Dictionary of Philosophy.* Cambridge: Cambridge University Press, 1995.

Auge, Mark. *Non-Places: An Introduction to Supermodernity.* Translated by John Howe. London: Verso, 2009.

Bachelard, Gaston. *The Poetics of Space: The Classic Look at How We Experience Intimate Places.* Translated by Maria Jolas. Boston: Beacon Press, 1994.

Bakhtin, Mikhail. *The Dialogic Imagination: Four Essays.* Edited by Michael Holquist. Austin: University of Texas Press, 1982.

Banerjee, Sukanya. "Political Economy, the Gothic, and the Question of Imperial Citizenship." *Victorian Studies* 47, no. 2 (2005): 260–71.

Bank, Rosemarie. "The Theater Historian in the Mirror: Transformation in the Space of Representation." *Journal of Dramatic Theory and Criticism* (spring 1989): 219–28.

Bao, Weihong. *Fiery Cinema: The Emergence of an Affective Medium in China, 1915–1945.* Minneapolis: University of Minnesota Press, 2015.

Barber, Stephen. *Projected Cities: Cinema and Urban Space.* London: Reaktion Books, 2004.

Barsacq, Léon. *Caligari's Cabinet and Other Grand Illusions: A History of Film Design.* Boston: New York Graphic Society, 1976.

Barthes, Roland. *Camera Lucida: Reflection on Photography.* Translated by Richard Howard. New York: Noonday Press, 1981.

Baskaran S. Theodore. *The Message Bearers: The Nationalist Politics and the Entertainment Media in South India, 1880–1945.* Madras: Cre-A, 1981.

Basu, Anustup. *Bollywood in the Age of New Media: The Geotelevisual Aesthetic.* Edinburgh, UK: Edinburgh University Press, 2010.

Battaglia, Giulia. *Documentary Film in India: An Anthropological History.* New York: Routledge, 2018.

Battersby, Christine. *The Sublime, Terror, and Human Difference.* New York: Routledge, 2007.

Bazin, André. "An Aesthetic of Reality: Cinematic Realism and the Italian School of the Liberation." In *What Is Cinema?*, Vol. 2. Selected and translated by Hugh Gray, 16–40. Berkeley: University of California Press, 1971.

Bazin, André. "De Sica; Metteur en Scène." In *What Is Cinema?*, Vol. 1. Selected and translated by Hugh Gray, 61–68. Berkeley: University of California Press, 1971.

Bazin, André. "The Evolution of the Language of Cinema." In *What Is Cinema?*, Vol. 1. Selected and translated by Hugh Gray, 23–40. Berkeley: University of California Press, 1967.

Bazin, André. *Jean Renoir.* Edited by François Truffaut. Translated by W. M. Halsey II and William H. Simon. New York: Da Capo Press, 1992.

Bazin, André. "The Myth of Total Cinema." In *What Is Cinema?*, Vol. 1. Selected and translated by Hugh Gray, 17–22. Berkeley: University of California Press, 1967.

Bazin, André. "The Ontology of the Photographic Image." In *What Is Cinema?*, Vol. 1. Selected and translated by Hugh Gray, 9–16. Berkeley: University of California Press, 1967.

Bazin, André. "A Pure Masterpiece: The River." In *Jean Renoir.* Edited by François Truffaut. Translated by W. M. Halsey II and William H. Simon, 104–19. New York: Da Capo Press, 1992.

Bazin, André. "The Virtues and Limitations of Montage." In *What Is Cinema?*, Vol. 1. Selected and translated by Hugh Gray, 41–52. Berkeley: University of California Press, 1967.

Bazin, André. *What Is Cinema?* Vol. 1. Selected and translated by Hugh Gray. Berkeley: University of California Press, 1967.

Bazin, André. *What Is Cinema?* Vol. 2. Selected and translated by Hugh Gray. Berkeley: University of California Press, 1971.

Bean, Jennifer M., Anupama Kapse, and Laura Horak, eds. *Space and the Politics of Silent Cinema*. Bloomington: Indiana University Press, 2014.

Beeton, Sue. *Film-Induced Tourism*. Clevedon, UK: Channel View Publications, 2005.

Behdad, Ali. *Belated Travelers: Orientalism in the Age of Colonial Dissolution*. Durham, NC: Duke University Press, 1999.

Behind the Frames: A Rendezvous with Evolution of Cinema. Mumbai: Ministry of Information and Broadcasting, Government of India, 2008.

Benjamin, Walter. *The Arcades Project*. Translated by Howard Eiland and Kevin McLaughlin. Cambridge, MA: Harvard University Press, 1990.

Benjamin, Walter. "Brief History of Photography." In *One-Way Street and Other Writings*, 240–57. London: Verso Books, 1997.

Benjamin, Walter. *The Origin of German Tragic Drama*. London: Verso, 2003.

Benjamin, Walter. "Theses on the Philosophy of History." In *Illuminations*, edited by Hannah Arendt, translated by Harry Zohn, 253–64. New York: Schocken Books, 1968.

Benjamin, Walter. *The Work of Art in the Age of Its Technical Reproducibility and Other Writings on Media*. Edited by Michael W. Jennings et al. Translated by Edmund Jephcott et al. Cambridge, MA: Harvard University Press, 2008.

Benjamin, Walter. "The Work of Art in the Age of Mechanical Reproduction." *In Illuminations: Essays and Reflections*, 217–53. New York: Harcourt Brace Jovanovich, 1968.

Benjamin, Walter. *The Writer of Modern Life: Essays on Charles Baudelaire*. Cambridge, MA: Belknap Press of Harvard University Press.

Bergan, Ronald. *Eyewitness Companions: Film*. New York: DK Publishing, 2006.

Bergan, Ronald. *Jean Renoir: Projections of Paradise*. Woodstock, NY: Overlook Press, 1994.

Bergstrom, Janet. "Jean Renoir and the Allied War Effort: Saluting France in Two Languages." *Historical Journal of Film Radio and Television* 26 (March 2006): 45–56.

Bergstrom, Janet. "Jean Renoir's Return to France." *Poetics Today* 17, no. 3 (fall 1996): 453–87.

Bergstrom, Janet. "Oneiric Cinema: The Woman on the Beach." *Film History* 11 (1999): 114–25.

Berman, Marshall. *All That Is Solid Melts into Air: The Experience of Modernity*. London: Verso, 2010.

Bhabha, Homi. *The Location of Culture*. London: Routledge, 2004.

Bhaskar, Ira, and Richard Allen. *Islamicate Cultures of Bombay Cinema*. New Delhi: Tulika Books, 2009.

Bhatia, Nandi. "Whither the Colonial Question." In *Cinema, Colonialism, Postcolonialism*, ed. Dina Sherzer, 51–64. Austin: University of Texas Press, 1996.

Bhaumik, Kaushik. "Consuming 'Bollywood' in the Global Age: The Strange Case of an 'Unfine' World Cinema." In *Remapping World Cinema: Identity, Culture, and Politics in Film*, edited by Stephanie Dennison and Song H. Lim, 188–99. London: Wallflower Press, 2006.

Bhaumik, Kaushik. "The Emergence of the Bombay Film Industry: 1913–1936." PhD diss., Oxford University, 2001.

Biswas, Moinak. *Apu and After: Revisiting Ray's Cinema*. Calcutta: Seagull Books, 2006.

Biswas, Moinak. "Her Mother's Son: Kinship and History in Ritwik Ghatak." *Rouge*. Last modified 2004. Accessed February 2015. http://www.rouge.com.au/3/ghatak.html.

Biswas, Moinak. "Mourning and Blood Ties: Macbeth in Mumbai." *Journal of the Moving Image*, no. 5 (December 2006): 78–85.

Blackburn, Simon. *The Oxford Dictionary of Philosophy*. Oxford: Oxford University Press, 1996.

Blaney, Aileen, and Chinar Shah. "The Aesthetics of Contemporary Indian Photography in an 'Incredible India.'" *Photography and Culture* 20, no. 1 (January 2018): 1–16.

Bloom, Peter J. *French Colonial Documentary: Mythologies of Humanitarianism*. Minneapolis: University of Minnesota Press, 2008.

Bois, Yve-Alain. "Introduction: Sergei Eisenstein: Montage and Architecture." Translated by Michael Glenny. *Assemblage*, no. 10 (December 1989): 110–31.

Bordwell, David, Janet Staiger, and Kristen Thompson. *The Classical Hollywood Cinema: Film Style and Mode of Production to 1960*. New York: Columbia University Press, 1985.

Borges, Jorge Luis. *Collected Fictions*. Translated by Andrew Hurley. New York: Viking, [1949] 1998.

Borges, Jorge Luis. "Funes, His Memory." In *Collected Fictions*, translated by Andrew Hurley, 131–39. New York: Viking, 1998.

Bose, Nandana. "Between the Godfather and the Mafia: Situating Right-Wing Interventions in the Bombay Film Industry (1992–2002)." *Studies in South Asian Film and Media* 1, no. 1 (2009): 23–43.

Bose, Nandana. "Situating Right-Wing Interventions in the Bombay Film Industry (1992–2002)." *Studies in South Asia Film and Media* 1, no. 1 (2009): 23–43.

Bosley, Rachael K. "Cultural Immersion." *American Cinematographer* 88, no. 9 (September 2007): 44–53.

Bourdieu, Pierre. *Distinction: A Social Critique of the Judgement of Taste*. Translated by Richard Nice. London: Routledge, 2015.

Bourne, Samuel. "Narrative of a Photographic Trip to Kashmir (Cashmere) and Adjacent Districts." *British Journal of Photography* 13 (October 5, 1866): 24–61.

Bourne, Samuel. *Photographic Journeys in the Himalayas 1863–1866*. Bath, UK: Pagoda Tree Press, 2009.

Bourne, Samuel. "Ten Weeks with the Camera in the Himalayas." In *Photographic Journeys in the Himalayas*, edited by Hugh Ashley Rayner. Bath, UK: Pagoda Tree Press, 2004.

Bowles, Ryan, and Rahul Mukherjee. "Documentary and Space: Introduction." *Media Fields Journal*, no. 3 (2011): 1–13.

Boym, Svetlana. *The Future of Nostalgia*. New York: Basic, 2001.

Boym, Svetlana. "Nostalgia and Its Discontents." *Hedgehog Review* (summer 2007): 9.

Braudy, Leo. *Jean Renoir: The World of His Films*. Garden City, NY: Doubleday, 1972.

Brenner, Neil, and Stuart Elden. "Henry Lefebvre on State, Space, Territory." *International Political Sociology* 3, no. 4 (2009): 353–77.

Brenner, Neil, and Stuart Elden. *Henri Lefebvre: State, Space, World: Selected Essays*. Translated by Gerald Moore, Neil Brenner, and Stuart Elden. Minneapolis: University of Minnesota Press, 2009.

British Instructional Films. *Catalogue of Films for Non-Theatrical Exhibition* (1928).

Brosius, Christiane. *India's Middle Class: New Forms of Urban Leisure, Consumption, and Prosperity*. New Delhi: Routledge, 2010.

Brown, Bill. *Things*. Chicago: University of Chicago Press, 2004.

Brown, Bill. "Thing Theory." *Critical Inquiry* 28, no. 1 (August 2001): 1–22.

Brown, Wendy. *States of Injury*. Princeton, NJ: Princeton University Press, 1995.

Bruno, Giuliana. *Atlas of Emotion: Journeys in Art, Architecture, and Film*. New York: Verso, 2002.

Bruno, Giuliana. *Streetwalking on a Ruined Map: Cultural Theory and the City Films of Elvira Notari*. Princeton, NJ: Princeton University Press, 1993.

Brunsdon, Charlotte. *London in Cinema: The Cinematic City since 1945*. London: British Film Institute, 2007.

Bryden, Inga. "There Is No Outer without Inner Space: Constructing the *Haveli* as Home." *Cultural Geographies* 11 (2004): 26–41.

Buchan, John. Foreword to *First over Everest: The Houston-Mount Everest Expedition*, edited by P. F. M. Fellowes et al. New York: Robert M. McBride, 1934.

Buck-Morss, Susan. *The Dialectics of Seeing: Walter Benjamin and the Arcades Project*. Cambridge, MA: MIT Press, 1991.

Burch, Noël, and Helen R. Lane. *Theory of Film Practice*. Princeton, NJ: Princeton University Press, 1981.

Burchell, Graham, Colin Gordon, and Peter Miller, eds. *The Foucault Effect: Studies in Governmentality with Two Lectures by and an Interview with Michel Foucault*. Chicago: University of Chicago Press, 1991.

Burke, Edmund. *A Philosophical Enquiry into the Origins of our Ideas of the Sublime and the Beautiful*. 1757. Edited by Adam Phillips. Oxford: Oxford University Press, 1990.

Burman, J. J. Roy. "Hindu-Muslim Syncretism in India." *Economic and Political Weekly* 31, no. 20 (May 18, 1996): 1211–15.

Burnier, Radha. "The Urgency for a New Perspective." *Quest* 91, no. 4 (July–August 2003): 146–48.

Butler, Judith. *Frames of War: When Is Life Grievable?* London: Verso, 2009.

Butler, Judith. *The Psychic Life of Power: Theories in Subjection*. Stanford, CA: Stanford University Press, 1997.

Caldwell, John Thornton. *Production Culture: Industrial Reflexivity and Critical Practice in Film and Television*. Durham, NC: Duke University Press, 2008.

Caminati, Luca. *Roberto Rossellini Documentarista / Una Cultura della Realta*. Roma: CSC Carocci Editore, 2012.

Carey, Daniel, and Lynn Festa, eds. *The Postcolonial Enlightenment: Eighteenth-Century Colonialism and Postcolonial Theory*. Oxford: Oxford University Press, 2009.

Casey, Edward S. "The Edge(s) of Landscape: A Study in Liminology." In *The Place of Landscape: Concepts, Contexts, Studies*, edited by Jeff Malpas, 91–110. Cambridge, MA: MIT Press, 2011.

Casey, Edward S. *The Fate of Place: A Philosophical History*. Berkeley: University of California Press, 1998.

Casey, Edward S. *Getting Back into Place: Toward a Renewed Understanding of the Place-World*. Bloomington: Indiana University Press, 1993.

Castells, Manuel. *The Urban Question: A Marxist Approach*. Cambridge, MA: MIT Press, 1979.

Castree, Noel, and Derek Gregory, eds. *David Harvey: A Critical Reader*. Oxford: Blackwell, 2006.

Chabon, Michael. Introduction to *The Wes Anderson Collection*, edited by Matt Zoller Seitz, 21–23. New York: Abrams Books, 2013.

Chakrabarty, Dipesh. *Habitations of Modernity: Essays in the Wake of Subaltern Studies*. Chicago: University of Chicago Press, 2002.

Chakrabarty, Dipesh. "Of Garbage, Modernity and the Citizen's Gaze." *Economic and Political Weekly* 27, no. 10/11 (March 7–14, 1992): 541–47.

Chakrabarty, Dipesh. *Postcolonial Thought and Historical Difference*. Princeton, NJ: Princeton University Press, 2007.

Chakrabarty, Dipesh. *Provincializing Europe*. Princeton, NJ: Princeton University Press, 2000.

Chakrabarty, Dipesh. "The Time of History and the Times of Gods." In *The Politics of Culture in the Shadow of Capital*, edited by Lisa Lowe and David Lloyd, 35–61. Durham, NC: Duke University Press, 1997.

Chakravarty, Gautam. *The Indian Mutiny and the British Imagination*. Cambridge: Cambridge University Press, 2005.

Chanana, Opender. *The Missing 3 in Bollywood: Safety, Security, Shelter*. Switzerland: UNI Global Union, 2011.

Charney, Leo, and Vanessa R. Schwartz. *Cinema and the Invention of Modern Life*. Berkeley: University of California Press, 1995.

Chatterjee, Partha. *Nationalist Thought and the Colonial World: A Derivative Discourse?* Minneapolis: University of Minnesota Press, 1993.

Chatterjee, Partha. *The Nation and Its Fragments: Colonial and Postcolonial Histories*. Princeton, NJ: Princeton University Press, 1994.

Chatterjee, Partha. "The Sacred Circulation of National Images." In *Traces of India: Photography, Architecture, and the Politics of Representation, 1850–1900*, edited by Maria Antonella Pelizzari, 276–92. New Haven, CT: Yale University Press, 2003.

Chatterjee, Partha. *Texts of Power: Emerging Disciplines in Colonial Bengal*. Minneapolis: University of Minnesota Press, 1995.

Chaudhary, Zahid. "Phantasmagoric Aesthetics: Colonial Violence and the Management of Perception." *Cultural Critique*, no. 59 (winter 2005): 63–119.

Chaudhuri, Amit. *Clearing a Space: Reflections on India, Literature, and Culture*. Oxford: Peter Lang, 2008.

Chaudhuri, Amit. "In the Waiting Room of History: A Review of Dipesh Chakrabarty's *Provincializing Europe*." *London Review of Books*, December 16, 2009, 4–7.

Chopra, Anupama. *Dilwale Dulhania le Jayenge (The Brave-Hearted Will Take the Bride)*. London: BFI Macmillan, 2002.

Chopra, Anupama. *First Day First Show: Writings from the Bollywood Trenches*. New Delhi: Penguin Books, 2011.

Chopra, Anupama. *The Front Row: Conversations on Cinema*. New Delhi: HarperCollins, 2015.

Chopra, Anupama. *King of Bollywood: Shah Rukh Khan and the Seductive World of Indian Cinema*. New York: Warner Books, 2007.

Chung, Hye Jean. "Media Heterotopia and Transnational Filmmaking: Mapping Real and Virtual Worlds." *Cinema Journal* 51, no. 44 (2012): 87–109.

Chung, Hye Jean. *Media Heterotopias: Digital Effects and Material Labor in Global Film Production*. Durham, NC: Duke University Press, 2018.

Colomina, Beatriz, ed. *Sexuality and Space*. New York: Princeton Architectural Press, 1992.

Conley, Tom. *Cartographic Cinema*. Minneapolis: University of Minnesota Press, 2006.

Cons, G. J., ed. *Handbook for Geographers*. London: Methuen, 1955.

Cook, Pam. *Screening the Past: Memory and Nostalgia in Cinema*. New York: Routledge, 2005.

Coorlawala, Uttara Asha. "Ruth St. Denis and India's Dance Renaissance." *Dance Chronicle* 15, no. 2 (1992): 123–52.

Cortade, Ludovic. "Cinema across Fault Lines: Bazin and the French School of Geography." In *Opening Bazin: Postwar Film Theory and Its Afterlife*, edited by Dudley Andrew and Hervé Joubert-Laurencin, 13–31. Oxford: Oxford University Press, 2011.

Cosgrove, Denis. *Apollo's Eye: A Cartographic Genealogy of the Earth in the Western Imagination*. Baltimore, MD: Johns Hopkins University Press, 2001.

Couldry, Nick, and Anna McCarthy, eds. *MediaSpace: Place, Scale, and Culture in a Media Age*. New York: Routledge, 2004.

Crampton, Jeremy, and Stuart Elden, eds. *Space, Knowledge, and Power: Foucault and Geography*. Surrey, UK: Ashgate, 2007.

Crary, Jonathan. *Techniques of the Observer: On Vision and Modernity in the 19th Century*. Cambridge, MA: MIT Press, 1992.

Crenshaw, Kimberlé. "Demarginalizing the Intersection of Race and Sex: A Black Feminist Critique of Antidiscrimination Doctrine, Feminist Theory and Antiracist Politics." *University of Chicago Legal Forum*, no. 1, article 8 (1989): 139–67.

Crone, G. R. "The Future of the International Million Map of the World." *Geographical Journal* 128, no. 1 (1962): 36–38.

Crouch, David, Rhona Jackson, and Felix Thompson. *The Media and the Tourist Imagination: Convergent Cultures*. London: Routledge, 2005.

Crowther, Paul. *The Kantian Sublime: From Morality to Art*. Oxford: Clarendon Press, 1991.

Dalrymple, William. *The Last Mughal: The Fall of a Dynasty: Delhi, 1857*. New York: Vintage Books, 2008.

Dass, Manishita. *Outside the Lettered City: Cinema, Modernity, and the Public Sphere in Late Colonial India*. New York: Oxford University Press, 2016.

Davies, Ann. *Spanish Spaces: Landscape, Space, and Place in Contemporary Spanish Culture*. Liverpool: Liverpool University Press, 2012.

Davis, Mike. *City of Quartz: Excavating the Future in Los Angeles*. London: Verso, 2006.

Dear, Michael. "Postmodern Bloodlines." In *Space and Social Theory: Geographical Interpretations of Postmodernity*, edited by G. Benko and U. Strohmayer, 49–71. Cambridge, MA: Blackwell, 1996.

de Certeau, Michel. *The Practice of Everyday Life*. Translated by Steven Rendall. Berkeley: University of California Press, 1984.

Debord, Guy. *The Society of the Spectacle*. Cambridge, MA: MIT Press, 1995.

Dehaene, Michiel, and Lieven De Cauter. *Heterotopia and the City: Public Space in a Postcivil Society*. New York: Routledge, 2008.

Deichmann, Catherine Lynch. *Rogues and Runners: Bermuda and the American Civil War*. Bermuda: Bermuda National Trust, 2003.

DeLanda, Manuel. *Intensive Science and Virtual Philosophy*. London: A&C Black, 2013.

Deleuze, Gilles. *Cinema 1: The Movement-Image*. Translated by Hugh Tomlinson and Barbara Habberjam. Minneapolis: University of Minnesota Press, 1986.

Deleuze, Gilles. *Cinema 2: The Time Image*. Translated by Hugh Tomlinson and Robert Galeta. Minneapolis: University of Minnesota Press, 1989.

Dennison, Stephanie, and Song H. Lim, eds. *Remapping World Cinema: Identity, Culture, and Politics in Film*. London: Wallflower Press, 2006.

Deprez, Camille. "The Films Division of India, 1948–1964: The Early Days and the Influence of the British Documentary Film Tradition." *Film History: An International Journal* 25, no. 3 (2013): 149–73.

Deren, Maya. "Cinematography: The Creative Use of Reality." In *Critical Visions in Film Theory: Classic and Contemporary Readings,* edited by Tim Corrigan, Patricia White and Meta Mazaj, 144–55. Boston: Bedford/St. Martin's Press, 2011.

Derrida, Jacques. *Aporias: Dying—Awaiting (One Another at) the Limits of Truth*. Translated by Thomas Dutoit. Stanford, CA: Stanford University Press, 1993.

Derrida, Jacques. "Hostipitality." In *Acts of Religion*, edited with an introduction by Gil Anidjar, 356–420. New York: Routledge, 2002.

Derrida, Jacques. *Of Grammatology*. Translated by Gayatri Chakravorty Spivak. 1974. Baltimore, MD: Johns Hopkins University Press, 1976. First published in 1974.

Derrida, Jacques. *Of Hospitality: Anne Dufourmantelle Invites Jacques Derrida to Respond*. Stanford, CA: Stanford University Press, 2000.

Derrida, Jacques. *Specters of Marx: The State of the Debt, the Work of Mourning, and the New International*. New York: Routledge, 2006.

Di Bello, Patrizia. *Women's Albums and Photography in Victorian England: Ladies, Mothers, and Flirts*. Aldershot, UK: Ashgate, 2007.

Dimendberg, Edward. *Film Noir and the Spaces of Modernity*. Cambridge, MA: Harvard University Press, 2004.

Dimendberg, Edward. "The Limits to Emplacement: A Reply to Philip Ethington." *Rethinking History* 11, no. 4 (December 2007): 513–16.

Doane, Mary Ann. "Information, Crisis, Catastrophe." In *Logics of Television: Essays in Cultural Criticism*, edited by Patricia Mellencamp, 222–39. Bloomington: Indiana University Press, 1990.

Dorrian, Mark, and Frédéric Pousin, eds. *Seeing from Above: The Aerial View in Visual Culture*. London: I. B. Tauris, 2013.

Dudrah, Rajinder. *Bollywood: Sociology Goes to the Movies*. New Delhi: SAGE, 2006.

Dudrah, Rajinder. *Bollywood Travels: Culture, Diaspora, and Border Crossings in Popular Hindi Cinema*. London: Routledge, 2012.

Dudrah, Rajinder, Elke Mader, and Bernhard Fuchs, eds. *SRK and Global Bollywood*. Oxford: Oxford University Press, 2015.

Duncan, Nancy, ed. *Bodyspace: Destabilizing Geographies of Gender and Sexuality*. London: Routledge, 1996.

Durgnat, Raymond. *Jean Renoir*. Berkeley: University of California Press, 1976.

Dussel, Enrique. "World-System and 'Trans'-Modernity." *Nepantla: Views from the South* 3, no. 2 (2002): 221–44.

Dutta, Sangeeta. *Shyam Benegal*. London: BFI Publishing, 2002.

Dwyer, Rachel. *Bollywood's India: Hindi Cinema as a Guide to Contemporary India*. London: Reaktion Books, 2016.

Dwyer, Rachel. "Bombay Gothic: On the 60th Anniversary of Kamal Amrohi's Mahal." In *Beyond the Boundaries of Bollywood*, edited by Rachel Dwyer and Jerry Pinto, 130–55. New Delhi: Oxford University Press, 2011.

Dwyer, Rachel. "I Am Crazy about the Lord: The Muslim Devotional Genre in Hindi Film." *Third Text* 24, no. 1 (2010): 123–34.

Dwyer, Rachel. "Mumbai Middlebrow: Ways of Thinking about the Middle Ground in Hindi Cinema." In *Middlebrow Cinema*, edited by Sally Faulkner, 51–68. London: Routledge, 2016.

Dwyer, Rachel. *Yash Chopra*. London: BFI Publishing, 2002.

Dwyer, Rachel. "Zara Hatke!: The New Middle Classes and the Segmentation of Hindi Cinema." In *A Way of Life: Being Middle-Class in Contemporary India*, edited by Henrike Donner, 184–208. New York: Routledge, 2011.

Dwyer, Rachel, and Divia Patel. *Cinema India: The Visual Culture of Hindi Film*. New Brunswick, NJ: Rutgers University Press, 2002.

Dwyer, Rachel, and Jerry Pinto. *Beyond the Boundaries of Bollywood: The Many Forms of Hindi Cinema*. New Delhi: Oxford University Press, 2011.

Easen, Sarah. "Mary Field." In *The Concise Routledge Encyclopedia of the Documentary Film*, edited by Ian Aitken, 248. London: Routledge, 2013.

Edwards, Paul, ed. *The Encyclopedia of Philosophy*. Vols. 1 and 2. New York: Macmillan/Free Press, 1967.

Eisenstein, Sergei. *Film Form: Essays in Film Theory*. Edited and translated by Jay Leyda. San Diego, CA: HBJ, 1977.

The "Elge" List: Gaumont and Company, 1902. BFI: World Microfilms, 1982.

Eliot, T. S. "Gerontion." In *Collected Poems, 1909–1935*, 43–46. New York: Harcourt, Brace, 1936.

Elison, William. *The Neighborhood of Gods: The Sacred and the Visible at the Margins of Mumbai*. Chicago: University of Chicago Press, 2018.

Elkins, James, ed. *Landscape Theory: The Art Seminar*. London: Routledge, 2008.

Elliott, B., and A. Purdy. "A Walk through Heterotopia: Peter Greenaway's Landscapes by Numbers." In *Landscape and Film*, edited by Martin Lefebvre, 267–90. London: Routledge, 2006.

Ellis, Jack C. *John Grierson: Life, Contributions, Influence*. Carbondale: Southern Illinois University Press, 2000.

Ellwood, Robert S. "Theosophy." In *America's Alternative Religions*, edited by Timothy Miller, 315–24. Albany: State University of New York Press.

Elmer, Greg, and Mike Gasher, eds. *Contracting Out Hollywood: Runaway Productions and Foreign Location Shooting*. Lanham, MD: Rowman and Littlefield, 2005.

Elsaesser, Thomas. "A Bazinian Half-Century." In *Opening Bazin: Postwar Film Theory and Its Afterlife*, edited by Dudley Andrew, 3–12. New York: Oxford University Press, 2011.

Elsaesser, Thomas. "The New Film History as Media Archeology." In *Cinémas: Journal of Film Studies* 14, no. 2–4 (2004): 75–117.

Elsaesser, Thomas. "Tales of Sound and Fury: Observations on the Family Melodrama." In *Imitations of Life: A Reader on Film and Television Melodrama*, edited by Marcia Landy, 68–91. Detroit: Wayne State University Press, 1991.

Ethington, Philip. "Placing the Past: 'Groundwork' for a Spatial Theory of History." *Rethinking History* 11, no. 4 (December 2007): 465–93.

Ezra, Elizabeth, and Terry Rowden. *Transnational Cinema: The Film Reader*. London: Routledge, 2006.

Faulkner, Christopher. *The Social Cinema of Jean Renoir*. Princeton, NJ: Princeton University Press, 1986.

Fay, Jennifer. *Inhospitable World: Cinema in the Time of the Anthropocene*. New York: Oxford University Press, 2018.

Fellowes, P. F. M., et al. *First over Everest: The Houston-Mount Everest Expedition*. New York: Robert M. McBride, 1934.

Fernandes, Leela. *India's New Middle Class: Democratic Politics in an Era of Economic Reform*. Minneapolis: University of Minnesota Press, 2006.

Fernandes, Leela. "The Politics of Forgetting: Class Politics, State Power and the Restructuring of Urban Space in India." *Urban Studies* 41, no. 12 (November 2004): 2415–30.

Fernandes, Leela. "Restructuring the New Middle Class in Liberalizing India." *Comparative Studies of South Asia, Africa and the Middle East* 20, no. 1 (2000): 88–104.

Field, Mary, and Percy Smith. *Secrets of Nature*. London: Faber and Faber, 1934.

Films Division Manual: Finance, Accounts, and Administration. New Delhi: Ministry of Information and Broadcasting, Government of India, March 1960 (Chaitra 1882 [Hindu Calendar]).

Fletcher, Catherine. "Science Teaching Films." *Sight and Sound* 6, no. 23 (autumn 1937): 156–61.

Forster, E. M. *Howards End*. New York: Alfred A. Knopf, 1910.

Forster, E. M. *A Passage to India*. Edited by Oliver Stallybrass. Harmondsworth, UK: Penguin, 1983.

Forster, E. M. *A Passage to India*. Revised ed. Harmondsworth, UK: Penguin Books, 1984.

Fortmueller, Kate. "Encounters at the Margins of Hollywood: Casting and Location Shooting for Bhowani Junction." *Film History* 28, no. 4 (winter 2016): 100–124.

Fortmueller, Kate. "Part Time Work, Full Time Dreams: Extras, Actors and Hollywood's On-Screen Labor." PhD diss., University of Southern California, 2014.

Foucault, Michel. *The Archaeology of Knowledge: And the Discourse on Language*. Translated by A. M. Sheridan Smith. New York: Pantheon Books, 1972.

Foucault, Michel. *Discipline and Punish: The Birth of the Prison*. New York: Vintage Books, 1995.

Foucault, Michel. "The Eye of Power." In *Power/Knowledge: Selected Interviews and Other Writings, 1972–1977*. Edited by Colin Gordon, 146–65. New York: Pantheon, 1980.

Foucault, Michel. "Governmentality." In *The Foucault Effect: Studies in Governmentality with Two Lectures by and an Interview with Michel Foucault*, edited by Graham Burchell, Colin Gordon, and Peter Miller, 87–104. Chicago: University of Chicago Press, 1991.

Foucault, Michel. "Of Other Spaces." Translated by Jay Miskowiec. *Diacritics* 16, no. 1 (spring 1986): 22–27.

Foucault, Michel. *Power/Knowledge: Selected Interviews and Other Writings, 1972–1977*. Edited by Colin Gordon. New York: Pantheon, 1980.

Fowler, Catherine, and Gillian Helfield, eds. *Representing the Rural: Space, Place, and Identity in Films about the Land*. Detroit: Wayne State University Press, 2006.

Franklin, Adrian. "The Tourist Syndrome: An Interview with Zygmunt Bauman." *Tourist Studies* 3, no. 2 (2003): 205–17.

Fraser, Nancy. *Scales of Justice: Reimagining Political Space in a Globalized World*. New York: Columbia University Press, 2010.

Friedberg, Anne. "The Mobilized and Virtual Gaze of Modernity: Flâneur/Flâneuse." In *Window Shopping: Cinema and the Postmodern*, 15–32. Berkeley: University of California Press, 1993.

Friedberg, Anne. *The Virtual Window: From Alberti to Microsoft*. Cambridge, MA: MIT Press, 2006.

Friedrichsmeyer, Sara, Sara Lennox, and Susanne Zantop. *The Imperialist Imagination: German Colonialism and Its Legacy*. Ann Arbor: University of Michigan Press, 1998.

Fusco, Coco. "The Other History of Intercultural Performance." *TDR: Journal of Performance Studies* 38, no. 1 (spring 1994): 143–67.

Gaines, Jane M. "What Happened to the Philosophy of Film History?" *Film History* 25, nos. 1–2 (2013): 70–80.

Gaines, Jane. *Pink Slipped: What Happened to Women in the Silent Film Industries?* Urbana: University of Illinois Press, 2018.

Galt, Rosalind. *Pretty: Film Theory, Aesthetics, and the History of the Troublesome Image*. New York: Columbia University Press, 2011.

Galt, Rosalind, and Karl Schoonover. *Global Art Cinema: New Theories and Histories*. Oxford: Oxford University Press, 2010.

Gandhi, Ramchandra. *Sita's Kitchen: A Testimony of Faith and Inquiry*. New Delhi: Penguin Books, 1992.

Ganti, Tejaswini. *Bollywood: A Guidebook to Popular Hindi Cinema*. New York: Routledge, 2004.

Ganti, Tejaswini. *Producing Bollywood: Inside the Contemporary Hindi Film Industry*. Durham, NC: Duke University Press, 2012.

Garga, B. D. *From Raj to Swaraj: The Non-Fiction Film in India*. New Delhi: Viking, 2007.

Gaur, Madan. *Other Side of the Coin: An Intimate Study of Indian Film Industry*. Delhi: Universal Book Service, 1973.

Gaycken, Oliver. *Devices of Curiosity: Early Cinema and Popular Science*. New York: Oxford University Press, 2015.

Gehlawat, Ajay. *Twenty-First Century Bollywood*. London: Routledge, 2015.

Ghatak, Ritwik. *Cinema and I*. Calcutta: Ritwik Memorial Trust, 1987.

Giedion, Sigfried. *Space, Time, and Architecture: The Growth of a New Tradition*. 5th ed. Cambridge, MA: Harvard University Press, 1967.

Gilbert, Elizabeth. *Eat, Pray, Love*. New York: Viking, 2006.

Gleich, Joshua. *Hollywood in San Francisco: Location Shooting and the Aesthetics of Urban Decline*. Austin: University of Texas Press, 2018.

Gleich, Joshua, and Lawrence Webb, eds. *Hollywood on Location: An Industry History*. New Brunswick, NJ: Rutgers University Press, 2019.

Godden, Rumer. *The River*. Boston: Little, Brown, 1946.

Goldsmith, Ben, and Tom O'Regan. "The Policy Environment and the Contemporary Film Studio." In *Contracting Out Hollywood: Runaway Productions and Foreign Location Shooting*, edited by Greg Elmer and Mike Gasher, 41–66. Lanham, MD: Rowman and Littlefield, 2005.

Golsan, Katherine. "Desperately Seeking Radha: Renoir's 'The River' and Its Reincarnations." Special issue, "Re-Framing Renoir," edited by K. Golsan, *South Central Review* 28, no. 3 (fall 2011): 103–25.

Goodstein, Elizabeth S. *Experience without Quality: Boredom and Modernity*. Stanford, CA: Stanford University Press, 2004.

Gopal, Sangita. *Conjugations: Marriage and Form in New Bollywood Cinema*. Chicago: University of Chicago Press, 2011.

Gopalan, Lalitha. *Cinema of Interruptions: Action Genres in Contemporary Indian Cinema*. London: British Film Institute, 2002.

Gordon, Sophie. "A City of Mourning: The Representation of Lucknow, India in Nineteenth Century Photography." *History of Photography* 30, no. 1 (spring 2006): 80–91.

Goswami, Manu. *Producing India: From Colonial Economy to National Space*. Chicago: University of Chicago Press, 2004.

Gould, Rebecca. "The Geography of Comparative Literature." *Journal of Literary Theory* 5, no. 2 (2011): 167–86.

The Government of India White Paper on Indian States. New Delhi: Manager Government of India Press, 1950.

Govil, Nitin. "Hollywood's Effects, Bollywood FX." In *Contracting Out Hollywood: Runaway Productions and Foreign Location Shooting*, edited by Mike Gasher and Greg Elmer, 92–114. Lanham, MD: Rowman and Littlefield, 2005.

Govil, Nitin. *Orienting Hollywood: A Century of Film Culture between Los Angeles and Bombay*. New York: New York University Press, 2015.

Govil, Nitin. "Producing 'India' as Location." In *The Routledge Companion to the Cultural Studies*, edited by Kate Oakley and Justin O'Connor, 232–45. New York: Routledge, 2015.

Graff, Violette. *Lucknow: Memories of a City*. Oxford: Oxford University Press, 1999.

Green, Penelope. "The Wildebeest in the Room." *New York Times*, March 6, 2014, D1, D6.

Gregory, Derek. *Geographical Imaginations*. Cambridge: Blackwell, 1994.

Grewal, Inderpal, and Caren Kaplan, eds. *Scattered Hegemonies: Postmodernity and Transnational Feminist Practices*. Minneapolis: University of Minnesota Press, 1994.

Grieveson, Lee. "The Cinema and the (Common)Wealth of Nations." In *Empire and Film*, edited by Lee Grieveson and Colin McCabe, 73–114. London: Palgrave Macmillan, 2011.

Grieveson, Lee. *Cinema and the Wealth of Nations: Media, Capital, and the Liberal World System*. Berkeley: University of California Press, 2017.

Grieveson, Lee. "Discipline and Publish: The Birth of Cinematology." *Cinema Journal* 49, no. 1 (fall 2009): 168–76.

Grieveson, Lee. "On Governmentality and Screens." *Screen* 50, no. 1 (2009): 180–87.

Grieveson, Lee, and Colin McCabe, eds. *Empire and Film*. London: Palgrave Macmillan, 2011.

Grieveson, Lee, and Colin McCabe, eds. *Film and the End of Empire*. London: BFI Palgrave Macmillan, 2011.

Grieveson, Lee, and Haidee Wasson. *Inventing Film Studies*. Durham, NC: Duke University Press, 2008.

Griffiths, Alison. *Wondrous Difference*. New York: Columbia University Press, 2001.

Grim, John A. *Indigenous Traditions and Ecology: The Interbeing of Cosmology and Community*. Cambridge, MA: Harvard University Press, 2001.

Grosfoguel, Ramón. "World-System Analysis and Postcolonial Studies: A Call for a Dialogie from the 'Coloniality of Power' Approach." In *The Postcolonial and the Global*, edited by Revathy Krishnaswamy and John Charles Hawley, 94–104. Minneapolis: University of Minnesota Press, 2008.

Grossberg, Lawrence. *Bringing It All Back Home: Essays on Cultural Studies*. Durham, NC: Duke University Press, 1997.

Grossberg, Lawrence. "The Space of Culture, the Power of Space." In *The Post-Colonial Question: Common Skies, Divided Horizons*, edited by Iain Chambers and Lidia Curti, 169–89. Oxon: Routledge, 1996.

Grosz, Elizabeth. *Space, Time and Perversion: Essays on the Politics of Bodies*. London: Routledge, 1995.

Guha, Ramachandra. *India after Gandhi: The History of the World's Largest Democracy*. New York: HarperCollins, 2007.

Guha-Thakurta, Tapati. *Monuments, Objects, Histories: Institutions of Art in Colonial and Postcolonial India*. Ranikhet, India: Permanent Black, 2004.

Gunning, Tom. "Animating the Nineteenth Century: Bringing Pictures to Life (or Life to Pictures?)." *Nineteenth Century Contexts* 36, no. 5 (2014): 459–72.

Gunning, Tom. *D. W. Griffith and the Origins of American Narrative Film: The Early Years at Biograph*. Urbana: University of Illinois Press, 1994.

Gunning, Tom. *The Films of Fritz Lang: Allegories of Vision and Modernity*. London: British Film Institute, 2000.

Gunning, Tom. "Hand and Eye: Excavating a New Technology of the Image in the Victorian Era." *Victorian Studies* 54, no. 3 (spring 2012): 495–516.

Gunning, Tom. "Modernity and Cinema: A Culture of Shocks and Flows." In *Cinema and Modernity*, edited by Murray Pomerance, 297–315. New Brunswick, NJ: Rutgers University Press, 2006.

Gunning, Tom. "Moving Away from the Index: Cinema and the Impression of Reality." *Differences* 18, no. 1 (2007): 29–52.

Gunning, Tom. "Tracing the Individual Body: Photography, Detectives and Early Cinema." In *Cinema and the Invention of Modern Life*, edited by Leo Charney and Vanessa R. Schwartz, 15–46. Berkeley: University of California Press, 1995.

Gunning, Tom. "The Whole World within Reach: Travel Images without Borders." In *Virtual Voyages: Cinema and Travel*, edited by Jeffrey Ruoff, 25–41. Durham, NC: Duke University Press, 2006.

Gunning, Tom. "The World in Its Own Image: The Myth of Total Cinema." In *Opening Bazin*, edited by Andrew Dudley, 119–26. Oxford: Oxford University Press, 2011.

Gupta, Akhil. "The Reincarnation of Souls and the Rebirth of Commodities: Representations of Time in 'East' and 'West.'" *Cultural Critique*, no. 22 (autumn 1992): 187–211.

Gupta, Akhil. "Reliving Childhood? The Temporality of Childhood and Narratives of Reincarnation." *Ethnos: Journal of Anthropology* 67, no. 1 (2002): 33–55.

Haddu, Miriam. *Contemporary Mexican Cinema, 1989–1999: History, Space, and Identity.* Lewiston, NY: Edwin Mellen Press, 2007.

Hake, Sabine. *German National Cinema*. London: Routledge, 2007.

Halberstam, Jack. *In a Queer Time and Place: Transgender Bodies, Subcultural Lives.* New York: New York University Press, 2005.

Hall, Stuart. "Introduction to the Verso Classics Edition." In *State, Power, Socialism*, edited by Nicos Poulantzas, vii–xvii. London: Verso, 1978.

Hansen, Miriam Bratu. "Benjamin, Cinema and Experience: 'The Blue Flower in the Land of Technology.'" Special issue, "Weimar Film Theory," *New German Critique*, no. 40 (winter 1987): 179–224.

Hansen, Miriam Bratu. Introduction to *Theory of Film: The Redemption of Physical Reality*, by Sigfried Kracauer, vii–xlvi. Princeton, NJ: Princeton University Press, 1997.

Hansen, Miriam Bratu. "The Mass Production of the Senses: Classical Cinema as Vernacular Modernism." *Modernity/Modernism* 6, no. 2 (April 1999): 59–77.

Haraway, Donna. "Situated Knowledges: The Science Question in Feminism and the Privilege of Partial Perspective." *Feminist Studies* 14, no. 3 (autumn 1998): 575–99.

Hariharan, Veena. "Private Modernities: The 'I' in Contemporary Indian Documentary and Visual Culture." PhD diss., University of Southern California, 2012.

Harootunian, Harry D. *History's Disquiet: Modernity, Cultural Practice, and the Question of Everyday Life.* New York: Columbia University Press, 2000.

Harvey, David. "Between Space and Time: Reflections on the Geographical Imagination." *Annals of the Association of American Geographers* 80, no. 3 (1990): 428.

Harvey, David. *The Condition of Postmodernity*. Cambridge, MA: Blackwell, 1990.

Harvey, David. *Cosmopolitanism and the Geographies of Freedom.* New York: Columbia University Press, 2009.

Harvey, David. "Space as a Keyword." In *David Harvey: A Critical Reader*, edited by N. Castree and D. Gregory, 270–93. Oxford: Blackwell, 2006.

Harvey, David. *Spaces of Global Capitalism.* London: Verso, 2006.

Heath, Stephen. "Narrative Space." In *Narrative, Apparatus, Ideology*, edited by Phil Rosen, 379–420. New York: Columbia University Press, 1986.

Heidegger, Martin. "The Age of the World Picture." In *Martin Heidegger: Off the Beaten Track*, edited and translated by Julian Young and Kenneth Haynes, 57–73. Cambridge: Cambridge University Press, 2002.

Hell, Julia, and Andreas Schönle, eds. *Ruins of Modernity*. Durham, NC: Duke University Press, 2010.

Higson, Andrew. "The Concept of National Cinema." *Screen* 3, no. 4 (1989): 36–47.

Higson, Andrew. *English Heritage, English Cinema: Costume Drama since 1980*. Oxford: Oxford University Press, 2003.

Higson, Andrew. "The Limiting Imagination of National Cinema." In *Cinema and Nation*, edited by Mette Hjort and Scott MacKenzie, 63–74. Oxon: Routledge, 2000.

Hodgson Burnett, Frances. *The Secret Garden*. New York: F. A. Stokes, 1911.

Holmes, J. B. "G.P.O. Films." *Sight and Sound* 6, no. 23 (1937): 159.

Honderich, Ted, ed. *The Oxford Companion to Philosophy*. 2nd ed. Oxford: Oxford University Press, 2005.

Hosagrahar, Jyoti. "Mansions to Margins: Modernity and the Domestic Landscapes of Historic Delhi, 1847–1910." *Journal of the Society of Architectural Historians* 60, no. 1 (2001): 26–45.

Hoyt, Eric. *Hollywood Vault: Film Libraries before Home Video*. New York: Columbia University Press, 2014.

Huhtamo, Erkki, and Jussi Parikka, eds. *Media Archeology: Approaches, Applications, and Implications*. Berkeley: University of California Press, 2011.

Hull, Matthew S. *Government of Paper: The Materiality of Bureaucracy in Urban Pakistan*. Berkeley: University of California Press, 2012.

India Business Law Handbook: Strategic Information and Basic Laws. Intl Business Pubns, 2012.

Jackson, John Brinckerhoff. *Discovering the Vernacular Landscape*. New Haven, CT: Yale University Press, 1986.

Jackson, John Brinckerhoff. *The Necessity for Ruins: And Other Topics*. Boston: University of Massachusetts Press, 1980.

Jackson, John Brinckerhoff. *A Sense of Place, a Sense of Time*. New Haven, CT: Yale University Press, 1996.

Jacobson, Brian R. *Studios before the System: Architecture, Technology, and the Emergence of Cinematic Space*. New York: Columbia University Press, 2015.

Jaikumar, Priya. "An 'Accurate Imagination': Place, Map, and Archive as Spatial Objects of Film History." In *Empire and Film*, edited by Lee Grieveson and Colin McCabe, 167–88. London: BFI Publishing, 2011.

Jaikumar, Priya. *Cinema at the End of Empire: A Politics of Transition in Britain and India*. Durham, NC: Duke University Press, 2006.

Jaikumar, Priya. "A Dialogue on *The River* with Shanay Jhaveri." In *Outsider Films on India, 1950–1990*, edited by Shanay Jhaveri, 17–47. Mumbai: Shoestring, 2009.

Jaikumar, Priya. "DVD Review: A Throw of Dice." *Modernism/Modernity* 16, no. 4 (2009): 845–48.

Jaikumar, Priya. "Feminist and Non-Western Interrogations of Film Authorship." In *The Routledge Companion to Cinema and Gender*, edited by Kristin Hole et al., 205–14. New York: Routledge, 2017.

Jaikumar, Priya. "Hospitality in the Time of Regulation: 1970s Films Division Tourism Shorts." In "Documentary Now," edited by Ravi Vasudevan. *MARG: A Magazine of the Arts* 70, no. 1 (September-December 2018): 32–35.

Jaikumar, Priya. "Insurgent Place as Visual Space: Location Shots and Rival Geographies of 1857 Lucknow." In *Silent Cinema and the Politics of Space*, edited by Jennifer M. Bean, Anupama Kapse, and Laura Horak, 45–70. Bloomington: Indiana University Press, 2014.

Jaikumar, Priya. "Out of Sync." In *Gendered Sounds of South Asia*, edited by Praseeda Gopinath and Monika Mehta. *Sounding Out*, archived November 6, 2017. https://soundstudiesblog .com/2017/11/06/.

Jain, Anuja. "The Curious Case of the Films Division: Some Annotations on the Beginnings of Indian Documentary Cinema in Postindependence India, 1940s–1960s." *Velvet Light Trap* 71 (2013): 15–26.

Jain, Anuja. "Suffering and Spectatorship: Sectarian Violence in Indian Documentary Film and Media." PhD diss., New York University, 2013.

James, David. *The Most Typical Avant-Garde: History and Geography of Minor Cinemas in Los Angeles*. Berkeley: University of California Press, 2005.

Jameson, Fredric. *The Geopolitical Aesthetic: Cinema and Space in the World System*. Bloomington: Indiana University Press and BFI, 1992.

Jameson, Fredric. *Postmodernism, or, the Cultural Logic of Late Capitalism*. Durham, NC: Duke University Press, 1999.

Jameson, Fredric. "Third-World Literature in the Era of Multinational Capital." *Social Text*, no. 15 (autumn 1985): 65–88.

Jameson, Fredric. "Walter Benjamin, or Nostalgia." *Salmagundi* 10/11 (fall 1969–winter 1970): 52–68.

Jani, Pranav. "Karl Marx, Eurocentrism, and the 1857 Revolt in British India." In *Marxism, Modernity and Postcolonial Studies*, edited by Crystal Bartolovich and Neil Lazarus, 81–97. Cambridge: Cambridge University Press, 2002.

Jenkins, Henry. *Convergence Culture: Where Old and New Media Collide*. New York: New York University Press, 2008.

Jhaveri, Shanay. *Outsider Films on India, 1950–1990*. London: Shoestring, 2010.

Johnson, Peter. "The Geographies of Heterotopia." *Geography Compass* 7, no. 11 (2013): 790–803.

Kabir, Ananya Jahanara. *Territory of Desire*. Minneapolis: University of Minnesota Press, 2009.

Kant, Amitabh. *Branding India: An Incredible Story*. Uttar Pradesh, India: Collins Business, 2009.

Kant, Immanuel. *Critique of Judgment*. Translated by Walter S. Pluhar. Indianapolis, IN: Hackett Publishing, 1987.

Kaplan, Caren. *Aerial Aftermaths: Wartime from Above*. Durham, NC: Duke University Press, 2018.

Kaplan, Caren. "The Politics of Location as Transnational Feminist Critical Practice." In *Scattered Hegemonies: Postmodernity and Transnational Feminist Practices*, edited by Inderpal Grewal and Caren Kaplan, 137–52. Minneapolis: University of Minnesota Press, 1994.

Kaplan, Caren. *Questions of Travel: Postmodern Discourses of Displacement*. Durham, NC: Duke University Press, 1996.

Kapse, Anupama, and Meheli Sen. "Introduction to Dossier: Fan as Doppelgänger." *Framework: The Journal of Cinema and Media* 58, nos. 1–2 (spring–fall 2017): 121–27.

Kapur, Geeta. *When Was Modernism: Essays on Contemporary Cultural Practice in India*. New Delhi: Tulika, 2000.

Kapur, Jyotsna. *The Politics of Time and Youth in Brand India: Bargaining with Capital*. London: Anthem Press, 2013.

Kasbarian, J. A. "Mapping Edward Said: Geography, Identity, and the Politics of Location." *Environment and Planning D: Society and Space* 14, no. 5 (1996): 529–57.

Kaushik, Ritika. "'Sun in the Belly': Film Practice at Films Division of India, 1965–1975." *Bioscope* 8, no. 1 (June 1017): 103–23.

Kavoori, Anandam P., and Aswin Punathambekar, eds. *Global Bollywood*. New York: New York University Press, 2008.

Kearns, Gerry. *Geopolitics and Empire: The Legacy of Halford Mackinder*. Oxford: Oxford University Press, 2009.

Kent, Ashley. "Geography: Changes and Challenges." *Teaching Geography in Secondary Schools: A Reader*, edited by Maggie Smith, 3–20. London: RoutledgeFalmer, 2002.

Kirby, Lynne. "Male Hysteria and Early Cinema." *Male Trouble*, edited by Constance Penley and Sharon Willis, 67–85. Minneapolis: University of Minnesota, 1993.

Kirby, Lynne. *Parallel Tracks: The Railroad and Silent Cinema*. Durham, NC: Duke University Press, 1997.

Kishore, Shweta. *Indian Documentary Film and Filmmakers: Practicing Independence*. Edinburgh, UK: Edinburgh University Press, 2018.

Klaver, Claudia. "Domesticity Under Siege: British Women and Imperial Crisis at the Siege of Lucknow, 1857." *Women's Writing: The Elizabethan to Victorian Period* 8, no. 1 (2001): 21–58.

Klinger, Barbara. "Film History Terminable and Interminable: Recovering the Past in Reception Studies." *Screen* 38, no. 2 (1997): 107–28.

Knowles, Anne Kelly, et al., eds. *Geographies of the Holocaust*. Bloomington: Indiana University Press, 2014.

Koch, Gerhard, ed. *Franz Osten's Indian Silent Films*. New Delhi: Max Müller Bhavan, 1983.

Koenig-Archibugi, Mathias. *Debating Cosmopolitics*. London: Verso, 2003.

Kontopoulos, Kyriakos. *The Logic of Social Structures*. Cambridge: Cambridge University Press, 1993.

Koo, Hagen. "The Global Middle Class: How Is It Made, What Does It Represent?" *Globalizations* 13, no. 4 (2016): 440–53.

Kosambi, D. D. "Indian Feudalism." In *Rural Sociology in India*, edited by A. R. Desai, 148–49. Mumbai: Popular Prakashan, 1994.

Kracauer, Siegfried. *Theory of Film: The Redemption of Physical Reality*. Princeton, NJ: Princeton University Press, 1997.

Krause, Linda, and Patrice Petro, eds. *Global Cities: Cinema, Architecture, and Urbanism in a Digital Age*. New Brunswick, NJ: Rutgers University Press, 2003.

Kuhn, Annette. "*Screen* and Screen Theorizing Today." *Screen* 50, no. 1 (spring 2009): 1–12.

Kuhn, Annette, and Guy Westwell. *A Dictionary of Film Studies*. Oxford: Oxford University Press, 2012.

Kuleshov, Lev. *Kuleshov on Film*. Translated and edited by Ronald Levaco. Berkeley: University of California Press, 1974.

Kumar, Ashok. "The Inverted Compact City of Delhi." In *Compact Cities: Sustainable Urban Forms for Developing Countries*, edited by Mike Jenks and Rod Burgess, 153–66. London: Spon Press, 2000.

Kumar, Shanti. *Gandhi Meets Primetime: Globalization and Nationalism in Indian Television*. Urbana: University of Illinois Press, 2006.

Kumar, Shanti. "Mapping Tollywood: The Cultural Geography of 'Ramoji Film City' in Hyderabad." *Quarterly Film and Video* 23, no. 2 (2006): 129–38.

Kumar, Shanti, and Aswin Punathambekar, eds. *Television at Large in South Asia*. New York: Routledge, 2014.

"La Carte Internationale du Monde au Millionème." *Geographical Journal* 43, no. 2 (1914): 178–82.

Laine, Tarja. *Feeling Cinema: Emotional Dynamics in Film Studies*. New York: Continuum, 2011.

Lamster, Mark. *Architecture and Film*. New York: Princeton Architectural Press, 2000.

Larkin, Brian. *Signal and Noise: Media, Infrastructure, and Urban Culture in Nigeria*. Durham, NC: Duke University Press, 2008.

Larkin, Brian. "Imperial Circulation: Cinema and the Making of Anxious Colonialists." In *Globalizing American Studies*, edited by Brian Edwards and Dilip Gaonkar, 155–83. Chicago: Chicago University Press, 2010.

Latour, Bruno. "The Berlin Key or How to Do Words with Things." In *Matter, Materiality, and Modern Culture*, edited by P. M. Graves-Brown, translated by Lydia Davies, 10–21. London: Routledge, 2000.

Latsis, Dimitrios. "Nature's Nation on the Move: The American Landscape between Art and Cinema, 1867–1939." PhD diss., University of Iowa, 2015.

Lazzarato, Maurizio. "Immaterial Labor." In *Radical Thought in Italy: A Potential Politics*, edited by Paolo Virno and Michael Hardt, 133–48. London: University of Minnesota Press, 1996.

Lefebvre, Henri. *The Production of Space*. Translated by Donald Nicholson-Smith. Malden, MA: Wiley-Blackwell, 1991.

Lefebvre, Henri. *Writings on Cities*. Edited by Eleonore Kofman and Elizabeth Lebas. Malden, MA: Wiley-Blackwell, 1996.

Lefebvre, Martin. *Landscape and Film*. New York: Routledge, 2006.

Legg, Stephen. "Beyond the European Province: Foucault and Postcolonialism." In *Space, Knowledge, and Power: Foucault and Geography*, edited by Jeremy Crampton and Stuart Elden, 265–91. Aldershot, UK: Ashgate, 2007.

Leyda, Jay. *Kino: A History of Russian and Soviet Film*. London: George Allen and Unwin, 1960.

Liang, Lawrence, and Ravi Sundaram. "India." In *Media Piracy in Emerging Economies*, edited by Joe Karaganis, 339–98. Social Science Research Council, US, 2011. (Creative Commons) http://piracy.americanassembly.org/wp-content/uploads/2011/06/MPEE-PDF-1.0.4.pdf.

Lifson, Ben. "Beato in Lucknow." *Artforum* (May 1988): 99–103.

Lim, Bliss Cua. *Translating Time: Cinema, the Fantastic and Temporal Critique*. Durham, NC: Duke University Press, 2009.

Limbrick, Peter. "Contested Spaces: Kamal Aljafari's Transnational Palestinian Films." In *A Companion to German Cinema*, ed. Andrea Mensch and Terri Ginsberg, 218–48. Oxford: Blackwell, 2012.

Limbrick, Peter. *Making Settler Cinemas: Film and Colonial Encounters in the United States, Australia, and New Zealand*. New York: Palgrave Macmillan, 2010.

Lipsitz, George. *Time Passages: Collective Memory and American Popular Culture*. Minneapolis: University of Minnesota Press, 2006.

Lively, Penelopy. *Moon Tiger*. 1987. London: Penguin Books, 2006.

Llewellyn-Jones, Rosie. *A Fatal Friendship: The Nawabs, the British, and the City of Lucknow*. Delhi: Oxford University Press, 1986.

Lloyd, David. "Ruination, Partition, and the Expectation of Violence (On Allan de Souza's Irish Photography)." *Social Identities* 9, no. 4 (December 2003): 475–509.

Lloyd, David, and Paul Thomas. *Culture and the State*. London: Routledge, 1998.

LoBianco, Lorraine, and David Thompson, eds. *Jean Renoir: Letters*. Translations by Craig Carlson, Natasha Arnoldi, and Michael Wells. London: Faber and Faber, 1994.

Lock Swarr, Amanda, and Richa Nagar, eds. *Critical Transnational Feminist Praxis*. Albany: State University of New York Press, 2010.

Longinus. *On the Sublime*. Edited by D. A. Russell. Oxford: Clarendon Press, 1964.

Low, Rachael. *The History of the British Film, 1918–1929*. London: George Allen & Unwin, 1971.

Lowenthal, David. *The Past Is a Foreign Country*. Cambridge: Cambridge University Press, 1985.

Lyon, James, and John Plunkett, eds. *Multimedia Histories: From the Magic Lantern to the Internet*. Exeter, UK: University of Exeter Press, 2007.

Lyotard, Jean-François. *Lessons on the Analytic of the Sublime*. Translated by E. Rottenberg. Stanford, CA: Stanford University Press, 1994.

Mackinder, Halford. "The Teaching of Geography from an Imperial Point of View, and the Use Which Could and Should Be Made of Visual Instruction." *Geographical Teacher* 6, no. 2 (1911): 79–86.

Maddrell, Avril. "Discourses of Race and Gender and the Comparative Method in Geography School Texts 1830–1918." *Environment and Planning D: Society and Space* 16 (1998): 81–103.

Mahadevan, Sudhir. *A Very Old Machine: The Many Origins of Cinema in India*. Albany: State University of New York Press, 2015.

Mahal, Zeenat. *Haveli*. Toronto: Indireads, 2013.

Maier, Robert G. *Location Scouting and Management Handbook: Television, Film, Still Photography*. Boston: Focal Press, 1994.

Maingard, Jacqueline. "African Cinema and *Bamako* (2006): Notes on Epistemology and Film Theory." *Critical African Studies* 5 (2013): 103–13.

Majumdar, Rochona. *Marriage and Modernity: Family Values in Colonial Bengal, 1870–1956*. Durham, NC: Duke University Press, 2009.

Majumdar, Rochona. *Writing Postcolonial History*. New York: Bloomsbury Academic, 2010.

Makdisi, Saree. *Romantic Imperialism: Universal Empire and the Culture of Modernity*. Cambridge: Cambridge University Press, 1998.

Malitsky, Joshua. "Science and Documentary: Unity, Indexicality, Reality." *Journal of Visual Culture* 11, no. 3 (2012): 250.

Mani, Lata. *Sacred Secular: A Contemplative Cultural Critique*. New Delhi: Routledge, 2009.

Marin, Louis. *Utopics: Spatial Play*. Translated by Robert A. Vollrath. Atlantic Highlands, NJ: Humanities Press, 1984.

Marks, Laura U. *Enfoldment and Infinity: An Islamic Genealogy of New Media Art*. Cambridge, MA: MIT Press, 2010.

Marks, Laura U. *The Skin of the Film: Intercultural Cinema, Embodiment, and the Senses*. Durham, NC: Duke University Press, 2000.

Martineau, Harriet, et al. "The India Question—Its Present Aspects and Teachings." *Calcutta Review* 30 (January–June 1858): 358–94.

Massey, Doreen. "A Global Sense of Place." *Marxism Today* (June 1991): 24–29.

Massey, Doreen. *Space, Place, and Gender*. Cambridge: Polity Press, 1994.

Massumi, Brian. *Parables for the Virtual: Movement, Affect, Sensation*. Durham, NC: Duke University Press, 2005.

Mathur, Saloni. *India by Design: Colonial History and Cultural Display*. Berkeley: University of California Press, 2009.

Mazaj, Meta. *Critical Visions in Film Theory: Classic and Contemporary Readings*. London: Macmillan, 2011, 154.

Mazumdar, Ranjani. "Aviation, Tourism and Dreaming in 1960s Bombay Cinema." *Bioscope: South Asian Screen Studies* 2, no. 2 (2011): 129–55.

Mazumdar, Ranjani. *Bombay Cinema: An Archive of the City*. Minneapolis: University of Minnesota Press, 2007.

Mazumdar, Ranjani. "Cosmopolitan Dreams." *Seminar* 598 (June 2009): 14–20.

Mazzarella, William. *Censorium: Cinema and the Open Edge of Mass Publicity*. Durham, NC: Duke University Press, 2013.

Mbembe, Achille. "Necropolitics." Translated by Libby Meintjes. *Public Culture* 15, no. 1 (2003): 11–40.

McCabe, Colin. "Theory and Film: Principles of Realism and Pleasure." In *Narrative, Apparatus, Ideology*, edited by Phil Rosen, 179–97. New York: Columbia University Press, 1986.

McCarthy, Anna. *Ambient Television: Visual Culture and Public Space*. Durham, NC: Duke University Press, 2001.

McCarthy, Todd, and Charles Flynn, eds. *King of the Bs: Working within the Hollywood System: An Anthology of Film History and Criticism*. New York: E. P. Dutton, 1975.

McClintock, Anne. *Imperial Leather: Race, Gender, and Sexuality in the Colonial Context*. London: Routledge, 1995.

McPherson, Tara. *Reconstructing Dixie: Race, Gender, and Nostalgia in the Imagined South*. Durham, NC: Duke University Press, 2003.

Mecklai, Noorel, and Brian Shoesmith. "Religion as 'Commodity Images': Securing a Hindu Rashtra." In *Hindu Nationalism and Governance*, edited by John McGuire and Ian Copland, 316–33. New Delhi: Oxford University Press, 2007.

Mehta, Monika. *Censorship and Sexuality in Bombay Cinema*. Austin: University of Texas Press, 2011.

Mehta, Rama. *Inside the Haveli*. New Delhi: Penguin, 1977.

Mehta, Suketu. *Maximum City: Bombay Lost and Found*. New York: Vintage Books, 2004.

Mehta, Uday. *Liberalism and Empire: A Study in Nineteenth-Century British Liberal Thought*. Chicago: University of Chicago Press, 1999.

Mérigeau, Pascal. *Jean Renoir: A Biography*. Translated by Bruce Benderson. Burbank, CA: Ratpac Press, 2016.

Metz, Christian. "The Imaginary Signifier." In *Narrative, Apparatus, Ideology*, edited by Phil Rosen, 244–80. New York: Columbia University Press, 1986.

Mezzadra, Sandro, and Brett Neilson. *Border as Method, or, The Multiplication of Labor*. Durham, NC: Duke University Press, 2013.

Mignolo, Walter. *Local Histories / Global Designs: Coloniality, Subaltern Knowledges, and Border Thinking*. Princeton, NJ: Princeton University Press, 2012.

Minteer, Ben A. *The Landscape of Reform: Civic Pragmatism and Environmental Thought in America*. Cambridge, MA: MIT Press, 2009.

Mishra, Vijay. *Bollywood Cinema: Temples of Desire*. London: Routledge, 2002.

Mishra, Vijay. *Devotional Poetics and the Indian Sublime*. Albany: State University of New York Press, 1998.

Mitchell, Donald. *Cultural Geography: A Critical Introduction*. Oxford: Blackwell, 2000.

Mitchell, William John. *Placing Words: Symbols, Space, and the City*. Cambridge, MA: MIT Press, 2005.

Mitchell, W. J. T., ed. *Landscape and Power*. 2nd ed. Chicago: University of Chicago Press, 2002.

Mittal, Ashok. *Cinema Industry in India: Pricing and Taxation*. New Delhi: Indus Publishing, 1995.

Moon, William Least Heat. *PrairyErth: (A Deep Map)*. New York: Houghton Mifflin Harcourt, 1999.

Moore, Rachel O. *Savage Theory: Cinema as Modern Magic*. Durham, NC: Duke University Press, 2000.

Morgan, Daniel. "The Afterlife of Superimposition." In *Opening Bazin*, edited by Andrew Dudley, 127–41. Oxford: Oxford University Press, 2011.

Morgan, Daniel. "Rethinking Bazin: Ontology and Realist Aesthetics." *Critical Inquiry* 32 (spring 2006): 443–81.

Morley, David. *Home Territories: Media, Mobility, and Identity*. London: Routledge, 2000.

M. R. Morarka Foundation. *Painted Heritage*. New Delhi: Popular Prakashan, 2012.

Mufti, Aamir. "A Greater Story-Writer than God: Genre, Gender and Minority in Late Colonial India." In *Community, Gender and Violence: Subaltern Studies* 11, edited by Partha Chatterjee and Pradeep Jeganathan, 1–36. New York: Columbia University Press, 2000.

Mukherjee, Debashree. *Cine-Ecology: Practicing Modernity in Colonial Bombay*. Unpublished manuscript.

Mukherji, Rahul. "India's Aborted Liberalization—1966." *Pacific Affairs* 73, no. 3 (autumn 2000): 375–92.

Mulvey, Laura. "Notes on Sirk and Melodrama." In *Home Is Where the Heart Is: Studies in Melodrama and the Woman's Film*, edited by Christine Gledhill, 75–79. London: BFI, 1987.

Mulvey, Laura. "Visual Pleasure and Narrative Cinema." In *Narrative, Apparatus, Ideology*, edited by Phil Rosen, 198–209. New York: Columbia University Press, 1986.

Murthy, M. V. K. Foreword to *The Boy from Lambata: Memoirs of a Combat Cameraman and Documentary Maker*, by N. S. Thapa. Nainital, India: Pahar Pothi, 2004.

Musser, Charles. *Thomas A. Edison and His Kinetographic Motion Pictures*. New Brunswick, NJ: Rutgers University Press, 1995.

Musser, Charles. "The Travel Genre in 1903–1904: Moving towards Fictional Narrative." In *Early Cinema: Space, Frame, and Narrative*, edited by Thomas Elsaesser, 123–32. London: BFI, 1990.

Naficy, Hamid. *An Accented Cinema: Exilic and Diasporic Filmmaking*. Princeton, NJ: Princeton University Press, 2001.

Naficy, Hamid. "Lured by the East: Ethnographic and Expedition Films about Nomadic Tribes—The Case of *Grass* (1925)." In *Virtual Voyages*, edited by Jeffrey Ruoff, 117–38. Durham, NC: Duke University Press, 2006.

Naipaul, V. S. *An Area of Darkness*. New York: Vintage Books, 1992.

Nair, Kartik. "Taste, Taboo, Trash: The Story of the Ramsay Brothers." *Bioscope: South Asian Screen Studies* 3, no. 2 (2012): 123–45.

Narwekar, Sanjit. *Films Division and the Indian Documentary*. New Delhi: Ministry of Information and Broadcasting, Government of India, 1992.

Narwekar, Sanjit. "Rewind to 1948." *Documentary Today* 1, no. 4 (2008): 6–17.

Nayar, Kuldip. "Averting Religious-Sites Disputes." *India Abroad* 19, no. 16 (January 1989): 24.

Nehru, Jawaharlal. *The Discovery of India*. New Delhi: Penguin Books, 2010.

Neumann, Dietrich, and Donald Albrecht. *Film Architecture: Set Designs from Metropolis to Blade Runner*. Munich: Prestel Publishing, 1996.

Ng, Andrew Hock Soon. *Asian Gothic: Essays in Literature, Film and Anime*. Jefferson, NC: McFarland, 2008.

Ngai, Sianne. *Our Aesthetic Categories: Zany, Cute, Interesting*. Cambridge, MA: Harvard University Press, 2012.

Ngai, Sianne. *Ugly Feelings*. Cambridge, MA: Harvard University Press, 2005.

Nichols, Bill. *Introduction to Documentary*. Bloomington: Indiana University Press, 2001.

Nichols, Bill. *Representing Reality: Issues and Concepts in Documentary*. Bloomington: Indiana University Press, 1992.

Nochimson, Martha. *World on Film: An Introduction*. Malden, MA: Wiley-Blackwell, 2010.

Nora, Pierre. "Between Memory and History: Les Lieux de Memoire." *Representations* 26 (spring 1989): 7–24.

Norrish, P. J. *Drama of the Group*. Cambridge: Cambridge University Press, 1958.

Nowell-Smith, Geoffrey and Christophe Dupin. *The British Film Institute, the Government, and Film Culture, 1933–2000*. Manchester, UK: Manchester University Press, 2012.

Oberoi, Patricia. "The Diaspora Comes Home: Disciplining Desire in DDLJ." *Contributions to Indian Sociology* 32, no. 2 (1998): 305–36.

O'Donnell, Erin. "'Woman' and 'Homeland' in Ritwik Ghatak's Films: Constructing Post-Independence Bengali Cultural Identity." *Jump Cut* no. 42 (2004). Online archive https://www.ejumpcut.org/archive/jc47.2005/ghatak/.

Oettermann, Stephan. *The Panorama History of a Mass Medium*. Translated by Deborah Lucas Schneider. New York: Zone Books, 1997.

Oever, Annie van den. *Ostrannenie: On "Strangeness" and the Moving Image; the History, Reception, and Relevance of a Concept*. Amsterdam: Amsterdam University Press, 2010.

Ondaatje, Michael. *The English Patient*. New York: Vintage Books, 1993.

Orgeron, Devin, Marsha Orgeron, and Dan Streible, eds. *Learning with the Lights Off: Educational Film in the United States*. Oxford: Oxford University Press, 2012.

Palmer, Barton R. *Shot on Location: Postwar American Cinema and the Exploration of Real Place*. Rutgers, NJ: Rutgers University Press, 2016.

Pandian, Anand. "Reel Time: Ethnography and the Historical Ontology of the Cinematic Image." *Screen* 52, no. 2 (2011): 192–214.

Pandian, Anand. *Reel World: An Anthropology of Creation*. Durham, NC: Duke University Press, 2015.

Parks, Lisa. *Cultures in Orbit: Satellites and the Televisual*. Durham, NC: Duke University Press, 2005.

Parks, Lisa. "Kinetic Screens: Epistemologies of Movement at the Interface." In *Mediaspace: Place, Scale, and Culture in a Media Age*, edited by Nick Couldry and Anna McCarthy, 37–58. New York: Routledge, 2004.

Parks, Lisa, and Caren Kaplan, eds. *Life in the Age of Drone Warfare*. Durham, NC: Duke University Press, 2017.

Parmar, V. S. *Haveli: Wooden Houses and Mansions of Gujarat*. Ahmedabad, India: Mapin Publishing, 1989.

Patke, Rajeev S. "Benjamin's Arcades Project and the Postcolonial City." In *Postcolonial Urbanism: Southeast Asian Cities and Global Processes*, edited by Ryan Bishop, John Phillips, and Wei Wei Yeo, 287–305. New York: Routledge, 2003.

Paul, Arunima. "Unraveling Countryside: Provincial Modernities in Contemporary Popular Indian Cinema." PhD diss., University of Southern California, 2015.

Pendakur, Manjunath. *Indian Popular Cinema: Industry, Ideology, and Consciousness*. Cresskill, NJ: Hampton Press, 2003.

Penz, Francois, and Maureen Thomas, eds. *Cinema and Architecture: Melies, Mallet-Stevens, Multimedia*. London: British Film Institute, 1997.

Penz, Francois, and Richard Koeck, eds. *Cinematic Urban Geographies*. New York: Palgrave Macmillan, 2017.

Peterson, Jennifer. *Education in the School of Dreams: Travelogues and Early Non-Fiction Films*. Durham, NC: Duke University Press, 2013.

Phadnis, Urmila. *Towards the Integration of Indian States, 1919–1947*. Bombay: Asia Publishing House, 1968.

Pierce, Steven, and Anupama Rao. *Discipline and the Other Body: Correction, Corporeality, Colonialism*. Durham, NC: Duke University Press, 2006.

Pinney, Christopher. *Camera Indica: The Social Life of Indian Photographs*. Chicago: University of Chicago Press, 1997.

Pinney, Christopher. *The Coming of Photography in India*. London: British Library, 2008.

Pinney, Christopher. "Future Travel: Anthropology and Cultural Distance in an Age of Virtual Reality: Or, a Past Seen from a Possible Future." *Visualising Theory*, edited by L. Taylor, 409–28. New York: Routledge, 1994.

Pinney, Christopher. "Introduction: How the Other Half . . ." In *Photography's Other Histories*, edited by Christopher Pinney and Nicholas Peterson, 1–14. Durham, NC: Duke University Press, 2003.

Pinney, Christopher. *Photos of the Gods: The Printed Image and Political Struggle in India.* London: Reaktion Books, 2004.

Pinney, Christopher, and Nicolas Peterson. *Photography's Other Histories*. Durham, NC: Duke University Press, 2003.

Poduval, Satish. "The Affable Young Man: Civility, Desire and the Making of a Middle-Class Cinema in the 1970s." In *The 1970s and Its Legacies in Indian Cinema*, edited by Priya Joshi and Rajinder Dudrah, 36–49. New York: Routledge, 2014.

Poulantzas, Nicos. *State, Power, Socialism.* London: Verso, 1978.

Power, Marcus, and Andrew Crampton. *Cinema and Popular Geo-Politics.* New York: Routledge, 2006.

Prakash, Gyan. *Another Reason: Science and the Imagination of Modern India.* Princeton, NJ: Princeton University Press, 1999.

Prakash, Gyan. "Writing Post-Orientalist Histories of the Third World: Perspectives from Indian Historiography." *Comparative Studies in Society and History* 32, no. 2 (April 1990): 383–408.

Pramar, Vickram Singh. *Haveli: Wooden Houses and Mansions of Gujarat.* Ahmedabad, India: Mapin, 1989.

Prasad, M. Madhava. *Ideology of the Hindi Film: A Historical Construction.* New Delhi: Oxford University Press, 1998.

Prasad, M. Madhava. "Surviving Bollywood." In *Global Bollywood*, edited by Anandam P. Kavoori and Aswin Punathambekar, 41–51. New York: New York University Press, 2008.

Prasad, Rajendra, ed. *A Historical Developmental Study of Classical Indian Philosophy of Morals.* Vol. 12. New Delhi: Concept, 2009.

Presner, Todd. "Hegel's Philosophy of World History via Sebald's Imaginary of Ruins." In *Ruins of Modernity*, edited by Julia Hell and Andreas Schönle, 193–211. Durham, NC: Duke University Press, 2010.

Puar, Jasbir. *Terrorist Assemblages: Homonationalism in Queer Times.* Durham, NC: Duke University Press, 2007.

Punathambekar, Aswin. *From Bombay to Bollywood: The Making of Global Media Industry.* New York: New York University Press, 2013.

Rai, Amit. *Untimely Bollywood: Globalization and India's New Media Assemblage.* Durham, NC: Duke University Press, 2009.

Raimondo-Souto, Mario H. *Motion Picture Photography: A History, 1891–1960.* Jefferson, NC: McFarland, 2007.

Rajadhyaksha, Ashish. "The 'Bollywoodization' of the Indian Cinema: Cultural Nationalism in a Global Arena." In *Global Bollywood*, edited by Anandam P. Kavoori and Aswin Punathambekar, 17–41. New York: New York University Press, 2008.

Rajadhyaksha, Ashish. "Dossier: Kumar Shahani." *Framework*, nos. 30/31 (1986): 67–111.

Rajadhyaksha, Ashish. *Ritwik Ghatak: A Return to the Epic*. Bombay: Screen Unit, 1982.

Rajadhyaksha, Ashish, and Paul Willemen. *Encyclopedia of Indian Cinema*. New rev. ed. London: BFI, 1999.

Rajagopal, Arvind. *Politics after Television: Hindu Nationalism and the Reshaping of the Public in India*. Cambridge: Cambridge University Press, 2001.

Rajagopalachari, C. *Upanishads*. New Delhi: Bharatiya Vidya Bhavan, 1991.

Ram, Harsha. *The Imperial Sublime: A Russian Poetics of Empire*. Madison: University of Wisconsin Press, 2003.

Ramaswamy, Sumathi. *The Goddess and the Nation: Mapping Mother India*. Durham, NC: Duke University Press, 2010.

Ramaswamy, Sumathi. *The Lost Land of Lemuria: Fabulous Geographies, Catastrophic Histories*. Berkeley: University of California Press, 2004.

Ramaswamy, Sumathi. *Terrestrial Lesson: The Conquest of the World as Globe*. Chicago: University of Chicago Press, 2017.

Ramaswamy, Sumathi. "Visualizing India's Geo-Body: Globes, Maps, Bodyscapes." *Contributions to Indian Sociology* 36, nos. 1–2 (2002): 151–89.

Ramirez, Juan Antonio. *Architecture for the Screen: A Critical Study of Set Design in Hollywood's Golden Age*. Jefferson, NC: McFarland, 2004.

Rancière, Jacques. "From One Image to Another? Deleuze and the Ages of Cinema." In *Film Fables*, 107–24. Translated by Emiliano Battista. London: Berg, 2006.

Rancière, Jacques. *The Names of History: On the Poetics of Knowledge*. Translated by Hassan Melehy. Minneapolis: University of Minnesota Press, 1994.

Renoir, Jean. "André Bazin's Little Beret." In André Bazin, *Jean Renoir*, edited by François Truffaut, translated by W. M. Halsey II and William H. Simon, 11–12. New York: Da Capo Press, 1992.

Renoir, Jean. "Introduction to the Film from 1962 by Jean Renoir." *The River*, Criterion Collection DVD special feature, April 21, 2015, spine no. 276.

Renoir, Jean. *My Life and My Films*. Translated by Norman Denny. New York: Atheneum Press, 1974.

Renoir, Jean. "Quelque chose m'est arrivé." *Cahiers du Cinéma* 2, no. 8 (1952): 31–32.

Renoir, Jean. *Renoir, My Father*. Introduction by Robert L. Herbert. Translated by Randolph and Dorothy Weaver. New York: New York Review of Books, 1958.

Renoir, Jean. *Renoir on Renoir: Interviews, Essays, and Remarks*. Translated by Carol Volk. Cambridge: Cambridge University Press, 1989.

Renov, Michael. *The Subject of Documentary*. Minneapolis: University of Minnesota Press, 2004.

Renov, Michael, ed. *Theorizing Documentary*. London: Routledge, 1999.

Report of the Film Inquiry Committee. New Delhi: Government of India Press, 1951.

Report of the Working Group on National Film Policy. Government of India, Ministry of Information and Broadcasting, 1980.

Rhodes, John David. *Spectacle of Property: The House in American Film*. Minneapolis: University of Minnesota Press, 2017.

Rhodes, John David. *Stupendous, Miserable City: Pasolini's Rome*. Minneapolis: University of Minnesota Press, 2007.

Rhodes, John David, and Elena Gorfinkel. *Taking Place: Location and the Moving Image*. Minneapolis: University of Minnesota Press, 2011.

Rice, Tom. "Exhibiting Africa: British Instructional Films and the Empire Series (1925–8)." In *Empire and Film*, edited by Lee Grieveson and Colin McCabe, 115–33. London: Palgrave Macmillan, 2011.

Rice, Tom. *Films for the Colonies: Cinema and the Preservation of the British Empire*. Berkeley: University of California Press, 2019.

Rice, Tom. "Indian News Parade." *Colonial Film Moving Images of the British Empire*. January 2010. http://www.colonialfilm.org.uk/production-company/indian-news-parade?sort =year&rpp=48.

Rich, Adrienne. *Blood, Bread, and Poetry: Selected Prose 1979–1985*. New York: W. W. Norton, 1986.

Richter, Linda K. *The Politics of Tourism in Asia*. Honolulu, HI: University of Hawaii Press, 1989.

Riegl, Alois. "The Modern Cult of Monuments: Its Character and Its Origin." *Oppositions*, no. 25 (fall 1982): 21–51.

Roan, Jeanette. *Envisioning Asia: On Location, Travel, and the Cinematic Geography of U.S. Orientalism*. Ann Arbor: University of Michigan Press, 2010.

Rodowick, David N. *Elegy for a Theory*. Cambridge, MA: Harvard University Press, 2015.

Rodowick, David N. *Gilles Deleuze's Time Machine*. Durham, NC: Duke University Press, 1997.

Rodowick, David N. *The Virtual Life of Film*. Cambridge, MA: Harvard University Press, 2007.

Rohdie, Sam. *Promised Lands: Cinema, Geography, Modernism*. London: British Film Institute, 2008.

Rojek, Chris, and John Urry, eds. *Touring Cultures: Transformations of Travel and Theory*. New York: Routledge, 1997.

Rose, Gillian. *Feminism and Geography: The Limits of Geographical Knowledge*. Cambridge: Polity Press, 1993.

Rose, Jay. *Producing Great Sound for Film and Video: Expert Tips from Preproduction to Final Mix*. New York: Focal Press, 2015.

Rosen, Philip. "Belief in Bazin." In *Opening Bazin*, edited by Andrew Dudley, 107–18. Oxford: Oxford University Press, 2011.

Rosen, Philip. "Border Times and Geopolitical Frames: The Martin Walsh Memories Lectures, 2006." *Canadian Journal of Film Studies* 15, no. 5 (fall 2006): 2–16.

Rosen, Philip. *Change Mummified: Cinema, Historicity, Theory*. Minneapolis: University of Minneapolis Press, 2001.

Rosen, Philip, ed. *Narrative, Apparatus, Ideology*. New York: Columbia University Press, 1986.

Rosen, Philip. "Screen and 1970s Film Theory." In *Inventing Film Studies*, edited by Lee Grieveson and Haidee Wasson, 267–97. Durham, NC: Duke University Press, 2008.

Rosenbaum, Jonathan. "The Creation of the World: Rossellini's *India Matri Bhumi*." In *Outsider Films*, edited by Shanay Jhaveri, 48–75. Mumbai: Shoestring, 2009.

Rosenberg, Daniel, and Anthony Grafton. *Cartographies of Time: A History of the Timeline*. New York: Princeton Architectural Press, 2010.

Rosenberg, Jordana. "The Molecularization of Sexuality: On Some Primitivisms of the Present." *Theory and Event* 17, no. 2 (2014). Project MUSE, muse.jhe.edu/article/546470.

Rosenstone, Robert A. *History on Film / Film on History*. Harlow, UK: Longman/Pearson, 2006.

Rosenstone, Robert A. *Visions of the Past: The Challenge of Film to Our Idea of History*. Cambridge, MA: Harvard University Press, 1995.

Rotha, Paul. *Documentary Film*. London: Faber, 1952.

Rowland, Richard. "Films from Abroad: Fact and Fiction." *Quarterly of Film, Radio and Television* 7, no. 2 (winter 1952): 135–39.

Roy, Arundhati. "The Greater Common Good." *Outlook*, May 24, 1999. http://www .outlookindia.com/article.aspx?207509.

Roy, Srirupa. *Beyond Belief: India and the Politics of Postcolonial Nationalism*. Durham, NC: Duke University Press, 2007.

Roy, Srirupa. "The Postcolonial State and Visual Representations of India." *Contributions to Indian Sociology* 36 (February 2002): 233–63.

Roychoudhuri, Ranu. "Documentary Photography, Decolonization, and the Making of 'Secular Icons': Reading Sunil Janah's Photographs from the 1940s through the 1950s." *Bioscope: South Asia Screen Studies* 8, no. 1 (September 12, 2007): 46–80.

Rudolph, Susanne Hoeber, and Lloyd I. Rudolph. *Essays on Rajputana: Reflections on History, Culture, and Administration*. New Delhi: Concept Publishing, 1984.

Ruoff, Jeffrey. *Virtual Voyages: Cinema and Travel*. Durham, NC: Duke University Press, 2006.

Ryan, James. *Picturing Empire: Photography and the Visualization of the British Empire*. Chicago: University of Chicago Press, 1998.

Said, Edward. "Always on Top." *London Review of Books* 25, no. 6 (March 20, 2003): 3–6.

Said, Edward. *Beginnings: Intention and Method*. New York: Columbia University Press, 1985.

Said, Edward. *Culture and Imperialism*. New York: Vintage Books, 1994.

Said, Edward. *Orientalism*. New York: Vintage Books, 1978.

Sakai, Naoki. *Translation and Subjectivity: On Japan and Cultural Nationalism*. Minneapolis: University of Minnesota Press, 1997.

Salazkina, Masha, ed. "Dossier on Geopolitics of Film and Media Theory." *Framework* 56, no. 2 (fall 2015): 325–491.

Sandberg, Mark. "Location, 'Location': On the Plausibility of Place Substitution." In *Silent Cinema and the Politics of Space*, edited by J. M. Bean, A. P. Kapse and L. E. Horak, 23–46. Bloomington: Indiana University Press, 2014.

San Miguel, Helen. *World Film Locations: Mumbai*. Bristol, UK: Intellect Books, 2012.

Sanogo, Aboubakar. "The History of Documentary in Africa in the Colonial Era." PhD diss., University of Southern California, Los Angeles, 2009.

Santos, Boaventura de Sousa. "Beyond Abyssal Thinking: From Global Lines to Ecologies of Knowledges." June 29, 2007. http://www.eurozine.com/beyond-abyssal-thinking, 15.

Sarkar, Bhaskar. "The Melodramas of Globalization." *Cultural Dynamics* 20, no. 1 (2008): 31–51.

Sarkar, Bhaskar. *Mourning the Nation: Indian Cinema in the Wake of Partition*. Durham, NC: Duke University Press, 2009.

Sarkar, Bhaskar, and Nicole Wolf. "Indian Documentary Studies: Contours of a Field." *Bioscope: South Asian Screen Studies* 3, no. 1 (January 2012): 1–6.

Sassen, Saskia. *The Global City: New York, London, Tokyo.* Princeton, NJ: Princeton University Press, 2001.

Schama, Simon. *Landscape and Memory.* New York: Vintage Books, 1996.

Schiller, Nina Glick, and Andrew Irving. *"Whose Cosmopolitanism?" Critical Perspectives, Relationalities and Discontents.* New York: Berghahn Books, 2015.

Schivelbusch, Wolfgang. *The Railway Journey: The Industrialization of Time and Space in the 19th Century.* Berkeley: University of California Press, 1986.

Schultze, Suzanne. "'Dissolved Boundaries and Affective Labor': On the Disappearance of Reproductive Labor and Feminist Critique in *Empire.*" Translated by Frederick Peters. *Capitalism Nature Socialism* 17, no. 1 (2006): 77–82.

Schwartz, Vanessa R. "Dimanche à Orly: The Jet Age Airport and the Spectacle of Technology between Sky and Earth." *French Politics, Culture and Society* (December 2014): 24–44.

Schwartz, Vanessa R. *It's So French!: Hollywood, Paris, and the Making of Cosmopolitan Film Culture.* Chicago, IL: University of Chicago Press, 2007.

Schwartz, Vanessa, and Jeannene Przyblyski, ed. *The Nineteenth-Century Visual Culture Reader.* London: Routledge, 2004.

Scott, James C. *Seeing Like a State: How Certain Schemes to Improve the Human Condition Have Failed.* New Haven, CT: Yale University Press, 1999.

Scott, Joan Wallach. *Gender and the Politics of History,* rev. ed. New York: Columbia University Press, 1999.

Seiberling, Grace. *Amateurs, Photography, and the Mid-Victorian Imagination.* Chicago, IL: University of Chicago Press, 1984.

Seitz, Matt Zoller. "*The Darjeeling Limited*: The 5,284-Word Interview." In *The Wes Anderson Collection,* edited by Matt Zoller Seitz, 203–33. New York: Abrams Books, 2013.

Sen, Meheli. "Haunted Havelis and Hapless Heroes: Gender, Genre and the Hindi Gothic Film." In *Figurations in Indian Film,* edited by Meheli Sen and Anustup Basu, 116–36. London: Palgrave Macmillan, 2013.

Sen, Meheli. *Haunting Bollywood: Gender, Genre, and the Supernatural in Hindi Commercial Cinema.* Austin: University of Texas Press, 2017.

Seton, Marie. *Portrait of a Director: Satyajit Ray.* Bloomington: Indiana University Press, 1971.

Shahani, Kumar. "Film as Contemporary Art." *Social Scientist* 18, no. 3 (March 1990): 33–48.

Shankar, Priyadarshini. "Star Gazing via Documentary." *Framework: The Journal of Cinema and Media* 58, nos. 1–2 (spring–fall 2017): 100–118.

Shapiro, Michael. *Violent Cartographies: Mapping Cultures of War.* Minneapolis: University of Minnesota Press, 1997.

Sharar, Abdul Halim, Rosie Llewellyn-Jones, and Veena Talwar Oldenburg. *The Lucknow Omnibus.* New Delhi: Oxford University Press, 2001.

Sharma, Aparna. *Documentary Films in India: Critical Aesthetics at Work.* London: Palgrave Macmillan, 2015.

Shaw, Philip. *The Sublime.* New York: Routledge, 2006.

Shelvankar, K. S. "Indian Feudalism, Its Characteristics." In *Rural Sociology in India*, edited by A. R. Desai, 150–54. Mumbai: Popular Prakashan, 1994.

Shiel, Mark. *Hollywood Cinema and the Real Los Angeles*. London: Reaktion Books, 2012.

Shiel, Mark, and Tony Fitzmaurice, eds. *Cinema and the City: Film and Urban Societies in a Global Context*. Oxford: Blackwell, 2001.

Shih, Shu-mei. "Globalisation and Minoritization: Ang Lee and the Politics of Flexibility." *New Formations*, no. 40 (spring 2000): 86–101.

Shohat, Ella, and Robert Stam. *Unthinking Eurocentrism: Multiculturalism and the Media*. New York: Routledge, 1994.

Silverman, Kaja. "Suture (excerpts)." In *Narrative, Apparatus, Ideology*, edited by Phil Rosen, 219–35. New York: Columbia University Press, 1986.

Simmel, Georg. *The Philosophy of Money*. London: Routledge, 2004.

Soja, Edward. *Postmodern Geographies: The Reassertion of Space in Critical Social Theory*. London: Verso, 1989.

Soja, Edward. *Seeking Spatial Justice*. Minneapolis: University of Minnesota Press, 2010.

Soja, Edward. *Thirdspace: Journeys to Los Angeles and Other Real-and-Imagined Spaces*. Malden, MA: Blackwell Publishing, 1996.

Sontag, Susan. *Regarding the Pain of Others*. London: Penguin, 2004.

Spivak, Gayatri Chakravorty. *An Aesthetic Education in the Era of Globalization*. Cambridge, MA: Harvard University Press, 2012.

Spivak, Gayatri Chakravorty. *A Critique of Postcolonial Reason: Toward a History of the Vanishing Present*. Cambridge, MA: Harvard University Press, 1999.

Spivak, Gayatri Chakravorty. *Death of a Discipline*. New York: Columbia University Press, 2003.

Spivak, Gayatri Chakravorty. "'Draupadi' by Mahasveta Devi." Writing and Sexual Difference. *Critical Inquiry* 8, no. 2 (winter 1981): 381–402.

Spivak, Gayatri Chakravorty. "Subaltern Studies: Deconstructing Historiography." In *Subaltern Studies IV*, edited by Ranajit Guha, 330–61. New Delhi: Oxford University Press, 1988.

Spivak, Gayatri Chakravorty. "Time and Timing: Law and History." In *Chronotypes: The Construction of Time*, edited by John Bryant Bender and David E. Bellbery, 99–118. Stanford, CA: Stanford University Press, 1991.

Srinivas, Priya. *Sweating Saris: Indian Dance as Transnational Labor*. Philadelphia, PA: Temple University, 2011.

Srinivas, S. V. *Megastar: Chiranjeevi and Telugu Cinema after N.T. Rama Rao*. New Delhi: Oxford University Press, 2009.

Srinivas, S. V. *Politics as Performance: A Social History of the Telugu Cinema*. Ranikhet, India: Permanent Black, 2013.

Srivatsava, Sanjay. *Passionate Modernity: Sexuality, Class, and Consumption in India*. New Delhi: Routledge, 2007.

Staples, Suzanne Fisher. *Haveli*. New York: Random House, 1993.

Staples, Suzanne Fisher. *Shabanu: Daughter of the Wind*. New York: Ember, 1989.

Starosielski, Nicole. *The Undersea Network*. Durham, NC: Duke University Press, 2015.

Steimatsky, Noa. *Italian Locations: Reinhabiting the Past in Postwar Cinema*. Minneapolis: University of Minnesota Press, 2008.

Stoler, Ann. *Along the Archival Grain: Epistemic Anxieties and Colonial Common Sense*. Princeton, NJ: Princeton University Press, 2010.

Street, Sarah. *Black Narcissus*. London: I. B. Taurus, 2005.

Stubblefield, Thomas. "Ritwik Ghatak and the Role of Sound in Representing Post-Partition Bengal." *Post Script* 25, no. 3 (summer 2006): 17–29.

Sturken, Marita. *Tourists of History: Memory, Kirsch, and Consumerism from Oklahoma City to Ground Zero*. Durham, NC: Duke University Press, 2007.

Sukhdev, S. "The Documentary in Theory and Practice." In Jag Mohan, *S. Sukhdev: Film Maker: A Documentary Montage*, 10–18. Pune: National Film Archive of India, 1984.

Sundaram, Ravi. *Pirate Modernities: Delhi's Media Urbanism*. London: Routledge, 2010.

Sutoris, Peter. *Visions of Development: Films Division of India and the Imagination of Progress, 1948–75*. Oxford: Oxford University Press, 2016.

Talukdar, Shashwati. "Picturing Mountains as Hills: Hill Station Postcards and the Tales They Tell." In *Tasveer Ghar: A Digital Archive of South Asian Popular Visual Culture*. Accessed December 7, 2018. http://bit.ly/cR528c.

Tandan, Banmali. *The Architecture of Lucknow and Its Dependencies, 1722–1856: A Descriptive Inventory and an Analysis of Nawabi Types*. London: Sangam Books, 2001.

Taneja, Anand Vivek. *Jinnealogy: Time, Islam, and Ecological Thought in the Medieval Ruins of Delhi*. Stanford, CA: Stanford University Press, 2018.

Taneja, Anand Vivek. "Muslimness in Hindi Cinema." *Seminar* (2009). Accessed February 13, 2015. http://www.india-seminar.com/2009/598/598_anand_vivek_taneja.htm.

Teverson, Andrew, and Sara Upstone, eds. *Postcolonial Space: The Politics of Place in Contemporary Culture*. Basingstoke, UK: Palgrave Macmillan, 2011.

Thapa, N. S. *The Boy from Lambata: Memoirs of a Combat Cameraman and Documentary-Maker*. Nainital, India: Pahar Pothi, 2004.

Thapa, N. S. "Life behind the Camera." *Documentary Today* 1, no. 4 (May 2008): 21–22.

Thapar, Romila. "Cyclic and Linear Time in Early India." *Museum International* 57, no. 3 (2005): 19–31.

Thapar, Romila. *The Past as Present: Forging Contemporary Identities through History*. New Delhi: Aleph Book Company, 2014.

Thapar, Romila. *Time as a Metaphor of History: Early India*. New Delhi: Oxford University Press, 1996.

Thomas, Rosie. "Indian Cinema: Pleasures and Popularity." *Screen* 26, nos. 3–4 (1985): 116–31.

Thompson, Hilary. "Encrypted Ancestries: Kazuo Ishiguro's *The Remains of the Day* and Its Uncanny Inheritances." In *Asian Gothic*, edited by Andrew Hock Soon Ng, 73–87. Jefferson, NC: McFarland, 2008.

Thompson, Kristen. *Breaking the Glass Armour: Neoformalist Film Analysis*. Princeton, NJ: Princeton University Press, 1988.

Tiedemann, Rolf. "Dialectics at a Standstill: Approaches to the Passengen-Werk." In Walter Benjamin, *The Arcades Project*. Translated by Howard Eiland and Kevin McLaughlin, 929–45. Cambridge, MA: Harvard University Press, 1990.

Tierney, Thérèse F. *The Public Space of Social Media: Connected Cultures of the Network Society*. London: Routledge, 2013.

Tillotson, Sarah. *Indian Mansions: A Social History*. Cambridge: Oleander Press, 1994.

Todorov, Tzvetan. *Mikhail Bakhtin: The Dialogic Principle*. Translated by Wlad Godzich. Minneapolis: University of Minnesota Press, 1985.

Tongson, Karen. *Relocations: Queer Suburban Imaginaries*. New York: New York University Press, 2011.

Topinka, Robert. "Foucault, Borges, Heterotopia: Producing Knowledge in Other Spaces." *Foucault Studies*, no. 9 (2010): 54–70.

Tribe, John. *The Economics of Recreation, Leisure, and Tourism*. New York: Routledge, 2011.

Trigg, Dylan. *The Memory of Place: A Phenomenology of the Uncanny*. Athens: Ohio University Press, 2012.

Tuan, Yi-Fu. *Space and Place: The Perspective of Experience*. Minneapolis: University of Minnesota Press, 1977.

Uberoi, Patricia. "The Diaspora Comes Home: Disciplining Desire in *DDLJ*." *Contributions to Indian Sociology* 32, no. 3 (1998): 305–36.

Urry, John. *Consuming Places*. London: Routledge, 1995.

Vasudevan, Ravi S., ed. "Documentary Now." *MARG: A Magazine of the Arts* 70, no. 1 (September–December 2018): 14–115.

Vasudevan, Ravi S. "A British Documentary Film-Maker's Encounter with Empire: The Case of Alexander Shaw, 1938–42." *Historical Journal of Film, Radio and Television* (January 2018): 1–19.

Vasudevan, Ravi S. "Geographies of the Cinematic Public: Notes on Regional, National and Global Histories of Indian Cinema." *Journal of the Moving Image* (2001): 94–117.

Vasudevan, Ravi S. "Official and Amateur: Exploring Information Film in India, 1920s–40s." *Film and the End of Empire*, edited by Lee Grieveson and Colin MacCabe, 73–94. London: BFI Palgrave Macmillan, 2011.

Vertov, Dziga. "From Kino-Eye to Radio-Eye." In *Kino-Eye: The Writings of Dziga Vertov*, edited by Annette Michelson, translated by Kevin O'Bren, 85–91. Berkeley: University of California Press, 1985.

Vertov, Dziga. "Kino-Eye." In *Kino-Eye: The Writings of Dziga Vertov*, edited by Annette Michelson, translated by Kevin O'Bren, 60–78. Berkeley: University of California Press, 1985.

Vidler, Anthony. *The Architectural Uncanny: Essays in the Modern Unhomely*. Cambridge, MA: MIT Press, 1994.

Vidler, Anthony. Foreword to *Public Intimacy: Architecture and the Visual Arts*, by Giuliana Bruno. Cambridge, MA: MIT Press, 2007.

Vidler, Anthony. *Warped Space: Art, Architecture, and Anxiety in Modern Culture*. Cambridge, MA: MIT Press, 2002.

Vismann, Cornelia. "The Love of Ruins." *Perspectives on Science* 9, no. 2 (summer 2001): 196–209.

Viswanathan, Gauri. "The Ordinary Business of Occultism." *Critical Inquiry* 7, no. 1 (2000): 1–20.

Vitali, Valentina. "Film Historiography as Theory of the Film Subject: A Case Study." *Cinema Journal* 50, no. 1 (fall 2010): 141–46.

Vora, Rajendra. *The World's First Anti-Dam Movement: Mulshi Satyagraha, 1920–24.* New Delhi: Permanent Black, 2009.

Waldman, Harry. *Hollywood and the Foreign Touch: A Dictionary of Foreign Filmmakers and Their Films from America, 1910–1995.* Boston: Scarecrow Press, 1996.

Watts, Philip. "The Eloquent Image: The Postwar Mission of Film and Criticism." In *Opening Bazin,* edited by Andrew Dudley, 215–24. Oxford: Oxford University Press, 2011.

Wheeler, Edward J., ed. "The International Map of the World." In *Current Literature* 53 (July–December 1912): 55–56.

Wilkinson-Weber, Clare M. *Fashioning Bollywood: The Making and Meaning of Hindi Film Costume.* London: Bloomsbury, 2014.

Weems, Jason. *Barnstorming the Prairies: How Aerial Vision Shaped the Midwest.* Minneapolis: University of Minnesota Press, 2015.

Wessinger, Catherine. "Hinduism Arrives in America: The Vedanta Movement and the Self Realization Fellowship." In *America's Alternative Religions,* edited by Timothy Miller, 173–79. Albany: State University of New York Press, 1995.

White, Hayden. *Metahistory: The Historical Imagination of Nineteenth-Century Europe.* Baltimore, MD: Johns Hopkins University Press, 2014.

White, Hayden. *Tropics of Discourse: Essays in Cultural Criticism.* Baltimore, MD: Johns Hopkins University Press, 1997.

Williams, Rosalind. *Notes on the Underground: An Essay on Technology, Society, and the Imagination.* Cambridge, MA: MIT Press, 2008.

Winston, Brian. *Claiming the Real: The Documentary Film Revisited.* London: BFI, 1995.

Wojcik, Pamela Robertson. *The Apartment Complex: Urban Living and Global Screen Cultures.* Durham, NC: Duke University Press, 2018.

Wojcik, Pamela Robertson. *The Apartment Plot.* Durham, NC: Duke University Press, 2010.

Wolfe, Charles. "From Venice to the Valley: California Slapstick and the Keaton Comedy Short." In *Taking Place,* edited by John David Rhodes and Elena Gorfinkel, 3–30. Minneapolis: University of Minnesota Press, 2011.

Wolfe, Charles. "Response to 'Wrong Living: Cinema and the Bungalow' by John David Rhodes." GRI-SCA Seminar, University of Southern California, April 23, 2013.

Wollen, Peter. "'Ontology' and 'Materialism' in Film." *Screen* 17, no. 1 (March 1, 1976): 7–25.

Wood, Denis. *Rethinking the Power of Maps.* New York: Guilford Press, 2010.

Woods, Philip. "From Shaw to Shantaram: The Film Advisory Board and the Making of British Propaganda Films in India, 1940–1943." *Historical Journal of Film, Radio and Television* 21, no. 3 (2001): 293–308.

Woodward, Christopher. *In Ruins: A Journey through History, Art, and Literature.* New York: Pantheon Books, 2001.

Younger, Prakash. "Re-thinking Bazin through Renoir's *The River* Part 1: Bazin and *The River* as a Problem in the History of Film Theory." *Off Screen* 7, no. 7 (July 2003). Accessed July 27, 2007. http://offscreen.com/issues/view/vol7_7.

Younger, Prakash. "Re-thinking Bazin through Renoir's *The River* Part 2: The French Renoir and *The River*." *Off Screen* 7, no. 7 (July 2003). Accessed July 27, 2007. http://offscreen .com/issues/view/vol7_7.

Younger, Prakash. "*The River*: Beneath the Surface with André Bazin." In *A Companion to Jean Renoir*, edited by Alastair Phillips and Ginette Vincendeau, 166–75. Wiley Blackwell, 2013.

Zhen, Zhang. *An Amorous History of the Silver Screen: Shanghai Cinema, 1896–1937*. Chicago: University of Chicago Press, 2005.

Zielinski, Siegfried. *Deep Time of the Media: Toward an Archeology of Hearing and Seeing by Technical Means*. Translated by Gloria Custance. Cambridge, MA: MIT Press, 2006. (2002).

Žižek, Slavoj. *The Sublime Object of Ideology*. London: Verso, 1989.

INDEX

commercial film industry, 24–25, 79–81, 111–20.
  See also Bollywood; Bombay film industry
commodification: of leisure, 262, 268–70; of life,
  256–57; of space, 27, 207, 239–49
concrete abstraction, 147, 172, 176, 333n82
Conley, Tom, 148, 291–92, 301
Conrad, Joseph, 135–36
Cons, G. J., 52, 58–59, 62, 65, 207
consumerism, 256, 268–80, 276–78, 286
consumption certificate, 110–13
corporatization, 237–38, 240, 251–53, 264, 273,
  285–86
counterinsurgency, 188, 194–98, 207
Crary, Jonathan, 291
credibility, 281, 303
credit economy, 276–77
cultures of production, 237–40. *See also* commercial film industry; production practices

dance: classical Indian, 178–79. *See also*
  Bharatanatyam
Darjeeling, 28, 41, 77, 96–97, 102, 108, 272,
  295–96
Darjeeling (film), 294. *See also Indian Town
  Studies* (film series)
Dasgupta, Hari, 128
Dawley, J. Searle, 191
Dear, Michael, 289
de Certeau, Michel, 4, 291, 315n43
Defence of India Act, 116–17
Deleuze, Gilles, 301–2, 351n72
Delhi, 41, 49, 87, 89, 119, 188, 194, 203, 219;
  New, 87, 89, 203; Old, 208
density, spatial, 135, 172, 304
depth staging, 148
Derrida, Jacques, 143, 300
desire, 251, 274–78, 280
developmentalism, 18, 80, 82, 95–96
Dewey, John, 53
Dharma Productions, 235, 285
Dil (film), 281
Dil Chahta Hai (film), 259
Dillywood (production company), 246

Dimendberg, Edward, 9, 86, 184–85, 287
disciplinary, the, 18, 35–74; boundaries, 300; habit,
  302; instruction, 129; space, 288; use, 96
disciplinary delirium, 96–101, 115
disciplinary power, 197, 217. *See also* state: power
dispositifs, 308. *See also* epistemic dispensations
documentary, 75–121, 140–41, 284; colonial,
  39–41, 47–50, 73. *See also* cinema: colonial;
  colonial films
Douglas-Hamilton, Douglas, 48
Dupin, Christophe, 65
Dutt, Guru, 204–5
Dwyer, Rachel, 208, 218, 222, 276

educational films, 66–68, 95–98
Egoyan, Atom, 187
Eisenstein, Sergei, 28, 177, 200
Ellis, Jack, 103
Elsaesser, Thomas, 300, 341n118
Empire Film Library, 67
Empire Marketing Board (EMB), 67
encounter, 133, 135, 153, 292
epistemic dispensations, 18–21. *See also dispositifs*
estrangement, 153, 162, 195
ethnographic: films, 45, 55, 96; images, 45; mode,
  170–72
ethnography, 12, 20, 125, 130–34, 180, 292; reverse,
  131, 154–64; visual, 55
Evening in Paris (film), 272–73, 275, 279–80
Everest (film), 99–110
exile, 134, 153–54, 163, 168, 207
expedition, 48, 100, 109; films, 37, 54, 75, 101–6.
  See also mountaineering films
exterior spaces, 168–69

Fairgrieve, James, 58–59
Fatehpur Sikri, 224–26
Faulkner, Christopher, 140
Fellini, Federico, 177
Fellowes, Peregrine, 48
feminine, the, 175, 202–3, 207
feminization, 196, 204
Fernandes, Leela, 251–52

Morgan, Daniel, 150–51, 350n55
mountaineering films, 84–85, 98–101. *See also* expedition: films
Mountain Vigil (film), 98–99
Mount Everest, 47, 100–110
mourning, 200–201
Mughal Empire, 183, 188, 202, 208, 219, 224
muhurat, 138–39
music videos, 243–44
Muslim socials, 207
Mystery of Marriage (film), 54

Naficy, Hamid, 187
Nanda, Lekhraj, 261–62, 264–66
National Film Development Corporation (NFDC), 111
nationalism, 5, 18, 106, 243–44, 250; religious, 95; secular, 115; statist, 115
nature films, 53–55
nawabs, 198, 200, 202, 213
Negri, Antonio, 256
Nehru, Jawaharlal, Prime Minister, 78, 80, 84–85, 94, 99, 117, 170, 183, 279
neoliberalism, 233, 240, 268, 278
neorealism, 141, 292, 294, 304–5, 352n84
neo-Vedantism, 158–64
New Delhi, 87–89
Nichols, Bill, 141, 169, 339n52
noir, 9, 185
No Objection Certificates, 118–19. *See also* licensing
Norgay, Tenzing, 100, 107
The North West Frontier (film), 43, 69
nostalgia, 162–63, 207–8, 228
Nostalgia for the Light (film), 187
Nowell-Smith, Geoffrey, 65

O'Regan, Tom, 236
Oetterman, Stephan, 86, 325n25
ontology: of cinema, 151, 172, 289, 302–3, 350n59; flat, 297–98, 350n44; of ruins, 185–86; of the state, 330n107
Open General License (OGL) list, 110

Orgeron, Devin, 95
Orgeron, Marsha, 95
orientalism, 51, 128–29, 131, 135, 146
Osten, Franz, 26, 56

Padamsee, Alique, 275
Pal, Niranjan, 56
Pandian, Anand, 12, 292
panorama, 86–91, 95
paramountcy, 216–21; social, 226–27
Parekh, Asha, 279
participative management, 256
partition: of Bengal, 146, 174–75, 177–78; of India, 19, 78, 120, 174–75, 216; refugees, 156, 171, 173; of space, 120, 219, 228
Patel, Divia, 218, 276
Patel, Sardar Vallabhbhai, 184
Pather Panchali (film), 284
Patil Committee Report, 25, 118–19
patriarchal authority, 146, 184, 188, 215, 219, 227–28
Peterson, Jennifer, 201, 315n37
Phalke, Dadasaheb, 26
photographic album, 196–203
place-images, 4, 7, 12, 294, 308
politics of location, 308–9
postcolonial: films, 184–85, 211–28; state, 82, 96, 270; theory, 135, 183, 351n71
post-Independence period, 82, 89, 189, 207, 214–18, 279, 286
postindustrial society, 256
Poulantzas, Nicos, 77, 82
Prabhat Studio, 26
Pragati Maidan, 87
Prakash, Gyan, 93
Prasad, Madhava, 237, 279–80, 290
pre-production, 257, 266, 286, 294. *See also* below-the-line work; line producers; location managers; production managers; production practices
Presner, Todd, 30
princely states, 55–57, 184, 216–17, 337n5. *See also* Rajputana states

privatization, 233, 256, 274

production managers, 245–46

production practices, 235–86

professionalization, 245, 264, 266, 286

profilmic, the, 1, 5–7, 9, 21–22, 49, 132, 148–49, 152–54, 179–80, 249, 293–94, 299, 303, 313n2

property, 213–16. *See also* land ownership

propriety, 213–16

Pudovkin, Vsevolod, 177

Purani Haveli (film), 214

Raees (film), 238

Rafi, Mohammad, 204

raga, 166

Rahman, A. R., 243

Rai, Amit, 241–42

Rai, Himansu, 26, 56–58

Rajadhyaksha, Ashish, 178, 237, 336n157

Raja Harishchandra (film), 26

Rajputana states, 43, 56, 213, 219, 222, 337n6. *See also* Bikaner; princely states; Udaipur

Ram, Sunitha, 245, 253–55

Ramaswamy, Sumathi, 94

Ramsay Brothers, 214

Rancière, Jacques, 301–2

rangoli, 133, 138–44, 173

rape, 214–15, 223, 225, 227–28. *See also* violence: sexual

Ray, Satyajit, 28, 108, 128, 134, 141, 153, 284, 295, 327n68

realism, 150–51, 177, 280–85, 303, 347n105; cinematic, 146–47

reality, 132–33, 289, 296, 298–99, 302–5

regimes of value, 81–82

regulation, 268–73; licensing, 117–20; statist, 24–25, 80–82, 110–13, 229

The Relief of Lucknow (film), 189–95, 198

Renoir, Claude, 149, 157, 167

Renoir, Jean, 19, 125–80, 293–94, 299, 307

Renoir, Pierre-Auguste, 162

Renov, Michael, 132

Rhodes, John David, 5–6, 17, 184

Rice, Tom, 66

Rich, Adrienne, 308–9

right-wing: ideologies, 245; political parties, 264–68; populism, 20, 244

The River (film), 19, 127–80, 293, 307; color in, 167–68, music in, 166–67. *See also* Renoir, Jean

Rohmer, Eric, 147

Romains, Jules, 158

Romantic India (film), 51, 68

Rosen, Phil, 302–5

Rosenbaum, Jonathan, 170

Rossellini, Roberto, 128, 134, 141, 170–72

Roy, Srirupa, 82, 85, 87

Royal Air Force, 48–49

Royal Geographical Society, 47, 52, 59

ruins, 19–20, 184–89, 194–99, 203–8

Rukhsana, 266–68

Rule 44A, 116–18

The Rules of the Game (film), 147, 151, 155, 163, 333n83

rupee, 273–74

Ryan, James, 60

Sadiq, M., 203

SAG-AFTRA, 262

Sahib Bibi aur Ghulam (film), 19

Said, Edward, 27, 40, 51, 135–36, 208, 297

Samanta, Shakti, 28, 272

Sarkar, Bhaskar, 173, 175, 216

scenics, 17. *See also* travelogue

Schönle, Andreas, 185–86

Schwartz, Vanessa, 291

Scott, James, 99

Screen theory, 3, 30, 313n4

Secrets of India (film series), 50–53. *See also* Field, Mary; Woolfe, H. Bruce

Secrets of Nature (film series), 53. *See also* Field, Mary; Woolfe, H. Bruce

secularism, 18, 95

segregated spaces, 213, 218–21

Self-Realization Fellowship, 158

Sen, Meheli, 208, 222

Sen, Mrinal, 1, 7, 306